CATALOGUE OF
CHAMBER MUSIC FOR
WOODWIND INSTRUMENTS

Da Capo Press Music Reprint Series
GENERAL EDITOR
FREDERICK FREEDMAN
VASSAR COLLEGE

CATALOGUE OF
CHAMBER MUSIC FOR
WOODWIND INSTRUMENTS

BY
ROY HOUSER

DA CAPO PRESS · NEW YORK · 1973

Library of Congress Cataloging in Publication Data

Houser, Roy.
   Catalogue of chamber music for woodwind instruments.

   (Da Capo Press music reprint series)
   Reprint of the 1962 ed.
   1. Woodwind ensembles—Bibliography. 2. Chamber
music—Bibliography. I. Title.
ML128.W5H7   1973   016.7856   76-166093
ISBN 0-306-70257-6

This Da Capo Press edition of
*Catalogue of Chamber Music
for Woodwind Instruments* is an
unabridged republication of the
1962 edition published by the
Indiana University School of Music.

Da Capo Press, Inc.
A Subsidiary of Plenum Publishing Corporation
227 West 17th Street, New York, New York 10011

CATALOGUE OF
CHAMBER MUSIC FOR
WOODWIND INSTRUMENTS

ACKNOWLEDGMENT

With deep appreciation for invaluable suggestions of procedure and organization of the catalogue, as well as vital financial assistance, from Dean Wilfred C. Bain, School of Music, Indiana University.

Also, John W. Ashton, Vice President of Indiana University and Dean of the Graduate School, for grant-in-aid which enabled the completion of this edition.

I wish to acknowledge the help of Dr. Charles Leonhard, University of Illinois, for the principles of music education as applied to woodwind chamber music. Dr. Max Risch, of St. Louis, for contributions of unknown chamber works for woodwind combinations and to Joseph Marx, of New York City, for his invaluable suggestions in the quintet literature. To my wife, Kathryn Irene, for the preparation of the multilith masters.

TABLE OF CONTENTS

PREFACE

CHAMBER MUSIC has long had an honored place in the hierarchy of Music. Chamber Music reached its zenith during the life of Beethoven. We think of the string quartet when we think of chamber music. Hence, woodwind chamber music by heritage, does not enjoy the prestige accorded to the string quartet; however, this does not mean that to play a stringed instrument in a chamber music medium is to be more honored than in any other medium.

Prestige and hierarchy are two-fold swords, pleasant and wonderful when enjoyed and not so pleasant and wonderful when not enjoyed.

If the answer to the age old remarks concerning the dismal lack of good literature for woodwinds is a catalogue of what does exist, good and bad, then my efforts have not been in vain. However, this is not the answer to the question. The answer has gone before our time - back to the days of the classic composers - days when such composers were composing for posterity. Wind instruments, and woodwinds in particular, were highly inferior during the classic period. We so often enjoy the masters today as the masters never heard their own compositions performed.

Inspiration is the breath of success. Woodwind instruments during the classical period did not especially inspire the composers to write for woodwind. We must not blame the performers. They, no doubt, in many cases played far beyond the capacity of the physical equipment available. The fault lies with the manufacture and the physics of the conical and cylindrical air columns. Our task as woodwind artists, then, is to foster in every way possible the performance and literature of chamber music for woodwinds on all levels. Certainly no one can refuse to acknowledge that the formation of the National Association of College Wind and Percussion Instrument Instructors is a step in the right direction. Today we have no excuse to give the modern composers.

Chamber Music is its only excuse for being. Far from the commercialism of the big production, Chamber Music sells only itself. Composers that compose for chamber ensemble know that composing requires the utmost in craftmanship and cannot be covered by size of ensemble and distracting elements of the stage.

We well know for these reasons the benefits derived, from an educational standpoint, from Chamber Music. We also recognize that Chamber Music cannot support itself financially.

The author makes no pretense of claiming completeness for this catalogue and the controversial aspects of the various sections of the contents are fully realized. However, if the listings presented here accomplish nothing more than the stimulation of the reader's thinking, the catalogue has been of value.

OBJECTIVES FOR A PROGRAM OF WOODWIND CHAMBER MUSIC

This paper is based on a set of questionnaires prepared and distributed for the sole purpose of determining teaching content desired in the woodwind training field. Such a listing of items to be evaluated, as appears on the sheet, is believed to be of use in the planning of classroom procedures. Those persons who were contacted, either in person or through the mail, are to be found in one of the following categories:

    (1)   Professional performer
    (2)   Private teacher
    (3)   Public school work
    (4)   College or university instructor
    (5)   Composer or arranger

Each person was asked to check which position he holds at present. The leaflet then specified a series of desirable teaching implements to be utilized in the classroom—altogether thirty-seven items. Each item was to be rated according to its value as felt by the person questioned. These ratings were divided into six parts:

    (1)   Extreme importance
    (2)   Considerable importance
    (3)   Average importance
    (4)   Less than average importance
    (5)   Only slight importance
    (6)   No importance

It is natural that individual persons would feel the need of a particular type of teaching content more than others. What one teacher would rate as extremely important, another would list as only of average importance due to the natural demands of his students, for most of them are quick to agree with the writer that no rigid standard can be applied to all situations. And too, the private lesson involves a completely personal approach, primarily based on the need of a single student in a closed situation.

It is not our purpose or intent to lay down any set mode of classroom conduct as a result of this survey. The writer merely hopes to shed some light on the type of thinking that has evolved through the teaching experience of the interviewed persons. In the case of the student there arises the fresh approach which remains unique to that individual yet uninitiated at the other side of the desk.

For purposes of clarity we intend not only to summarize (as best as possible from such a short collection of contacts) the median of thought evolved out of this study, but also to establish some sort of basic precedent or train of thought which might be said to be generally characteristic of the professionally inclined person.

From the questionnaire results we hope to gain a set of objectives which might well be used in the guidance of a program of chamber music teaching.

Implications from the questionnaire, in terms of objectives for a woodwind program, would be experienced learnings acquired in a functional manner. We may define functional as opposed to the formalized memorization, recitation, etc.

A. Musical Skills and Knowledge Necessary for Program

The teacher-training course in woodwind ensemble should:

(1) Provide experience with the representative instruments of the woodwind family so that generalizations may be made to facilitate transfer to other wind instruments.

(2) Provide a functional presentation of woodwind music materials.

(3) Provide seminar and laboratory courses to give a wide range of experience and acquaintance with the problems and practice in woodwind education, musical resources, materials and media in woodwind chamber music.

(4) Emphasize the importance of coordinated presentation of subject matter in musical skills and knowledge as they pertain to woodwind chamber ensemble.

(5) Emphasize the importance of relating musical performance and practice to theory of interpretation of chamber music.

(6) Provide opportunity for practice teaching experience in a realistic atmosphere to develop individual approach to future problems of organization, method and interpretation of ensemble problems.

(7) Provide opportunity for knowledge of basic techniques of instruments of the woodwind family and knowledge of repair and maintenance of said instruments.

(8) Provide opportunity for interested individuals to arrange or adapt music to the woodwind groups which can be played by those groups in which they perform.

(9) Provide basic principles of tone production and pitch variation as they pertain to the idiosyncrasies of the individual woodwind instruments.

(10) Encourage performance in an aesthetic and satisfying manner at least in one musical medium.

(11) Encourage score reading and conducting of participating groups by capable and interested individuals.

(12) Stress organizational procedures and methodology for participants in the woodwind ensemble program.

(13) Stress knowledge of harmony, form and theory, also the different periods such as classical, romantic and contemporary woodwind literature.

(14) Provide style treatment of composers so that the performer may relate such treatment to all periods of the individual composer's life.

(15) Provide opportunity for individuals to arrange seasonal melodies for the woodwind media.

(16) Provide opportunity for groups to perform for high school and elementary grade school groups in order that the performers might appreciate the effect of the performance of woodwind literature upon such an audience.

B. Habits, Attitudes and Appreciation

The teacher-training program in woodwind ensemble should:

(1) Provide experiences in study and performance in all styles of music found in woodwind chamber literature.

(2) Provide varied musical resources including record players, recording equipment, library facilities, practice facilities, and musical instruments necessary for good musical conduct in woodwind chamber ensemble.

(3) Provide experience in opportunities presented for the application of valid, evaluated, judgment techniques to cover musical performance, literature and method in woodwind ensemble training.

(4) Emphasize the importance of providing musical experience for elective students irrespective of their professional interest in music at the advanced level.

(5) Provide opportunities for teaching-training participation in woodwind groups at three developmental levels--secondary, advanced and graduate--as an aid to better understanding and appreciation of the problems peculiar to these levels.

(6) Provide a recognition of the objectives of the woodwind program with general music education.

(7) Relate musical experience in chamber music activities in the classroom to outside informal experience, both in professional and educational situations.

(8) Bring about an appreciation of related musical fields of endeavor to woodwind chamber ensemble so that these contributions are evaluated to the total development of the woodwind student.

(9) Provide an opportunity for students to appreciate and distinguish musical timbres, pitch relationships and tonalities as related to the woodwind instruments.

(10) Provide stimuli for students to listen to chamber music performance regularly, both live and recorded.

(11) Provide for discriminatory judgment in the selection of recorded music for woodwinds.

(12) Promote democratic relations with all persons and within groups.

(13) Provide for the welfare of groups and individuals within the groups above the personal aspirations of the teacher.

(14) Promote appreciation of knowledge and utilization of scientific and theoretical principles of sound as it relates to better musical production and intonation.

(15) Provide appreciation for principles of good program presentation and selection of program materials.

(16) Encourage promotion of research, literature, and experimental procedures that pertain to ensemble playing for the betterment of individuals concerned.

In order that one might acquire a clear conception of what woodwind ensemble teachers stress in their teaching, one must determine what these teachers desire in the material that they use.

The questionnaire for the establishing the teaching method desired in the teaching of woodwind ensemble attempts to find conclusive trends in the thinking of teachers and the students of the

woodwind field. This is for the benefit of educators who are
interested in building objectives toward more effective teaching of woodwind chamber music.

Because the return of the questionnaire is not great in
size, the evidence of a trend is not as large as it might be.
Therefore we might say that the conclusions are somewhat inadequate.
These conclusions are not, however, to be disregarded, since they
do represent the thought-out opinions of a selected number of peo-
ple. The questions asked ranged from those of a more practical
nature to those of aesthetic value. The composite information
appears on the sample sheet and represents the needs of the persons who contributed the information. As previously indicated, the
questions were rated from extensive importance to no importance
relative to the teaching of woodwind ensemble classes. A power rating has been set up showing the relative value of these aspects of
teaching and the materials with which the teaching is augmented.
With the number five as high rating and 0 as low rating, the aver-
ages were determined so that the number which appears on the sample sheet represents the considered importance of that item concerned.

The value of work in developing ear-training, availability
of score for conductor, musical value or aesthetic worth of a composition, interest of the composition to the student arrangement
of voicing, difficulty of individual parts, value of the material
in developing musical subtleties (nuances, phrasing, and dynamics)
as criteria for choice of material -- were selected by the con-
tributors to the questionnaire. Educational value of the work to
the student (value which would promote later interest) and material that would provide a challenge to the performers were also
selected.

The above information is the subject for treatment of objectives of woodwind ensemble teaching (part two of this paper).
The questionnaire provided also for additional comment by the con-
tributors. A great deal of interesting comment was noted and gives
some insight into the concern of the individual who filled out the
questionnaire.

A most important requirement of the material to be used for
woodwind ensemble teaching is that all parts must be of the same
comparable difficulty. No particular instrument or instruments
should have a part which is more difficult than the other instruments in the group comparably speaking. This important aspect is
readily understood when one played within the group has more difficulty with his part than do the others; it is much the same thing
as a weak link in a chain. Apathy and disinterest actually set
in when one member is continually struggling to keep up with the
rest of the performers.

The validity of this questionnaire cannot be determined, as
a greater number of participants would be needed to add weight to

the findings. Of the many letters sent out, only five percent were returned filled in. Because of the vacation season, we cannot necessarily say that apathy was the sole reason for the lack of returns on the part of those to whom the questionnaire was sent.

In the final analysis we turn from the objectives above discussed directly to the interpretation of music for woodwind chamber groups wherein our objectives must apply. The terms composition, material, ensemble, reproductive analysis, program of reproduction, rebuilding, phrasing, tone and intonation are defined in the following body of the paper.

INTERPRETATION OF MUSIC FOR WOODWIND CHAMBER MUSIC GROUPS

Composing music is drawing ideas and emotions from the primary source of sound. Music is committed to writing by notation. We read notations to form a conception. With this conception we set a pattern for reproduction.

The material of music is sound. Sounds are combined to give the music form. In form we include ideas and expressions to portray and re-create music. We project the composer's message to the listener so that he may comprehend it fully.

An ensemble is a conformation of individual players into a unified whole. Any function performed simultaneously by more than one person is possible only by the joint conception and uniform execution of the component parts of the group. The music to be performed must be measured, differentiated, related and proportioned among the instruments and then integrated.

I. Reproductive Analysis

1. Reading the notation.
2. Forming a general conception about the ideas of the music.
3. Actually playing the music in its entirety.
4. Remembering the impression the music made in specific places.
5. Remembering the emotions connected with it.

II. Program of Reproduction

A. Reconstruction of structure.

1. The great form -- family of sentences, sentences out of periods, all as compared to language.

2. A period -- out of phrases.
   Idea expressed in many sentences (in language).

3. A phrase -- out of motives.
   Gramatic expression - many words make a sentence.

4. Motive -- out of syllables.
   A word out of syllables (language).

5. Syllables -- out of intervals and tones.
   Syllables out of letters (language).

B. Reconstruction of elements of expression.

1. The objective consists of theoretical elements.

(a) Rhythm
(b) Melody
(c) Harmony

2. The subjective.

    (a) The conception of singing, decorating rhythmic and dynamic elements.

    (b) Materialization by technical means.

    (c) Materialization by division of rhythm.

        (1) Mechanical repetition of beats.
        (2) Meter of a measure.
        (3) Phrasing -- carrying across an idea through meter.

    (d) Grading the intensities of up and down beats.

        (1) Follow up the ideas and emotions of the composition.

        (2) Re-create the music in an auditory way.

III. Rebuilding

A. Start from a sound.

Conception of sound characteristic -- pitch, length, quality, quantity, timbre-coloring.

B. Materialization.

Tone is produced on a woodwind instrument by the speed of air entering, intensity of air, reed and embouchure.

IV. Phrasing

A. Phrasing in music is an organized use of taste. It relates the individual parts and brings them into an overall unity. It is the opposite of analysis; analysis sub-divides, whereas phrasing combines.

B. Two or more notes in succession played with the same intensity do not form a group. We form a group of two or more notes by organizing their intensity so that the tones compliment each other in a progression. We colate them as a group. Group expression is practical phrasing.

C. Stages of expressing music compared to language. <u>In lan-guage</u>:

    1. Phonetically -- spelling (words).
    2. Orthographically -- speaking.
    3. Grammatically -- sentence structure.
    4. Declamatory -- interpretation of ideas and emotions.

<u>In Music</u>:

    1. Different bowings, embouchure, air support, resulting in different sounds.
    2. Forming of syllables and musical words.
    3. Phrases -- periods into sentences.
    4. Forming sentences into a group.

V. Ensemble

A. Ensemble playing is a steady progression of balancing and pro-portioning. We must distinguish, differentiate, relate, co-ordinate, subordinate and integrate. It is not just an accom-paniment to a solo voice. It is also an inter-weaving of voices in coloring, phrasing and interpreting. It portrays in different voices the different elements of expression.

B. Ensemble technique.

    1. Tone: volume, coloring, intensity, balance, vibrate, accompaniment, solo tone.

    2. Rhythm: absolute, relative meter of the measure, group meter.

    3. Leadership principle: alternating.

    4. Expressive playing: use of all elements of expression.

    5. Interpretation: unity of style, expression of emotion.

    6. Adaptation of the score: relative arrangement of voices in intensity projection.

VI. Volume of Tone

A. The volume of tone in an ensemble is relative. The dynamics of a composition are the dynamics of the total group of players, so that the dynamics of each is relative. If a solo voice is accompanied by other voices, the sum of their dynamics must be added to the leading dynamic. Thus, the members first have to collate their voices and add them to the solo voice.

1. The solo tone has more air, pressure, less speed.

2. The accompaniment tone has less air, pressure, and
    more speed.

3. The solo tone is heavier and darker; the accompaniment
    tone brighter and lighter.

B. The vibration has to be equalized. Equal starting direction --
    down or upward. Amplitude is equal swinging in both directions
    in space and numbers. For coloring there is an organized diff-
    erence of vibration. The solo voice has more swinging and less
    breadth in space; the accompaniment is the opposite.

1. For imitation of different styles: French, German, classic
    and modern, etc. We need different vibration.

2. French: brighter swingings, less in numbers.

3. German: less bright, more in number.

VII. Intonation

A. The solo voice is absolute; the accompaniment is relative.

B. Dynamic approach to intonation: Experience shows that only
    equalized dynamics result in good intonation in an ensemble. A
    soft tone is low. A loud tone sounds too high. In ensemble
    playing the different instruments at times express the same
    group phrasing and other times part of the voices have their
    own phrasing.

The Leadership Principle

Generally the flutist in the woodwind quintet is responsible
for the leadership (the agreed tempo, phrase). The flute is the
most agile of the five instruments; flute, oboe, clarinet, bassoon,
and french horn. If the solo is in the other instrument, it has to
be responsible for the "carrying" of the music. The quintet, as a
group, must "feel" the continuity of the music and anticipate the
whim of the solo instrument. The quickest passages in the accompaniment have to be respected, also.

The Interpretation of Styles

The interpretation of the different styles requires different
phrasing, intensity and vibration. In Mozart, for example, we need
a concentrated vibrato with a light air stream. In Beethoven both
are concentrated. In Brahms both are heavy. In French music the
air stream is light, the vibration broad in both directions and
less in numbers. In Bartok a heavy charging air stream is required.

Conclusion

The average music listener cannot fully appreciate a well
performed concert of five such instruments as the flute, oboe,
clarinet, bassoon, and french horn, each with his different over-
tones and timbre, blending only when played in perfect intonation and balance. To know one of the many intonational hazards
of each of the basic woodwind instruments is to know that the oboe
is generally low in pitch in its extreme low register and that the
bassoon is sharp in pitch in its lower register, while the french
horn is generally sharp to A-440 throughout its entire range. The
clarinet will, when performing softly in the Chalemeau register,
be sharp, and in the throat register will be flat when blown forte.
The high register or clarion will generally be sharp if the performer has a strong embouchure, or flat unless he does not have
such a strong embouchure and does not use enough air support. The
flute will be sharp in the high register and flat in the bottom
register. The ability of the student to understand these inher-
ent acoustical difficulties and to correct these difficulties, as
well as many other components of musical performance, is a great
step forward in building a more artistic level of musical standards
in the school systems.

ORGANIZATION AND PROCEDURES OF A WOODWIND ENSEMBLE PROGRAM ON A COLLEGE LEVEL

Problems and procedures of a newly organized woodwind ensemble program will usually be quite similar, whether the music department be small or large. Of course the larger department, both in personnel and in facilities, would be an asset, and could more easily overcome the immediate problems involved in a newly organized woodwind program. After some consideration I thought it best to establish my procedures on a basis of a reputable and average college level music department. The college would contain a student body of around 3000 students, a certain percentage of whom would be in the school of music. So, let us consider a total of 175 music majors and fifty music minors. Those students interested in a BM degree in orchestral instruments would total a high of about ten. Combining these two mentioned degrees would give us a total of twenty-five persons, with possibilities of forming four complete woodwind quintets. I would require those students working toward a BM in orchestral instruments to have four semesters of woodwind ensemble experience. Those working for a BM in woodwinds would be required to have at least five semesters of woodwind ensemble experience. It has been learned that private study alone on an instrument is not sufficient to allow the student to facilitate quickly enough for the high standards of expectations, therefore this emphasis of four to five semesters of ensemble work would definitely and desirably aid in his required instrumental performance.

The accepted woodwind teacher will have definite capabilities allowing him to fulfill his position as instructor. His having an MM degree in woodwinds would enable him to have a thorough knowledge of the woodwinds, including fingerings, embouchures, tonal production and execution. Since the horn is used in quintet ensemble, it will be necessary that he at least know the fundamentals of the horn such as the fingerings, tonal productions and the various transpositions. With a good background of music history, he will be able to enlighten the students in the ensemble of the period of music they are about to play and something about the composer and his contemporaries. This knowledge will more or less correlate with his vast experience of playing ensemble repertoire and provide him with an ability to choose adequate repertoire. The instructor's past contacts with instrument deals and necessary equipment of excellent make will aid in this ensemble program. Last, but not least he must enjoy to the utmost this specialized work. An extensive ensemble program will absorb most of his school hours and he will find it quite difficult to have adequate time to do some private instrumental teaching. He must be a good teacher with good presence, personality, and sincerity. He must be able to present the materials with a certain element of finesse.

It is now understood that the BM in orchestral instruments requires four semesters of ensemble training and the BM in woodwinds requires five semesters. There will be three one hour meetings each week, giving the students a one hour credit for the semester. Other students from the various musical degrees will definitely be encouraged to participate in this ensemble program and will receive one hour elective credit. The pianists who are asked to perform for quintets with piano will receive one hour of credit toward their required ensemble fulfillments each semester. For advanced ensemble playing such as septets and octets and others, there is a need for a few strings players, and it will be necessary to be dependent on the department of strings and their cooperation as to provide string talent for the necessary rehearsals toward a performance.

The scheduling of one hour rehearsals during the actual school hours when setting up this department of woodwinds will be one of the major problems. It is almost impossible to work this scheduling to a most satisfactory degree without some conflicts, but with some cooperation the department can operate smoothly. The first objective is to avoid conflicts with major music courses, i.e., theory, ear training, method courses, counterpoint, etc. So it will be necessary to schedule on weak or off hours such as 8:30, 10:30, (11:30), 1:30, and (2:30). With departmental cooperation, there will be no necessity for evening or week-end scheduling. The biggest problem will be the student's programs and their conflicts, but with a few alterations and changes as to their definite scheduled times for ensemble, scheduling should be fairly smooth. For some students it will be necessary to wait possibly for the coming semester or to take it non-credit and "sit in" at times until the following semester, depending, however, upon how deep is the student's interest.

The next immediate problem will be the lack of balanced instrumentation for a complete quintet -- flute, oboe, clarinet, bassoon, and horn. This often results from the lack of double reeds in the secondary schools and also an inadequacy of instrumental training. The variance in capabilities on an instrument among the students will there parallel, but with time, musical experience and instruction, this problem evens itself out. But if there is a shortage of double reeds, or of flutes, oboes, or clarinets, the only alternative left is to form smaller ensembles until the higher ensemble goal is reached. Many combinations can be formed. In trio ensemble it is possible to acquire repertoire for three flutes; three clarinets; oboe, flute or clarinets; flute, clarinet and bassoon; one oboe, two clarients; two clarinets and bassoon. Many more will be shown in my materials list. When using quartet repertoire, combinations exist such as clarinet quartets; oboe, clarinet, horn, and bassoon, etc., and some repertoire has been prepared as to four sections - A, B, C, and D. Whereas supplementary parts are provided in each section to fit any instrumentation. If personnel and instrumentation is so weak that the department must resolve to duet ensemble, I would suggest closing the department until adequate facilities present themselves.

Once the newly organized ensemble department is well under way, whether it be of small ensembles or of quintet size or larger, there remains an existing problem that must be considered throughout the school year. We have our attending personnel, but I find it drastically necessary that they realize the importance of woodwind ensembles and that every instrumentalist concerned acquires an interest, initiative and drive for the program. If the correct procedures are taken, I believe there will be no problem.

First of all the department must have interesting and graded repertoire for training purposes and for performing purposes and in all categories from EASY TO HARD. If there is not an existing faculty in the school of music solo performances on the various woodwinds would suffice. In this way the students would hear well organized ensemble in good blend and musicianship at a high level of achievement. Having a tape or disc recorder would enable the ensemble groups to record repertoire and tape recordings of their performances could be played back for criticism and amusement as well. This naturally would be quite an aid to the instructor as well as to the students, especially for constructive criticism.

While on the topic of initiative and interest, I would like to suggest that a woodwind ensemble program would be most ideal for the students to experience supplementary training in regards to original composition and arranging. I believe the instructor should definitely encourage and aid students to write for quintet or other ensemble idioms or to take organ works and others to be arranged for these ensembles. I'm sure the steps the instructor would take in this direction would receive the fullest cooperation from the compositional department. Composition and arranging in itself would hold strong towards keeping the initiative and interest of the students concerned toward the ensemble program, and may also help bring forth other talents from within the student.

And, last but not least, the instructor should schedule two or more quintet or ensemble recitals each semester, whereas the students would be "pressurized" to work toward a performance level. Rather than just one person being responsible -- such as the flutist -- for the group or performance, every member of the quintet should have the chance for leadership and responsibility, more or less on a rotation plan. And along with this rotation plan, it should be enforced that the students perform on the other instruments of the ensemble, especially if their degree is of an instrumental nature and they are receiving instruction in secondary woodwind instruments. This most likely wouldn't be offered to the student until his junior and senior years, performing on a secondary instrument. This rotation plan also helps keep up the interest among the personnel. It would also help the student to better understand the problems of intonation of every instrument concerned and problems thereof, along with bettering his musicianship and instrumental achievement.

As the BM in woodwinds and BM orchestral instrument students reach their senior year, I believe it would be most applicable to provide as one hour courses "Problems and Procedures of a Woodwind Ensemble Program." The students could work on a catalogue of chamber music for woodwind instruments and work on a report as to the problems of this woodwind department.

It is necessary that the school provide the required equipment for such a department such as school oboes, flutes and the other winds; a large enough rehearsal room with good lighting and ventilation, music stands, chairs, a piano, filing cabinet, desk, folios for training and selective purposes and woodwind repair material and equipment and materials for reed making.

As for the grading and selection of adequate repertoire for a woodwind ensemble program, it will not be mentioned here but as a preface to my catalogue of wind literature. Let us just hope that the school will have appropriations for an extensive repertoire and equipment.

As a goal is reached in obtaining complete woodwind quintets, then the instructor is able to proceed toward occasional work with sextets, septets, octets, nonets, dixtours and wind ensembles for more than ten instruments. If the department is under good instructorship, results and achievements will show rapidly in the students as to a betterment in musicianship, performance and initiative.

TRIOS WITHOUT PIANO

Selective List

ALLEN, P. H., Song of Venus (ob, cl, bn); Whitney Blake.

ANDRE, ANTON, Original Trio, Op. 29 (3 fl) G major, Me; Andre, 1883; Andraud; Baxter-Northrup (now Keynote Music Service.)

BACH, J. S., Prelude and Fugue, (ob, cl, bn) MH (Bach-Arnell arr.) Boosey-Hawkes; Belwin, Inc.

BACH, J. S., Prelude et Fugue (ob, cl, bn) (Arr. by Fernand Oubradous) L'Oiseau Lyre (Lyre Bird Press); Baron.

BEETHOVEN, LUDWIG VAN, Theme and Variations, Op. 25 (3 fl) ME (rec) (Arr. Fetherston) Belwin, Inc.
---Serenade, Op. 25 (3 fl) (Arr. Fetherston) Belwin, Inc.

BENNETT, DAVID, Clarinet Polka (3 cl) EMB

BERBIGUIER, TRANQUILLE, Six Concert Trios, Op. 5 (2 fl, va) Andraud (probably also in B&H edition)

BLATT, FRANCOIS-THADEE, Trio (3 cl) Eb Major, Ed. by Bellison, Ricordi.

BONNEAU, Three Old Christmas Carols (ob, Eng h, bn or alt cl) Andraud.

BORNEFELD, HELMUT, New Music (3 fl), 1932 Nagel.

BOZZA, EUGENE, Fughette, Sicilienne, Rigaudon (ob, cl, bn) MH, Andraud; Ricordi.

BUSCH, ADOLF, Four Miniatures: Solitude, Contentment, Frolic, Joyfulness (3 cl) Me, Andraud; Fischer, Carl (score, parts separately)

CASSEL-GEARHEART, Clarinet Sessions (A variety of style from Palestrina to Jazz) (3 cl) ME-MH, EMB.

CAZDEN, NORMAN, Trio (No. 2 from "Six discussions for Wind Ensemble) (fl, ob, cl) Kalmus Editions--score.

CHANDLER, EUDORA (3 cl) MH, Pro-Art Publications.

CHIAFFARELLI, ALBERT, Serenade, Woodwind Trio (fl, ob, cl) Alfred Music Co.

CIARDI, CESARE, Trio, Op. 24, "Trio Scolastico" (3 fl) 1853, Ricordi.
---Petit Trio Concertant, Eb major (3 fl) Andraud; Ricordi.

COHEN, SOL B., Madrigale (2 Bb cl, bass-cl) MH (rec) Belwin, Inc.

CORROYEZ, G., Seven Trios (3 cl) Andraud; Leduc (scored for ob, cl, bn)
---Brilliant Variations on a Mozart These (3 cl) Andraud.

DAQUIN, LOUIS CLAUDE, La Joyeuse (fl, fl or ob, cl) Andraud.

DAVID, HANS T., Introduction & Fugue in 18th Century Style, Ms. at University of Michigan.

DELORENZO, LEONARDO, Two Divertimenti, Op. 24 and 29 (fl, cl, bn) Andraud.
---I tre Virtuosi, op. 31 (The Three Virtuosos) Capriccio brillante (3 fl) (rec) 1930, Zimmermann; Andraud; Baxter Northrup (Keynote Music Service)

DIETRICH, FRITZ, Wenn alle Brunnlein fliessen. Variationen (3 fl) 1938 Barenreiter.
---Nordische Volksweisen (aus Normigers Tabulatur 1598) (3 fl) Barenreiter.
---Three Small Suites (Kleine Suiten) (3fl) 1938 Barenreiter.

ENDRESEN, R. M., Woodwind Moods (3 Bb cl) ME, EMB; Rubank.
 ---Woodwind Revels (3 Bb cl) ME. EMB; Rubank.
ENKE, FERD., Trio, Zusammenspiel (3 fl) 1932 Lienau.
ETLER, ALVIN, Sonata (ob, cl, va) Valley Music Press.
FABER, FRANK, Trio, Ein neuer Tag ist angebrochen. Kleine Mor-
 genmus. An der Fahne. (3 fl) 1939 Moeck.
FABER, JOHANN CHRISTOPHER, Partita for Three flutes, C major (3
 fl) 1932 Nagel.
FAHRBACH, JOSEPH, Trio, Op. 58 (3 fl) 1865 Ricordi.
FEDDER, AMANDUS, Serenade. Studien im alten Stil (3 fl) 1932
 Nagel, score.
FLEGIER, ANGE, Concert Trio (Suite) (fl, cl, bn) Bb major MH (rec)
 Rubank; Gallet (scored for ob, cl, bn)
FRANGKISER, CARL, Fugue a la Valse (3 cl) EMB, Boosey-Hawkes
 (score, parts)
 ---Les Lavalettes (2 Bb cl, bn) ME, Boosey-Hawkes (score,
 parts)
 ---Trion A Belle (fl, cl, bn) ME, Belwin, Inc.
FUCHS, GEORG FRIEDRICH, Six Trios, Op. 1 (3 bn) Lemoine; Andraud.
FUCIK, JULIUS, Suite (2 cl, bn) 1939 Editions Continental (score,
 parts) Prague.
 ---Symphonie Scandaleuse (2 cl, bn) 1939 Editions Continen-
 tal (score, parts) Prague.
FURSTENAU, A. B., Trios, No. 1, 2, 3, op. 14 (3 fl) in D major. F
 major, G major, Breitkopf and Rartel.
 ---Trios, No. 1, 2, 3, Op. 22 (3 fl) in A minor, G major,
 E major, Hansen (new edition) (Trios with fugues)
 ---Trios, Op. 66 (with fugues) (3 fl)
 ---Trio, Op. 118 (3 fl) in F Major, 1841, Bote & Bock; An-
 draud.
GALLON, NOEL, Suite en Trio (ob, cl, bn) Eble.
GERSHWIN, GEORGE, Liza (3 cl) (Arr. Sears) EMB.
GIRNATIS, WALTER, Festival Music "Festliche Hausmusik" (3 fl or
 3 cl) 1941, Litolff.
GOLESTAN, STAN, Divertimento (ob, cl, bn)
GRAF, FRIEDRICH HERMANN, Two Works of Trios (2 fl, bass) Breit-
 kopf Thematic Catalogue; Fetis.
GUERICKE, WALRAD, Trio (Festl. Musik u. dt. Tanze) (3 fl) 1937,
 Schott.
HAHN, REYNALDO, Eglogue (ob, cl, bn) Andraud.
HAUBIEL, CHARLES, In the Phrygian Mode (3 fl) ME, Composers Press.
JACOBSEN, KARSTEN, Preludes (Niederdeutsche Praludien) (3 fl)
 1942, Moeck.
JADIN, LOUIS EMMANUEL, Symphonie Concertante (cl, h, bn) Sieber,
 Paris; Fetis.
 ---Symphonie Concertante (fl, h, bn) Fetis; Dufaut et
 Dubois, Paris.
JEAN-MARTINON, Sonatina No. 4 for Reed Trio (ob or fl, cl, bn)
 VH, Costallat; Baron.
JELINEK, HANNS, Six Small Works, Op. 10, No. 3 (2 cl, bn) 1922,
 Universal Edition.
JENSEN, P., Trio, Op. 22 (3 cl) Andraud.
KOECHLIN, CHARLES, Three Divertissements, Op. 91 (2 fl, bass-fl
 or cl) Andraud.

KOHS, ELLIS B., Night Watch (fl, h, tymp) School of Music, University of Southern California, Los Angeles, California.

KOTCHAU, JOHANN, Divertimento, Op. 12 a, Bb major (fl, cl, bn) MH (rec) 1932, Zimmermann (min. score, parts); Rubank; Andraud.

KRAKAMP, EMANUELE, Il Maestro e gli allievi, Scherzo (3 fl) Andraud.

KUBIK, GAIL T., Little Suite (fl, 2 cl) MH (rec) Hargail Music Press.

KUFFNER, JOSEF, Trio on L'Italiana in Algeri, Op. 34, D major (3 fl) Andraud.

KUGELMANN, HANS, Trio, 1942 (3 fl)

KUMMER, KASPAR, Trio in G, Op. 24, No. 1, G major (3 fl) E-H, (rec), Dedicated to Captain Hempel; 1879 Andre (new edition, L. Doppler; Offenbach--Bonn & Leipzig; Andraud; Cundy-Bettoney Co. (Score, parts, scored for 3 cl)

   ---Trio Brilliant, Op. 30, No. 2 D major (3 fl) MH, (rec) Dedicated to Mons. Constantin Loeffler; 1879 Andre (new edition, Doppler) Offenbach--Bonn & Leipzig; Andraud; Cundy-Bettoney Co., Baxter-Northrup (Keynote Music Service)

   ---Trio, Op. 52, No. 3, E minor (3 fl) Dedicated to J. W. Gabrielsky; Offenbach--Bonn & Leipzig; Fetis.

   ---Trio in C, Op. 53, No. 4, C major (3 fl) MH (rec) Dedicated to Mons. H. Fischer; 1879, Andre (new ed. Doppler); Offenbach--Bonn & Leipzig; Andraud; Cundy-Bettoney Co. (score, parts, scored for 3 cl); Keynote Music Service.

   ---Trio, Op. 58, No. 5, D major (3 fl) Dedicated to Karl Keller; Offenbach--Bonn & Leipzig; Fetis.

   ---Sixth Trio, Op. 59, No. 6, A major (3 fl) H (rec) Dedicated to F. Kuhlau; 1923 Zimmermann; Cundy-Bettoney Co. (score, parts, scored for three cl.); Andraud; Keynote Music Service.

   ---Trio, Op. 65, No. 7, D minor (3 fl) Dedicated to A. B. Furstenau; Zimmermann; B&H; Offenbach--Bonn & Leipzig.

   ---Trio, Op. 72, No. 8, G major (3 fl) Dedicated to Eug. Walkiers, Zimmermann; B&H; Offenbach--Bonn & Leipzig; Cundy-Bettoney Co.

   ---Trio, Op. 77, No. 9, A major (3 fl) Dedicated to Mons. Schwarz. Offenbach--Bonn & Leipzig; Fetis.

   ---Nine Trios (3 fl) Ashdown (ed. by Clinton)

   ---Trio, Op. 32 (fl, cl, bn) F major MH (rec) 1864 Andre (second edition); Andraud; Rubank (first movement); Schott.

KUMMER, GOTTHOLD HEINRICH, Trios, Op. 12 and 13 (3 bn) Peters, Leipzig; B&H; Fetis.

LANGE, GUSTAVE FRIEDRICH, Weber's Invitation Waltz. Trio. (2 cl, bn) Andraud.

LAUBER, JOSEPH, Serenade. Trio (fl, cl, bn) Andraud.

LERICH, RUDOLF, Trio: Kleine Russ. Suite in d minor (3 fl) 1940, Lienau.

LOYON, ERNEST, Scherzo in D major (ob, cl, bn) Costallat, Paris.

LUBIN, First Scherzo (3 cl) ME David Gornston.

MALER, WILHELM, Sechs Kleine Spielmusiken, Op. 13a (v, fl or ob, ob or cl) 1931, Schott.

MARAIS, MARIN, Petite Trio d'Alcyone (2 ob, bn) Andraud.

MARKEVITCH, IGOR, Serenade (ein langer Satz) (v, cl, bn) polytonal. 1931 Schott (Schott Sohne in Mainz, min. score, parts); Andraud; AMP.

MARTINI, GIOVANNI BATTISTA, Les Moutons (fl, fl or ob, cl) Arr. by Milhaud. Andraud.
   ---Gavotte. Trio (ob or fl, cl, bn) Sansone; Andraud; Fischer, score, parts.

MATTHESON, JOHANN, Sonatas, Op. 1, Nos. 3-5; 8-10 (3 fl) Ed. by F. J. Giesbert. 1932-35 Nagel; 1940 Nagel; Fetis.

MCBRIDE, ROBERT, Fugue (ob, 2 cl)

MERCADANTE, SAVERIO, Three Serenades (3 fl) ME 1859 Ricordi (ed. IIa); Belwin, Inc.; Andraud.

MIHALOVICI, MARCEL, Sonata, Op. 35 (3 cl--Eb, A, bass-cl) H (rec) 1933 Salabert (scored for 3 cl, Eb, Bb, bass); Andraud; Baron.

MORITZ, EDWARD, Divertimento (3 cl) ME Mercury.

NEUMANN, H., Grand Trio, Op. 14 in A jamor (3 fl) 1883 Andre; Andraud; Cundy-Bettoney Co., Inc.; Keynote Music Service; Offenbach; Fetis.

ORBAN, MARCEL, Prelude, Pastoral, Divertimento (ob, cl, bn) Andraud.

OUBRADOUS, FERNAND, Four Pieces de Schumann in Eb major (ob, cl, bn) Selmer, Paris.
   ---Sonatine (ob, cl, bn) ME, M. Baron; Andraud; Selmer.

PAGANI, LUIGI, Trio, Op 7 (b) (3 fl) Ricordi.

PARADISI-HORTON, Sonata (fl or ob, cl, bn) MH, Transc. by Lewis H. Horton. Gamble-Hinged Music Co.; Music Publishers Holding Corp. (score, parts); Remick.

PASQUINI, BERNARDO, Sonata-Fuga. Trio (2 cl, bn) Andraud.
   ---Rocereto, Volkwein.

PERCEVAL, J., Serenata (fl, cl, bn) H-VH Southern Music Publishing Co.; Editorial Cooperative Interamericana.

PIKET, Legend and Jollity (3 cl) ME, Omega Music Edition.

PISK, PAUL AMADEUS, Trio (ob, cl, bn)

PORTER, COLE, Begin the Beguine (3 cl) Arr. by Sears, EMB

RAULT, FELIX, Six Trios, Op. 8 (2 fl, bn)
   ---Trios, Op. 25 (2 fl, bn) Pleyel, Paris; Fetis.

REIN, WALTER, Serenade I. & II. (3 woodwinds) 1937 Hanseat. Vertl-Anst. (score)

RIEGGER, WALLINGFORD, Duos for Three Woodwinds, Metropolitan Music School, NYC.

RIVIER, JEAN, Humoresk, Idyl, Waltz, Depart, "Petit Suite" (ob, cl, bn) Andraud.

RORICH, CARL, Trio in Counterpoint Style, Op. 81b (fl, cl, bn) Andraud.

ROSENBERG, Trio (ob, cl, bn) H. (rec) Borup.

ROUSSEL, ALBERT CHARLES PAUL, Andante from Unfinished Trio (ob. cl, bn) Andraud.

RUST, FRIEDRICH WILHELM, Trio in D major (vla d'am, 2 fl or fl. and v) 1939 Kallmeyer (score) in Das Erbe dt. Musik Metteldeutschland Bd 1.

SAALFELD, RALF VON, Drei kleine Spielmusiken fur 3 Melodie Instru-
    ments, Barenreiter.
SALIERI, ANTOINE, Dance from "Tarare" (fl, ob, cl, or 3 fl) ME
    Edition Musicus.
SAMUEL, HAROLD, Suite (3 fl) 1934 Boosey-Hawkes (score, parts)
SCARLATTI, ALESSANDRO, Swing Fugue (3 cl) EMB
SCHARFF, ERICH, Trio (3 fl) 1939 Vieweg.
SCHMUTZ, ALBERT D., Trio (fl, ob, cl) MH, Boosey-Hawkes.
SCHUMANN, ROBERT ALEXANDER, Four Pieces (ob, cl, bn) E (rec)
    Arr. by Fernand Oubradous. M. Baron; Andraud; Selmer.
SHAW, MARTIN FALLAS, The Rivenhall Suite (3 fl) 1936, Cramer.
SPIES, FRITZ, Serenade (3 fl) 1934 Kallmeyer.
STRINGFIELD, LAMAR, Chipmunks (fl, cl, bn) MH (rec) Edition-
    Musicus; Baron.
SUPPIGER, RUSSELL S., Improvisation and Gypsy Dance (3 Bb cl)
    ME (rec) Gamble-Hinged Music Co; Music Publishers Holding
    Corp. (score, parts).
    ---Nocturne (3 Bb cl) ME Gamble-Hinged Music Co; Music
    Publishers Holding Corp. (score, parts).
TCHEREPNINE, A., Trio (3 fl) Hug.
THOMPSON, RANDALL, Suite (ob, cl, va) Eschig, Paris; AMP.
TOMASI, HENRI, Concert Champetre (ob, cl, bn) Andraud; Baron.
TULOU, JEAN LOUIS, Trio, Op. 65 "Les Trois Amis" in F major
    (3 fl) Cocks.
    ---Trio, Op. 24 "Grand Trio" in Eb Major (3 fl) Cimrock;
    Pleyel, Paris; Fetis.
TUSTIN, WHITNEY, Tarantella (fl, ob, cl) H. C. L. Barnhouse, Inc.
VALENTIN(I), ROBERTO, Sonatas for 2 fl, bass. Published in Italy.
VOGT, G. Adagio Religioso (3 cl or 2 ob, Engl. h) ME (rec)
    Arr. by Hymie Voxman; Rubank; Costallat; Andraud.
WALCKIERS, EUGENE, Three Trios, Op. 12, in Bb major, F major,
    and C minor (fl, cl, bn) Richault.
    ---Three Trios, Op. 93, in Eb major, A major, C major (3 fl)
    Andraud; Richault; Costallat.
    ---Trio, Op. 3 in D major (3 fl)
    ---Two Trios, Op. 29, 37, in D major, Bb major (3 fl) Joubert.
WALKER, RICHARD, Bagatelle Trio (fl, ob, cl) AMP.
WEISMANN, WILHELM, Prelude, Elegie and Dance (3 fl or 3 reco)
    1932 Nagel.
    ----Theme and Variations on an Old German Folksong (3 fl)
    1932 Nagel.
WEISS, ADOLPH, Trio "Ricercare" (fl, cl, bn)
WEISS, CHARLES N., Seven Trios for Three Flutes, Published in
    London.
    ---Trios, Op. 29, 30. (3 fl) Clementi, London; Fetis.
WEISS, HELMUTH, Serenade (3 cl or 3 ob, or 3 fl) 1941-42 Moeck.
WILLAERT, ADRIAN, Nine Ricercari in Three Parts (3 winds, sop,
    alto, bass) Schott, AMP.
YODER, PAUL, Clarumba (3 cl) EMB.
    ---Dark Eyes (arr) (3 cl) EMB.
ZIMMERMANN, H., Trios, No. 1, 2 (ob, bn, vc) in F major, C major.
    1885 Schmidt, Heilbr. Cefes-Edition; Andraud.

Cumulative List

ALBISI, ABELARDO, Miniature Suites, Nos. 1 and 2 (3 fl) VH (rec)
    Andraud; Cundy-Bettoney Co., Inc.; Baxter-Northrup.
    ----Suite No. II (fl, 2 cl) Cundy-Bettoney.
    ----Trio from Miniature Suite No. 2 (3 fl) VH Cundy-Bettoney.
ARDEVOL, JOSE, Dos Sonatas a Tres, Sonata No. 1 (ob, cl, cello)
    Southern Music Publishing Co; Editorial Cooperative Inter-
    americana; Grupo de Musical Renovacion.
    ----Dos Sonatas a Tres, Sonata No. 2 (2 fl, va) Southern Music
    Publishing Co; Editorial Cooperativa Interamericana; Grupo
    de Musical Renovacion.
    ----Curata Sonata a Tres (2 ob, Eng h) Sonata No. 4, VH Sou-
    thern Music Publishing Co; Editorial Cooperativa Inter-
    americana; Grupo de Musical Renovacion.
ARNOLD, M., Trio (fl, va, bn) Lengnick.
BAAREN, KEES VAN, Trio, 1936 (fl, cl, bn) Stichting Donemus.
BACH, J. S., Three Pieces (fl or ob, cl, bn) MH M. Witmark & Sons;
    ----Three Little Classics, Andraud.
    ----Trio and Polonaise in G minor (ob, cl, bn) ME, arr. by
    Page. Oliver Ditson Co.
    ----Gavotte and Musette (ob, cl, bn) MH, arr. by Van Leeuwen.
    Gamble-Hinged Music Co; Music Publishers Holding Corp.
    (score, parts); Remick.
BADINGS, HENK, Trio II, 1943 (ob, cl, bn) Stichting Donemus.
    ----Trio IV, 1946 (2 ob, alto ob) Stichting Donemus.
BANES, ANTOINE, Shepherd's Pipe, Villanelle (ob, cl, bn) Andraud;
    Societe Nouvelle.
BANTOCK, GRANVILLE, Dance of Witches, Rondo (3 bn) 1927 Swan &
    Co; Eble.
BARNARD, Merriment Polka (3 cl, pf. if desired) EMB
BARRERE, GEORGES, Deux Pieces Breves, 1. Preludiettino, 2. Ver-
    lainade (3 fl) VH (rec) Andraud; Carl Fisher; Baxter-
    Northrup (Keynote Music Service); Hug.
BECKERATH, ALFRED VON, Kleine Hausmusik. Tag fur Tag. Kleine
    Spielmusik (3 fl or 3 cl) 1941 Moeck.
BEETHOVEN, LUDWIG VAN, Allegretto, Op. 2 (2 ob, Eng h or 3 cl)
    Andraud; Cundy-Bettoney Company.
    ----Variations on a Mozart theme (fl, cl, bn) Andraud.
    ----Celebrated Original Trio--Variations, Op. 87 "La ci darem
    la mano" (2 ob, Eng h) MH Andraud; Sansone.
    ----Trio, Op. 87, in C major (fl, ob, cl) H, arr. by Langemus.
    1882 Kistner & Siegel; Fischer; Costallet (scored for 2
    ob, Eng h); Andraud (scored for 3 cl, 3 fl or 2 ob and
    Eng h); Sansone (scored for 2 ob, Eng h).
    ----Allegro from Trio, Op. 87 in C major (3 cl) H Andraud;
    Remick.
BERBIGUIER, TRANQUILLE, 32 Trios for Three Flutes.
    ----Trio, Op. 110 (3 fl) Ashdown; B&H.
    ----Trios, Op. 40, Nos. 1, 2, and 3, in F major, E minor and
    D major (3 fl) Andraud; B&H.
    ----Trios, Op. 13, Nos. 1, 2, and 3, in G major, F major and
    E minor (3 fl) Ashdown; B&H.

---Trios, Op. 51, Nos. 1, 2, and 3, in Bb major, A minor and
 D major (3 fl) Schlesinger; B&H.
BERBIGUIER, TRANQUILLE, Trios, Op. 33, Nos. 1, 2, and 3, in G
 major, Eb major and A major (3 fl)
---Trios, Op. 62, Nos. 1, 2, and 3 in G minor, A major, and
 D major (3 fl)
---Trios, Op. 70, Nos. 1, 2, and 3 in Eb major, F major and
 G major (3 fl)
BERGT, ADOLF, Trio in 4 movements (3 bn) 1880 Merseburger & Hof-
 meister; 1933 Hofmeister; Andraud.
BEVILAQUA, M., Three Trios (2 cl, bn) Fetis.
BLASIUS, MATHIEU-FREDERIC, Trios, Op. 31 (fl, cl, bn) Fetis.
BLATT, FRANCOIS THADEL, Trio, Op. 27 (3 cl) MH, Andraud; Bossey-
 hawkes (score, parts).
 ---Trios, Op. 3 (3 cl) Prague, Berra; Fetis.
BORNEFELD, HELMUT, New Music (Neue Musik) (3 cl or 3 fl) 1932
 Nagel.
BOUFFIL, JACQUES JULES, Trios No. 1, 2, 3, Op. 7 in G major, A
 minor, F major (3 cl) MH Cundy-Bettoney Co; Andraud; A.
 Petit, Paris; Fetis. (rec)
 ---Trios, (2 cl, bn) A. Petit, Paris; Fetis.
 ---Grand Trio, Op. 8, Nos. 1, 2, and 3 in G major, A minor,
 and F major (3 cl) MH 1886 Schott; Andraud; Cundy-
 Bettoney Co; A. Petit; Fetis.
BRANDENBURG, "The Ash Grove", Welsh Folk Song (3 cl) Fischer;
 Andraud.
BRUSTAD, BJORNE, Serenade, Trio No. 2 (v, cl, bn) Ms. Photostats
 from scores from Norwegian Composers Society.
BUHL, H., Suite (3 fl) 1939 Kallmeyer.
CAMBINI, JEAN JOSEPH, Trios (3 fl) Fetis.
CHERON, ANDRE, Trios, Op. 1 (3 fl) Fetis.
 ---Trios, Op. 2 (3 fl) Fetis.
CRUSELL, BERNARD HENRIK, Trio, Symphonie Concertante, Op. 3 (cl,
 h, bn) Fetis; Peters, Liepzig.
DAUBE, JOHANN FRIEDERICH, Trio in D minor (fl, cl, guit) 1927
 (H. Neemann) Vieweg.
DAVID, ANTOINE, Six trios (cl, basset-horn, bn) 1790 Ms to Boehme
 (l'editeur de musique) in Hamburg; Fetis.
DECRUCK, FERNANDE, Capriccio. Le P'tit Quinquin (ob, cl, bn)
 Andraud; Editions de Paris.
DEROSIERS, NICOLAS, Three Books of Trios for various instruments,
 Fetis.
D'HARCOURT, M. BECLARD, Rhapsodie Peruvienne (ob, cl, bn) C major,
 Lemoine, Paris; Elkan-Vogel.
DIETTER, CHRETIEN LOUIS, Several pieces (airs, etc.) (fl, bn,
 cl) Fetis.
DOUGLAS, R., Six Dance Caricatures (fl, ob, cl) Hinrichsen.
DRESDEN, SEM, Klein Trio (2 ob, Eng h) Stichting Donemus.
DRESSLER, RAPHAEL, Trio Concertante, Op. 64 (3 fl) D major; Sim-
 rock.
DROUET, LOUIS, Trios (3 fl) Fetis.
DUCREUX, EMMANUEL, Duos, taken from works of J. Haydn and Mozart,
 Books I, II (2 fl, bn) 1795 Sieber; Fetis.

DUMONCHAU, CHARLES FRANCOIS, Symphonie Concertante (fl, ob, bn)
      Fetis.
EGIDI, ALBERT, Trio
EHRHARDT, ELSE, Trio 5 Flotensprunge (Pitsch) (3 fl) 1942 Moeck.
EMMERT, ADAM JOSEPH, Harmonie, Premier recueil (2 h, bn) Salz-
      bourg, 1799; Fetis.
ESCHER, RUDOLF, Trio d'anches, Op. 4 (ob, cl, bn) Stichting Do-
      nemus.
ESSER, BEN, Small Suite in F major (Kleine Suite) (3 fl), 1932
      Nagel.
FABRE, C., Serenade, (3 cl) Andraud.
FAHRBACH, JOSEPH, Le Telegraphe musical, recueil periodique de
      pots-pourris (fl, cl, or ob, bn) sur des motifs d'operas,
      Op. 21. Fetis Supplement.
   ---Deux Fantaisies sur Aida, Op. 78 (3 fl) Fetis Supplement.
FLEDERHOF, JAN, Thema met variaties, 1943 (ob, cl, bn) Stichting
      Donemus.
FERGUSON, HOWARD, Five Pieces (3 fl) 1935 Cramer (score, parts)
   ---5 Pipe Pieces for treble, alto and tenor pipe.
FIALA, JOSEPH, Trios concertants, Book I & II (fl, ob, bn) Ratis-
      bonne, 1806; Fetis.
FLOTHUIS, MARIUS, Nocturne, Op. 11, 1941 (fl, ob, cl) Stichting
      Donemus; Chester.
FORCK, WILHELM, Introduction, Prelude, Fuge (3 fl) 1938 Moeck;
      (Introduction u. Doppelfuge--lyd. Praludium u. Fuge--
      phryg.)
FORTNER, WOLFGANG, Serenade 1945 (fl, ob, bn) Schott (B. Schott
      Sohne in Mainz); Baron; AMP; Hug.
FRANCK, MAURICE, Pastoral, Andante, Scherzo, Finale (ob, cl, bn)
      Andraud.
FREDERICK THE GREAT, Andante (2 fl, v) Andraud.
FUCHS, GEORG FRIEDRICH, Two works of trios (cl, h, bn) Fetis
      Sieber, Paris.
   ---Symphonies concertantes (cl, fl, h) Naderman, Paris;
      Fetis.
GABRIELSKY, JOHANN WILHALM, Trios, Op. 6, Nos. 1, 2, and 3 in
      G major, A minor and D major (3 fl) ed. by Clinton; Ashdown.
   ---Trios, Op. 10, Nos. 1, 2, and 3 in A major, Eb major and
      E minor, (3 fl) B&H.
   ---Trio, Op. 31 in D major (3 fl) Schlesinger.
   ---Grand Trio Concert, Op. 31 (3 fl) Andraud.
   ---Trios, Op. 32 in F major (3 fl) Ashdown.
   ---Trios, Op. 33 in G major (3 fl) B&H.
   ---Trio, Op. 34, in F major (3 fl) B&H.
   ---Trios, Op. 41 in Bb major (3 fl) B&H.
   ---Trios, Op. 55, Nos. 1, 2, and 3 in D major, F major and
      E minor (3 fl) Ashdown.
   ---Trios, Op. 56, Nos. 1, 2, and 3 in G major, D major and
      C major (3 fl) Ashdown.
   ---Trios, Op. 58, Nos. 1, 2, and 3 in D major, E minor and
      Eb major (3 fl) Ashdown.
   ---Trio, Op. 104, Nos. 1, 2, and 3 in G major, A major and
      D minor (3 fl) Ed. by Clinton. Ashdown.

GABRIELSKY, JOHANN WILHELM, Trios, Op. 78, Nos. 1, 2, and 3 in
Eb major, A major, and G minor (3 fl) B&H.
GARNIER, FRANCOIS JOSEPH, Symphonie Concertante, Op. 4 (fl, ob,
bn) Naderman; Fetis.
---Trios, (fl, h, bn or vc) Janet & Cotelle; Fetis.
GEBAUER, FRANCOIS RENE, Trios, Op. 29, 32, 39, 42, 46 and letter
D, for various wind instruments, Pleyel; Sieber; Hentz;
Lemoine; Fetis.
GIANELLA, LOUIS, Trios-Nocturnes, Op. 12 (2 fl, bn) Carli; Fetis.
GIORDANI, THOMAS, Six Trios (taken from Opera airs) Op. 9 (2 fl,
vc) Fetis.
GOETZEL, FRANCOIS JOSEPH, Trios (3 fl) Ms. in Dresden, Germany.
Fetis.
GOUE, Bagatelle, Melopee and Scherzo (ob, cl, bn) Andraud.
GRENZER, JEAN FREDERIC, Six Trios (3 fl) 1779, Hummel; Fetis.
HANKE, CHARLES, Trios (2 ob, bn) Fetis.
HARRER, GOTTLOB, Trios for oboe (3 ob) Fetis.
HECKEL, WILHELM, Burlesk in G major (ob, h, bn) Ms. Heckel--
Wiesbaden, Germany.
HERMANN, PAUL, Music for Three Flutes (Flotenmusik) 1943 Moeck
HERRMANN, HUGO, Music for Three Flutes, Op. 57a (3 fl) 1931 Bote
and Bock.
HERX, W., Trios, Op. 65 (2 fl, guit) 1845 Schloss (Ries & Erler).
HOFFER, PAUL, Three Kleine Suiten (Three Small Suites) (3 fl)
1938 Vieweg (score, parts).
HOFFMEISTER, FRANCOIS ANTOINE, Symphonies Concertantes (2 cl, bn)
Fetis.
HOLST, GUSTAV, Terzetto in two movements, Op. 44 (fl, ob, va) poly-
tonal, Allegretto and Scherzo. M. Baron; Andraud; Eble.
HURRELL, Two Impressions (3 cl) EMB.
JEMNITZ, ALEXANDER, Trio, Op. 20 (fl, ob, cl) Zimmermann, 1928.
KETTING, PIET,. Trio, 1929 (fl, cl, bn) Stichting Donemus.
---Sonata, 1935-36 (fl, ob, pf) Stichting Donemus.
KINSCELLA, Folk Tune Trios.
KOCHFR-KLEIN, HILDA, Kleine Serenade, Op. 26 (Petite Serenade)
(fl, ob or v, vc) 1928 Bohm (score, parts); Andraud.
KOECHLIN, CHARLES, Three Divertissements, Op. 91 (2 fl, bass-
fl or cl) Andraud.
KOLB, JEAN BAPTISTE, Trios (ob, cl, bn) Ms. in le magasin de
Westphall a Hambourg; Fetis.
KONINK, SERVAAS DE, Trios, (2 fl, v or ob) Roger, Amsterdam;
Fetis.
KRAMER, Swing Fuge (3 cl) MH Pro Art.
KREJEL, ISA, Divertimento. Trio (ob, cl, bn) Andraud; Hudebni
Matice.
KREUTZER, JOS., Trio in A major (fl, cl, guit) Zimmermann.
KRIENS, C., Rone des Lutins (fl, ob, clar) Fischer.
KROLIMANN, A., Trios, Op. 13, Nos. 1, 2, and 3 in D major, F
major, and E minor (3 fl) Three Grand Trios. Hannover-
Bachmann; Fetis.
KROMMER, FRANZ, Concertante, Op. 70 (fl, cl, v) Haslinger; Fe-
tis.
---Concertante, Op. 80. (fl, cl, v) Haslinger; Fetis.

KUFFNER, JOSEPH, Trios (five works) (3 fl, and duos for 2 fl)
      Richault, Paris; Fetis.
KUGELMANN, HANS, Trio, Kleine Messe (3 ob or 3 cl or 3 fl) 1942
      (Fritz Jode); Moek.
KURPINSKI, CHARLES, Nocturne, Op. 16 (h, va, bn) Brzczina, Varso-
      vie; Fetis.
KURZWEIL, Trio (cl, va, bn) Fetis.
LABARRE, MICHEL DE, Trios (3 fl) Fetis.
LAFAGE, JUSTE-ADRIEN LENOIR DE, Air Varie en Trio (2 fl, v) Fetis.
LAMBERTI, LOUIS, Pieces (v, cl, fl) Fetis.
LANGE, F.G., The Three Gay Brothers Trio (2 cl, bn) Andraud; 1881
      (Erdmann, Ein heiteres Trio) Seeling; (Die drei lustigen
      Bruder Trio).
LEFEVRE, JEAN-XAVIER, Six Trios (2 cl, bn) Fetis.
   ---Concertante (ob, cl, bn) Janet, Paris; Fetis.
LIADOW, Mosquito Dance (3 fl) E (rec) EMB; Concord Music Publish-
      ing Co.
MAGANINI, QUINTO E., Ars Contrapunctus (fl, cl, bn) MH Edition-
      Musicus; Baron.
   ---Gaeta (fl, Eng h, tamb) comp. 1897.
MAHAUT, ANTON, Trios (3 fl) Probably publ. in Amsterdam or Paris.
MARKEVITCH, IGOR, Serenade (v, cl, bn) Schott; AMP.
MARTINENGHI, G., Terzetto (3 fl) Ricordi.
MARTINN, JACQUES JOSEPH BALTHAZAR, First Symphony Concertant (2 fl,
      bn) Frey, Paris; Fetis.
MARTINON, JEAN, Sonatine No. 4 in C, Op. 26, No. 1 (ob, cl, bn)
      Baron.
MARX, KARL, Trio, Op. 27c, Kleine Weihnachtmusik (3 fl) Barenreiter.
MAYR, A., Kleine suite (fl, cl, h) Hug.
MEISTER, KARL, Little Suite (3 fl) 1940 Moeck.
MELCHIOR, A.J.B., Three trios tres-brillants et faciles (Bb cl, h,
      bn) Op. 7. Fetis Supplement.
MELNIK, Eighteen Trios from Classic Masters in score form (2 fl,
      cl or fl, ob, cl) EMB.
MENGELBERG, KAREL, Trio No. 5, 1939 (fl, ob, bn) Stichting Done-
      mus.
MOHR, A., Landliches Idyl. Trio (fl, cl, bn) Andraud.
MOZART, W. A., Allegretto from Sixth Sonata (fl, cl, bn) MH. 1932
      Leuckart; Kay & Kay Music Publishing Co., Trinkaus-Frank-
      lin Publishing Co. (scored for ob, cl, bn); Andraud (scored
      for fl, cl, bn)
MULLER, ERNEST LOUIS, Trio (3 fl) Publ, ca 1760 in Berlin; Fetis.
NAUDOT, JEAN JACQUES, Twelve Petite Pieces in Trios for German
      Flutes. Publ. in Paris between 1720 and 1726; Fetis.
NAUMANN, ERNSTGUIDO, Trio: Nun lasset uns beginnen. Ein Spiel.
      (3 fl or 3 ob or 3 cl) 1943, Simrock (score, parts)
OLIVADOTI, JOSEPH, Trio, Scherzetto (fl, ob, cl or fl, 2 cl) MH
      (rec) Gamble-Hinged Music Co.; Music Publishers Holding
      Corp. (score, parts); Remick.
PAINTER, PAUL, Alla Camera (3 fl or 3 C-cl) M Gamble-Hinger Mu-
      sic Co., Music Publishers Holding Corp. (score, parts).
PEZEL, JOHANN, Works for Three Flutes. Stucke. (3 fl) 1935,
      Barenreiter (J. Bacher).

PHILIDOR, PIERRE, Pieces for flute, oboe and violin together with
three books of duos in a single volume in a second edition.
---Premier oeuvre, 3 suites a deux flutes traversieres, Paris,
1717, Fetis Supplement.
---Deuxieme oeuvre, 2 suites a deux flutes traversieres, Paris,
1718, Fetis Supplement.
---Troisieme oeuvre, 1 suite a deux flutes traversieres, Paris,
1718, Fetis Supplement.
---Trio, premier oeuvre, 6 suites (a collection of the three
groups listed above) Paris, Fetis Supplement.
PICCHIANTI, LUIGI, Trio (cl, bn, guit) B&H; Fetis.
PIJPER, WILLEM, Trio (fl, cl, bn) Stichting Donemus.
PITSCH, Trio (3 fl) Moeck, 1942.
PLA, JUAN AND MANUEL, Three trios, (2 fl, bn)
PLATS, JOSEPH, Twenty Trios (2 ob, bn) Fetis.
PLEYEL, IGNACE JOSEPH, Six Trios, Op. 8, arr. for clarinet from
Duets, Op. 8 (3 cl) Andraud; Cundy-Bettoney Co.
PLOUVIER, PIERRE JOSEPH, Serenades, Books I, II, III, IV (2 fl,
bn) Brussells, Plouvier; Fetis.
POESSINGER, FRANZ ALEXANDER, Pieces, Op. 5 (3 fl) Artaria, 1799;
Fetis.
PONSE, LUCTOR, Trio (fl, cl, bn) Stichting Donemus.
PORTA, BERNARDO, Trios, Op. 1, 6, 11 (3 fl) Sieber; Janet; Fetis.
QUOINTE, LE P., Pieces en trio composees a la maniere ita-
lienne et a la maniere francaise (fl, v, ob) Fetis Supple-
ment.
RODGERS, RICHARD, Blue Room (3 cl) Arr. by Sears. EMB.
ROTHENBERG, THEOPHIL, Variations (3 fl) 1939, Hug.
RUBARDT, PAUL, 3 Kleine Terzette (3 fl) 1932, Nagel.
SCARLATTI, ALESSANDRO, Tempo di Ballo (3 cl) MH Music Service
Press; Masterworks Publications (scored for ob, cl, bn)
SHANKS, ELLSWORTH, Sonata of Moods and Humors (3 Bb cl) MH (rec)
1935, Gamble Hinged Music Co. (score, parts); Andraud.
SIMONET, FRANCOIS, Three Trios (cl, h, bn) Fetis.
STETKA, FRANZ, Kleine Suite (2 fl, guit) 1944 Universal Edition.
TAK, P. C. Preludium, koraal en fuga (ob, cl, bn) 1935 Stichting
Donemus.
THEIL, KARL, Trio, Op. 33, Kammertrio (3 fl) 1937, Nagel.
THOMAS, KURT, Trio, Op. 33b, Kleine Hausmusik (3 fl) 1939, B&H.
THURNER, FREDERICK EUGENE, Trio, Op. 56 (ob, 2 h) Fetis; Probst.
TSCHAIKOWSKY, PETER ILITCH, Dance des Mirlitons (Dance of the Reed
Flutes) (3 fl) Fischer; Andraud; Rubank (scored for 3
cl, arr. by Colby).
TULOU, JEAN LOUIS, Symphonie Concertante (fl, ob, bn) H. Lemoine;
Fetis.
TUSTIN, Scherzo (fl, ob, cl) MH. C. L. Barnhouse, Inc.
TUTHILL, BURNET CORWIN, Scherzo, Op. 1, No. 1, 1909 (3 cl or 2Bb
and 1 Eb alto) H. Fischer (score, parts); Andraud.
---Intermezzo, Op. 1, No. 2, 1927 (2 cl, bassethorn) MH.
Fischer (score, parts, also scored for 3 cl, 2 Bb and 1
Eb alto); Andraud (scored for 2 cl, and alto cl).
VANDENBROECH, OTHON JOSEPH, Symphonie Concertante No. 2 (cl, h.
bn) Naderman; Fetis.

VIERDANCK, JOHANN, Trio-Suite (2 ob, bn) Andraud.
   ---Capricci, for two or three instruments, Engel.
WALCKIERS, EUGENE, Grand Trio Concertant, Op. 2 in F major (3
      fl) Ricordi; 1923, Zimmermann; Andraud; Baxter-
      Northrup; Hug.
WALTHEW, RICHARD HENRY, Triolet in Bb (ob, cl, bn) VH (rec)
      Andraud; 1934, Boosey-Hawkes (score, parts).
   ---Prelude & Fugue (2 cl, vn or vc)
WATERSON, JAMES, First Grand Trio Concertant (3 cl) in G minor.
      H. Boosey-Hawkes (score, parts); Andraud; Cundy-Bettoney
      Co. (rec)
WEHRLI, WERNER, Trio, Op. 32 (3 fl) 1932, Hug.
WEISS, CHARLES, Trios (3 fl) London, Longman; Fetis.
WEISSENBORN, JULIUS, Six Trios, Op. 4 (3 bn) 1933, Hofmeister;
      1882, Merseburger; Andraud.
WERTHEIM, ROSY, Trio, 1942 (fl, bn, cl) Stichting Donemus.
WIDERKEHR, JACQUES CHRETIEN MICHEL, Symphoney Concertant, No. 7,
      (fl, cl, bn) Erard; Fetis.
   ---Thtree Trios, Op. 12 (fl, cl, bn) Gaveaux; Fetis.
WOEHL, WALDEMAR, Music for Three Flutes (3 fl) 1931, Nagel.
WOELFFL, JOSEF, Two Trios (2 cl, bn) Steiner, Vienna; Fetis.
WOEMPNER, HENRY C., Trio (3 fl)
WORTH, Music Box and Miniature Song, arr. by Tustin (fl, ob, cl)
      EMB.
WRANICZKY, PAUL, Three Trios, Op. 53 (2 fl, vc) Andre Offenbach;
      Fetis.
ZAGWIJN, HENRI, Trio I, 1944 (fl, ob, cl) Stichting Donemus.
   ---Trio II, 1949 (fl, ob, cl) Stichting Donemus.
ZOELLER, CARL, On an Alpine Meadow (2 cl, bn) Andraud.

Training Trios

ANDRAUD, A. J., Eighteen Trios from the Classic Masters (fl, ob, cl)
    ME-H (rec) Leeuwen; Andraud, (also scored for 2 fl and cl).
ARDEVOL, JOSE, Curata Sonata a Tres (2 ob, Engl h) VH Southern Mu-
    sic Publishers.
ARNE, THOMAS AUGUSTINE, Affettuoso (3 cl) ME Oliver Ditson.
ARTOT, J. B., Twelve Trios (2 cl, fl; or 3 cl; or fl, cl, Eb sax; or
    2 cl, Eb sax) Cundy-Bettoney.
AURIC, GEORGES, Trio (ob, cl, bn) ME (rec) Andraud; Eble; L'Oi-
    seau Lyre.
BACH, JOHANN SEBASTIAN, Three Part Inventions, arr. by Tustin
    (3 ob or 2 ob and Eng h) Spratt.
    ---Sinfonia in A Minor, arr. by Taylor (fl, ob, bn) E Mills
      Music, Inc.
    ---Trio and Polonaise in G minor (ob or fl, cl, bn) ME Oliver
      Ditson; Andraud; Presser.
    ---Three Fugues (2 cl, bn) Arr. by Thurston. ME Boosey-
      Hawkes (score, parts).
    ---Fugue in C Minor (cl, h, bn) Arr. by Foreman. Andraud.
    ---A variety of Bach music, transc. by Simon (3 cl) E-MH.
      EMB; Schirmer.
    ---Fugue in C minor from the Well-Tempered Clavichord, arr.
      by Tarlow (fl, cl, bn) E-MH, Elkan-Vogel Co., Inc.
    ---Fughetta, arr. by Taylor (3 fl) ME Mills Music, Inc.
BEETHOVEN, LUDWIG VAN, Minuet in G, No. 2, arr. by Trinkhaus (2
    cl, bn) E Fischer (score, parts).
BLATT, FRANCOIS-THADEE, Trio, Op. 27 (3 cl) ME Boosey-Hawkes-
    Belwin, Inc.
BOVE, J. HENRY, Petit Trio (fl or ob, cl, bn) E (rec) 1934 Fis-
    cher (score, parts); Andraud; Hug.
    ---Andante and Allegro (2 cl, bass-cl or bn) E-ME Leeds
      Music.
BROOKE, ARTHUR, The Three Musketeers (3 fl) Cundy-Bettoney Co.
    Inc.
CAMARA, JUAN ANTONIA, Suite (fl, cl, bn) ME-MH Southern Music
    Publishing Company; Editorial Cooperative Interamericana;
    Grupo De Musical Renovacion.
CARMAN, A., Petit Rondo (Forme Classique) (2 cl or fl and cl, bn)
    Cundy-Bettoney Co., Inc.
CARULLI, BENEDICT, Trio in Bb major, ed. by Bellison (3 cl) Ri-
    cordi.
CHAPPELL, Chappell's Famous Melodies, including Bells of St.
    Mary's, Roses of Picardy, etc., arr. by Carver (3 cl) ME EMB
CHEMIN-PETIT, HANS, Trio im alten stil (ob, cl, bn) ME Eble.
CLINTON, JOHN, Trio for three flutes, Op. 7 in A, Op. 9 in G and
    Op. 30 in F, Ashdown.
COBB, SCRIBNER, Woodland Dance (fl, 2 cl) ME Gamble Hinged
    Music Co.; Music Publishers Holding Corp. (score, parts);
    Remick.
COLBY, CARLETON L., Three Blind Mice, Scherzo (3 fl or 3 cl, op-
    tional pf) ME Gamble Hinged Music Co.; EMB; Music Pub-
    lishers Holding Corp. (score, parts). (rec)

CORROYEZ, G., Second Collection: Trio-Sonatas from the Old Masters: Ph. E. Bach, Boccherini, Couperin, Corelli, Gluck, Haydn, Mozart. (Part A: Fl, ob, or v, cl) (Part B: 2nd Cl, 2nd v) (Part C: 3rd cl, bn or vc; Eb Tenor-sax; Bb bar-sax; Bass-cl; fr h in F; Va) MH Andraud.

---First Collection: Little Trios. La Steinkerque, Joyous Fanfare, Fr. Couperin; Menuet de Castor et Pollux, J. Ph. Rameau; Air tendre et Bourree, J. Mouret; Andante Expressivo, C. Tessarini; Rondo, J. Haydn; Sicilienne, J. Walond; Andante de la Sonatine, Op. 36, No. 4, M. Clementi; Gavotte, W. Boyce; Andante Cantabile et Menuet, Mozart; Marche Solennelle, Mendelssohn; Adagio de la Sonate, Op. 2, Beethoven; Menuet, Mozart; Air d'Orphee, Gluck; Allegro Moderato, Mozart; Marche Solennelle, Handel; Andante et Menuet, J. S. Bach; Sarabande, Handel; Menuet, J. Stamitz; Marche religieuse en forme de fugue, G. Ph. Teleman; Andante du Concerto pour orgue, Ch. Wesleg; Gigue, Corelli; Sarabande et Allegro, Corelli. (Part A: fl, ob, or v; cl or sop.-sax; Bb tr; C tr) (Part B: Cl; Eb alto-sax; 2nd v; Bb tr; C tr) (Part C: fr h in Eb or Alto-cl; Bb ten-sax; Bb bass-sax or Bb bass-cl; Eb bar-Sax; bn or vc or str-bass; Bb trom or Bb euph; tr or tuba in C) Andraud.

CRIST, Old Spanish Melody (3 fl) E Concord Music Publishing Co.

---Tap Dance (3 fl) ME Concord Music Publishing Co.

ECKER, Six pieces by Bach, Brahms, Martini, Mendelssohn, Rameau and Schubert, arr. by Ecker. (cl, fl, ob, bn in different combinations) ME Boston Music Co; EMB.

FELDMAN, First Round for all Instruments (3 cl or c fl) VE Mercury Music.

FRANGKISER, Les Lavalette (2 cl, bn) Boosey & Hawkes.

---Inventriole, (2 cl, bn) ME-MH Belwin.

GIRNATIS, WALTER, Trio (3 cl)

GLUCK, CHRISTOPH WILLIBALD VON, Gavotte from Iphigenia en Aulis, (ob or fl, cl, bn) E (rec) Andraud; Kay & Kay.

---Gavotte (fl, cl, bn) E Kay & Kay Music Publishing Co. (scored for 3 cl) Andraud (scored for ob, cl, bn); Ed. by Trinkaus, Franklin Co.

---Gavotte (3 Bb cl) ME Arr. by Brandenburg, Fischer; Arr. by Harry S. Hirsch, scored for fl, or ob, cl, bn, Music Publishers Holding Corp.

HANDEL, GEORGE FRIEDRICK, Minuet, arr. by Angel del Busto (fl, cl, bn) E (rec) Fischer (score, parts); Andraud (scored for ob, cl, bn).

HAUBIEL, CHARLES, In the Dorian Mode (3 fl) ME The Composers Press.

---In the Lydian Mode (3 fl) ME The Composers Press.

HAYDN, FRANZ JOSEPH, Rondo Scherzando, arr. by Taylor (3 fl) ME Boosey-Hawkes (score, parts).

HEIDRICH, MAXIMILIAN, Clarinet trio, Op. 33 (3 cl)

HIRSCH, HARRY S, Three Little Classics: Gavotte and Musette, Bach; Fugue, Bach; Gavotte, von Gluck, arr. by Hirsch. (fl or ob, cl, bn) Music Publishers Holding Corp. (score, parts).

HOOK, JACQUES JAMES, Sonata in G major, Op. 83, No. 4 (3 fl) ME
    Boosey-Hawkes (score, parts); Hug.
JAVAULT, LOUIS, Trios, Books I and II (cl, h, bn) Janet, Paris;
    Fetis.
KEITH, GEORGE D., Scherzo and Continuo (3 fl) E Gamble Hinged
    Music; Music Publishers Holding Corp. (score, parts,
    called Scherzet and Continuo).
LEEUWEN, ARY VAN, Sonatina in the Old Style (3 fl) Fischer; Hug.
MAGANINI, QUINTO E., La Rubia, Spanish Serenade (Fairest One) (ob,
    cl, bn or fl, cl, bn) ME Fischer; Andraud.
   ---Vienna, (fl, ob or cl, bn) Fischer (score, parts).
MATHESON, JOHANN, Air, Minuet and Sarabande, arr. by Taylor (2 cl,
    bass-cl, bn optional) ME Mill Music, Inc.
MOORE, DOUGLAS, Twenty Trios for Clarinet Ensembles (3 cl) E-ME
    Willis Music Co.
MOZART, WOLFGANG A., German Dance arr. for 3 winds. McGinnis &
    Marx.
   ---March from Titus (Clemenza di Tito, K. 621), arr. by Tay-
    lor (3 fl) E Mills Music, Inc.
MULLER, IWAN, Trio in G minor (3 cl) Ed. by Bellison. Ricordi.
NEUMANN, H., Rondo Brilliante, arr. by Taylor (fl, ob, bn) ME
    Willis Music, Inc.
OLIVADOTI, JOSEPH, Scherzetto (fl, ob, cl) ME Gamble Hinged
    Music Co. (scored for ob, cl, bn); Andraud.
OLSEN, SPARRE, Suite for Three Treblasere, Op. 10 (fl, ob, cl)
    ME Peters; M. Baron; C. F. Peters; Hug.
OWEN, BLYTHE, Trio, (ob, cl, bn)
PAINTER, PAUL, Semplicia (3 fl) MH Gamble Hinged Music; Music
    Publishers Holding Corp. (score, parts)
QUINET, FERNAND, Rhapsody (3 cl)
RAMEAU, DE FILIPPI, The Hen (fl, ob, bn) ME (rec) Concord Mu-
    sic Publishing Co.
RATHAUS, K., Gavotte Classique (fl, ob, bn) ME Boosey-Hawkes
    (score, parts) (rec).
RIETHMULLER, H., Miniautres (fl, cl, bn) Hug.
ROBERTS, CHARLES J., The Harmony: Solo, Duet and Trio Album,
    trans. and arr. by Charles J. Roberts: Songs My Mother
    Taught Me, Dvorak; Dreamland Shadows, Hoelzel; The Old
    Refrain, Kreisler; Serenade Espagnole, Bizet; The Magic
    Song, Meyer-Helmund; Estrellita, Ponce; Torna a Sor-
    rento, de Curtis; Cielito Lindo, Fernandez; Largo from
    New World Symphony, Dvorak; Dreams, Chenoweth; Stances
    (Love Song), Flegier; La Paloma, de Yradier. (Instru-
    mentation: Melody of first part: fl, Bb cl. Duet or 2nd
    Parts: Bb cl, alto cl. Trio or 3rd Parts: Bb cl, alto
    cl-Eb, hn in F, bn) (With piano accompaniment.) Fischer.
ROOT, GEORGE F., There's Music in the Air, transc. by M.A. Sprin-
    ger (2 cl, bn) Music Publishers Holding Corp. (score,
    parts).
ROPARTZ, J. GUY, Entrata a Scherzetto (ob, cl, bn) ME Eble.
ROSENTHAL, C. A., Clarinet Trios from Corelli to Beethoven, arr.
    by Rosenthal (3 cl) E-ME (rec) Edwin H. Morris & Co.
    (White & Smith); EMB.
   ---Clarinet Trios (18th Century) arr. by Rosenthal (3 cl) E-
    ME (rec) Edwin H. Morris & Co. (White & Smith); EMB.

SCARMOLIN, A. LOUIS, Barcarolle and Petite Humoresque (2 cl, bn
    or bass-cl) E Ludwig Music Publishing Co.
SCHUMANN, ROBERT ALEXANDER, Chant du Soir (fl, cl, bn) E (rec)
    Ricordi.
    ---First Loss, Op. 68, No. 16, Transc. by M. A. Springer (3
    cl) Music Publishers Holding Corp. (score, parts).
SHOSTAKOVICH, DMITRI, Preludes (fl or ob, cl, bn) arr. by Mag-
    anini E-ME (rec) Edition-Musicus; Baron.
SPRATT, JAC, Three Miniatures for Three Woodwinds (fl or ob, cl,
    bn) E-ME Spratt; Baron.
STAEPS, HANS, Variations "On Our Little Farm" (3 reco) AMP; Os-
    terreichischer Bundesverlag, Vienna.
TARTINI, GIUSEPPE, Two Trio Sonatas in D major (3 cl) ME Edition-
    Musicus.
TAYLOR, LAWRENCE, Suite Classique (3 fl) Kay & Kay.
TRINKAUS, GEORGE J., Sixteen Original and Transcribed Compositions,
    (fl or ob, cl, bn) E-MH (rec) Fillmore Music House.
TUSTIN, Tarantella (2 cl, bass-cl) MH C. L. Barnhouse.
UGGEN, Playwell Trios, a collection (fl, ob, cl) VE-E (rec) Paul
    A Schmitt Music Co.
WALTER, JOHANN, Canons for equal instruments, arr. by Ehmann (3
    fl, 3 cl, etc.) especially suitable for recorders. (rec)
    Hortus Musicus, Musica Rara, London.
VAUBOURGOIN, MARC, Trio (ob, cl, bn) MH (rec) Eble; Baron; Sel-
    mer.
WELSH FOLK SONG, The Ash Grove (3 Bb cl) Carl Fischer (score,
    parts).
WISSMER, Serenade (ob, cl in A, bn) MH (rec) Andraud; Costal-
    lat.
VOXMAN, HYMIE, Trio (3 fl) ME Rubank.
    ---Trios, Vol. I (3 cl) E (rec) Rubank.
    ---Trios, Vol. II (3 cl) M (rec) Rubank.
    ---Trios for Three Woodwinds (fl, cl, bn or bass-cl) ME
    Rubank.
ZEISL, ERIC, Greek Melody (3 cl) E Mills Music, Inc.
ZOLLER, CARLI, Auf Der Alm (2 cl, bn) ME Boosey-Hawkes (score,
    parts).
    ---Sonate, Op. 150 (3 cl) 1885, Boosey-Hawkes-Belwin, Inc.

Collections:

Three & Four Part Canons & Rounds (3 or 4 fl, ob, or cl, or reco)
    Mercury.
TRITONE FOLIO, selected, edited and arranged by Joseph E. Maddy,
    T. P. Giddings and Charles J. Roberts. Contents: The
    Starting Point, Maddy; Choral, Minnema; Choral, McKay;
    Choral, Chase; Ascension, Shaw; The Clock, Part; Cho-
    ral, Bellstrom; Hymn of Prayer, Maddy; The Crusader,
    Gilman; Camp Hymn, Mattern; The Cossack, Monger; Tip-
    Top, Wilson; Memories, Hawkinson; The Cavalier, Maddy;
    Jeanne, Williams; Integer Vitae, Flacci; Go, Forget Me,
    Mozart; Lullaby, Maddy; As a Little Girl, Weber; Amici,
    College Song; The Log Cabin, Evanson; Away with Melan-
    choly, Mozart; Romance, Benson; Boat Song, Weber; Slum-
    ber Song, French Lullaby; Prayer, Maddy; Hard Times
    Come Again No More, Foster; The Call, Zoeller; Stars of
    the Summer Night, Anonymous; Cradle Song, Schubert; What
    Care We for Gold or Silver, Anonymous; Children's Hosan-
    na, King; Come and See Me, Anonymous; Dickory, Dickory
    Dock, Traditional; Days of Absence, Rosseau; Darling,
    Go to Rest, Anonymous; Ellie Rhee, Winner; The Farmer,
    Anonymous; Home Again, Pike. Instrumentation: Parts for
    fl, ob, Bb cl, Eb alto cl, Bb bass cl, bn Carl Fischer.

Classic Trios

ALLIER, G., Rustic Scene (fl or ob, cl, bn; 2 ob, bn or h; 3 cl)
    Andraud.
AUBER, D.F.E., Fra Diavolo Overture (2 cl, bn) Manuscript.
BACH, J.C.F., Allegretto Piacevole, arr. by Quinto Maganini (fl,
    cl, bn) Andraud; Carl Fischer (score, parts).
BACH, J.S., Fughetta, arr. by E. Cafarella (ob, eng h, bn) An-
    draud; Music Publishers Holding Corp. (score, parts);
    Witmark.
    ---Gavotte, Musette, Fuge, (Trio), transc. by Harry S. Hirsch
      (ob or fl, cl, bn) MH Gamble; Andraud; Music Publishers
      Holding Corp. (I. Gavotte and Musette, 2. Fugue).
    ---Choral Prelude, arr. by Lawrence Taylor (2 fl, bn or bass-
      cl) ME Kay & Kay.
    ---I Call Upon Thy Name, O Jesus (Trio) (ob or fl, cl, bn)
      Sansone; Andraud; Carl Fischer (score, parts).
    ---Sinfonia IX, XI and Gavotte (ob or fl, cl, bn) Andraud;
      Witmark; Music Publishers Holding Corp. (arr. by Theo-
      dore M. Finney, "Three Pieces").
    ---Sinfonia in C Minor (cl, alto-cl, bass-cl) Andraud; Wit-
      Mark; Music Publishers Holding Corp. (arr. by E. Cafarel-
      la, score, parts).
    ---First and Second Gavotte Favorites (ob, cl, bn) Andraud.
    ---Canonical Fugue (3 cl, Bb, Eb alto, Bb bass) Fischer.
    ---Musical offering, I. Ricercar a 3 (3-Part fugue) (3 reeds)
      Schirmer.
    ---Musical offering, II-VI, Canons for 3 instruments. Schir-
      mer.
    ---Prelude and Fugue, arr. by Arnell (ob, cl, bn) MH Boosey
      & Hawkes (score, parts).
    ---Trio Album (3 fl, 3 ob, 3 reco or 3 bn) Mercury Music Co.
    ---Three Little Classics (fl or ob, cl, bn) Transc. by
      Hirsch ME Gavotte and Musette, Bach; Fugue, Bach; Ga-
      votte, C. W. von Gluck. Andraud: Witmark; Music Publish-
      ers Holding Corp. (score, parts).
BACH, WILHELM FRIEDRICH ERNST, Trio in G, arr. by Ermeler (2 fl,
    va) Hortus Musicus, Musica Rara.
    ---Trio in G major, arr. by Ermeler (2 fl, va) 1943, Baren-
      reiter (score, parts).
BARRAUD, HENRI, Trio (ob, cl, bn) 1939 Lyre d'Oiseau; Broude
    Bros.; Andraud; Baron.
BARRERE, GEORGES, Deux Pieces Breves (Two Short Pieces) (3 fl)
    VH 1. Preludiettino, 2. Verlainade. Carl Fischer.
BASSANO, GIOVANNI, Seven Trios (3 wind instruments) Musica Rara.
BECK, FREDERICK W., Second Trio for Three Flutes (3 fl)
BECKERATH, ALFRED VON, Trio Musik (v or ob or fl, cl, bn or vc)
    MH 1938 Litolff (score, parts).
BEETHOVEN, LUDWIG VAN, Dondo from Sonate Pathetique (3 cl) arr. by
    R. Toll. Andraud; Cundy-Bettoney Co.
    ---Clarinet Trio in Bb, contained in Beethoven, 11 Trios (3
      Bb cl) C. F. Peters Corp., NYC.
    ---Opus 87 in C major, also op. 29, op. 55 (2 ob, eng h) ME
      (rec) 1863, B&H: Simrock; 1866, Andre (ed. by Woolhouse);
      Costallat; 1894, Feldman; 1894, Sander (ed. by Jockisch);

1894, Schott; 1898, C. F. Schmidt; 1877, Schweers & Haake,
(ed. by A. C. Prell); Osterreichischer Bundesverlag; AMP;
Carl Fischer; Boosey & Hawkes; Andraud; B&H Crit. Ed, 1862-5.
---Op. 87, Celebrated Oboe Trio in C major, E-ME (arr. for
oboes, bassoons, strings, flutes, clarinets in any desired
combination) Andraud; Costallat (scored for 2 ob, eng h,
or ob, eng h, vn); B&H (score, parts); Sander (min. score)
(scored for 2 ob or cl or fl, bn, eng. h); Langenus (scored
for fl, ob, cl); Leuckart (arr. by G. Weigelt, for fl, cl,
bn); Remick; Baron; Boosey & Hawkes (2 ob, eng h).
---Trio, Op. 29 (2 ob, eng h or 2 fl, va) Andre.
---Trio, Op. 55 (3 cl or 2 cl, alto-cl) Andraud.
---Variations, "La ci Darem la mano" from Mozart's <u>Don Juan</u>.
(fl, cl, bn) Andraud; B&H (arr. by F. Stein, for 2 ob,
eng h, score, parts); Leuckart (arr. by G. Weigelt, for
fl, cl, bn).
---Adagio, Trio, Op. 87 (3 Bb cl) (rec) Cundy-Bettoney Co.
---Allegretto, Op. 2 (2 ob, cl; ob, 2 cl; 2 cl, eng h; 3 cl)
E Andraud; Cundy-Bettoney Co.
---Minuet from Trio, Op. 87 (3 cl) Cundy-Bettoney Co; Boo-
sey & Hawkes.
---Adagio Cantabile from Trio, Op. 2 (3 cl) Cundy-Bettoney Co.
BENTZON, JORGEN, Sonatine Trio, Op. 7 (fl, cl, bn) MH 1926, Bo-
rup (min. score, parts); Eble; Andraud; Skandinavisk og
Borups; Hug.
---Racconto No. 3, Op. 31 (ob, cl, bn) Skandinavisk og Bor-
ups; McGinnis & Marx.
---Intermezzo (fl, cl, v) Skandinavisk og Borups.
BOCCHERINI, LUIGI, Terzetto, arr. by Waln (fl, ob, or cl, cl)
Kjos, Chicago.
BORNEFELD, HELMUT, New Music (fl, ob, cl) 1931, Barenreiter.
BOZZA, EUGENE, Suite Breve en Trio (ob, cl, bn) MH-VH (rec) M.
Baron; Andraud; Leduc.
BULLING, BURCHARD, Suite, Op. 30 (fl, ob, bn) 1942, Grosch.
BYRD, WILLIAM, English Fantasy, Wind Trio from the 17th century.
1934, Barenreiter-Bote; Musica Rara.
CADOW, PAUL, Kleine Suite (2 ob or ob, fl, eng. h) 1942, Grosch.
CARION, FERNAND, Bagatelles, Op. 19 (fl, ob, cl) H (rec) Ba-
ron; Brogneaux.
---Trio (fl, ob, cl) MH Eble.
CONSTANT, MARIUS, Trio (ob, cl, bn) MH Eble; Baron.
COUPERIN, FRANCOIS, Les Petite Moulins a vent (The Little Wind
Mills, Trio) (fl, ob, bn) H (rec) Ricordi; Andraud.
DAHLHOFF, WALTER, Three Movements, Burlesque, Allegro, Scherzando
(ob, cl, bn) Andraud; Eble.
---Drei Satze (ob, cl, cl) C. F. Schmidt (Cefes-Edition, Al-
legro mvt only).
DECRUCK, FERNANDE, Trio, Capriccio (ob, cl, bn) 1934, Les Edi-
tions de Paris (min. score, parts); Baron.
DELORENZO, LEONARDO, Capriccetto eccentrico (fl, cl, bn) Ms.
---Divertimento quasi moderno (fl, ob, cl) Ms.
---Two Divertimenti brillanti, Op. 24, 29. (fl, cl, bn) H
(rec) 1931, Zimmermann; Andraud.

DEVIENNE, FRANCOIS, Six trios, Op. 27 (2 cl, bn) Sieber, Paris;
  Fetis.
  ---Six trios, Books I & II (3 fl) Imbault, Paris; Fetis.
  ---Six trios, Op. 61, books I & II (fl, cl, bn) Andre; Fetis.
  ---Three trios, Op. 75 (2 cl, bn) Sieber, Paris, Fetis.
  ---Sonata, Op. 77 (2 fl, bn or vc).
  ---Six Trios for 2 fl, bn, Op. 77. Sieber, Paris; Fetis.
  ---Symphonie concertante (fl, cl, bn) Fetis.
FABER, JOH. CHRISTOPHER, Partita Trio (3 cl) E Cundy-Bettoney
  Co.; 1932, Ricordi (scored for 3 fl).
  ---Six Melodies in Ancient Style (3 cl) E (rec) Cundy Bet-
  toney Co. (score, parts).
FABRE, C., Second Reverie (3 cl) Cundy-Bettoney Co.
FERNANDEZ, OSCAR LORENZO, Duas Invencoes Seresteiras a Tres Vozes
  (fl, cl, bn) Boletin Latinoamericano de Musica.
FERROUD, P. O., Trio in E major (ob, cl, bn) H 1934, Durand; An-
  draud; Elkan-Vogel.
FLEGIER, ANGE, Trio (ob, cl, bn) ME (rec) 1897, Gallet; An-
  draud; Rubank.
FOSS, LUKAS, Four Preludes (fl, cl, bn).
FRANCK, MAURICE, Trio (ob, cl, bn) MH (rec) Baron; Eble; Sel-
  mer.
FRANCO, JOHAN, Sonata for Three (fl, cl, bn) 1935, Ricordi.
FUCHS, GEORG FRIEDRICH, Trio, Op. 1 (fl, cl in C, bn) Sieber, Pa-
  ris.
FUCIK, JULIUS, Fantasy on a Bohemian Folksong (2 cl, bn) 1939,
  Editions Continental, Prague (score, parts).
GALLON, NOEL, Suite en Trio, Allemande, Fugue, Sarabande, Tambou-
  rin (ob, cl, bn) MH-VH (rec) Baron; Andraud; Selmer.
GENNARO, MARCEL, Trio in G major (fl, ob, cl) H 1922, Buffet-
  Crampon; M. Baron; Andraud; Leduc; Evette & Cie.
GIBBONS, ORLANDO, English Fantasy. (See Byrd)
GLINKA, MICHAEL IVANOVITCH, Trio Pathetique.
GLUCK, C. W. VON, See Bach, Three Little Classics, for Gluck Gavotte.
GOEB, ROGER, Suite for Woodwind Trio.
GRAUPNER, Suite in F (Ouverture a 3 Chalumeaux ((3 reco) (Urtext)
  Peters, C. F.; Hug (scored for 3 fl).
HANDEL, GEORGE FRIEDRICK, Sonata in D major (2 cl, h, orig. corno
  di caccia, or 3 cl) Mercury Music Corporation; McGinnis
  & Marx. Edited by LaRue Coopersmith.
  ---Kammertrios (2 fl, or fl & ob, bn) See Piano Quartets.
  ---Bouree, arr. by Brandenburg (3 Bb cl) ME Fischer, (score,
  parts).
  ---Celebrated Gavotte and Bourree (3 cl) Andraud; Fischer,
  (Gavotte, arr. by Paul de Ville for 3 Bb cl or Eb cl and 2
  Bb cl).
HAYDN, FRANZ JOSEPH, Six Divertimenti, Op. 38 (2 fl, vc) Geir-
  inger, British Museum, Haydn Catalogue.
  ---Four London Trios, in C major, G major, G major and G ma-
  jor (2 fl, vc) 1931, Nagel (arr. by L. Balet) Baron;
  Andraud; McGinnis & Marx.
HAYDN, FRANZ JOSEPH, Three Trios, No. 1 in C major, No. 2 in G
  major, No. 3, in G major (2 fl, vc) 1927, Vieweg (arr. by
  Gustav Lenzewski, score, parts); Andraud.

    ---Allegro Giocoso, arr. by Taylor (3 fl) MH Mills Music.
    ---Divertimento in C major (3 fl) arr. by F. Jode, 1941,
        Moeck.
    ---First Sonata Finale (2 cl, alto-cl) Andraud.
HENNESSY, SWAN, Trio, Op. 70 in Ab major (v, fl, bn) 1926, Es-
        chig, Schott (min. score, parts); Andraud.
    ---Trio, Op. 54 in G major (2 cl, bn) MH 1921, Eschig (min.
        score, parts); Baron; Eble; Andraud; AMP.
HINDEMITH, PAUL, Trio for Three Flutes (3 fl or 3 reco) 1932,
        Schott.
HOFFMAN, PAUL, German Dance (fl, ob, cl) 1936, Hofmeister.
HUGENIN, CHARLES, First Trio, Op. 30, Marcietta, Sicilienne, Men-
        uet, Gavotte (ob, cl, bn) Andraud.
    ---Second Trio, Op. 31, Reverie, The Spinner, My Villate Cho-
        rister, The Hen, Donkey & Cuckoo (ob, cl, bn) Andraud.
IBERT, JACQUES, Cinq Pieces en Trio (ob, cl, bn) MH (rec) An-
        draud; Leduc.
IKONOMOV, BOYAN, Trio, Op. 14 in E minor (ob, cl, bn) 1937, Oi-
        seau Lyre (min. score, parts); Baron; Andraud.
INGENHOVEN, JAN, Drei Stucke (fl, cl, bn) in C Tischer & Jagen-
        berg.
IPPOLITOV-IVANOV, MIKHAIL MIKHAILOVICH, Two Kirghizian Songs (ob,
        cl, bn, with optional pf) Mercury Music Corp.; Andraud;
        McGinnis & Marx.
JELINEK, HANS, Trio, Op. 10, No. 3, 6 Kleine Stucke. (2 cl, bn)
        1922 Universal Edition; Peters.
JONGEN, JOSEPH, Trio (ob, cl, bn) VH Andraud.
JOSTEN, WERNER, Trio 1940 (fl, cl, bn) Arrow Press; Hug.
JUON, PAUL, Arabeskes, Op. 73 (Kleines Trio) (ob, cl, bn) H 1941
        Schott (score, parts); Eble; Lienau.
KAMMELER, HANS, Hausmusik (2 fl, str) Barenreiter.
KARG-ELERT, SIEGFRIED, Trio, Op. 49, No. 1 in D minor (ob, cl,
        eng h or waldhorn) MH 1905 Hofmeister; Andraud; Zim-
        mermann.
KNAB, ARMIN, Pastorale and Allegro (2 fl, guit or laute) Baren-
        reiter.
KNUDAGE-RIISAGER, Trio (cl, bn, va) Andraud.
KOECHLIN, CHARLES, Trio, Op. 92 in G major (fl, cl, bn) MH (rec)
        1927 Senart (min. score, parts); Sansone; Andraud.
KOELLREUTTER, HANS JOACHIM, Inventions for Oboe, Clarinet and
        Bassoon, Koellreutter.
KRIENS, CHRISTOPH, Ronde des Lutins (fl, ob, cl) H (rec) An-
        draud; Fischer (score, parts).
KUHLAU, FRIEDRICH DANIEL RODOLPHE, Trios concertants, Op. 13, No.
        1 in D major, No. 2 in G minor, No. 3 in F major (3 fl)
        Andraud; B&H; Farrenc; Fetis; Costallat; Baron; Hug
        (Trio No. 1).
    ---Three Grand Trios, Op. 86, No. 1 in E minor, No. 2 in D
        major, No. 3 in Eb major (3 fl) MH Andraud; M. Baron;
        Cranz; Bohme; Baxter-Northrup; Costallat.
    ---Sonatina, Op. 20, No. 1 (fl, ob, cl) arr. by Whitney Tus-
        tin. Spratt.
KUHLAU, FRIEDRICH DANIEL RODOLPHE, Allegro, Op. 20, No. 2 (fl,
        cl, bn or bass-cl) arr. by Whitney Tustin; Spratt.
    ---Trio, Op. 90, No. 7 in B minor. Andraud; Baster-Northrup;
        Costallat; 1861, Schott.

LOEILLET, JEAN-BAPTISTE, Sonates (2 fl, ob) Catalogue British
  Museum.
MAGANINI, QUINTO E., Havana (Rhumba), Istanboul (Turkish March),
  Vienna, in Bb (ob or fl, cl, bn) E Fischer, (score,
  parts).
  ---Danse from Tarare (fl, ob, cl) in D major. Musicus, NY.
  ---The Troubadors (3 ob, or 2 ob, eng h.) in G major; Musi-
  cus, NY; Baron.
MARTELLI, HENRI, Trio, Op. 45 in C (ob, cl, bn) MH Eble; Ba-
  ron, NY; Andraud.
MAYEUR, Trio (fl, ob, cl) Andraud.
MELKIKH, DMITRY MICHAELOVITCH, Trio, Op. 17 in F# minor (ob, cl,
  bn) H (rec) 1928, Universal Edition; Andraud; Peters.
MIGOT, GEORGES, Trio (ob, cl, bn) H Leduc; Baron; Eble; An-
  draud.
  ---Threnody (ob, cl, bn) Leduc; Baron.
MILHAUD, DARIUS, Pastorale (ob, cl, bn) MH 1937, Senart; An-
  draud; Elkan-Vogel.
  ---Suite d'apres Corrette: Entree et rondeau; Tambourin,
  Serenade, Rondeau, Le Coucou, Musette, Fanfare, Menuets.
  (ob, cl, bn) MH (rec) Eble; Broude Bros; Lyre Bird
  Press.
MONDONVILLE, JEAN-JOSEPH CASSANEA DE, Tambourine (G. Barrere re-
  pertoire) (ob or fl, cl, bn) Andraud.
MOSER, FRANZ JOSEF, Trio, Op. 38 in C major (2 ob, eng h) 1926
  Bosworth; Andraud.
MOSER, RUDOLPH, Divertimento, Op. 51, No. 1 (fl, ob, cl) 1933,
  Steingraber; Andraud.
MOZART, WOLFGANG AMADEUS, Five Divertimenti, K 229 in Bb major
  (2 cl, bn) ME (rec) B&H (Arr. by E. Lewicki, score,
  parts); M. Witmark & Sons; Music Publishers Holding Corp.
  (arr. by Theodore M. Finney, score, parts); Andraud (arr.
  by Oubradous, scored for fl or ob, cl, bn).
  ---Divertimento No. 1, arr. by G. Weigelt (fl, cl, bn or 2
  cl, bn) ME (rec) Leuckart.
  ---Divertimenti Nos. 1 and 2, K 229 in Bb (2 cl, bn) ME
  (rec) Boosey-Hawkes (score, parts).
  ---Divertimento No. 3, K 229 in Bb (fl, cl, or ob, bn) Leuckart.
  ---Divertimento No. 4, K 229 in Bb (fl, cl, bn) Broude; Andraud; Leuckart (arr. by G. Weigelt, scored for 2 cl, bn);
  L'Oiseau Lyre (arr. by Oubradous, scored for ob, cl, bn).
  ---Serenaden (3 wind instruments) (Irmer-Marguerre) vols. 1,
  2, 3, 4. Barenreiter-Bote (score, parts).
  ---Brilliant Variations, arr. by Corroyez (fl, cl, bn) An-
  draud.
  ---Allegro from Fifteenth Sonata (2 cl, alto-cl) Andraud.
  ---Harmonika Andante, Canonic Adagio (fl, ob, va) Andraud.
  ---Rondo from Piano Sonata No. 1, arr. by R. Toll (3 cl) An-
  draud; Cundy-Bettoney Co. (parts).
MOZART, WOLFGANG AMADEUS, Excerpts from Piano Sonata Nos. 4 and
  10, arr. by R. Toll (3 cl) Andraud; Cundy-Bettoney Co.
  ---Andante for a Music Box, trans. (fl, ob, va) Andraud.
  ---Divertimenti (7 mvts) (3 cl with Tymp ad lib) ME EMB.
  ---Rondo from 8th violin Sonata, arr. by George J. Trink-
  aus (fl, cl, bn or fl, Bb, Eb alto-cl) Fischer, (score,
  parts).

---German Dance in A minor (fl, ob, bn) C. F. Peters.

---Four small pieces (2 basset h, bn) B&H.

---Clarinet Trio in Eb, K 498, contained in Mozart, 7 Trios (3 cl) C. F. Peters, (score, parts).

---Kanonisches Adagio in F major (2 alto-cl, bn or 2 basset h, bn) 1885 B&H; Andraud.

MOZART, W. A. (The Younger) Six Trios, Op. 11 (fl, 2 h) Haslinger; Fetis.

OVALLE, JAYME, Dois improvisos (3 cl) Boletin Latinoamericano de Musica.

PANNIER, OTTO, Trio, No. 2, Op. 40 in Eb major (cl, h, bn) 1938, Grosch; Andraud.

PFEIFFER, GEORGES JEAN, Musette, Op. 47 (ob, cl, bn) E (rec) Sansone; Andraud; Salabert, Inc; Rouart.

PIERNE, GABRIEL, Pastorale Variee (ob, cl, bn) Eble.

---Bucolique Variee (ob, cl, bn) H (rec) Andraud; Costallat.

PILLEVESTRE, J., Nocture (fl, ob, cl) Andraud.

PISTON, WALTER, Three Pieces, 1926 (fl, cl, bn) H (rec) 1935, Oxford University Press; Andraud; New Music Edition.

PURCELL, HENRY, Spielkanons (3 fl, other instrument) Barenreiter.

---Chaconne in G minor, arr. by Maganini (3 cl) MH Edition-Musicus.

QUANTZ, JOHANN JOACHIM, Sonata in D major (3 fl) 1935, Nagel; Andraud; Baxter-Northrup; Zimmerman; McGinnis & Marx; Hug.

REDA, SIEGFRIED, Kleine Spielstucke uber alte Weihnachtslieder (2 fl, str) Barenreiter.

REICHA, ANTON, Trio, Op. 26 in D major (3 fl) Spehr (Brunswick).

---Trio, Op. 51 (3 fl) Spehr (Brunswick).

REIN, WALTER, Kleine Spiel Musik 1938, Vieweg.

RHEIN, FREDERIC, Trios (six, Op. 5) 2 fl, bn) Fetis; Bossler.

RIVIER, JEAN, Petite Suite (ob, cl, bn) VH (rec) Baron; Andraud; Eble; Fougeres.

RONTGEN, JULIUS, Trio, Op. 86 in G major (fl, ob, bn) MH (rec) 1931, Alsbach.

RORICH, CARL, Trio in C major, Op. 81b (fl, cl, bn) 1930, Zimmermann (min. score, parts); Andraud. (rec)

SAMUEL, HAROLD, Suite for Alto Pipe and Two Tenor Pipes (3 fl) 1934 Boosey-Hawkes-Belwin (score, parts).

SCARLATTI, ALESSANDRO, Pastorale (fl, ob, bn) MH Ricordi; Andraud; Music Press, Inc.

---Allegro in G minor (2 cl, bass-cl) Ricordi.

---Allegro from Eighth Suite (2 cl, bass cl, or ob, cl, bn) Andraud.

SCHALLER, ERWIN, Trio, Nordische Volks-Musik (2 fl, bn, or 2 fl or ob or cl, bn) 1941, Barenreiter.

SCHANTL, H., Der Freischutz, Scherzo (cl, h, bn) Sansone; Andraud.

SCHMID, HEINRICH KASPAR, Serenade, Op. 99 (fl, ob, cl) (3 fl) 1935, Hieber.

SCHMIT, CAMILLE, Trio (ob, cl, bn) Baron.

SCHUBERT, FRANZ PETER SERAPH, Impromptu, Trio (fl, ob, cl) Andraud.

SCHULHOFF, ERWIN, Divertissement (ob, cl, bn) atonal H (rec)
      1928, Schott (min. score, parts) Baron; Andraud; AMP.
SCHWARZ, L., Die schone Sommerzeit (folktune) (3 fl) Barenreiter.
SCHWER, HUGO, Always Happy, Humoristic Trio (ob, 2 bn) Andraud.
   ---Something Comical, Humoristic Trio (ob, 2 bn) Andraud.
SHOSTAKOVITCH, DMITRI, Preludes, arr. by Quinto E. Maganini, in
      G major (ob or fl, cl, bn) Musicus, NY.
SLAVICKY, KLEMENT, Trio, 1937. Largo, Allegro vivo, Molto tran-
      quillo, Presto (ob, cl, bn) H. Eble; 1948, Hudebni Ma-
      tice.
SOBECK, JOHANN, Trio, Op. 20 in F major (2 cl, bn or vc) 1898,
      Ehrler; Andraud.
STAMITZ, KARL, Trio in G major (2 fl, vc) 1939, Barenreiter, (arr.
      by F. Schnapp.)
STARK, ROBERT, Sonata in G minor (2 cl, bn or basset h or alto-cl)
      1897 C. F. Schmidt, Cefes-Edition; Andraud.
SZALOWSKI, A., Trio (ob, cl, bn) H (rec) M. Baron; Eble; Ches-
      ter.
TAYLOR, LAWRENCE, Suite Classique in D, from the 18th century.
      Prelude, Bach; Courante, Croft; Minuet, Boccherini; Ron-
      do, Steilbelt, arr. by Taylor (3 fl) Franklin Co.
TELEMANN, GEORG PHILIPP, Kammer Sonate No. 5 in G major (ob, fl,
      bn) Andraud.
   ---Trio in C major (fl, ob or cl, bn) Andraud.
   ---Trio in C minor (fl, ob or cl, bn) Andraud.
TSCHAIKOWSKY, PETER ILITCH, Danse des Mirlitons (Dance of the
      Reed Flutes) from the Nutcracker Suite. (3 cl) H Rubank;
      EMB.
VERDI, GIUSEPPE, Aida, Second Fantasy Trio (fl, ob, or cl, bn)
      Andraud.
   ---Aida, First Fantasy Trio (fl, ob or cl, bn) Andraud.
VIERDANCK, JOHANN, Capricci for two or three instruments, arr. by
      Engel (2 or 3 wind inst) VE Musica Rara, London.
VILLA-LOBOS, HEITOR, Trio (ob, cl, bn) VH 1929, Eschig; Schott;
      Baron; Marks; International Music Corp; Andraud; Eble;
      AMP; Musica Rara, London.
   ---Trio, (fl, ob, cl) 1921.
VIVALDI, A., Concerto in D major (fl, vn, bn or vc) Ricordi.
   ---Concerto in G minor (fl, ob, bn) Ricordi.
VOGT, G., Adagio Religioso (2 ob, eng h) Costallat, (score, parts)
      Andraud.
WAGNER-REGENY, RUDOLF, Suite in F major (ob, cl, bn) 1929, Uni-
      versal Edition (score, parts); Andraud.
WAILLY, P. DE PAUL, Aubade (fl, ob, cl) H (rec) Sansone; An-
      draud; Rubank; Rouart; Baxter-Northrup.
WEBER, CARL MARIA FRIEDRICH ERNST VON, Scherzo from Der Freis-
      chutz (cl, h, bn) Andraud.
   ---Overture from Oberon in Bb (3 cl) Ms.
VERALL, JOHN, Divertissement (cl, h, bn) ACA.
WEIS, FLEMMING, Trio (fl, cl, bn) 1930, Kistner; McGinnis &
      Marx.
   ---Trio Music (fl, cl, bn) 1930, Edition Dania (min. score
      parts); Kistner & Siegel; Andraud; McGinnis & Marx,
      (score, parts).

WEISS, ADOLPH, Petite Suite (fl, cl, bn) ACA.
   ---Trio 1937 (fl, cl, bn) Boletin Latino Americano de Musica.
WIENER, KARL, Trio, Op. 20, No. 3 Terzett, atonal (fl, eng h, cl) 1931 Universal Edition; Andraud.
   ---Trio, Op. 20, Nos. 1, 2, 3, atonal (fl, eng h, cl) Andraud; 1931, Universal Edition (No. 3).
ZACHOW, FRIEDRICK WILHELM, Kammertrio (fl or ob, bn, general bass) Andraud.
ZODER, Dorfmusik (2 fl or 2 v, or 2 cl and guit) Barenreiter.
ZOELLER, CARL, Three Virtuosos (fl, cl, bn) Andraud; Boosey-Hawkes.
   ---Musical Joke (fl, cl, bn) Andraud; Boosey-Hawkes.

Collections:

Classic Pieces for Small Ensembles: 1, Beethoven, Three Duets
      for Flute or Oboe and Clarinet. 2, Marais, Petit Trio
      d'Alcyone for Three Woodwinds. 3, Fischer, A Little 17th
      Century Banquet Music for Flute, Oboe, Clarinet and Bas-
      soon. 4, Mondonville, Tambourin for Flute or Oboe, Clar-
      inet, and Bassoon. Andraud.

Fifteen Trios from the Classic Masters, arr. by Ary Van Leeuwen.
      (fl, ob, cl or 2 fl, cl) Bach: Two Gavottes. Caix
      D'Hervelois: Musette. Daquin: The Merry Maiden. Hay-
      dn: Allegro Marziale, Andante, Allegro, Two Presti. Le-
      clair: Musette. Lotti: Allegro. Mondonville: Tam-
      bourin. Mozart: Larghetto, Two Adagi. Rameau: Rigo-
      don de Dardanus.

PIANO TRIOS

Selective List

ADDISON, JOHN, Trio (fl, ob, pf) Angener.

AGNEL, EMILE, Pastoral, Op. 1 (eng h, bn, pf) 1864 Costallat.
---Trio in D major, Op. 2 (ob, bn, pf) Costallat; Baxter-Northrup.

ALEXANDER, FRIEDRICH LANDGRAF VON HESSEN, Trio, Op. 3 in A major (cl, h, pf) 1897 Simrock; AMP.

AMBROSIO, W. F., Album of Selected Trio Arrangements of Favorite Compositions (fl, cl, pf) Fischer.

ANDERSEN, CARL JOACHIM, Allegro Militaire, Op. 48 (2 fl, pf) Andraud; Zimmermann; Baxter-Northrup.

AUSTIN, ERNEST, Pastorale in Field and Forest, Op. 15, No. 2 (fl or v, h or vc, pf) 1908 Larway.

BACH, CARL PHILIPP EMANUAL, Spring's Awakening, (2 cl, pf) MH Baxter-Northrup; Fischer (scored for cl, fl, pf).
---Frulingserwachen Romanze (2 fl, pf) C. F. Schmidt, Cefes-Edition.

BACH, CARL PHILIPP EMMANUEL, 12 Kleine stucke (2 fl, pf) Zimmerman.
---Six Little Sonatas (cl, bn, pf)
---Trio in E major (2 fl, pf) Zimmermann,(ed. by Walther); Andraud; Baxter-Northrup.

BACH, JOHANN CHRISTIAN, Divertissement, arr. by Moyse (2 fl, or fl, ob, and pf) Andraud.

BACH, JOHANN CHRISTOPH FRIEDRICH, Sonate in C major (fl, ob, pf) Andraud.

BACH, JOHANN SEBASTIAN, Trio in G minor (2 fl, pf) Royal Library in Berlin; Fetis.
---Choral Prelude (2 fl, bn) MH Kay & Kay.
---Adagio, arr. by H. Sarlit (fl, ob or v or cl, pf) Baron.
---Trio Sonata in Bb arr. by Woehl (2 alto reco, pf, vc ad lib) C. F. Peters.
---Trio in G major (2 fl, pf, vc ad lib) Andraud; 1920, B&H (arr. by Max Seiffert); 1937, Peters (arr. by Ludw. Landshoff, in Trio Sonaten, Bd. 1).
---Musik for two solo instruments and bass, arr. by J. Altemark. 1940, Kallmeyer.

BACH, WILHELM FRIEDEMANN, Siziliano (ob, bn, pf) 1911, B&H, London (arr. by G. B. Weston); Andraud.
---Sonata in D major (2 fl, pf) arr. by Ary van Leeuwen. Andraud; 1933, Zimmermann.
---Three Trios, D major, D major, A minor (2 fl, pf, vc ad lib) Andraud; B&H (arr. by Max Seiffert).
---Sonata in Eb (2 fl, pf) Andraud.
---Trio (2 fl, bass) Royal Library, Berlin; Fetis.

BALFE, M. W., I Dreamt I Dwelt in Marble Halls (2 cl, pf, or fl, cl, pf) E Fischer; Baxter-Northrup (Keynote Music Service).

BARMANN, CARL, Concertant Duet, Op. 33 (2 cl, pf) Andraud.

BARNARD, Merriment Polka (2 cl, pf) EMB.

BECKERATH, ALFRED VON, Sonatine (2 fl, pf, or fl, ob, pf) 1939, Moeck.

BEETHOVEN, LUDWIG VAN, Trio, Op. 11 in Bb major, transc. (ob, bn, pf or cl, bn, pf) Andraud.

---Trio, Op. 38 in Eb major, transc. (ob, bn, pf or cl, bn, pf) Andraud.

---Two Trios, C major, F major (cl, bn, pf) B&H Critical Edition, 1862-5; Supplementary volume, 1904.

---Three Trios, Op. 1, transc. (ob, bn, pf) Andraud (Op. 1, No. 2, scored for fl, bn, pf. Op. 1, No. 3, scored for ob, bn, pf, arr. by Jancourt).

---Trio (fl, bn, pf) B&H, Critical Edition, 1862-5; Supplementary volume, 1904.

---Sonata in G major, Op. 259 (fl, bn, pf) B&H, 1888; AMP.

---Trio in G major (fl, bn, pf) 1888, B&H; Schweers & Haake; Andraud; Hug (arr. by W. Lyman).

---Trio, Op. 83 in Eb major, trans. (ob, bn, pf) Andraud.

---Minuet in G (2 cl, pf) Cundy-Bettoney Co. (score, parts).

---Three Original Duos, No. 1 in C major, No. 2 in F major, No. 3 in Bb major (cl, bn, pf) Op. 147. Andraud; 1900, B&H (arr. by G. Gohler).

BEHR, F., Two Nocturnes and Evening on the Sea (2 fl, pf) Baxter-Northrup (Keynote Music Service) Carl Fischer.

BELLINI, VINCENZO, Duo Concertant on Norma (2 fl, pf or 2 cl, pf or fl, cl,, pf) MH Andraud; Fischer; Cundy-Bettoney Co.

---La Somnambule (2 cl, pf) Andraud.

BENDIX, TH., Polka de Concert, "Je vous salue". (fl, cl, pf) Carl Fischer; Baxter-Northrup.

BENNET, ROBERT RUSSELL, Six Souvenirs, 1948 (2 fl, pf) 530 Park Ave., NYC.

BENT, R., Swiss Boy (Air varie) in C and Db major (2 fl, pf or 2 picc, pf or fl, cl, pf or 2 cl, pf) Cundy-Bettoney Co.

BERLIOZ, HECTOR, Trios des Jeunes Ismaelites from L'Enfance du Christ (The Childhood of Christ) Op. 25 (2 fl, harp or pf) Baxter-Northrup; AMP; M. Baron; Andraud; B&H (ed. by Schuecker).

BERR, FREDERICH, Fantaisie in F (cl, bn, pf) Richault.

BERTONI, FERDINANDO GIUSEPPE, Canzona (2 fl, pf) EMB.

BEYER, Duos Classiques (2 fl, pf) Fischer.

BEIBER, C., Under the Linden, Romance (fl, h, pf) Andraud.

---Blissful Hour (fl, h, pf) Andraud.

---Happy Moments (fl, h, pf) Andraud.

BISHOP, H. F., Lo, Hear the Gentle Lark, arr. by Lax (fl, cl, pf) Andraud; Fischer.

---Pretty Mocking Bird (fl, cl, pf) Andraud.

BIZET, GEORGES, Three Pieces: Entr'act, Third Act of Carmen; Intermezzo Religioso and Valse-Menuet from l'Arlesienne. (2 fl, pf or fl, cl, pf or fl, ob, pf, with optional h, eng h and bn parts) Andraud; Choudens.

---Entr'act, Third Act of Carmen (fl, ob, harp) Andraud.

---Valse-Menuet from l'Arlesienne (fl, cl, pf or fl, ob, pf) Edition Musicus; Andraud (2 fl, harp or pf).

BLANC, ADOLPHE, Trio, Op. 14 in C major (ob, bn, pf) Costallat; Andraud.

---Romance, Op. 43 (ob, h, pf) Andraud.

BODINUS, SEBASTIAN, Sonata in Eb major (2 ob, pf) arr. by Hans Fischer. 1939 Vieweg.

BOEDIJN, GERARD H., Folkloristische suite; vier impressies voor trio (fl, ob, pf) Stichting Donemus.

BOHM, KARL, Calm as the Night (fl or cl, h, pf) E Fischer.

BOISMORTIER, J. BODIN DE, Six Gentillesses (2 ob or fl, pf)
       Andraud; Fetis (called Les Gentillesses, cantatilles).
   ---Two Sonatas, in C major and G major (2 fl, pf) Baxter-
       Northrup (Keynote Music Service).
BONNER, EUGENE, Over the Hills (2 fl, pf) Edition Musicus.
BONONCINI, GIOV. BATTISTA, Seven Suites (2 fl or fl, ob, pf)
       arr. by F. J. Giesbert. 1939, Schott.
BORODIN, ALEXANDRE, Cavatina from Prince Igor (fl, cl, pf) Edi-
       tion Musicus.
BOUSQUET, N., Golden Robin Polka (2 picc. pf or 2 cl, pf or fl,
       cl, pf) Cundy-Bettoney Co.; Carl Fischer.
   ---L'Adige, Tyrolienne (ob, bn, pf) (2 cl, pf) Andraud.
BOUSSAGOL, E., En Badinant (2 A-cl, pf) Andraud.
BRAGA, GAETANO, Angels' Serenade in Eb major (fl, ob, pf or fl,
       cl, pf) Cundy-Bettoney Co.; Fischer (2 Eb cl, pf).
BRAHMS, JOHANNES, Famous Waltz, Op. 39, No. 15 (fl, cl, pf or
       2 cl, pf) Andraud; Cundy-Bettoney Co. (score, parts).
   ---Hungarian Dance No. 5 (2 cl, pf or fl, cl, pf) Cundy-
       Bettoney Co. (score, parts).
   ---Eight Hungarian Dances (2 fl, pf) Andraud.
   ---Lullaby (2 fl, pf) Andraud.
BRAUN, the younger, Trios (2 fl, pf) Fetis.
BRAUN, the elder, Two Books, Trios (2 fl, pf) Fetis.
BRESGEN, CESAR, Music on Two Old Folksongs (2 fl, pf) 1940,
       Schott.
BRICCIALDI, GUILIO, Soirees Musicales de Rossini, Op. 49 (2 fl,
       pf) Andraud; Baxter-Northrup (Keynote Music Service).
   ---Duo, Op. 67 in D major (Portafogli per i Dilettanti) 1853
       Schott. (2 fl, pf)
   ---Duo Brillant, Op. 130 in A major (2 fl, pf) 1881, Schott;
       Andraud; Baxter-Northrup (Keynote Music Service).
   ---Serenade, Op. 137 (2 fl, pf) Andraud; Baxter-Northrup.
BROD, HENRI, Trio, Op. 1, No. 1 (ob, bn, pf) 1877 Costallat.
   ---Trio, Op. 11, No. 2 (2 winds, pf) Theme autriche. Le-
       moine.
   ---Trio, Op. 24, No. 5 (2 winds, pf) Lemoine.
   ---Trio, Op. 5 (ob, bn, pf) Sansone.
   ---Trio, Op. 56, No. 7 (2 winds, pf) Lemoine.
   ---Trio, Op. 43 (ob, bn, pf) Sansone.
   ---Premiere Fantasie-Air Espagnol (cl, bn, pf) Schonen-
       berger.
   ---Troisieme fantaisie sur le "Crociato", Op. 17 (ob, bn, pf)
       Ricordi, Milan; Fetis.
BRUNO, FILIPO, Recreation (fl, cl, pf)
BUCHNER, FERDINAND, Sophien Waltzer, Op. 43 (2 fl, pf)
   ---Hungarian Dance, Op. 44 (2 fl, pf)
   ---Spring, Op. 49 (2 fl, pf)
   ---Sixteen Characteristic Pieces, Op. 65 (2 fl, pf)
BUCHTEL, FORREST L, Bonita (2 fl, pf) EMB: Mills Music, Inc.
BUOT, Song of the Nests (2 cl, pf) Andraud.
BURGHARDT, HANS GEORG, Trio-Sonata, Op. 42 in C major (2 fl, pf)
       1941, Barenreiter.
   ---Partita Brevis II (2 fl, pf) Op. 44 1940, Barenreiter.
BURKHARD, WILLY, Canzone (2 fl, pf or fl, ob, pf) (or organ),
       Op. 76a. Barenreiter.

CAMPANA, Do You Remember? (2 cl, pf) Carl Fischer.
CARL, M., Serenade, Op. 37 (fl, ob, pf) Andraud.
CARMICHAEL, HOAGI, Star Dust (2 cl, pf) EMB.
CAVALLINI, ERNESTO, La Bacana, Bizzarria (2 cl, pf) Andraud.
   ---Reverie Russe (fl, cl, pf) Andraud.
CHEDEVILLE, NICOLAS, Two Pastorales (2 fl, pf) Andraud.
CHERUBINI, Ave Maria (2 ob, pf or 2 cl, pf or cl, bn, pf) An-
     draud; Cuney-Bettoney Co.
CHOPIN, FREDERIC FRANCOIS, Minute Waltz, arr. by A. Van Leeuwen
     (2 fl, pf) Andraud.
CHRETIEN, HEDWIGE (Madame) Serenade Sous Bois (fl, ob, pf) An-
     draud; Baxter-Northrup (Keynote Music Service).
CIMAROSA, DOMINIQUE, Concerto, arr. by Moyse, in G major (2 fl,
     pf or fl, ob, pf) Andraud.
CIMR, E. O., Instructive Trio, Op. 9 (cl, bn, pf) 1905, Fr. A.
     Urbanek; Andraud.
CLINTON, JOHN, Trios for Two Flutes and Piano, Op. 2 in Bb, Op.
     3 in A, Op. 10 in F, Op. 33 in G, Op. 34 in G minor, Op.
     35 in Eb, Ashdown.
   ---Two Trios Ongarese in G major (2 fl, pf) Op. 11 and 12.
     Ashdown.
   ---Grand Duo, Op. 43 (fl, Bb cl, pf) Ashdown.
CORBETT, WILLIAM, Sonatas, Op. 3 (2 fl, pf) London, 1701; Fetis.
   ---Sonatas, Op. 2 (2 fl pf) London, 1706; Fetis.
CORELLI, ARCANGELO, Sonatas, Op. 2, Nos. 1, 5, 7 (2 alto reco,
     pf, vc ad lib) C. F. Peters.
   ---Trio Sonata, Op. 3, No. 2 (2 fl, p) arr. by Dietz Degen
     1944, Rieter-Biedermann; (2 ob, pf, bn ad lib) Music
     Press, Inc. ME
   ---Sarabande and Minuet (2 ob, pf) Andraud.
   ---Gigue (2 fl or 2 cl, pf) Baron.
CORTICELLI, GAETANO, Terzetto (ob, bn, pf) Ricordi; Andraud.
COSTE, Fantaisie de Concert (2 ob, pf) Andraud.
CZIBULKA, A., Stephanie (Gavotte de la Princesse) E (2 cl, pf or
     fl, cl, pf) Carl Fischer; Baxter-Northrup (Keynote Mu-
     sic Service).
DAHLHOFF, WALTER, Pan and Nymphs (fl, ob, harp) Andraud; 1925,
     Schmidt, Cefes-Edition; Baxter-Northrup.
DAVID, Brilliant Bird "Pearl of Brazil" (fl, cl, pf) Andraud;
     (fl, ob, pf) Cundy-Bettoney Co. (called "Thou Brilliant
     Bird".)
DE FESCH, WILLIAM, 3 Sonatas (2 fl, pf, vc ad lib) C. F. Pet-
     ers; McGinnis & Marx.
DEMERSSEMAN, JULES, Six Petities Fantaisies, Op. 28 (2 fl, pf)
     Andraud.
   ---Fantaisie Concertante, Op. 36 (fl, ob, pf) Baxter-
     Northrup.
DEROSIERS, NICOLAS, La Fruite du Roi d'Angleterre (2 fl, pf)
     1689 Roger, Amsterdam; Fetis.
DESTENAY, E., Trio, Op. 27 in B minor (ob, cl, pf) 1906, Ha-
     melle; Andraud.
DEVIENNE, FRANCOIS, Six Trios, Op. 19 (2 fl, pf) Sieber, Paris;
     Fetis.
DE VILLE, P., The Swiss Boy, Air Varie (2 cl, pf) MH Fischer;
     EMB.

D'HERVELOIS, CAIX, La Gracieuse (2 fl, pf or fl, ob, pf or 2 ob,
     pf) Edition Musicus.
DONIZETTI, GAETANO, Sextet from Lucis di Lammermoor (2 fl, pf or
     2 cl, pf or fl, cl, pf) E Cundy-Bettoney Co., Inc. (score
     parts) Fischer.
   ---La Favorita, Divertissement, arr. by Lazarus (2 cl, pf)
     Cundy-Bettoney Co. (score, parts).
   ---Mad Scene from "Lucia" (fl, cl, pf) Andraud; Cundy-
     Bettoney Co. (score, parts).
   ---Lucrezia Borgia, arr. by Lazarus (2 cl, pf) Cundy-Bettoney
     Co. (score, parts).
DOPPLER, FRANZ, Souvenir du Rigi. Idyl (fl, h, pf or cl, h, pf)
     Andraud; Cundy-Bettoney Co., Inc.
   ---Andante and Rondo, Op. 25 (2 fl, pf) (rec) Andraud;
     Fischer.
   ---Fantasy on Hungarian Themes, Op. 35 (2 fl, pf) Andraud.
   ---Souvenir de Prague, Op. 24 (2 fl, pf) Andraud.
   ---Rigoletto, Fantaisie, Op. 38 (2 fl, pf) Andraud.
   ---La Sonnambula, Paraphrase, Op. 42 (2 fl, pf) Andraud.
   ---Valse di Bravura, Op. 33 (2 fl, pf) Andraud.
   ---Hungarian Duettino, Op. 36 (2 fl, pf) Andraud.
DORADO-WHEELER, Dos Amigos (2 cl, pf) Volkwein.
DOUARD, Third and Fourth Duetto (fl, ob, pf) Andraud; Baxter-
     Northrup.
DOUJON, JOHANNES, Tracoline (2 picc, pf) Andraud.
DUBOIS, CLEMENT FRANCOIS THEODORE, Trio: Two Canons in F (ob, bn,
     pf) Heugel, Paris.
DUKELSKY, VLADIMIR, Trio. Theme and Variations, 1903 (fl, bn,
     pf) Andraud; 1933 Russischer Musikverlag.
DURAND-MARLIN, Chaconne (fl, cl, pf) Pro Art.
DVORAK, ANTONIN, Humoreske (2 cl, pf or fl, cl, pf) MH Carl
     Fischer; Baxter-Northrup.
ENRICH, J., Dreamy Moments, Op. 32 (fl, cl, pf) Carl Fischer;
     Baxter-Northrup.
EMMANUEL, MAURICE, Trio-Sonata (fl, cl, pf) 1907 Lemoine; San-
     sone; Andraud; Durand; Baron.
ENDRESEN, R. M., Pepperino (2 cl, pf) EMB.
   ---Prarie Warblers (2 cl, pf or fl, cl, pf or 2 fl, pf) EMB.
   ---Two Flyers (2 cl, pf or fl, cl, pf or 2 fl, pf) EMB.
   ---Promenade (2 cl, pf or fl, cl, pf) EMB.
ERSFELD, CHR., Slumber Song (2 cl, pf or fl, cl, pf) E Carl
     Fischer; Baxter-Northrup.
ESSEX (le docteur) Duos (2 fl, pf) Fetis.
EVANS, DAVID MOULE, Suite in Three Movements, 1, Capriccio 2, Duo
     3, Rondo (fl, ob, pf) Joseph Williams, London (this work
     on hire).
FABRE, C., Reverie (2 fl, pf or fl, cl, pf or 2 cl, pf) Cundy-
     Bettoney Co., Inc.
   ---Second Reverie (2 fl, pf or fl, cl, pf) Cundy-Bettoney
     Co., Inc; (2 cl, pf) Carl Fischer.
FAHRBACH, JOSEPH, Variations de concert sur un "Ballo in Mas-
     chera", Op. 56 (2 fl, pf) Fetis Supplement.
FASCH, JOHANN FRIEDRICH, Sonata for Three, No. 1, Op. 3 in Bb
     major (2 ob or fl, pf or harp) 1930 Nagel, arr. by Lud-
     wig Schaffler; Andraud; Baxter-Northrup.

FAURE, J., The Palms (2 cl, pf) Carl Fischer.
FESCH, WILLIAM DE, Three Sonatas (2 fl, pf, vc ad lib) C. F.
    Peters; McGinnis & Marx.
FILLIAUX-TIGER, Drifting Waters (fl, ob, pf) Andraud; Baxter-
    Northrup.
   ---On a Fine Day, Pastorale (fl, ob, pf) Andraud; Baxter-
    Northrup.
FINGER, GODEFROID, Twelve Sonatas, Op. 4, 6 (2 fl, pf) Edition
    Roger; Fetis.
   ---Sonata in D Minor (fl, ob, pf) Nagel.
FOSTER, STEPHEN COLLINS, Come Where My Love Lies Dreaming (fl,
    cl, pf) Cundy-Bettoney Co. (score, parts).
FRIEDMANN, C., Dialogue of a Married Couple (ob, bn, pf) An-
    draud.
FURSTENAU, ANTON BERNHARD, Adagio et Variations, Op. 55 (2 fl,
    pf).
   ---Concertino, Op. 87 (2 fl, pf)
   ---Introduction et Variations, Op. 102 (2 fl, pf)
   ---L'Union, Op. 115 (2 fl, pf)
   ---La Ravalite, Op. 116 (2 fl, pf)
   ---Deux Rondolettos, Op. 124 (2 fl, pf)
   ---Introduction et Rondeau, Op. 132, (2 fl, pf)
   ---William Tell, Op. 101 (2 fl, pf) Andraud.
   ---Rondo Brillant, Op. 102 in D major (in collaboration with
    Reissinger) (2 fl, pf) Collection Litolff; Baxter-
    Northrup.
FUX, JOHANN JOSEPH, Sinfonia. Trio in F major (fl, ob pf or 2 fl,
    pf) 1938, Nagel, ed. by Leo Kuntner.
   ---Nurnberger Partita, 1781 (fl, ob, pf or 2 fl, pf) (vc ad
    lib) ed. by Hoffmann, 1939, Kallmeyer.
GABRIEL, MARIE, In the Calm of the Night (ob, A-cl, pf) Andraud.
   ---Gaiety (ob, A-cl, pf) Andraud.
   ---Dialogue Tendre (ob, cl, pf) Andraud.
   ---Feuilles au Vent (Leaves in the Wind) Three Trios (ob,
    cl, pf) Andraud; Baron; Lemoine.
GANNE, LOUIS, Extase. Reverie (fl, h or cl, pf or harp or organ)
    Andraud; Carl Fischer; Baxter-Northrup.
GARIBOLDI, GIUSEPPE, Fourth Duo on Aida (2 fl, pf) Andraud.
GATTERMANN, P.H., Fantaisie Concertante, Op. 38 (fl or any combin-
    ation with cl or bn, pf) Andraud.
GAUBERT, PHILLIPE, Tarentelle (fl, ob, pf) H Andraud; Baxter-
    Northrup; Enoch.
   ---Divertissement Grec (2 fl, harp or pf) (rec) Andraud:
    M. Baron; Leduc.
GEBEL, GEORG, Two Trio-Sonatas (2 fl, pf) Andraud.
GENIN, PAUL AGRICOL, Concertant Duet, Op. 51 (fl or any combina-
    tion with cl or bn, pf) Andraud.
   ---Trio, Op. 9 in A minor (2 fl, pf) 1869, Costallat.
GILSON, PAUL, Trio in G minor (ob, cl, pf) MH 1924, Cranz;
    Andraud.
GIORDANI, THOMAS, Six Trios (2 fl, pf) Fetis.
GIRNATIS, WALTER, Festl. Hausmusik (2 fl, ob or cl, pf) 1941,
    Litolff.
GLINKA, MICHAEL IVANOVITCH, Trio (cl, of, pf) Fetis Supplement.
   ---Der Zweifel. Russische Romanze (2 fl, pf) C. F. Schmidt,

Cefes-Edition.
---Trio Pathetique in D minor (cl, bn, pf) 1889, Jurgenson;
Andraud; Leeds.
GLUCK, C. W. VON, Trio Sonata No. 2 in G minor (2 ob, pf, bn ad
lib) MH Music Press, Inc.
---Spirit Dance from Orpheus (2 cl, pf) EMB.
GOEPFART, KARL, Trio, Op. 74 in C minor (fl, ob, pf) MH (rec)
1898, F. Schuberth, Jr; Baxter-Northrup.
---Trio, Op. 75 in G minor (cl, bn, pf) MH (rec) Andraud;
Schuberth, Jr., 1898.
GOOSSENS, EUGENE, Pastorale and Harlequinade, Op. 39 (fl, ob, pf)
(rec) J. Curwen & Sons; Andraud; Baxter-Northrup.
GOSSEC, FRANCOIS JOSEPH GOSSE, Gavotte, arr. by Maganini (2 fl,
pf) E (rec) EMB; Fischer; Baxter-Northrup.
GOUNOD, CHARLES FRANCOIS, Serenade (2 cl, pf) MH Carl Fischer.
---Souvenir d'un Bal (2 fl, pf) E (rec) Andraud; Chou-
dens.
---Faust (fl, cl, pf) arr. by Ernesto Cavallini; Andraud;
---Flower Song from Faust (2 cl, pf) E Carl Fischer.
---Ave Maria (Meditation) on the prelude of J. S. Bach (2 cl,
pf or fl, cl, pf) E Fischer; Baxter-Northrup.
GRANDVAL, MARIE CLEMENCE DE, Grand Trio de Salon (ob or eng h,
bn, pf) Lemoine.
GRIFFES, CHARLES TOMLASON, Woodwind Harp Trio, Piano tone-pic-
tures.
GRIMM, FRIEDRICH KARL, Trio Sonata Op. 64 in Bb major (cl, bn,
pf) 1939, Moricke.
GYRING, ELIZBETH, Trio for oboe, clarinet and piano. ACA.
HALETZKI, PAUL, Father and Son (picc. bn, pf) Leduc.
HALEVY, J. F. E., Bright Star of Hope. Romance from L'Eclair.
(2 cl, pf) E Carl Fischer.
HAMM, J. V., Zwiegesprach ("Dialogue") Polonaise (ob, cl, pf or
fl, ob, pf or fl, cl, pf) Andraud; Fischer; Baxter-
Northrup.
HAMMERSCHMIDT, ANDREAS, Ballet and Canzone No. 2 in 3 parts (2
C rec, pf, and fl, ob, v ad lib) Moeck; McGinnis &
Marx.
HANDEL, GEORGE FRIEDRICK, Op. 1, No. 5 in G major (fl, bn, pf)
ed. by Max Seiffert, B&H.
---Sonatas or Trios, Op. 5 (2 fl or ob, pf) Ausgabe der
Handel-Gesellschaft, 1879, Vg. S. 66.
---Trio Sonata, Op. 5, No. 4 in Eb major (2 ob, pf, bn ad
lib) MH-H (rec) Music Press, Inc.
---Op. 1, No. 8 in C minor (ob, bn, pf) Ed. by Max Seif-
fert, B&H.
---Trio, Op. 2, No. 3 in Eb major (2 ob, pf, bn ad lib) MH
Heugel (ed. by H. Schikkel); Music Press, Inc.
---Sonatas or Trios, Op. 2 (2 fl, or 2 ob, pf) 1879, Aus-
gabe der Handel-Gesellschaft, Vgl. S. 66.
---Trio, Op. 2, No. 1 in C minor (2 fl or 2 ob, pf) 1903,
B&H, ed. by Seiffert. MH (rec)
---Six Sonatas or Trios, No. 1 in Bb major (1889), No. 2 in
D minor, (1889), No. 3 in Eb major (1908), No. 4 in F ma-
jor (1908), No. 5 in G major (1910), No. 6 in D major,
(1910), (2 ob, pf, bn ad lib) MH (rec) B&H; Schott,

Ed. by Emil Krause; 1879 Ausgabe der Handel-Gesellschaft, Vgl. S. 86.

---Op. 2, Sonate a tre (2 ob, or fl, pf) No. 1, C minor (1889), No. 2, G minor. (1889), No. 3, F major (1896), No. 4, Bb major, (1896), No. 5, F major, (1909), No. 6, G minor (1909), No. 7, G minor (1908), No. 9, E major (1910) Ed. by Emil Krause, Schott; No. 8, G minor, ed. by Hans Sitt, Peters.

---Sonatas Nos. 9 and 11 (2 ob, pf) Andraud.

HANDEL, GEORGE FRIEDRICK, Tochter Zion, from Judas Maccabaus. (2 fl, harp), Andraud; (2 fl, pf) C. F. Schmidt, Cefes-Edition.

---Nightingale Scene, from "Il Penseroso" (fl, ob, pf or fl, cl, pf or fl, bn, pf) Andraud; Carl Fischer; C. F. Schmidt, Cefes-Edition; Baxter-Northrup.

---Adagio and Allegro (2 cl, pf) Andraud.

---Kammersonaten Nos. 7, G minor and 9, C minor (ob, pf, vc or bn ad lib) Ed. by Max Seiffert. B&H.

---Op. 6, Sonatas (2 ob, fig. bass) Ed. by Handel Society, 1879.

---Trio Sonatas in D minor, Eb major, D major. International Music Co.

---Where E'er You Walk (fl, h, pf) E Arr. by Hamilton. Carl Fischer.

HASSELMANS, J., Duo Concertant (fl, h, pf) Andraud.

HAYDN, FRANZ JOSEPH, Four Trios, arr. by Moyse (fl, ob or cl, va or vc, pf) Andraud.

---Trio Sonata No. 29 (fl, bn, pf or cl, bn, pf) Baron.

---Trio No. 31 in G major (fl, bn, pf or fl, vc or bass-cl and pf) Cundy-Bettoney; Baron.

---Six Trios (2 fl, pf) Fetis; Ms. B&H (1771)

---Haydn's celebrated Oxen Minuet (2 cl, pf or 2 fl, pf or fl, cl, pf) Andraud; Cundy-Bettoney Co., Inc.

---Larghetto, arr. by Brearley (fl, ob or cl, and pf) J. Curwen & Sons.

HEIDRICH, MAXIMILIAN, Trio, Op. 25 in C minor (cl, h, pf) Andraud; 1894, Kistner & Siegel.

HENRICH, HERMANN, Triosuite, Op. 23 (ob, h, pf) 1937 Heinrichs-hofen.

HERBERT, L'Encore (fl, cl, pf) Music Publishers Holding Corp.

HERMAN, JULES ARTHUR, Turkish Rondo (2 fl, pf) Andraud; Baron.

---Tarentelle (2 fl, pf) Andraud; Baron.

HERZOGENBERG, HEINRICH VON, Trio, Op. 61 in D major (ob, h, pf) 1889, Rieter-Biedermann; Andraud; Peters.

HESSEN, F. L. VON, Trio, Op. 3 (cl, h, pf) Andraud.

HILDRETH, R. E., Ripples (2 cl, pf) Cundy-Bettoney Co., (score parts).

HILL, ALFRED, Miniature Trio, No. 2 in C major (fl or ob or cl, bn, pf) 1928 Schirmer; Andraud.

HOLBROOKE, JOSEPH A., Trio (fl or v, h, pf) Andraud; Modern Music Library, London.

---Trio in D major, Op. 28 (fl, h, pf) Modern Music Library, London.

---Trio (ob, bn, pf) Andraud; Modern Music Library.

---Tamerlane (cl, bn, pf) Modern Music Library.

HOLMES, G. E., Tyrolean Fantasia (2 cl, pf) MH Carl Fischer.
    ---Auld Lang Syne (2 cl, pf) MH Carl Fischer.
HOLST, GUSTAV THEODORE, A Fugual Concerto, Op. 40, No. 2 (fl,
        ob, pf) Andraud; Baxter-Northrup.
    ---Terzetto (fl, ob, va) MH Eble.
HONEGGER, ARTHUR, Concerto da Camera (fl, eng h, pf) McGinnis
        & Marx; Hug.
    ---Petite Suite (2 woodwinds, pf) 1937 Editions Sociales
        Internationales.
HONEGGER, ARTHUR, Rapsodie (2 fl or 2 cl, pf) in C, Senart.
HOTTETERRE, LOUIS, Op. 5, Second Suite of pieces (2 fl, pf)
        Fetis.
HUGES, LUIGI, Carnevale di Venezia (2 fl, pf)
HUMMEL, arr. of Clarinet Polka by David Bennett (2 cl, pf) EMB
HUSSONMOREI, Invocation on Bach's Prelude (fl, bn, pf) Andraud.
IBERT, JACQUES, Aria (fl, cl, pf) Andraud; Baron.
    ---Five Pieces en Trio ME Eble
    ---Five Pieces, No. 3 ME Sansone
INGENHOVE, JAN, Trio (fl, cl, harp) Senart & Co., 1920; Andraud.
JANCOURT, EUGENE, Fantasy on the Italians in Algiers (ob, bn, pf)
        Andraud.
    ---Op. 7 (ob, bn, pf) Fetis; Fichault.
JOHNSON, HUNTER, Serenade (1937) (fl, cl, pf) Valley Music
        Press.
JOLIVET, Pastorales de Noel (fl, bn, harp) MH Eble; Mercury.
JUNGMANN, A., Longing for Home (Heimweh) (2 cl, pf or fl, cl,
        pf) MH Fischer; Baxter-Northrup.
KAHN, ROBERT, Serenade, Op. 73 (ob, h, pf or fl, h, pf) Andraud;
        1923, Simrock; AMP.
KALINNIKOW, BASILE, Chanson Triste (fl, cl, pf or cl, bn, pf or
        ob, pf, bn or 2 cl, pf) Edition Musicus.
KELLER, GODERFROID, Six Sonatas (2 fl, pf) Amsterdam, Roger Edi-
        tion; Fetis.
KESNAR, MAURITS, Un Petit Rien (2 fl, pf) Edition Musicus.
KETTING, PIET., Sonata, 1935-36 (fl, ob, pf) Stichting Donemus.
KINSCELLA, H. G., Folk Tune Trios, A collection of Ten Favorite
        Airs (fl, bn, pf) Carl Fischer; (ob, bn, pf) Baxter-
        Northrup. Contents: An Old Round; All Thro' the Night;
        Brother John; Little Valse; Evening Song; O Sanctissi-
        ma; It Was a Shepherd; O Believe Me; If All Those En-
        dearning Young Charms; Looby Loo; How Can I Leave Thee.
KLEINKNECHT, JOHANN FRIEDRICH, Three Trios (2 fl, pf) Fetis.
    ---Six Trios (2 fl, pf) Fetis.
KLING, HENRI, Two Little Bullfinches, Polka (picc, cl, pf or 2
        picc, pf or fl, cl, pf) Carl Fischer; Andraud; Baxter-
        Northrup; Cundy-Bettoney Co., Inc.
    ---Nightingale and Thrush. Concert-Polka (2 picc, pf) An-
        draud; Carl Fischer.
KLOSE, OSCAR, Op. 42, Fruhlingstraum. Nocturne (2 fl, pf) C. F.
        Schmidt, Cefes-Edition.
    ---Op. 43, Salve Regina, Andante Religioso (2 fl, pf) C. F.
        Schmidt, Cefes-Edition.
    ---Romance, Op. 34 (fl, ob or cl, bn, pf) Andraud; (fl, ob
        or cl, or bn or h, pf) C. F. Schmidt, Cefes-Edition
    ---Concertant Duet (2 cl, pf) Andraud.
    ---Duettino Concertant (2 cl, pf) Andraud.

KNAB, ARMIN, Sonata in D minor (2 fl, pf) 1939, Barenreiter.
KNAPP, F., Two Trios (winds, pf) B&H.
KOECHLIN, CHARLES, Three Pieces, Op. 34 (fl, bn,pf) Andraud.
KOHLER, ERNESTO, Concert-Duet on Schubert's Melodies, Op. 67
        (2 fl, pf) Andraud.
    ---Concert-Duet on Chopin's Melodies, Op. 68 (2 fl, pf) An-
        draud.
KOHLER, ERNESTO, The Magic Flute Collection of 100 Popular Oper-
        atic and Folk Melodies, Dances (2 fl, pf) Andraud.
    ---Flower Waltz, Op. 87 (2 fl, pf)
KONINK, SERVAAS DE, Twelve Sonatas (fl, ob or v, pf) Amsterdam,
        Roger; Fetis.
KOPSCH, JULIUS, Trio in A minor (ob, cl, pf) 1929, Universal
        Edition; Andraud.
KREBS, JOHANN LUDWIG, Loving, I Think of Thee (2 cl, pf) E
        Carl Fischer.
KREISLER, FRITZ, Liebesfreud, Schon Rosmarin, arr. by Erik Leid-
        zen; Midnight Bells, arr. by Heuberger (2 cl, pf) Foley.
KREJEI, ISA, Trio (cl, contrabass, pf) ME Eble; Nakcadem
        Vlastnim.
KREUTZER, KON-RADIN, Trio, Op. 43 in Eb major (cl, bn, pf) Pe-
        ters, Leipzig; Fetis.
KRONKE, EMIL, Suite, Op. 164, A minor, in Ancient Style (2 fl,
        pf) MH (rec) 1922, Zimmermann; Andraud; Baxter-
        Northrup.
    ---Two Butterflies, Op. 165 (2 fl, pf) Andraud.
    ---Romance and Scherzo, Op. 200 (2 fl, pf) Andraud.
KUHLAU, FREIDRICH DANIEL RODOLPHE, Grand Trio, Op. 119 in G ma-
        jor (2 fl, pf) Raabe & Plothow, 1905 (now Simrock), ed.
        by A. G. Kurth; Andraud; Simrock; Baxter-Northrup.
KUHN, EDMUND, Friendship and Confidence, Tyrolienne (2 cl, pf)
        Andraud.
KUMMER, KASPAR, Concertino, Op. 101 (cl, fl, pf or ob, fl, pf)
        Andraud.
    ---Grand Trio Brillant (2 fl, pf).
LABARRE, THEODORE, Trios, Op. 6 (bn, h, harp) Pacini; Fetis.
LABITSKY, The Herd Girl's Dream, Trio (2 fl, pf or fl, cl, pf or
        2 cl, pf) Cundy-Bettoney, Inc.
LACOMBE, PAUL, Serenade of Autumn, Op. 47 in G major (fl, ob,
        pf) Hamelle; Andraud; Baxter-Northrup.
    ---Dialogue Sentimental (fl, bn, pf) 1917 Heugel; Andraud.
LAFAGE, JUSTE-ADRIEN LENOIR DE, Air Varie (2 fl, pf) Fetis.
LAKE, M. L., Annie Laurie. Fantasia (2 cl, pf) MH Carl Fischer.
LALBER, Trio, Op. 22 (ob, bn, pf) Peters, 1872.
LALLIET, C. THEOPHILE CASIMIR, Terzetto, Op. 22 in D major (ob,
        bn, pf) 1872 Hamelle; Andraud.
    ---Souvenir de Mendelssohn (fl, cl, or ob, pf) Andraud.
LANGE, FR. GUST., Chant du Nord (Song of the North) (2 cl, pf
        or fl, cl, pf) E Carl Fischer; Baxter-Northrup.
    ---Flower Song (fl, cl, pf or 2 cl, pf) Carl Fischer;
        Baxter-Northrup.
LANGENUS, G., Swallow's Flight, Scherzo (fl, cl, pf) EMB; Music
        Publishers Holding Corp.
LANGEY, OTTO, Gondolier and Nightingale, Op. 49 (ob, picc, pf)
        Andraud; Baxter-Northrup.

LAUBER, JOSEPH, Trio (fl, eng h, pf) Andraud.
LAVALLEE-BOURDON, The Butterfly (fl, cl, pf) MH (rec) Fischer.
LAX, FREDERICK, Lo! Hear the Gentle Lark. Fantasy on the ori-
      ginal song (fl, cl, pf) Fischer; Baxter-Northrup; Cundy-
      Bettoney Co., Inc.
   ---Twilight Carol Polka (2 fl, pf or 2 picc, pf)
      Cundy-Bettoney Co., Inc.
LE BEAU, LUISE ADOLPHA, Canon, Op. 38 in E minor (2 fl or ob or
      cl, pf) Schmidt, Cefes-Edition.
LECAIL, CLOVIS, Pastorale, Trio (fl, ob or cl, pf) Andraud;
      Baxter-Northrup.
LECHTHALER, JOS., Trio, Op. 53 Freundliche Abendmusik (fl, cl,
      pf or fl, cl, guit) Bohm, 1942.
LECLAIR, JEAN MARIE, Trio Sonate 8, Op. 2 in D major (fl, bn, pf)
      Schott, Mainz.
LEDUC, ALPHONSE, Trio Op. 66 (fl, bn, pf) Leduc.
LEEUWEN, ARY VAN, Chopin's Minute Waltz (arr.) (2 fl, pf) J.H.
      Zimmermann.
LEGRENZI, Sonata in D minor (2 fl, pf, vc ad lib) C.F. Peters.
LEMARE, E.H., Andantino (2 fl, pf) arr. by Long. EMB; Fischer;
      Baxter-Northrup; Volkwein (scored for any combination of
      instruments).
LEMIERE DE CORVEY, J.F.A., Trio (h, bn, harp) Naderman; Fetis.
LEROUX, XAVIER HENRY NAPOLEON, A Simple Thought (Une Simple
      Idee) (fl, ob, pf) Andraud; Baxter-Northrup.
LINICKE, JOHANN GEORG, Ouverture in C major (2 fl, pf) 1938,
      Vieweg, arr. by Hans Fischer.
   ---Suite (2 fl, pf) 1939, Vieweg, arr. by Hans Fischer.
LLOYD, CHARLES HARFORD, Trio in Bb major (cl, bn, pf) Boosey-
      Hawkes-Belwin, Inc.
LOCATELLI, PIETRO, Sonata in E minor (2 fl, pf) Baxter-Northrup.
LOEILLET, JEAN BAPTISTE, Trios in E minor and G minor (2 fl, pf)
      1911, Lemoine, ed. by A. Beon; Andraud; International;
      Elkan-Vogel; Hug.
   ---G minor Sonata a Trois (2 fl, pf) Cundy-Bettoney Co., Inc.
   ---Minuet (2 fl, pf or fl, ob, pf or 2 ob, pf) Edition Mus-
      icus; London, at Walsh; Amsterdam, at Roger.
   ---Trio Sonata in F major, Schott; AMP.
   ---Trio Sonata, No. 1, ed. by Bergmann (fl, ob, pf) Hug.
   ---Trio Sonatas No. 5 in C minor and No. 16 in D minor (fl,
      ob, pf) 1911, Lemoine (ed. by A. Beon); Andraud; Hug,
      (ed. by A. Beon); International; Elkan-Vogel; Walsh,
      London; Roger, Amsterdam. (rec)
   ---D minor Sonata (reco, ob, pf, vc ad lib) Music Press,
      inc; Mercury.
   ---Sonata in E major (2 fl, pf) Lemoine.
   ---Two Sonatas in c minor. Music Press, Inc.
LOSEY, F.H., Alita (Wild Flower) Gavotte (2 cl, pf or fl, cl,
      pf) E Fischer; Baxter-Northrup.
LOVREGLIO, DONATO, Grand Concert Duet, on themes from Verdi's
      opera "Simon Boccanegra", ed. by Bellison (fl, cl, pf)
      Ricordi.
LUIGINI, A.C.L.J., Pastorale, (2 ob, pf) Andraud.
MAGANINI, QUINTO E., Moonlight on the Painted Desert (fl, cl,
      pf) (2 cl, pf) Edition Musicus.

      ---Twins, Valse (2 fl, pf) E Carl Fischer; Baxter-
          Northrup.
      ---Fiesta, Spanish March (2 fl, pf) E Carl Fischer; Baxter-
          Northrup.
      ---An Old Song, Romance (2 fl, pf) E Fischer; Baxter-
          Northrup.
MANCINI, Pastorale (fl, ob, pf) Andraud; Baxter-Northrup.
MANGELSDORF, W., Edelweiss und Almenrausch, Oberlander (2 fl, pf)
          C. F. Schmidt, Cefes-Edition.
MARSAL, E., Nanine, Fantasie Polka (2 cl, pf or fl, cl, pf) (rec)
          EMB; Cundy-Bettoney Co., Inc.
MARTINI, G. B., Les Moutons (The Sheep) (cl or ob, bn pf) Andraud.
MASON, DANIEL GREGORY, Pastorale (fl, cl, pf) Andraud.
MAYR, S., Birds of the Forest, Polka de Concert (2 picc, pf)
          Carl Fischer.
MCCAUGHEY, Enchanted Isle (2 fl, pf or fl, cl, pf) EMB.
MCKAY, Two Movements (cl, bn, pf)
MEL-BONIS, MADAME ALBERT DOMANGE, Trio, Suite in Four Movements
          (fl, h, pf) Ms.
MENDELSSOHN-BARTHODY, Felix, Konzertstuck, No. 1 and No. 2, Op.
          113-114 (cl, alto-cl or basset h, pf) Andraud; Baron;
          B&H; Andre; AMP
      ---Spring Song (fl, cl, pf) Andraud; Cundy-Bettoney Co.,
          (score, parts).
MENZEL, FR., Susses Sehen, Beruhmte Romanze, Op. 40 (Sweet Long-
          ing) (fl, ob, pf or fl, cl, pf or fl, bn, pf or fl, h,
          pf) C. F. Schmidt, Cefes-Edition; Carl Fischer (fl, cl,
          pf); Baxter-Northrup.
MEREDITH, EVAN, Op. 28 in D major (fl, h, pf) Modern Music Li-
          brary.
METHFESSEL, ERNEST, Concertino, Op. 8 (ob, cl, pf) Fetis; Bale,
          Knop.
METZGER, JOHANN GEORG, Six Trios, Op. 2 (2 fl, pf) Hummel;
          Fetis.
MEYERBEER, GIACOMO, Robert Le Diable, arr. by Lazarus (2 cl, pf)
          Cundy-Bettoney Co., (score, parts).
      ---L'Africaine, Grand Duet (2 cl, pf) Andraud.
MICHEL, E., Spring Warbling (2 cl, pf) Andraud.
MIGOT, GEORGES, Divertissements Francais (fl, cl, harp) Andraud;
          Leduc; Hug.
      ---Prelude and Estampie (fl, cl, harp) Andraud; Leduc.
MOLBE, HEINRICH FREIHERR VON BACH, Air Arabe, Op. 77 in C major
          (ob, h, pf) Rorich, Vienna.
      ---Trio (Songe) Op. 80 in D Minor (cl, bn, pf) F. Rorich.
MONIUSHKO, STANISLAUS, Romance (eng h, bn, pf or h, bn, pf) Ed.
          by Maganini. Edition Musicus.
MONTI, Csardas (2 cl, or 2 fl, pf) EMB
MOREAU, LEON EUGENE, Flute Players from Dionysos (2 fl, pf)
          Andraud.
MOSZKOWSKI, MORITZ, Serenade (fl, cl, pf) Cundy-Bettoney Co.,
          (score, parts).
MOULE-EVANS, D., Suite (fl, ob, pf) Jos. Williams, London.
MOUQUET, JULES, Divertissement Grec, Op. 23 (2 fl, harp) An-
          draud; Baxter-Northrup.
MOZART, WOLFGANG AMADEUS, Fantasy for a Music-Box, trans. (fl,
          ob, pf) Andraud.

---Fantasy for Mechanical Organ in F Minor, arr. Baxter-
Northrup.

---Trio in Eb (ob or cl, bn, pf) Andraud.

---Clarinet Trio in Eb, K 498, contained in Mozart, 7 trios.
(3 cl) C. F. Peters Corp.; (2 cl, pf) Baron.

MOZART, WOLFGANG AMADEUS, Two Short Divertimenti (ob, bn, pf)
Andraud.

---Zwei Leichte Trios (Two Easy Trios, based on Divertimenti)
in Eb major, Op. 252 and Bb major, Op. 240 (ob, bn, pf)
1885 B&H; Andraud.

MUFFAT, GOTTLIEB, Gigue (2 fl, pf or 2 cl, pf or fl, cl, pf or
fl, ob, pf) Edition Musicus.

MULLER, IWAN, Concertante, Op. 23 (fl, cl, pf or 2 cl or 2 ob,
pf or fl, ob, pf) Andraud; Baxter-Northrup.

MULLER, BERNHARD ED., Serenade (fl, h, pf) Spratt.

NAPIERSKY, HERBERT, Trio, Op. 19, No. 1 (Frohliche Musik Sonatine) (2 fl, pf) 1939, Moeck.

NEUGEBOREN, H., Little Serenade (cl, bn, pf) Andraud.

NEVIN,ETHELBERT W., Narcissus, arr. by Hummel (2 cl, pf) EMB.

NICOLAI, O., The Lark Sings in the Grove (fl, ob, pf) Andraud.

---Horch die Lerche Singt im Hain (fl, ob, pf or fl, cl, pf
or fl, bn, pf) C. F. Schmidt, Cefes-Edition.

NIKOLSY, Elegie, Op. 40, No. 4 (cl, bn, pf) Andraud.

OBIOLS, Divertimento (fl, cl, pf) Union Musical Espanola.

OERTEL, Forty well-known Charales, ed. by Oertel (2 cl, pf) Andraud.

OFFENBACH, JACQUES, Barcarolle from Tales of Hoffmann (2 cl, pf)
E Carl Fischer; EMB.

PACINI, GIOVANNI, Trios (wind instruments and pf) Fetis Supplement.

PAGANINI, NICOLO, Carnival of Venice, variations de concert (2
fl, pf) Andraud.

PAISIBLE, JACQUES, Sonatas No. 1 in D minor, No. 2 in G minor,
No. 3 in F major, No. 4 in C minor and No. 5 in C major
(2 fl or fl, ob, pf, vc ad lib) 1939, Moeck; McGinnis
& Marx (scored for 2 alto reco or fl or ob or v, pf).

PAQUOT, P. H., Scene et Air de Mozart (2 cl, pf) Andraud.

---Pluie de Perles (2 cl, pf) Andraud.

PEPUSCH, JOHANN CHRISTOPHER, Sonata in G minor (2 fl, pf) 1939
Rieter-Biedermann; Peters, C. F. (Urtext); Hug (vc ad
lib, Urtext).

PERFECT, A., Two Little Chums. Polka di Concert (2 cl, pf) H
Fischer; EMB.

PEZ, JOHANN CHRISTOPHER, Trio Sonata in C Major (2 fl, pf) 1938
Peters; Rieter-Biedermann; (new edition, C. F. Peters,
Urtext, for 2 reco, pf. Aria, Rondeaux, Gavotte en Ron-
deaux, 2 Minuets, Gigue.)

---Trio Sonata (2 reco & pf) McGinnis & Marx.

---Trio-Sonata in D Minor (2 fl, pf) 1935, Nagel, ed. by
von Waldemar Woehl.

PFYFFER, F., Dialogue (fl, cl, pf) Andraud.

PILLEVESTRE, J., The Squeaky Reeds (2 cl, pf) Andraud.

---Duet (2 cl, pf) Andraud.

---Hero and Leandre (ob, eng h or cl, pf; or fl, ob, pf; or
fl, cl, pf; or 2 cl, pf; or ob, bn, pf; or ob, eng h, pf)

Andraud; Baxter-Northrup.

---Riccolinette (2 fl, or 2 picc, pf or 2 cl, pf) Andraud.

---Perpetual Motion, Old Style Gavotte (2 fl, pf or 2 cl, pf) Andraud.

PILLEVESTRA, J., Eglogue Auvergnate (2 ob, pf or ob, eng h, pf) Andraud.

---An Idyl in Brittany (2 ob, pf or cl, of, pf or ob, bn, pf 2 cl, pf or ob, eng h, pf) Andraud.

---Yvonette, Little Scene in Brittany (2 ob, pf or ob, eng h pf or ob, h, pf or 2 cl, pf) Andraud.

---Duettino (2 ob, pf or 2 cl, pf) Andraud.

---Phoebe, Nocturne (fl, ob, pf or fl, cl, pf) Andraud.

---Daphnis and Chloe (fl, ob, pf or fl, cl, pf) Andraud.

PLANEL, ROBERT, Andante et Scherzo (ob, bn, pf)

---Andante and Scherzo in A (ob, bn, pf) MH Andraud; Selmer; Baron.

POHL, J., Rosa and Roschen (fl, cl, pf) Andraud.

POLLET, JEAN JOSEPH BENOIE, Trio (h, bn, harp) Hanry; Fetis.

PONCE, LUCTOR, Estrellita (My Little Star) Mexican Serenade (2 fl, pf) arr. by Maganini. E (rec) EMB; Fischer; Baxter-Northrup.

PONCHIELLI, AMILCARE, Il Convegno (The Meeting) Divertimento (2 cl, pf) H Fischer.

---Divertimento (2 cl, pf) Andraud.

POPP, WILHELM, Lockvogel, Joyous Intermezzo, Op. 449 (2 fl, pf) Andraud.

---Evening Song, Op. 306 (fl, h, pf) Andraud.

POTTER, CIPRIANI, Three Trios, Op. 12, Nos. 1, 2, and 3 (cl, bn pf or v, vc, pf) Simrock; Bonn; Fetis.

POULENC, FRANCIS, Trio (ob, bn, pf) H (rec) 1926, Hansen; Baron; Andraud; Eble; AMP: McGinnis & Marx.

PROWO, P., Sonatas No. 5 and 6 in G minor and Bb major (2 fl or 2-ob, pf) 1940, Moeck, ed. by Wilh. Friedrich.

---Sonata No. 5 for 2 alto Recorders (or fl, ob, or v, pf) McGinnis and Marx.

PUCCINI, GIACOMO, Musetta's Waltz Song From La Boheme, arr. by Erik Leidzen (2 cl, pf or 2 fl, pf) EMB.

---Musetta's Waltz, arr. by Stebbing (2 fl or 2 cl, pf) (rec) Ricordi.

---Love and Music from Tosca, arr. by Leidzen, (2 cl, or 2 fl, pf) EMB.

---Vissi D'arte, Vissi D'Amore from Tosca (2 fl or 2 cl, pf) E (rec) Arr. by Stebbing. Ricordi.

PUGNI, CESARE, Russian Ballet Scene (fl, cl, pf) (rec) arr. by B. Bernards, Andraud; (fl, cl, pf, 2 v, vc, ad lib) Wilhelm Zimmermann, Leipzig.

QUANTZ, JOHANN JOACHIM, Trio-Sonata (reco, fl, pf) arr. by Ermeler. Hortus Musicus, Musica Rara.

---Trio-Sonata in C Minor (fl, ob, or 2 fl, pf) 1930, Zimmermann, arr. by Conrad Blumenthal; Andraud; Baxter-Northrup.

---Sonata in D Major (2 fl, pf) 1921, Robert Forberg.

---Trio Sonata in C Major (2 fl, pf) 1929, Barenreiter, arr. by W. Birke.

---Sonata No. 7, (2 fl, pf) Andraud.

   ---Sonata (Andante) in D major (2 fl, pf)   Cundy-Bettoney
         Co., Inc.
QUENSEL, A., Entracte (fl, cl, pf) Cundy-Bettoney Co., (score,
         parts).
ROBBONI, GIUSEPPE, Duos on Rigoletto, Stiffelio, Leonara, Il
         Trovatore, Op. 55, 57, 60 and 67 (posthumous) (2 fl, pf)
         Fetis Supplement.
RAMEAU, JEAN PHILIPPE, Menuet from Castor and Pollux (2 cl, pf)
         Andraud.
RANGER, A. R., Country Gardens (Handkerchief Dance) Traditional
         Morris Dance Tune (2 cl, pf) E Fischer; EMB.
   ---A Wreath of Holly (Selection of Christmas Songs: Adeste
         Fideles, Silent Night, Hark, the Herald Angels, It Came
         Upon the Midnight Clear, O Faithful Pine, Jingle Bells)
         (2 cl, pf) E Fischer.
RAPP, JOHANN DIETRICH, Six Trios (2 fl, pf) Riga; Fetis.
REBIKOFF, VLADIMIR IVANOVITCH, Valse from The Christmas Tree
         (fl, ob, pf or fl, cl, pf) Edition Musicus.
   ---Cradle Song (fl, cl, pf) Edition Musicus.
   ---A Little Girl Rocking Her Doll (2 fl, pf) Edition Musicus.
REICHEL, A., Trio (ob, bn, pf) Andraud.
REINECKE, CARL HEINRICH CARSTEN, Trio, Op. 188 in A minor (ob,
         h, pf) 1887 B&H; Sansone; Andraud; AMP.
   ---Trio, Op. 274 in Bb major (cl, h, pf) 1906 B&H; Sansone;
         Andraud; AMP.
REISSET, MARIE CLEMENCE DE, Grand Trio (ob, bn, pf) Lemoine.
   ---Trio de Salon (2 winds, pf) Lemoine.
RICHTER, CHARLES GOTTLIEB, Six Trios (2 fl, pf) Fetis.
RIEDT, FRIEDRICH WILHELM, Six Trios (2 fl, pf) Fetis.
RICHI, TEL, Fede e Follia, Bizzarria (fl, cl, pf) Andraud.
ROBBINS, Bagatelle (fl, ob, pf) ME Eble.
ROMAN, JOHAN HELMICH, Sonata for 2 Oboes and Piano (rec) MH
         McGinnis & Marx; Nordiska Musikverlaget.
ROMANO, H. J., Twelve Sonatas (2 fl, pf) Fetis.
ROSCHER, J., Musical Magic, Humoresque (ob or cl, bn, pf) An-
         draud.
ROSSINI, GIOACCHINO ANTONIO, Pastoral from William Tell Over-
         ture (fl, cl, pf) Andraud.
   ---Third Movement (cl, fl, pf) Cundy-Bettoney Co., (score,
         parts).
   ---Duo Brilliant on William Tell, arr. by Jules Demersse-
         mann (fl, ob or cl, pf) Andraud.
ROUGNON, Andante and Polonaise (ob, cl, pf) Andraud.
RUBINSTEIN, Anton Gregorovitch, Celebrated Melody in F, Op. 3
         (2 fl, pf) Andraud.
RUDINGER, GOTTFRIED, Divertissement, Op. 75 in G major (cl, bass-
         cl, pf) 1930, Bohm.
RUPPE, FRIEDRICH CHRISTIAN, Grand Trio (cl, bn, pf) Offenbach,
         Andre; Fetis.
SABON, E., Duo Concert Helvetie (ob, eng h. pf or fl, cl, pf or
         fl, ob, pf) Spratt; Costallat;
   ---Charite-Offertoire (fl, ob or eng h, pf) Costallat;
         Baxter-Northrup.
   ---The Scotch Pibrochs (2 cl, pf) Andraud.
   ---The Blue Bells (fl, ob, pf or any combination with cl or
         bn) Sabon and Coyon. Andraud.

SABON, J., and DOUJON, JOHANNES, Trio (fl, ob, pf) Chatot-
        Durand.
SAINT-SAENS, CHARLES CAMILLE, Serenade (fl, cl or h, pf) An-
        draud; Cundy-Bettoney Co., Inc.
    ---Tarentelle, Op. 6 (fl, cl, pf) MH (rec) Richault; Fe-
        tis; Sansone; Andraud; Durand; Elkan-Vogel; Fischer.
SALIERI, Danse from "Tarare" (2 fl, pf) Edition Musicus.
SAMMARTINI, GIUSEPPE, Twelve Sonatas, 2 vols. (2 fl, pf) 1935,
        Schott (ed. by F. J. Giesbert); Andraud.
SARGENT, W.A.B., Nip and Tuc (C and Db picc, pf or 2 cl in Eb
        or Bb, pf) Barrington-Sargent; Cundy-Bettoney Co., Inc.
SCHEYERMANN, GEORGES, Trio Concertant (fl, bn, pf) Fetis.
SCHICKHARDT, JOHANN CHRISTIAN, Sonata I (2 fl, pf) 1934, Moeck,
        ed. by H. Monkemeyer.
    ---Sonata, Op. 4 (2 fl, pf) Roger, Amsterdam; Fetis.
    ---Sonata, Op. 6 (2 fl, pf) Roger, Amsterdam; Fetis.
    ---Sonata, Op. 9 (2 fl, pf) Roger, Amsterdam; Fetis.
    ---Sonata, Op. 10 (2 ob, pf) Roger, Amsterdam; Fetis.
    ---Recueil de Menuets, Op. 11 (2 ob, pf) Roger, Amsterdam;
        Fetis.
    ---Twelve Sonatas, Op. 16 (2 fl, pf) Roger, Amsterdam; Fe-
        tis.
    ---Airs Spirituels des Lutheriens, Op. 21 (2 fl, pf) Roger,
        Amsterdam; Fetis.
SCHMITT, FLORENT, Sonatine, Op. 85, en trio in E major (fl, cl,
        pf) MH (rec) 1936, Durand; Eble; Andraud; Elkan-
        Vogel.
SCHNEIDER, J. C. FRIEDRICH, Trio, Op. 10 in Bb major (cl, bn, pf)
        Peters, Leipzig; Fetis.
SCHONICKE, WILHELM, Nocturne, Op. 27 (fl, h, pf) Andraud.
SCHOUWMAN, HANS, Trio, Op. 36, 1944 (cl, bn, pf) Stichting Don-
        emus.
SCHUBERT, FRANZ, Five Little Duets (2 fl, pf) EMB.
    ---Barcarolle (2 cl, pf) E Fischer.
    ---Serenade (fl, ob, pf) Andraud; (2 cl, pf) Fischer. MH
SCHULTZE, JOHANN CHRISTOPF, Ouverture No. 1 from Suite in F Ma-
        jor, arr. by W. Friedrich (2 fl, pf) 1939, Moeck.
    ---Overture No. 1 in F Major (2 alto reco or fl, v, and pf)
        McGinnis & Marx.
    ---Suite in D Minor, arr. by W. Friedrich (2 fl, pf) 1938,
        Schott.
SCHUMANN, ROBERT ALEXANDER, The Voice of Love, Serenade (fl, h,
        pf) Fischer; Baxter-Northrup.
    ---Evening Song and Reverie (2 fl, pf) Andraud.
SINGER, Concerto (2 ob, pf) Ricordi.
SITT, HANS, Moment Musical (fl, cl, pf) Andraud.
SLECHTA, T. J., Father of Waters (2 cl, pf or fl, cl, pf) EMB;
        Cundy-Bettoney Co., Inc. (score, parts.)
SMITH, CLAY, While the Fire Burns, Valse Caprice (2 cl, pf) E
        Fischer.
    ---The Spirit of Joy, Valse Caprice (2 cl, pf) E Fischer.
    ---On Pleasure Bent, Valse Caprice (2 cl, pf) E Fischer.
    ---Helen (2 cl, pf) E Fischer.
    ---De Die in Diem (From Day to Day) Waltz (2 cl, pf) E
        Fischer.

SMITH-HOLMES, Drink to Me Only with Thine Eyes and Old Black
       Joe (Airs Variees) (2 cl, pf) MH Fischer.
SMYTH, DAME ETHEL MARY, 2 Trios (fl, ob, pf) Oxford University
       Press.
    ---Two Interlinked French Folk-Melodies (fl, ob, pf) 1928,
       Oxford University Press; Andraud; Baxter-Northrup.
    ---Variations on "Bonny Sweet Robin" (Ophelia's Song) (2
       winds, pf) Andraud; 1928, Oxford University Press;
       Baxter-Northrup.
SOBECK, JOHANN, Duo on Mozart's Don Juan, Op. 5 (cl, h, pf) An-
       draud.
SOLNITZ, ANTON WILHELM, Six Trios, Op. 1 (2 fl or fl, v, pf)
       Publ. at Amsterdam; Fetis.
SONTAG, H., An Evening Serenade (fl, h, pf or fl, ob, pf or fl,
       cl, pf or cl, h, pf) Cundy-Bettoney Co., Inc.
SOULAGE, MARCELLE, Legende (fl, ob, harp) Andraud.
SOUSSMANN, HEINRICH, Trio Concertante, Op. 30 (2 fl, pf) Fetis;
       Richault; Hofmeister, Leipzig.
SPENCER, J. HENRY, Silvatones (fl, cl, pf or 2 cl, pf) MH (rec)
       Cundy-Bettoney Co., Inc. (score, parts).
SPITTA, HEINRICH, Trios, Op. 39, in D minor and F major (2 fl,
       pf) 1937, Nagel.
STADTFELD, CHRISTIAN, Trio (ob, bn, pf) Fetis.
STAES, WILLIAM, Grand Sonata, Op. 1 (fl, or v, by or vc, pf)
       Sieber, Paris; Fetis.
STAIGERS, DEL, Hazel, Valse Caprice (2 cl, pf) MH Fischer.
STEGEWY, A. C., Three Sonatas (2 fl, pf) Fetis.
STOHR, RICHARD, Trio, Op. 53 in A minor (2 bn, pf) E. Strache,
       Vienna.
STOLZEL, GOTTFRIED HEINRICH, Trio-Sonata in F minor (2 ob, pf)
       1937, Nagel (ed. by Hermann Osthoff); Andraud; Baxter-
       Northrup.
STRAUSS, JOHANN, Tales from the Vienna Woods, Valse, Op. 325
       (2 cl, pf or fl, cl, pf) Cundy-Bettoney Co., (score,
       parts).
STRAUSS, RICARD, Duet Concertino (cl, bn, pf) Boosey & Hawkes.
STRAUSS, RICHARD, The Duel, Polonaise (fl, bn, pf) Ms.
STRAVINSKY, IGOR FEDOROVICH, Dances of the Princesses from "The
       Firebird" (ob, bn, pf; or ob, fl, pf; or ob, cl, pf; or fl,
       h, pf; or fl, bn, pf; or fl, cl, pf; or ob, h, pf) Edition
       Musicus.
STRUBE, GUSTAVE, Trio (1936) (cl, h, pf)
SVAN, ALFRED J., Trio (fl, cl, pf) 1936, Belaieff; Andraud.
TADOLINI, GIOVANNI, Trio (ob, bn, pf) Cipriani, Florence; Fe-
       tis.
TAK, P.C., Trio, 1943 (fl, ob, pf) Stichting Donemus.
TELEMANN, GEORG PHILIPP, Triosonata in C (2 reco, pf) Der Ge-
       treue Musikmeister, Heft 5 (Degen) Musica Rara, London;
       McGinnis & Marx.
    ---Polish Sonata No. 2 (2 fl, pf) Andraud.
    ---Sonata (2 fl, pf) Andraud.
    ---Concerto in G major (fl, ob d'amour, organ or pf or harp-
       sichord) Litolff.
    ---Trio, D minor and G minor (2 fl or fl, ob, pf) Ed. by M.
       Ruetz, 1939, Schott.

TELEMANN, GEORG PHILIPP, Trio-Sonata in C minor (Aus Exercii
        Musici, fl, ob, pf) 1938, ed. by W. Woehl, Peters;
        Rieter-Biedermann; (reco, fl or v, and ob, v or va, pf,
        vc ad lib) C. F. Peters, new ed., 1951 (Urtext); Hug
        (Urtext, vc ad lib).
    ---Trio-Sonata in G major (2 fl, pf) Der Getreue Musik-
        meister, Heft 5, Degen; Barenreiter-Bote.
    ---Tafelmusik III, No. 5 (Banquet Music, G minor Sonata)
        1733, arr. by M. Seiffert, B&H, 1931 (ob, bn, pf, vc ad
        lib).
    ---G minor Sonata (ob, bn, pf) Andraud.
    ---Concert (ob, fl, pf) Andraud; Baxter-Northrup; Litolff.
    ---Trio Sonata in C major (fl, ob, pf) (Aus Exercicii Mu-
        sici) ed. by W. Woehl, 1938, Peters; (2 reco, fl or v,
        pf) Der Getreue Musikmeister, Heft 5, McGinnis & Marx;
        Musica Rara.
    ---Trio Sonata (2 fl, pf) Hug.
    ---Trio-Sonatas in F major and C major (2 fl, pf) ed. by
        Adolf Hoffmann, 1937, B&H.
    ---Sonata in A major (2 fl, pf, vc ad lib) ed. by H. Schrei-
        ter, 1938, B&H.
    ---Sonata in F major (2 fl, or fl, ob, pf, vc ad lib) ed. by
        A. Rodemann, 1939, Moeck; Hug; (alto reco or fl, ob and
        pf) McGinnis & Marx (Moecks Kammermusik).
    ---Trio Sonata in E minor (reco or fl, ob, pf) McGinnis &
        Marx; Musica Rara; Hug, ed. by Ruetz.
    ---Trio II in E minor (Tafelmusik II) (fl, ob, pf) 1928, ed.
        by Max Seiffert, D.D.T., Vol. I; Barenreiter-Bote, ed.
        by Ruetz (score, parts).
    ---Trio III in D major (Tafelmusik III) (2 fl, pf) 1928, ed.
        by Max Seiffert, D.D.T., Vol. I.
TERSCHAK, ADOLF, Duets (2 fl, pf)
THOME, FRANCIS, Simple Aveu, Romance (2 cl, pf or fl, cl, pf)
        E Fischer; EMB; Baxter-Northrup; Cundy-Bettoney Co.,
        Inc. (score, parts).
TICCIATI, FRANCESCO, Trios (ob, fl, pf)
    ---Trio (sonata form) Op. 17 in D minor (fl, ob, pf)
TILIMETZ, RUDOLF, Der Amsel Lockruf, Idyl, Op. 24 (2 fl or 2
        picc, pf) Andraud; C. F. Schmidt, Cefes-Edition.
    ---Nocturne, Op. 31 (fl, h, pf) Andraud.
TITL, A. E., Serenade (fl, cl, pf and any other combination) H
        Andraud; (2 cl, pf or fl, cl, pf) Fischer; (2 cl, pf; or
        fl, h, pf; or fl, ob, pf; or fl, bn, pf; or fl, cl, pf)
        Cundy-Bettoney Co., Inc.; Baxter-Northrup.
TOESCHI, CARLO GIUSEPPE, Trio in G major, No. 4 (string or wind
        instrument, pf) ed. by H. Riemann, D.T.B., Vol. 28; B&H
        1915.
TOVEY, DANIEL FRANCIS, Trio, Tragic Style, Op. 8 (cl, h, pf) in
        C minor MH (rec) 1906, Schott; Andraud.
TRINKAUS, GEORGE J., The Approach of Day, (fl, cl, pf) Music
        Publishers Holding Corp.
    ---The Approach of Night (fl, cl, pf) Music Publishers
        Holding Corp.
    ---The Ballet of the Birds (fl, cl, pf) Music Publishers
        Holding Corp.

TRINKAUS, GEORGE J., Dance of the Pixies, Scherzo (fl, cl, pf)
        Music Publishers Holding Corp.
    ---In Arcady, Meditation (fl, cl, pf) Music Publishers
        Holding Corp.
    ---Momo, Danse Villageoise, No. I (fl, cl, pf) Music Pub-
        lishers Holding Corp.
    ---Lolo, Danse Villageoise No. II (fl, cl, pf) Music Pub-
        lishers Holding Corp.
    ---Pollywogs at Play, The (fl, cl, pf) Music Publishers
        Holding Corp.
TROJE, Chinese Checkers, arr. by Miller (2 cl, pf) EMB.
Tschaikowsky, Peter Ilitch, Three Pieces from the Album for Chil-
        dren; 1, Organ Grinder's Song, 2, In the Church, 3, The
        Witch (ob, cl, pf or fl, cl, pf) Edition Musicus.
TULOU, JEAN LOUIS, Polonaise de Tancredi, Op. 32 (2 fl, pf)
        Schlesinger, Paris; Fetis.
    ---Trio, Op. 83 in A major (2 fl, pf) Schott.
    ---Air Varie, Op. 63 (2 fl, pf) Andraud.
UCCELLINI, DOM MARCO, Trio (2 ob or cl, pf) arr. by Gustave Len-
        zewski, Vieweg, 1930.
    ---Two Trio Sonatas, No. 16 in E minor, No. 17 in C minor
        (2 winds, pf) Ricordi, 1907).
VERDI, GIUSEPPE, Miserere from Il Trovatore (2 cl, pf) MH Carl
        Fischer.
    ---Dramatic Duo on Aida (2 fl, pf) Andraud.
    ---Simon Boccanegra, Concert Duo, arr. by Lovreglio (fl, cl
        pf) Andraud.
VERROUST, L'Elisire d'Amor (fl, bn, pf) Andraud.
VINEE, ANSELME, Trio-Serenade (fl, eng h or ob, harp or pf) F
        major. Hayet; Andraud; 1890, Gay & Teuton; Durdilly.
VIVALDI, ANTONIO, Sonata in A minor F XV, No. 1, arr. by F. Mali-
        piero (fl, bn, pf) Hug.
    ---Concerto in G minor (fl, vn, pf) Ricordi.
VIVIER, Contemplation, Andante (fl, ob, pf) Andraud.
VOGT, GUSTAVE, Grand Duo (fl, cl, bn, any combination, pf) An-
        draud.
    ---Duo for Two Oboes, pf. Richault, Paris; Fetis.
VOIGT, G.B., Brillante Serenade (fl, h, pf; or fl, ob, pf; cl, bn
        or h, pf) Andraud; (fl, h, pf; or fl, ob, pf; or cl, bn
        pf; cl, fl, pf) C.F. Schmidt, Cefes-Edition.
VOIGT, F.W., Nocturne, Op. 75 (cl, h, pf) Andraud.
VOLKMANN, FRIEDRICH ROBERT, Schlummerlied, Op. 76 (cl, h, harp)
        Andraud; 1882, Schott.
WALCKIERS, EUGUNE, Trio, Op. 95 in G minor (fl, cl, pf) Costal-
        lat; Richault.
WALLACE, W.V., Cavatina from Maritana (fl, cl, pf or 2 cl, pf)
        Cundy-Bettoney Co., Inc. (score, parts).
WECKERLIN, JEAN BAPTISTE, Pastorale (fl, ob, pf) Andraud; Hug;
        Baxter-Northrup.
WEHRLI, WERNER, Sonata in C major, Op. 38 d (2 fl, pf) 1937,
        Hug.
WEISSE, HANS, Concerto (fl, ob, harpsichord).
WETGE, Grand Duo (2 cl, pf) Andraud.
WIEDEMANN, L., Hunter's Farewell Serenade, Op. 13 (fl, h, pf or
        ob, h, pf or cl, h, pf) Andraud.

WILCOCKE, JAMES, Valse de Concert (fl, cl, pf) Rudall, Carte
      & Co.; Andraud; Boosey & Hawkes.
WILLIAMS, T., Larboard Watch (2 cl, pf) Carl Fischer.
WOEHL, WALDEMAR, Gesellige Spielmusik, in der Reihe der "Kleinen
      Hausmusikhefte," (Folk Music, 2 fl or other instrument,
      pf) Barenreiter-Bote.
YRADIER, C. DE, La Paloma, Spanish Serenade (2 cl or fl, cl, pf)
      E Carl Fischer; Baxter-Northrup.
ZACHOW, FRIEDRICH WILHELM, Trio No. 25, Kammertrio in F major
      (fl or ob, bn, pf or harpsichord) arr. by Max Seiffert,
      D.D.T. I., Vol. 21/22.
   ---Trio for two winds and piano, arr. by Max Seiffert. Kist-
      ner & Siegel.
ZAGWIJN, HENRI, Pastorale, 1937 (fl, ob, pf) Stichting Donemus.
ZOELLER, Petit Duo de Concert (cl, bn, pf) Boosey & Hawkes.

Collections

The Comrades' Repertory, Clarinet Duets (2 Bb cl, pf) Contents:
Nanine, Concert Polka, E. Marsal; Il Convegno, Fantasia,
A. Ponchielli; Reverie, C. Fabre; Two Little Bulfin-
ches, Polka, H. Kling; Nip and Tuc, Intermezzo, W. A.
Barrington Sargent; The Herd Girl's Dream, A. Labitsky;
Golden Robin, Polka, N. Bousquet; The Famous Waltz, J.
Brahms; Second Reverie, C. Fabre; Minuet in G, L. Beet-
hoven; Sextette from Lucia, G. Donizetti; Father of
Waters, Concert Waltz, T. Schlecta; The Swiss Boy (air
varie), Bent. Cundy-Bettoney Co., Inc.

Collections for Two Bb Clarinets and Piano, Album of Selected
Trio Arrangements. Contents: Spring's Awakening, Bach;
I Dreamt I Dwelt in Marble Halls, Balfe; Stephanie (Ga-
votte de la Princesse) Czibulka; Humoreske, Dvorak;
Slumber Song, Ersfeld; Ave Maria, Gounod; Longing for
Home, Jungmann; Chant du Nord, Lange; Flower Song,
Lange; Alita (Wild Flower, Losey; Simple Aveu, Thome;
La Paloma, Yradier, Carl Fischer; Baxter-Northrup.

Album of Selected Trio Arrangements, transc. and arr. by Charles
J. Roberts, 12 Favorite Compositions (2 cl, pf) Fischer.

Nordische Volksmusik (2 wind instruments, pf) Barenreiter (score
parts).

Masters of the Baroque, Trio Sonatas by Buxtehude, Reinken, Foerster, Schop, Becker (2 fl, pf, vc ad lib) C. F. Peters.

<u>QUARTETS</u>

<u>Selective List</u>

ABELTSHAUSER, Wind Quartets, Schott.
 ---Six Quartets, Op. 1 (2 fl, 2 h) Schott; Fetis.
 ---Six Quartets, Op. II, (2 fl, 2 h) Schott; Fetis.
 ---Six Pieces, Op. IV (fl, cl, h, bn) Schott; Fetis.
BABBITT, MILTON, Composition for Four Instruments (4 woodwinds)
  New Music Editions XXII No. 4, 1949.
BACHMEHKO, S.W., Quartet (fl, ob, cl, bn)
BECHER, HEINRICH, Heiteres Quartet (Potpourri) in Bb major (ob,
  cl, h, bn) VH 1933, Lausch & Zweigle.
BECKERATH, ALFRED VON, Quartet (4 fl) 1939, Moeck (score).
BENNETT, DAVID, Clarinet Rhapsody (2 cl, alto-cl, bass-cl) H
  (rec) Fischer; EMB.
 ---Way of the Wasp (2 cl, alto-cl, bass-cl) VH Fischer.
 ---Ciribiribin, by Alberto Pestalozza, arr. (4 cl) MH
  Gamble Hinged Music; Music Publishers Holding Corp.
  (score, parts).
 ---Clarinet Polka in Bb major (4 cl) Polish Folk Song, arr.
  MH Gamble Hinged Music; Music Publishers Holding Corp.
  (score, parts).
 ---Dark Eyes, Russian Folk Song (4 cl) MH Gamble Hinged
  Music; Music Publishers Holding Corp. (score, parts).
 ---Loch Lomond, Scotch Folk Song, transc. (4 cl) MH Gam-
  ble Hinged Music; Music Publishers Holding Corp. (score,
  parts).
 ---Prelude and Scherzo (4 cl) H (rec) Fischer.
 ---Swing Low, Sweet Chariot, spiritual (4 cl) MH Gamble
  Hinged Music; Music Publishers Holding Corp. (score,
  parts).
 ---Two Guitars, Russian Folk Song (4 cl) MH Gamble Hinged
  Music: Music Publishers Holding Corp. (score, parts).
 ---Argentine (4 cl) Fischer; EMB.
BOCCHERINI, LUIGI, Minuet from Quintet (fl, ob, cl, bn) An-
  draud.
 ---Minuet from Quintet in E major, arr. by G. J. Trinkaus
  (fl or ob, cl, h, bn) Franklin.
BODENHORN, AARON, Woodwind Quartet (fl, ob, cl, bn) 415 W.
  118th St., NYC 27.
BOROWSKI, Whimsies (4 cl) MH-H Belwin.
BOZZA,EUGENE, Andante and Scherzo (4 cl) Andraud.
BRAUN, CHARLES ANTOINE PHILIPPE, Quartet, Op. 1 (2 fl, 2 h)
  Peters, Leipzig; Fetis.
 ---Two Quartets (fl, ob, h, bn) B&H; Fetis.
BUSCH, C., Northland Suite, 1, Quietude, 2, Playful Mood, 3,
  Evening Promenade (fl, ob, c., bn) ME H. T. FitzSimons;
  (4 cl) Andraud; Fischer (score, parts).
CAPELLER, JOHANN NEPOMUK, Set of Quartets (2 fl, guit, vc)
CAZDEN, NORMAN, Round Dance, No. 6 from Six Discussions for Wind
  Ensemble (4 cl) Kalmus Editions.
 ---Insistence, No. 5 from Six Discussions for Wind Ensemble
  (2 ob, 2 bn) Kalmus Editions.
 ---Waltz, No. 1 from Six Discussions for Wind Ensemble (fl,
  ob, cl, bn) Kalmus Editions.

CHAMINADE, CECILE, Dance Creole, arr. by De Bueris (3 cl, bass-
cl or 4 cl or 2 cl, alto-cl, bass-cl) MH Belwin.
CHOULET, CHARLES, Two Quartets, 1850, Costallat.
CHWARTZ, LEO, Evening in the Turkestan Steppe (fl, eng h or ob,
cl, bn) 1937, Boosey-Hawkes-Belwin (score, parts).
COHEN, SOL B., Alabama Sketches (4 cl) MH (rec) Witmark; An-
draud; Music Publishers Holding Corp. (score, parts).
DALLIN, LEON, Autumn Vignette, arr. by F. W. Westphal (4 cl or
2 cl, alto-cl, bass-cl or 3 cl, bass-cl) ME Belwin.
DALLIN, LEON, Concert Rondo, arr. by F. W. Westphal (4 cl) ME
Mills Music.
---Fountains at Dawn, arr. by F. W. Westphal (4 cl) H Bel-
win.
DE BUERIS, Gavotte Classique (4 cl or 3 cl, bass-cl or 2 cl,
alto-cl, bass-cl) MH Belwin.
DELIBES, LEO, Pizzicato Polka (4 fl) ME Schirmer.
DEMANTIUS, CHRISTOPH, Deutsche Tanze (4 wind instruments) Ba-
renreiter.
DESPORTES, YVONNE, Normandie, Suite on Ancient Airs (4 cl) An-
draud.
---French Suite, 1. Prelude 2. Sarabande, 31 Gavotte,
4. Minuet, 5. Bourree, 6. Gigue (4 cl) H-VH (rec)
Andraud; Baron.
---Italian Suite (4 cl) Andraud.
DOFLEIN, ERICH, Fugenbuchlein (4 wind instruments) 1936, Baren-
reiter.
DUBENSKY, Prelude and Fugue (1933) (4 bn) VH Andraud; Ricor-
di (score, parts).
EDMUNDS, CHRISTOPHER MONTAGUE, Fieldside Suite (4 fl) 1935,
Cramer (score, parts).
EGGE, KLAUS, Quartet (4 woodwinds)
ENDRESEN, R.M., Quartet No. 1 (2 cl, alto-cl, bass-cl or 3 cl,
bass-cl or 4 cl) MH Belwin.
---Quartet No. 2 (2 cl, alto-cl, bass-cl or 3 Bb cl, bass-
cl or 4 cl) MH Belwin.
ETLER, ALVIN, Quartet (ob, cl, va, bn) Valley Music Press.
FETHERSTON, Valse Staccato (4 cl) MH Belwin (based on themes
from the pf etude, Op. 23, Anton Rubinstein.)
FILIPPI, DE, In Nostalgic Mood (fl, ob, cl, bn) E Concord Mu-
sic Publishing Co.
---Hornpipe for a Gay Dolphin (fl, ob, cl, bn) ME (rec)
EMB Concord Music Publishing Co.
---March of the Little Tumblers (fl, ob, cl, bn) E Concord
Music Publishing Co; EMB.
FINNEY, THEODORE M., Ballabile (fl, ob, cl, bn) in A minor ME
Witmark; Andraud; Music Publishers Holding Corp. (score,
parts).
FIORILLO, DANTE, Six Sketches (fl, ob, or cl, cl, bn) ME Edu-
cational Publishing Institute.
---Rustic Scenes (fl, ob or cl, cl, bn) ME Educational
Publishing Institute.
FISCHER, JOHANN KASPAR FERDINAND, A Little Seventeenth Century
Banquet Music (fl, ob, cl, bn or 2 ob, cl, bn, or 2 ob,
2 bn) Andraud.

FRANGKISER, CARL, Fuguerest (2 cl, alto-cl, bass-cl or 4 cl,
  or 3 cl, bass-cl) ME Belwin.
 ---En Escapades (2 cl, alto-cl, bass-cl or 4 cl, or 3 cl,
  bass-cl) MH Belwin.
 ---Stars At Dawn (4 cl or 2 cl, alto-cl, bass-cl) EMB
  Boosey-Hawkes (score, parts).
FRESCOBALDI, GIROLAMO, Fugue in C minor, arr. by Rocereto (fl,
  ob, cl, bn) MH Volkwein Bros., Inc.; Andraud.
GABRIELE, GIOVANNI, Two Ricercari (fl, ob, cl, bn)
GERVAISE, Six Dances (fl, ob, cl, bn) Senart
GLAZOUNOV, ALEXANDER CONSTANTINOVITCH, In Modo Religioso (4 cl or
  2 cl, alto-cl or sax, bass-cl or bn or fl, ob, cl, bn) MH
  E. B. Marks; Cundy-Bettoney Co., Inc. (score, parts).
GOEB, ROGER, Suite in Folk Style (4 cl) ME-MH (rec) Broadcast
  Music Inc.; Associated Music Publishers; Baron.
GRIEG, EDWARD, Melody by Grieg, arr. by Robert McBride (4 cl)
  EMB
 ---Three Little Pieces from Grieg, arr. by Lawrence Taylor
  (fl, ob, cl, bn) (alternate bass-cl) ME Cundy-Bettoney
  Co., Inc. (score, parts); EMB.
HANDEL, GEORGE FRIEDRICK, Fughetta of the Little Bells, arr. by
  Paul Painter (4 cl) ME (rec) Gamble Hinged Music;
  Music Publishers Holding Corp. (score, parts).
HOYER, KARL, Elegie, Third Canon (2 fl or v, va, vc or bn) 1937
  Portius.
HUGUES, LUIGI, Quartet, Op. 72 in G minor (fl, ob, cl, bn) An-
  draud; Ricordi.
 ---Quartet, Op. 76 in Bb (fl, ob, cl, bn) Ricordi; Andraud.
HURRELL, Three Impressions (4 cl) EMB.
IPPOLITOV-IVANOV, Procession of the Sardar, arr. by De Bueris
  (4 cl, 3 cl, bass-cl or 2 cl, alto-cl, bass-cl) MH Bel-
  win.
JEANJEAN, Twenty-Five Melodies & Technical Studies, eight of
  which are accompanied by 3 cl. Andraud.
JOHNSON, WILLIAM SPENCER, Fantasia (2 cl, alto-cl, bass-cl) H
  (rec) Witmark; Andraud; Music Publishers Holding
  Corp. (score, parts).
JONGEN, JOSEPH, Two Paraphrases on Walloon Christmas Carols (3
  fl, alto-fl or cl, eng h h) Andraud.
KEITH, GEORGE D., Character Sketches I and II (2 cl, alto-cl,
  bass-cl) MH No. I: 1, Temperamental, 2, Single Track.
  No. II: 1, Gossips, 2, Absent-Minded. Gamble Hinged
  Music; Music Publishers Holding Corp. (score, parts).
KOHLER, ERNESTO, Grand Quartet in D major, Op. 92 (4 fl) H
  (rec) 1904, Zimmermann (score, parts); Andraud; Baxter-
  Northrup.
KOLLESCHOWSKY, M., Adagio Religioso (2 cl, 2 bn) 1846 Hoffmann,
  Prague.
KRAEHENBUEHL, DAVID, Variations on a Pavane by H. Schein (3 cl,
  bass-cl) AMP.
KRENEK, ERNST, Country Dance (4 cl) MH (rec) Belwin; EMB.
KUNTZ, MICHAEL, Kleine Passacaglia from "So treiben wir den
  Winter aus" (4 fl) 1941, Moeck (score).
LANDRY, A., Musette (fl, ob, cl, bn) transc. by Georges Grisez
  Andraud; Cundy-Bettoney Co., Inc.
LANGE, HANS, Serenade, Op. 45 (ob, cl, bn, h) 1942.

LAUBE, P. X., Alsatian Dance (2 fl, alto-cl, bass-cl or 3 cl, bn
    or 4 cl, alternate bass-cl part, or fl, ob, cl, bn) ME
    Cundy-Bettoney Co., Inc. (score, parts); Andraud (pf
    acc. ad lib).
LAUBER, JOSEPH, Visions de Corse, Op. 54, Five Pieces (4 fl)
    1937 Zimmermann; Andraud.
LEEUWEN, ARY VAN, Turkey in the Straw. Theme and Variations on
    the original folk tune (2 fl, ob, cl, or 2 fl, 2 cl, or
    3 fl, cl, or 4 fl) Andraud.
LEFEBVRE, CHARLES EDOUARD, Intermezzo from 2nd Suite, Op. 122
    (4 cl) arr. by Waln. Kjos.
   ---Prelude from 2nd Suite, Op. 122 (2 cl, alto, bass) arr.
    by Waln. Kjos.
LOCKHART, LEE M., Several pieces, arr. by Lockhart (2 ob or ob
    and cl, bn or cl, bn) Witmark; Music Publishers Hold-
    ing Corp.
MALIPIERO, GIAN FRANCESCO, Epodi e Giambi (ob, v, va, bn) An-
    draud; McGinnis & Marx (score, parts).
MARCELLO, BENEDETTO, Toccato in C minor, arr. by Rocereto (2 cl
    2 bn) Volkwein; Andraud.
MARX, KARL, Kleine Suite, after Leopold Mozart's notebook of
    Wolfgang Mozart (4 fl or woodwinds) 1939, Hanseat.
MASSARANI, RENZO, Pastorale (ob, bn, va, vc)
MAYEUR, L., First Quartet (2 cl, alto-cl, bass-cl) H (rec) arr.
    by H. Voxman. Andraud; Rubank.
MCKAY, GEORGE FREDERICK, Chromatic Caprice (4 cl or 2 cl, alto-
    cl, bass-cl) EMB.
   ---With Gay Spirit (4 cl) EMB.
MEHAN, The Firefly, arr. by Louis Pietrini (fl, ob, cl, bn) Ms,
    Copy with Louis Pietrini, Bassoonist, Met.
MENDELSSOHN, FELIX, Spinning Song, arr. by A. Chiaffarelli (fl,
    ob, cl, bn) Alfred Music Co.
   ---Canzonetta, arr. by De Bueris (3 Bb cl, bass-cl, or 2 Bb
    cl, alto-cl, bass-cl or 4 cl) MH Belwin.
MENGAL, MARTIN JOSEPH, Three Quartets, Op. 18 (fl, cl, h, bn)
    Lemoine; Fetis.
   ---Quartets for wind instruments, Fetis.
   ---Three Quartets, Op. 19 (fl, cl, h, bn) Lemoine; Fetis.
MICHELIS, DE, A Mezzanote Ascoltami, Nocturne, Op. 37 (4 fl)
    Andraud.
MIELENZ, HANS, Scherzo (fl, eng h, cl, bn) 1938, 1940, Wilke.
MILLER, RALPH DALE, Prelude and Scherzo, Op. 20 (4 cl or 2 cl,
    alto-cl, bass cl or 3 cl, bass cl) MH (rec) Belwin.
   ---Prelude to Autumn (2 cl, alto-cl, bass-cl) MH (rec)
    Belwin; EMB.
MORTARI, VIRGILIO, Three Dances (fl, ob, va, vc) 1937, Carisch
    (score, parts).
MOSZKOWSKI, MORITZ, March of the Dwarfs, Op. 53, No. 4. arr. by
    Frank Vognar (2 cl, alto-cl, bass-cl) MH Gamble Hinged
    Music Co.; Music Publishers Holding Corp. (score, parts).
MOZART, WOLFGANG AMADEUS, Andante and Menuetto from String Quar-
    tet No. 21, arr. by G. Langenus (fl, ob, cl, bn) ME-MH
    (rec) Ensemble Music Press; Fischer.
MULLER, IWAN, Three Quartets (4 cl) Ricordi.

PAGANINI, NICOLO, La Chasse, transc. by Frank Vognar (fl, ob, cl, bn or bass-cl ad lib) H Music Publishers Holding Corp. (score, parts) Gamble Hinged Music Co.; Remick.

PAINTER, PAUL, Notturnine di Luna (4 fl) VH Gamble Hinged Music Co; Andraud; Music Publishers Holding Corp. (score, parts).

PAQUIS, Three Quartets, Op. 1 in F major, G major, F major (fl, cl, h, bn) Costallat.

---Three Quartets Concertant, Op. 2 (fl, cl, h, bn) Costallat.

PIKET, Reflection and Caprice (4 cl) MH Omega Music Edition.

PISK, PAUL, Elegy and Scherzino (ob, 2 cl, bn) Op. 70, No. 2, A.C.A.

---Little Woodwind Music (ob, 2 cl, bn) Baron; AMP.

---Suite: 1. March 2. Siciliana 3. Landler (slow waltz) (4 cl) ME-MH (rec) Carl Fischer.

PIZZI, F., Divertissement (4 fl) Ricordi.

RAKOV, N., Three Miniatures (fl, ob or eng h, cl, bn) Leeds.

READY, ELDON, Repartee (4 cl or 2 Bb cl, alto-cl, bass-cl) EMB; Music Publishers Holding Corp. (score, parts).

REICHA, ANTON, Quartet Op. 12 in D major (Sinfonico Quartett) (4 fl) VH 1861, Hofmeister; Andraud; Cundy-Bettoney Co., Inc; Boieldieu, Paris; Baxter-Northrup; Playel; Hug (score, parts).

RIEGGER, WALLINGFORD, Three Canons, Op. 9, 1931 (fl, ob, cl, bn) 1932 New Music Editions, No. 4, San Francisco.

SCARMOLIN, A. LOUIS, Scherzo (fl, ob, cl, bn) Fischer.

SCARLATTI, ALESSANDRO, Pastoral Sonata VIII in F major (fl, ob cl, bn) arr. by Rocereto MH Volkwein Bros.; Andraud.

---Sonata II, Tempo di Ballo (fl, ob, cl, bn) MH arr. by Rocereto. Volkwein Bros., Inc; Andraud.

SCHARWENKA, X., Andante (4 cl) Arr. by Liegl. Fischer; EMB.

SCHUMANN, ROBERT ALEXANDER, Scenes from Childhood, Op. 15 (fl, ob, cl, bn) MH (rec) Witmark; Andraud; Music Publishers Holding Corp. (arr. by James R. Gillette, score. parts).

SCHWARTZ, LEONID, Evening in the Turkestan Stepp (fl, ob or eng h, cl, bn) Hawkes, 1937.

---Variations in C (fl, ob, cl, bn) Russian American Music Publishers.

SCHRIABINE, Praeludium (fl, ob, cl, bn) Andraud.

SILCHER, PHILIPP FRIEDRICH, Loreley, Paraphrase (4 cl or 2 cl, alto-cl or sax, bass-cl or bn or fl, ob, cl, bn or 3 cl, bn or Eb alto-cl or sax or 2 cl, 2 Eb alto-cl or sax) arr. by A. Harris. Cundy-Bettoney Co., Inc. (parts); Andraud.

SKINNER, Scherzetto (4 Bb cl) VH Belwin.

---Capricietta (4 Bb cl) VH Belwin.

SLONIMSKY, NICHOLAS, Suite No. 2 (fl, ob, cl, percussion)

SMITH, T.S., Suite for Four Equal Clarinets (4 cl) MH (rec) C.L. Barnhouse; EMB.

SOUSSMAN, HENRI, Quartet Op. 27, No. 1, 2 in G major and C major (4 fl) Schuberth, Leipzig; Schubert and Niemeyer, Hamburg; Fetis.

---Quartet, Op. 5 in D major (4 fl) Lischke, Berlin; Fetis.

STARK, ROBERT, Entertaining Quartets, Three Books (3 cl, bn)
Andraud.
STEINFELD, A.J., Six Quartets, Op. 20 (2 cl, 2 h, drums ad lib)
Andre; Offenbach, 1802; Fetis.
STRINGFIELD, LAMAR, An Old Bridge in F (ob or fl, cl, h, bn)
Sprague Coleman, N.Y.; Mercury; Leeds.
SUPPIGER, RUSSELL S., Impressions (4 Bb cl or 2 Bb cl, alto-cl,
bass-cl) Music Publishers Holding Corp. (score, parts).
TARLOW, MARC, A Southland Sketch (fl, ob, cl, bn) Andraud;
Music Publishers Holding Corp. (score, parts).
TCHEREPNINE, A., Quartet (4 fl) Hug.
TEMPLETON, ALEC, Bach Goes to Town (4 cl) EMB
THOME, FRANCIS LUCIEN JOSEPH, Pizzicato (4 cl or 2 cl, alto-cl
or sax, bass-cl or bn or 3 cl, bn or Eb alto-cl or sax or
fl, ob, cl, bn or 2 Bb cl, 2 Eb cl or sax) arr. by A.
Harris. Cundy-Bettoney Co., Inc.; Andraud.
TURECHEK, EDWARD, Divertissement in F minor (fl, ob, cl, bn)
MH Witmark; Andraud; Music Publishers Holding Corp.
(score, parts).
VOLKMANN, FRIEDRICH ROBERT, The Knights (2 cl, 2 bn) Andraud.
arr. by Trinkaus, Franklin Publishing Co.
WAGNER, JOSEPH, Theme and Variations (fl, cl, v, vc) Southern
Music Publishing Co., Inc.
WALCKIERS, EUGENE, Grand Concert Quartet, Op. 46 in F# minor
(4 fl) H (rec) Zimmermann, 1923; Andraud; Ashdown;
Costallat; Baxter-Northrup.
---Quartet, Op. 48 in Bb major (fl, cl, h, bn) Schlesinger.
---Grand Quartet, Op. 70 (second Grant Quartet, F major)
(4 fl) Andraud; Ashdown.
---Quartet, Op. 73 in C minor (fl, cl, h, bn) B&H.
WATERSON, JAMES, Andantino and Scherzo, arr. by G. Langenus (4
cl) Fischer.
WILSON, K. L., Nocturne (fl, ob, cl, bn or bass-cl) ME Belwin,
Inc.
WUILLEUMIER, Prelude, Gavotte, Canon, Mazurka: First Suite (fl
cl, eng h, bn) Andraud.
---Second Suite: Pastorale, Minuet, Chanson, Serenade, Ca-
price. Andraud.
WYMAN, BYRON B., Tarantella (3 Bb cl, bn or 2 Bb cl, alto-cl,
bass-cl) Music Publishers Holding Corp. (score, parts).
YODER, PAUL, Dark Eyes (4 cl or 3 cl, bass-cl) arr. Neil A.
Kjos Music Co.

Cumulative Quartets

AGRELL, JEAN, 6 Sinfonias (2 v, va, vc or pf, with h, tromb, ob, or fl ad lib) Fetis.

ALBISI, ABELARDO, Divertimento No. 3 (fl, ob, cl, bn) MH-H (rec) Andraud.

ARENSKY, ANTON, The Cuckoo (4 cl) Andraud.

ASIOLI, BONIFACE, Quartet (v, fl, h, bn) Fetis.

BAYER, CARL, Ein Aufsitzer in F (ob, cl, bn, tromb) Oertel, Hanover.

BAYR, GEORG, Quartette, Op. 4 (flutes) Publ. in Vienna.

BITSCH, MARCEL, Divertimento (fl, ob, cl, bn) ME Eble.

BOCHSA, CHARLES, Andante and Minuetto, arr. by Schmidt (4 Bb cl) E Rubank.

BODDECKER, PHILIP FRIEDRICH, Sonata Sopra La Monica. 1936, arr. by Max Seiffert, Organum III, No. 33, Kistner.

BOURIE, HONORE, Quartets (4 wind instruments) MS. Fetis Supplement.

BRANDL, JEAN, Quatuors (fl, bn) Fetis.

BRIDGE, Divertimenti (fl, ob, cl, bn) VH (rec) Boosey-Hawkes (score, parts).

CAMBINI, JEAN JOSEPH, Quartets (4 ob) Fetis.

CAMBINI, JEAN JOSEPH, Quartets (4 fl) Fetis.

CARLE, Enchantment (Tone Poem) (3 cl, bass-cl, with pf score) arr. by Wheeler. Volkwein.

CARTER, ELLIOT COOK, JR., Eight Etudes and a Fantasia, 1950 (4 woodwinds or fl, ob, cl, bn) ACA.

CATEL, CHARLES SIMON, Three Quartets (fl, cl, h, bn) Paris, Fetis.

CROSSE, W. A., Three Pieces: Prelude, Andante, Scherzo (4 cl) MH 1906, Boosey-Hawkes; Andraud.

   ---Suite (4 cl) 1906, Boosey-Hawkes.

   ---Carnival of Venice (4 cl) Andraud; Boosey-Hawkes (score, parts).

   ---Petit Quartet (4 cl) ME (rec) Boosey-Hawkes (score, parts); Andraud.

DE BUERIS, Oboe Fantasie (4 ob) MH Belwin.

   ---Bassoon Fantasie (4 bn) MH Belwin.

DUPART, CHARLES, Methode Polyphonique (2, 3 or 4 wind instruments) Fetis Supplement.

DURAND, AUGUST, Chaconne in C, Op. 62, arr. by Lawrence Taylor (fl, ob, cl, bn or bass-cl) Ditson; Presser.

EGIDI, ARTHUR, Quartet, Op. 19 (fl, ob, cl, bn) H 1925, Kultur; Andraud; Wolbing.

FAHRBACH, JOSEPH, 2 Fantaisies on Aida, Op. 60 (4 fl) Fetis Supplement.

FELTRE, ALPHONSE CLARKE, Several quartets (4 wind instruments) Fetis.

FERNANDEZ, OSCAR LORENZO, Suite in F, Op. 37, Part II (fl, ob, cl, bn) ME (rec) AMP.

FOGELBERG, LAWRENCE, Danza (4 Bb cl or 2 Bb cl, alto-cl, bass-cl) Music Publishers Holding Corp. (score, parts); Remick.

FRANGKISER, CARL, Melodie Petite (4 cl) ME Pro Art; EMB.

FROHLICH, JOSEPH, Serenade in A major (fl, cl, va, vc or bn) Schott; Fetis; Muller.

FUCHS, GEORG FRIEDRICH, Quartets, Op. 5, 6, 7, 13, 19 (cl, var-
    ious other instruments) Imbault; Fetis.
FURSTENAU, ANTOINE BERNARD, Quartet (4 fl) Fetis.
    ---First Grand Quartet in F major, Op. 88 (introducing the
        Austrian National Anthem) (4 fl) Ashdown; Andraud;
        Baxter-Northrup.
FUTTERER, C., Quartet (ob, cl, h, bn) Andraud.
GABRIELSKY, JOHANN WILHELM, Quartets, Op. 53, No. 1 in G major,
    No. 2 in A major, No. 3 in E minor (4 fl) H-VH B&H
    ---Grand Quartet, No. 3 (Hommage a Kuhlau) (4 cl) Andraud;
    AMP.
    ---Grand Quartet, Op. 53, No. 5 (4 cl) Baron.
GAMBARO, GIOVANNI BATTISTA, Three Quartets Concertant, Op. 4
    fl, cl, h, bn) Fetis; B&H.
GARIBOLDI, GIUSEPPE, Andante Quasi Lento (4 cl) Andraud.
GASPARD, Six Quartets (cl, 2 str, bn or cl, v, va or vc, bn)
    Fetis.
GEBAUER, MICHAEL JOSEPH, Two Quartets (fl, cl, h, bn) Schonen-
    berger; Fetis.
GEBAUER, FRANCOIS RENE, Eight Symphony Concertants (fl, cl, h,
    bn) Hentz-Houve; Sieber; Fetis.
GEBAUER, FRANCOIS RENE, Quartets, Op. 20, 27, 41 (fl, cl, h, bn)
    Pleyel; Sieber; Hentz; Lemoine; Fetis.
GERMAN, SIR EDWARD, Pastoral Dance in Eb (fl, ob, cl, bn) arr.
    by Dahm. Carl Fischer (score, parts).
GIANELLA, LUDOVICO, Quartet in G, Op. 52 (4 fl) Andraud.
GODARD, BENJAMIN, Berceuse from Jocely, arr. by G. J. Trinkaus,
    (fl or ob, cl, h or eng h, bn) Franklin Publishing Co.
GRAF, FREDERIC HERMANN, Quartet (4 fl or ob, v, bn, vc) Fetis.
GRAINGER, PERCY ALDRIDGE, Died for Love, Folksong from Lincoln-
    shire (voice, fl, cl, bn) 1912, Schott, London.
GUILLOU, JOSEPH, Several Themes (4 fl) Fetis.
GUMLICH, FREDERIC, Two Quartets (4 bn) Bonn, Simrock; Fetis.
HAENSEL, PIERRE, Three Quartets (fl, cl, h, bn) Vienna, Artaria;
    Fetis.
HARRIS, A., A Kerry Tune, Farewell to Cucullain (fl, ob, cl, bn,
    see Quintets) Andraud; (4 cl) EMB; (2 Bb cl, 2 Eb alto-
    cl or sax; or 3 Bb cl, bn or Eb alto-cl or sax; or 3 fl,
    alto-fl or Bb cl; or 2 Bb cl, Eb alto-cl or sax, bn or
    bass-cl) Cundy-Bettoney Company, with piano accompaniment.
HASSE, JOHANN ADOLF, Two Quartets (v, ob, fl, bn) Fetis.
HAUBIEL, CHARLES, Nostalgia (4 cl) ME Composers Press.
    ---Will O'The Wisp (4 cl) ME Composers Press.
HERRMANN, HUGO, Quartet, Op. 57a Musiken (4 fl) 1931, Bote &
    Bock.
HUFFMAN, Autumn's Waning (4 cl) EMB.
ISAAK, HEINRICH, Six instrumental pieces (4 wind instruments)
    Musica Rara.
JACOBI, CONRAD, Quartet (bn, str) Simrock.
KAPPELER, JOHANN NEPOMUK, Quartet (2 fl, v, guit) Schott, May-
    ence: Fetis.
KAUDER, HUGO, Quartet (4 woodwinds) New Music Editions XXII,
    No. 3, 1949.
KRIEGER, JOHANN PHILIPP VON, Lustige Feld Musik (Gay Field-Music)
    in six overtures with suites, c. 1690 (4 wind instruments)
    Fetis.

KRONKE, EMIL, Quartet, Op. 184, Theme and Paraphrase (4 cl) Andraud.

KUCHLER, JOHANN, 18 Quartets for various instruments (including bn) Fetis.

KUHLAU, FRIEDRICH, Allegretto Grazioso from piano sonatina, Op. 55, No. 3 (fl, ob, cl, bn) Volkwein.

LEEMANS, Six Quartets, Op. 3 (three quartets for fl, bn, v, vc; three for ob, v, bn, vc) Fetis. Supplement.

LEONI, Conclave and Fugue Patrol (4 cl) E Pro Art; EMB.

LOVELOCK, Suite, Old Style (4 fl, bass-fl ad lib) Andraud.

MALZAT, JOHANN MICHAEL, Eleven Quartets (fl or ob or eng h or bn) Fetis; Vienna, catalogue of Traeg, 1799.

MARGERISON, L. A., Quartets (treble, alto, tenor and bass pipes) selected and arranged, 1935, Cramer (score, parts).

MARTINN, JACQUES JOSEPH BALTHAZAR, Second Symphony Concertant (fl, ob, h, bn) Publ. by the author in Paris; Fetis.

MAZOROV, Ten Russian Folk Songs in D (fl, ob, cl, bn) Russian-American Music Publishers.

MELKICH, DMITRY MICHAELOVITCH, Quartet, Op. 19 (fl, ob, cl, bn) Andraud.

MENEAU, LEON, Quartets for instruments (4 wind instruments) Fetis Supplement.

MOFFITT, In the Spotlight (4 cl or 2 cl, alto-cl, bass-cl) EMB

MULDER, ERNEST W., Quartett, 1938-46 (ob, bn, vc, harp) Stichting Donemus.

OSTBORN, RUDOLF VON, Epilog, Op. 7 in A (2 h, 2 bn) Ries & Erler.

PAULSON, Clarinet Quartet Moderne (2 cl, alto-cl, bass-cl) ME George F. Briegel.

PIRANI, EUGENIO, Govotte Rococo and Whirlwind, arr. by G. Langenus (fl, ob, cl, bn) Andraud; Fischer.

PLEYEL, IGNACE JOSEPH, Rondo, transc. by Harry C. Geiger (4 Bb cl) MH Music Publishers Holding Corp. (score, parts); (4 cl) Gamble Hinged Music.

---Andante and Rondo, Op. 48, No. 1 (4 cl) Andraud; (4 Bb cl; 2 Bb cl, 2 Eb alto-cl or sax; 3 Bb cl, bn or Eb alto-cl or sax; fl, bn, cl, ob; 2 Bb cl, Eb alto-cl or sax, bn or bass-cl) Cundy-Bettoney Co.

POLDINI, Q., Poupee Valsante (Dancing Doll) arr. by Harold Mueller (fl, ob, cl, bn) Cundy-Bettoney Co., Inc.

POWELL, LAURENCE, Quartet, 1936 (4 cl or 2 cl, alto-cl, bass-cl) MH 1938, Carl Fischer, (score, parts).

PRAAG, HENRI C. VAN, Kwartet, 1940 (fl, ob, cl, bn) Stichting Donemus.

---Drie Schetsen, 1939 (fl, ob, cl, bn) Stichting Donemus.

PUSCHMANN, JOSEPH, Three Quartets (2 cl, 2 h) Fetis.

RATHAUS, K., Country Serenade (4 cl) ME Boosey-Hawkes (score, parts).

RENZI, ARMANDO, Five Bagatelles; Preambolo, Duetto, Pastoraletta, Canzone Funebre, Sonatella (di commiato) (fl, ob, cl, bn) ME (rec) Eble; Edizione De Santis, 1948-49.

RHEINBERGER, JOSEPH GABRIEL, Quartet, Op. 80 (ob, eng. h. heckelphone, bn)

RIISAGER, KNUDAGE, Serenade, Op. 15 (fl, cl, v, vc) Hansen, (min score).

  ---Sonata, Op. 24 (fl, v, cl, vc) 1931 Hansen, (min score, parts); Andraud; AMP.
RODEN, Cerise (4 cl) EMB.
RUMLER, JOHN, Works for Wind Instruments.
SCARMOLIN, A. LOUIS, Plaisanterie (4 cl) MH Pro Art.
SCHLABACH, KARL W., Holiday, Gigue and Serenade (4 cl) EMB; Music Publishers Holding Corp. (score, parts).
SCHMUTZ, ALBERT D., Praeludial Fantasia on Lo How a Rose E'er Blooming (2 cl, alto-cl, bass-cl) ME H. T. Fitzsimons.
  ---Allegro Capriccioso (4 cl) ME Carl Fischer.
  ---Scherzoso (4 cl) H Clayton F. Summy Co; H. T. Fitz-Simons.
SCHNEIDER, GEORG ABRAHAM, Three Quartets, Op. 68 in Eb major. Op. 72 in F major, Op. 80 in D major (4 fl) Andraud.
SCHROTER, Foolish Fantasy (ob, cl, h, bn) Andraud (humorous).
SCHUMAN, WILLIAM, Quartettino, 1939 (4 bn) Boletin Latino-Americano, 1941.
SCHWARZ, L., Oriental Suite (fl, ob, cl, bn with drum) Andraud.
SCHWEGLER, JOHANN DAVID, Quartet, Op. 3, No. 2 in Eb major (2 fl, 2 h) B&H; Nagel, 1941, ed. by H. Schultz.
SCHWEGLER, JOHANN DAVID, Four Quartets, Op. 3 (2 fl, 2 h) B&H; Fetis.
SOLA, CHARLES MICHAEL ALEXIS, Quartet, Op. 21 (fl, cl, h, bn) Fetis; Leduc.
SOLNITZ, ANTON WILHELM, Twelve Pieces (2 cl, 2 h) Fetis.
TULOU, JEAN LOUIS, Symphonie Concertante, No. 2 (fl, ob, h, bn) Pleyel; Fetis.
TURNER, GODFREY, Quartet (fl, ob, cl, bn)
TUTHILL, BURNET CORWIN, Fugue for 4 clarinets, Op. 10, No. 4 (2 Bb cl, alto-cl, bass-cl) Burnet Tuthill.
VALENTINI, GIOVANNI, Quartet (fl, ob, cl, bn) 1933, published by composer in Modena.
VOGT, GUSTAVE, Three Nocturnes, pots-pourris of well-known airs (fl, ob, h, bn) Pleyel; Fetis.
WALCKIERS, EUGENE, Three Quartets, Op. 7 (fl, cl, h, bn) Costal-lat.
WEIS-OSTBORN, RUDOLF VON, Epilogue, Op. 7 (2 h, 2 bn) 1900, Ries & Erler (score, parts).
WEISS, ADOLPH, Classical Suite (fl, ob, cl, bn)
WHITE, FELIX HAROLD, Four Proverbs (fl, ob, v, vc) 1935, Stainer & Bell (score, parts).
WOLF, ERNST WILHELM, Two Quartets (fl, va, vc, bn) Fetis.
WOUTERS, FRANCOIS-ADOLPHE, Adagio in Eb Major and Scherzando in G Minor, Op. 77 (4 fl) MH (rec) 1889, Maison Beethoven, Brussels; Andraud; Rubank; Oertel, Brussels; Baxter-Northrup.

Collections

ANDRAUD, Fourth Collection of A. J. Andraud. 22 Celebrated Com-
      positions in quartet form. VE-MH Contents: Largo,
      Handel; Minuetto, Dittersdorf; Lied, Op. 102, No. 44,
      Mendelssohn; Menuet de la Fantaisie, Op. 78, Schubert;
      Chanson du Printemps, Schumann; Gavotte en Rondeau,
      from Les Talents Lyriques, J. Ph. Rameau; Reverie, Schu-
      mann; Menuet, Boccherini; Sarabande from French Suite,
      J. S. Bach; La Pentecote, Aria, J. S. Bach; Lied, Op.
      67, No. 35, Mendelssohn; Menuet de la Sonate, Op. 2, No.
      1, Beethoven; Gavotte from Nais, Rameau; Menuet from
      Symphony No. 3, J. Haydn; Marche Funebre, Op. 62, Men-
      delssohn; Lied, Op. 102, No. 48, Mendelssohn; Canzona,
      Hasse; Menuet from Sonata, Op. 27, No. 2, Beethoven;
      Andante from Sonata No. 2, Mozart; Menuet from Ballet
      Don Juan, Mozart; Pastorale, Scarlatti; Rigaudon from
      Dardanus, Rameau. (Instrumentation: Part A: fl, ob,
      cl or soprano sax; Part B: cl, Eb alto-sax; Part C:
      cl, Bb tenor-sax, fr h in F; Part D: bn, vc, bar-sax,
      bass-cl or tuba in Bb. Strings may be substituted.)

Training Quartets

ALLEN, P.H., Heaven's Gifts (4 cl) Whitney Blake.
ARRIOLA, Liseta, arr. by J. I. Tallmadge, MH (4 cl) Boosey-
      Hawkes.
ARTOT, ALEXANDRE, Twelve Quartetts, arr. by A. H. Harris (1st pt:
      cl, cornet, fl or ob; 2nd pt: cl; 3rd pt: Bb cl or
      alto cl; 4th pt: cl, bass-cl or bn) Cundy-Bettoney Co.
BACH, JOHANN SEBASTIAN, Gavotte from 5th Suite (fl, ob, cl, bn)
      arr. by Cox. Boosey & Hawkes.
   ---Minuet, arr. by Taylor (4 fl) E-ME Mills Music; Bel-
      win (arr. by Eck).
   ---Loure, arr. by A. E. Harris (4 Bb cl) (fl, ob, cl, bn)
      Cundy-Bettoney Co., Inc.
   ---A variety of Bach music, transc. by Joseph Simon (4 cl)
      E-MH G. Schirmer; EMB.
BAGLEY, E. E., Thistledown, arr. by A. E. Harris (4 Bb cl or 2
      Bb cl, 2 Eb alto-cl or sax; 3 Bb cl, bn or Eb alto-cl
      or sax; fl, ob, cl, bn; 2 Bb cl, Eb alto-cl or sax, bn
      or bass-cl) Cundy-Bettoney Co., Inc.
BALAY, GUILLAUME, Sarabande and Menuet from Petite Suite, arr.
      by Waln (2 cl, alto-cl, bass-cl) Kjos.
BEETHOVEN, LUDWIG VAN, Minuet from 1st Symphony (fl, ob, cl,
      bn) E-ME Cundy-Bettoney Co., Inc. (score, parts).
BIZET, GEORGES, Andante and Minuet, transc. by Arthur Brooke
      (3 fl, alto-fl or Bb cl) Cundy-Bettoney Co., Inc.
BOHNE, R., Andante from Quartet in D, arr. by Hymie Voxman (4
      cl) E Rubank.
BORNSCHEIN, The French Clock (4 fl) E-ME (rec) Presser.
BRADAC, JAROSLAV, Bohemian Suite (4 cl) E (rec) Rubank.
BROOKE, ARTHUR, Transcriptions: Rondo, Walckiers; Andante,
      Farrenc; Salut d'Amour, Elgar; Traumerei, Schumann;
      Andante and Minuet, Bizet. (3 fl, alto-fl or Bb cl)
      Cundy-Bettoney Co., Inc.
BROWN, T. P., Piece for Four Clarinets (4 cl) ME G. Schirmer.
BUCHTEL, FORREST L., ed. by Paschedag, First Ensemble Book
      (4 Bb cl or 4 fl) VE-ME Neil A. Kjos Music Co.; EMB.
   ---First Ensemble Book (4 fl) VE Kjos.
   ---Two Books for Woodwind Instruments (1st,2nd,3rd cl.with h.
      or bn,& 3 cl with bn or bass-cl) E Music Publishers
      Holding Corp (entitled "Harms Musical Americana, avail-
      able with piano acc.)
   ---Remick Musical Americana, Two books for woodwind instru-
      ments (cl, cl, cl. & h or bn, cl, or bn or bass-cl)
      E Music Publishers Holding Corp. (with pf acc).
CASSEL, Clarinet Sessions, A variety of style from Palestrina
      to Jazz, arr. by Gearheart (4 cl) ME-MH Shawnee; EMB.
CHAPPELL, Chappell's Famous Melodies, including Bells of St.
      Mary's, Roses of Picardy, and so forth, arr. by Carver
      (4 cl) ME EMB.
CHEYETTE, IRVING, See Fischer "Four-tone Folio" Collections,
      at end of this section.
CHOPIN, FREDERIC, Prelude, Op. 28, No. 7, arr. by Leopold Liegl
      (4 cl) E Carl Fischer.

---Prelude, Op. 28, No. 6, transc. by O. B. Wilson (3 Bb cl, bn) Music Publishers Holding Corp. (score, parts).

CLINTON, JOHN, Quartet for four flutes, Op. 32, in G major. (4 fl) Ashdown, London.

COHEN, SOL B., Colonial Sketches, Suite (4 fl) ME (rec) Boosey & Hawkes (score, parts).

CORELLI, ARCANGELO, Praludium, arr. by Skornicka (4 Bb cl) E Belwin.

COX, Minuet (fl, cl, ob, bn) Boosey & Hawkes.

DENZA, L., Funiculi, Funicula, arr. by A. Harris (4 Bb cl or 2 Bb cl, 2 Eb alto-cl or sax; 3 Bb cl, bn or Eb alto-cl or sax; fl, ob, cl, bn; 2 Bb cl, Eb alto-cl or sax, bn or bass-cl) Cundy-Bettoney Co. (parts, with pf acc. available).

DEWIT, A., Polonaise and On the Lake (4 Bb cl; 2 Bb cl, 2 Eb alto-cl or sax; 3 Bb cl, bn or Eb alto-cl or sax; fl, ob, cl, bn; 2 Bb cl, Eb alto-cl or sax, bn or bass-cl) Cundy-Bettoney Co., (parts).

---Summertime (4 Bb cl or 2 Bb cl, 2 Eb alto-cl or sax; 3 Bb cl, bn or Eb alto-cl or sax; fl, ob, cl, bn; 2 Bb cl, Eb alto-cl or sax, bn or bass-cl) Cundy-Bettoney Co., (parts).

---Hungarian Fantasie (2 Bb cl, 2 Eb alto-cl or sax; 4 Bb cl; 3 Bb cl, bn or Eb alto-cl or sax; fl, ob, Bb cl, bn; 2 Bb cl, Eb alto-cl or sax, bn or bass-cl) Cundy-Bettoney Co., (parts).

---Harvest Dance (4 Bb cl; 2 Bb cl, 2 Eb alto-cl or sax; 3 Bb cl, bn or Eb alto-cl or sax; fl, ob, cl, bn; 2 Bb cl, Eb alto-cl or sax, bn or bass-cl) Cundy-Bettoney Co., (parts).

---Spanish Waltz (4 Bb cl; 2 Bb cl, 2 Eb alto-cl or sax; 3 Bb cl, bn or Eb alto-cl or sax; fl, ob, cl, bn; 2 Bb cl, Eb alto-cl or sax, bn or bass-cl) Cundy-Bettoney Co., (parts).

D'HARCOURT, MARGUERITE BECLARD, Peruvian Inca Melodies, arr. by David Bennett (Bb cl quartet; mixed cl quartet) Ricordi (score, parts).

DONT, JACOB, Larghetto & Scherzo (4 cl) arr. by Waln, Kjos.

DUREY, LOUIS EDMOND, Quartet (4 winds)

ELGAR, EDWARD, Salut d'Amour, transc. by Arthur Brooke (3 fl, alto-fl or Bb cl) Cundy-Bettoney Co.

FARRENC, MME. JEANNE LOUIS, Andante (3 fl, alto-fl in G or cl) arr. by Arthur Brooke, Cundy-Bettoney.

FRANGKISER, CARL, Three Blind Mice (4 Bb cl; 3 Bb cl, bass-cl; 2 Bb cl, Eb alto-cl, bass-cl) ME Belwin.

GERSHWIN, GEORGE, Liza, arr. by Sears (3 Bb cl, bass-cl) Music Publishers Holding Corp.

GLUCK, CHRISTOPHE WILLIBALD, Dance of the Happy Spirits from "Orpheus" (4 cl) arr. by Leopold Liegl, E Carl Fischer.

GOSSEC, FRANCOIS JOSEPH GOSSE, Gavotte (4 fl) ME arr. by Eck Belwin.

---Tambourine, arr. by Lawrence Taylor (4 fl) ME Kay & Kay; Franklin.

GRAHAM, L'Venture (4 cl) ME Pro Art.

GRIEG, EDWARD HAGERUP, Ase's Death from Peer Gynt, arr. by L.
  Liegl (4 cl) E Carl Fischer.
GUILLEMAIN, GABRIEL, Tambourin, arr. by Lawrence Taylor (4 fl)
  E Mills Music.
GUILMANT, FELIX ALEXANDRE, Tempo di Minuetto (2 cl, alto-cl,
  bass-cl) E Mills Music Co.
GURLITT, CORNELIUS, Loss (2 ob, 2 bn or ob, 2 cl, bn) Music
  Publishers Holding Corp., transc. by Lee M. Lockhart
  (score, parts).
HANDEL, GEORGE FREDERICK, How Beautiful are the Feet (from the
  Messiah) arr. by T. Stang (4 Bb cl; 2 Bb cl, 2 Eb alto-
  cl or sax; 3 Bb cl, bn or Eb alto-cl or sax; fl, ob,
  Bb cl, bn; 2 Bb cl, Eb alto-cl or sax, bn or bass-cl)
  Cundy-Bettoney Co., (parts).
  ---Largo from Xerxes, arr. by T. Stang (4 Bb cl; 2 Bb cl,
  2 Eb alto-cl or sax; 3 Bb cl, bn or Eb alto-cl or sax;
  fl, ob, Bb cl, bn; 2 Bb cl, Eb alto-cl or sax, bn or
  bass-cl) Cundy-Bettoney Co., (parts).
  ---Sinfonia, from the Messiah, arr. by T. Stang (4 Bb cl;
  2 Bb cl, 2 Eb alto-cl or sax; 3 Bb cl, bn or Eb alto-cl
  or sax; fl, ob, Bb cl, bn; 2 Bb cl, Eb alto-cl or sax,
  bn or Bass-cl) Cundy-Bettoney Co., (parts).
  ---Sarabande, arr. by L. Liegl (4 cl) E Carl Fischer.
HARRIS, A., Two Transcriptions: Andante, Mme. Jeanne Louise
  Farrenc; Rondo, Eugene Walckiers (4 Bb cl; 2 Bb cl,
  2 Eb alto-cl or sax; 3 Bb cl, bn or Eb alto-cl or sax;
  2 Bb cl, Eb alto-cl or sax, bn or bass-cl) Cundy-Bettoney
  Co. (parts for Andante; score, parts for Rondo).
  ---Four Heart Songs: Sweet and Low, Drink to Me Only with
  Thine Eyes, When You and I were Young Maggie, Love's Old
  Sweet Song (4 Bb cl; 2 Bb cl, 2 Eb alto-cl or sax; 3
  Bb cl, bn or Eb alto-cl or sax; fl, ob, cl, bn; 3 fl,
  alto-fl or Bb cl; 2 Bb cl, Eb alto-cl or sax, bn or bass-
  cl) Cundy-Bettoney Co. (parts).
HERMANN, FRIEDRICH, Ensemble Studies (fl, ob, cl, bn) MH
  (rec) B&H.
  ---Quartets, Book I (ob, cl, bn, h) Variation on "Lord
  Preserve Franz den Kaiser," Haydn; Andante and Minuet
  from string quartet in D major, K575, Mozart; Beetho-
  ven, Allegretto alla Polacca from Serenade, Op. 8.
  1899, B&H.
HEROLD, LOUIS JOSEPH FERDINAND, Prayer, from Zampa, arr. by
  Skornicka (4 Bb cl) E Belwin.
HILDRETH, R. E., Three Songs: Londonderry Air, Old Irish;
  Poem, Fibich; Come Where My Love Lies Dreaming, Steph-
  en Foster (4 cl) Ludwig Music Publishing Co.
HOLMES, G. E., Clarinet Symphony Album, arr. by Holmes (4 cl)
  VE (rec) Rubank.
  ---Flute Symphony Album, arr. by Holmes (4 fl) VE (rec)
  Rubank.
HURRELL, Two Impressions (fl, ob, cl, bn) EMB.
JOHNSON, CLAIR W., Red Sunset (4 Bb cl) ME Belwin.
JONGEN, JOSEPH, Elgeie (4 fl) MH-H Andraud.
KEITH, GEORGE D., Interlude (4 cl) E-MF Boosey-Hawkes.

KREISLER, FRITZ, The Old Refrain and Schon Rosmarin, arr. by
      Erik Leidzen (4 cl) Foley.
KREUTZER, KONRADIN, Quartet in Eb major, first movement (fl,
      ob, cl, bn) ME-MH transc. by F. H. Klickmann, Alfred
      Music Company
LA CAPRIA, Notturnino, (fl, ob, cl, bn) E H. T. Fitzsimons Co.
LANDRY, A., Musette, transc. by Georges Griesez (fl, ob, cl, bn)
      Cundy-Bettoney Co., Inc.
LA VIOLETTE, WESLEY, Filigree and Charade (4 fl) MH Boosey-
      Hawkes (score, parts).
   ---Masquerade (fl, ob, cl, bn or bass-cl) ME Boosey &
      Hawkes; EMB.
LEEUWEN, ARY VAN, Curiosities, Set I: Largo, Kuntze, Allegro,
      Donjon; Set II. Old Spanish Church Tune in Bb Major (4
      fl) MH Remick; Gamble Hinged Music; Music Publishers
      Holding Corp. (score, parts).
   ---Four Miniatures, transcribed. Turish March, Mozart;
      Rain, Bohm; Paraphrase from the Nutcracker Suite (March,
      Waltz of the Flowers, Mirlitons Dance, Trepak) Tschai-
      kowsky; Flight of the Bumblebee, Rimsky-Korsakoff (4
      fl or 2 fl, 2 cl) MH Andraud; Baron.
LEONI, Southern Waltz (4 Bb cl; 3 Bb cl, bass-cl; 2 Bb cl,
      Eb alto-cl, bass-cl) ME Belwin.
LIADOW, HAYDN, Sarabande and Finale (2 cl, alto-cl, bass-cl)
      E (rec) Rubank.
LONG, NEWELL H., In the Aquarium (4 cl or fl, ob, 2 cl or 2 fl
      2 cl) Carl Fischer.
LORENZ, JOHANN, Casino Caprice (4 cl) ME Pro Art.
   ---Par Avion (4 fl) MH Pro Art.
LULLY, JEAN BAPTISTE DE, Sarabande, arr. by Lawrence Taylor
      (4 fl) Franklin Co., EMB.
   ---Courante (fl, ob, cl, bn) E Mills Music, Inc.
MACBETH, A., Intermezzo, Forget-Me-Not, arr. by A. Harris (4
      Bb cl; 2 Bb cl, 2 Eb alto-cl or sax; 3 Bb cl, bn or Eb
      alto-cl or sax; fl, ob, Bb cl, bn; 2 Bb cl, Eb alto-cl
      or sax, bn or bass-cl, pf acc ad lib) Cundy-Bettoney
      Co. (parts).
MAGANINI, QUINTO E., The Realm of Dolls, Op. 9. A Suite of
      Three Little Pieces, in 2 parts (4 fl) MH-H 1923, Carl
      Fischer; Andraud.
   ---Patrol of the Wooden Indians, Op. 9 (from the Realm of
      Dolls) (4 fl) Hug.
   ---The Rag Dolls Lullaby, Op. 9 (from the Realm of Dolls) (4
      fl) Hug.
   ---Fox-Trot Burlesque on a Simple Aveu (4 fl) Andraud;
      Carl Fischer; Baxter-Northrup.
   ---Shepherds in Arcadia (4 fl) VH Edition Musicus.
MATTESON-TAYLOR, LAWRENCE, Air, Minuet and Sarabande (2 cl,
      bass-cl, bn) Mills Music.
MCKAY, GEORGE FREDERICK, Christmas Morning (4 fl) ME (rec)
      Andraud.
   ---American Sketch (4 cl) ME C. L. Barnhouse.
   ---Two Promenades (4 cl) ME C. L. Barnhouse.
   ---American Panorama (4 cl) E-ME Carl Fischer.
MOLLOY, J., Kerry Dance, arr. by A. Harris (4 Bb cl; 2 Bb cl,
      2 Eb alto-cl or sax; 3 Bb cl, bn or Eb alto-cl or sax;

fl, ob, cl, bn; 2 Bb cl, Eb alto-cl or sax, bn or bass-
cl) Cundy-Bettoney Company (parts, with pf acc).
MORRISSEY, JOHN, Clarinet Quartetts, arr. by Morrissey (4 cl)
White & Smith.
MOZART, W. A., Andante (1791) arr. by Ary van Leeuwen (2 fl, 2
cl) Spratt.
---Minuet from Don Juan, arr. by L. Liegl (4 cl) E Carl
Fischer.
OWINGS, J.V., Rollicking Rover, March (4 Bb cl) E Belwin.
---Lamentoso (4 Bb cl) E Belwin.
---Quartet Album for Bb Clarinets, containing 16 original
compositions (4 cl) MH Belwin; EMB.
PAINTER, PAUL, Small Poem in Four Stanzas (4 Bb cl) Music Pub-
lishers Holding Corp. (score, parts); Gamble Hinged Mu-
sic.
PORTER, COLE, Begin the Beguine, arr. by Sears (3 Bb cl, bass-
cl) Music Publishers Holding Corp.
PRAETORIUS, MICHAEL, Preludial Fantasia (2 Bb cl, alto, bass-cl)
ME Clayton F. Summy.
PUCCINI, GIACOMO, "Un Bel Di" from Madame Butterfly, arr. by Erik
Leidzen (4 Bb cl or fl, ob, cl, bn) G. Ricordi (score,
parts) MH.
---"Vissi D'Arte" from Tosca, arr. by Erik Leidzen (4 Bb cl;
2 cl, alto-cl, bass-cl; fl, ob, cl, bn or alto-cl) EMB;
Ricordi (score, parts).
---"Si, Mi Chiamano Mimi" from La Boheme (4 Bb cl; 2 cl,
alto-cl, bass-cl; fl, ob, cl, bn or bass-cl) EMB; Ri-
cordi (score, parts).
---Musetta's Waltz Song from La Boheme (2 cl, alto-cl, bass-
cl; 4 cl; fl, ob, cl, bn or bass-cl) EMB; Ricordi,
(score, parts).
RAMEAU, Gavotte, arr. by Soeller (fl, ob, cl, bn) ME-MH H. T.
Fitzsimons Co.
READY, ELDON, Romance (4 cl; 2 cl, alto-cl, bass-cl) E Gam-
ble Hinged Music; Music Publishers Holding Corp. (score,
parts).
ROBERTS, CHARLES J., See Fischer "Four-Tone Folio", Collections,
at end of this section.
RODGERS, RICHARD, Blue Room arr. by Sears (3 Bb cl, bass-cl)
Music Publishers Holding Corp.
RUBINSTEIN, ANTON G., Valse Staccato, arr. by Fetherston (4 fl)
MH (rec) Belwin.
SALOME, THEODORE-CESAR, Canon. Marziale, arr. by Taylor (fl,
ob, cl, bn) E Mills Music, Inc.
SANDERS, ROBERT L., The Imp (2 cl, alto-cl, bass-cl) ME (rec)
Carl Fischer.
SCHLABACH, KARL W., Caprice (4 cl) E (rec) Gamble Hinged Mu-
sic; Music Publisher Holding Corp. (score, parts).
SCHMITT, FLORENT, Quartet (4 fl) Eble.
---Quartet, Op. 106 (4 fl) Durand; Elkan-Vogel; Hug.
SCHUBERT, FRANZ PETER SERAPH, Theme from D minor string quartet,
arr. by Del Busto (4 cl) VE Andraud; Carl Fischer.
SCHUMANN, ROBERT ALEXANDER, Traumerei, transc. by Arthur Brooke
(3 fl, alto-fl or Bb cl) Cundy-Bettoney Co.
---Allegretto from Sonata No. 1, Concert key of F (fl, ob, cl,

bn)   (2 Bb cl, Eb alto-cl or sax, bn or bass-cl)   Cundy-
    Bettoney (score, parts, also concert key of Eb).
SEVERN, EDMUND, Scherzo Brilliante (4 fl) ME Belwin.
SONTAG, HENRIETTE, Quartet on Old Tunes, arr. by Sontag (fl, ob,
    cl, bn) Presser.
SPINDLER, FRITZ, Andantino (2 ob, 2 bn or ob, 2 cl, bn) transc.
    by Lee M. Lockhart, Music Publishers Holding Corp. (score,
    parts).
STOLZ, Twilight in Blue (4 cl or 2 cl, alto-cl, bass-cl) E-ME
    Boosey-Hawkes (score, parts).
TELEMANN, GEORG PHILIPP, Concerto, arr. by Joseph Simon (4 cl,
    pf ad lib) ME (rec) E. B. Marks.
TOLL, R., Six Little Gems from the Masters, arr. by Toll (4 cl)
    EMB; Cundy-Bettoney Co., Inc. (score, parts).
TSCHAIKOWSKY, PETER ILITCH, Overture "1812", arr. by Skornicka
    (4 Bb cl) E Belwin.
TUFILLI, Charm (4 Bb cl) ME Belwin.
UGGEN, Playwell Trio and Quartet Album (4 cl) VE-E Paul A.
    Schmitt.
WEIGL-DANCLA, Air Varie (4 cl; 2 Bb cl, 2 Eb alto-cl or sax;
    3 Bb cl, bn or Eb alto-cl or sax; fl, ob, cl, bn; 2 Bb
    cl, Eb alto-cl or sax, bn or bass-cl) Cundy-Bettoney
    Co. (parts).
WHITNEY, Roulade (4 cl) ME Carl Fischer.
WILLAMAN, Six Easy Excerpts for 4 clarinets (4 cl) E Schirmer.
WINSLOE, RICHARD, Flute Player's Serenade (4 fl) MH Belwin.
WYMAN, BYRON B., Les Clarinettes Joyeux (2 cl, alto-cl, bass-cl)
    ME Gamble Hinged Music; Music Publishers Holding Corp.
    (3 Bb cl, bn, score, parts).
YODER, PAUL, Clarumba (4 cl or 3 cl, bass-cl, Maraccas and Claves
    ad lib) ME Neil A. Kjos.

Collections

Three and Four Part Canons and Rounds (3 or 4 fl, ob, cl, or
    reco) Mercury.
ANDRAUD, A. J., Collection Number 3, 20 Little Quartets. Con-
    tents: Larghetto, Handel; Chanson du ruisseau, Franz
    Schubert; Scenes d'Enfants, Mendelssohn; Marche So-
    lennelle, Handel; Menuet du Boeuf, J. Haydn; Andante
    from 4th Conata for Organ, Op. 65, Mendelssohn; Bour-
    ree from Suite for Trompettes, J. S. Bach; Tannhauser,
    (chorus from Act I), R. Wagner; Petite Piece in popu-
    lar style, R. Schumann; Andante Religioso, Gluck; Ba-
    gatelle, Beethoven; Choral en forme de fugue, Gretry;
    Deuxieme Ballade, Op. 38, Chopin; Andante Cantabile,
    Mozart; Le Curieux, F. Schubert; Menuet du Bourgeois
    Gentilhomme, Lully; First Piece caracteristique, A.
    Chauvet; Menuet, R. Wagner; Second Piece caracteris-
    tique A. Chauvet; Air de Chasse et le cavalier sau-
    vage, R. Schumann. (Instrumentation: Part A: fl or
    v, ob or v, cl or sop-sax, Bb tpt, C tpt; Part B: cl,
    Eb alto-sax, v, Bb tpt, C tpt; Part C: cl, Bb ten-sax,
    h, Euph or trom, va; Part D: bn or vc, bar-sax; bass-
    cl or tr, tuba.) A. J. Andraud.
ECK, Quartet Album, familiar melodies, by Bach, Handel, Haydn,
    Beethoven, etc., arr. (4 fl) ME (rec) Belwin; EMB.
THE FAMOUS FOUR-TONE FOLIOS, arr. by Irving Cheyette and Charles
    J.Roberts. Contents, Vol. I: Air de Ballet from "Al-
    ceste", Gluck; March of Harlech, Welsh Air; Lo, How a
    Rose E'er Blooming, Praetorius; Finlandia, (Introduction
    to Overture) Sibelius; The Log Cabin, Evanson; Chorale
    from "Die Meistersinger", Wagner; The Old Homestead, Ro-
    berts; Passion Chorale, Bach; Days of Wonder, Haydn;
    Go Down, Moses, Negro Spiritual; Evening and Morning,
    Eberling; Alleluia, Palestrina; The Crusader, Gilman.
    (Instrumentation: mixed ensemble, parts for fl, ob, sax,
    Bb cl, h in F, bn)
    Contents, Vol. II: The Spacious Firmament, Haydn; Cho-
    ral from "Sleepers Awake!", Bach; Minstrel Boy, Irish
    Air; Deep River, Negro Spiritual; Aria from "Orpheus",
    Gluck; Song of Farewell, Mendelssohn; March from "L'Ar-
    lesienne" Suite, Bizet; Ave Maria, Arcadelt; Theme from
    First Symphony, Brahms; Loreley, Silcher; Theme from
    Ninth Symphony, Beethoven; (Instrumentation: mixed en-
    semble, parts for bn, fl, ob, Bb cl, h in F)
    Contents, Vol. III: Praise ye the Lord (Choral), Vulpius;
    The Heavens Resounding, Beethoven; Dedication, Franz;
    Song of Thanksgiving, (Netherlands) Traditional; Sunday
    Morning, Abt; Whispering Winds, Mendelssohn; Air from
    "Martha", Flotow; Choral from "Die Meistersinger", Act
    III, Wagner; Air from "The Water Carriers", Cherubini;
    Proudly as an Eagle, Spohr; Ebening Song, Abt. (Instru-
    mentation: mixed ensemble, parts for bn, fl, ob, Bb cl,
    h in F) Fischer.

HARRIS, A., American Songs. Contents: Swanee River, Old Black
       Joe, My Old Kentucky Home, Kingdom Coming. (4 Bb cl; 2
       Bb cl, 2 Eb alto-cl or sax; 3 Bb cl, bn or Eb alto-cl or
       sax; fl, ob, cl, bn; 2 Bb cl, Eb alto-cl or sax, bn or
       bass-cl) Cundy-Bettoney Co., Inc.
   ---Scotch Airs. Contents: Annie Laurie, Loch Lomond, Co-
       min' Thru the Rye, Old Lang Syne, The Pipes-Tullochgorum.
       (4 Bb cl; 2 Bb cl, 2 Eb alto-cl or sax; 3 Bb cl, bn or
       Eb alto-cl or sax; fl, ob, cl, bn; 2 Bb cl, Eb alto-cl
       or sax, bn or bass-cl) Cundy-Bettoney Co., Inc.
   ---Sacred Melodies. Contents: Onward Christian Soldiers,
       Abide With Me, Nearer My God to Thee, Adeste Fideles,
       Dennis, Portuguese Hymn. (4 Bb cl; 2 Bb cl, 2 Eb alto-
       cl or sax; 3 Bb cl, bn or Eb alto-cl or sax; fl, ob,
       cl, bn; 2 Bb cl, Eb alto-cl or sax, bn or bass-cl) Cundy-
       Bettoney Co.
LIEGL, LEOPOLD, Collection of Clarient Quartets. Contents:
       Spanish Dance, Moszkowski; Humoreske, Dvorak; March Mi-
       litaire, Schubert; Moment Musical, Schubert; Poupee
       Valsant, Poldini; Scarf Dance, Chaminade; Anitra's
       Dance, Grieg; Hungarian Dance No. 5, Brahms. (2 cl,
       alto-cl, bass-cl or 4 Bb cl) ME Witmark; Music Pub-
       lishers Holding Corp.
SKORNICKA, Quartet Album for Bb cl, containing 14 compositions
       by Corelli, Mozart, Goldmark, Gluck, etc. (4 cl) ME
       EMB; Belwin.
VOXMAN, HYMIE, Ensemble Classics for Clarinet Quartets, arr. by
       Voxman (4 cl) VE-E Rubank; EMB.
   ---Ensemble Classic for Clarinet Quartets, Vol. II (2 cl,
       alto-cl, bass-cl) VE-E (rec) Rubank; EMB.
WARNER, Collection of Clarinet Ensembles, arr. by Hartmen-
       Mesang. (4 cl) E EMB.
WOOD, CHARLES, First Ensemble Album, arr. by Wood (4 Bb cl)
       VE Concord Music Publishing Co.
ZAMECNIK, J. S., Fox Ideal Instrumental Quartets. Contents:
       Morning Song, Country Dance, Fall in Line, A Bit of Har-
       mony, Jolly Hunters, Alpine Memories, Bagpipes, Minuet,
       College Tune, The Chapel Organ, An Old Ballad, Our Kindly
       Father, Cuban Dreams, Dancing Dolls, The Rolling Sea, Oh
       Hallelujah!, Old Monterey, Toy Soldiers, Gavotte Royal,
       The Happy Peasant, Softly Gliding, The Victor's Return.
       (Instrumentation: Part 1: Db picc, fl, ob, Eb cl, Bb
       cl. Part 2: ob, Bb cl, F h, Eb alto-cl. Part 3: Bb
       cl, F h, Eb alto-cl. Part 4: Bb cl. Tenor Banjo, drums,
       pf ad lib). Fox Publishing Co.

Classic Quartets

BACH, CARL PHILIPP EMANUEL, Allegro Brilliant (fl, ob, cl, bn)
    Andraud; Fischer (Maganini, arr. for fl, ob, cl, bn,
    score, parts).
BACH, JOHANN SEBASTIAN, Aria Suite in D (2 cl, v, vc, pf ad lib)
    Andraud.
   ---Bourree, arr. by L. A. Hahn (fl, ob, cl, bn) Fischer
    (score, parts).
   ---Bourree, arr. by Brandenburg (4 cl) Andraud; Fischer,
    (score, parts).
   ---Two Chorales (4 bn) arr. by Paul Bazelaire.
   ---Fughetta, Minuet, arr. by A. E. Cafarella (fl, ob, cl, bn)
    Volkwein; Andraud; Music Publishers Holding Corp. (score,
    parts); Witmark (Fughetta only).
   ---Quartet Fugue No. 1 (ob, eng h, 2 bn or cl)
   ---Fugue in Eb, arr. by Hirsch (fl or ob, cl, h, bn) San-
    sone; Andraud; Fischer (score, parts).
   ---Fugue in G minor (fl, ob, cl, bn) MH Fillmore Music
    House; Andraud (arr. by Hahn).
   ---Gavotte, arr. by De Bueris (4 cl; 3 cl, bass-cl; 2 cl,
    alto-cl, bass-cl) MH Belwin.
   ---Two Gavottes from French Suites (fl, 2 cl, bn) Master-
    works Publications.
   ---Gavotte from Partita in B minor, arr. by A. E. Cafarella,
    (4 cl; 2 cl, alto-cl, bass-cl; 3 cl, bn) Andraud;
    Music Publishers Holding Corp., (score, parts).
   ---Loure (fl, ob, cl, bn) arr. by A. E. Cafarella; Andraud.
   ---Prelude and Fugue, arr. by Ossek (fl, ob, cl, bn)
   ---Prelude and Fugue XIV, Vol. 2, arr. by Kessler (fl, ob,
    cl, bn) VH Rubank.
   ---Fugue in G minor from the Well-Tempered Clavichord, No.
    XVI (2 cl, alto-cl, bass-cl or 4 Bb cl) MH Belwin.
BACH, JOHANN SEBASTIAN, Sarabande in D minor from French Suite,
    arr. by Kessler (fl, ob, cl, bn) ME Witmark; Music
    Publishers Holding Corp. (arr. by Theodore M. Finney,
    score, parts).
   ---"Unschuld, Kleinodreiner Seelen", arr. by Friedrich
    Smend (sop, fl, ob, va) Music Rara; Barenreiter, (arr.
    by Bote).
   ---Preludes, Sarabandes, Courantes, Bourrees, arr. by Cor-
    royez (4 cl) Andraud.
   ---80 Preludes, Fugues, Chorales, Inventions, Canons, Var-
    iations, etc. (Instrumentation: Part A: fl, ob Eb
    cl, Bb cl. Part B: Bb cl. Part C: Eb alto-cl, bn.
    Part D: bn, bass-cl) Andraud.
BEETHOVEN, LUDWIG VAN, Adagio from Sonata Pathetique (4 Bb
    cl) Boosey-Hawkes (score, parts).
   ---Allegro con Brio, Op. 18, No. 1, arr. by K. L. Wilson
    (2 cl, alto-cl, bass-cl) H Carl Fischer, 1948.
   ---Andante Cantabile from Symphony No. 1, transc. by Harry
    C. Geiger (2 cl, alto-cl, bass-cl) ME Gamble Hinged
    Music; Remick; Music Publishers Holding Corp. (arr.
    by 4 Bb cl, score, parts).

————Andante Favori, Op. 3, from string quartet, Op. 3 (4 wind instruments) Fetis.

———Contredanse, arr. by L. A. Hahn (fl, ob, cl, bn) Andraud.

———Menuetto from piano sonata, Op. 10, No. 3, arr. by Marc Tarlow (fl, 2 cl, bn) Music Publishers Holding Corp. (score, parts).

————Minuet (fl, ob, cl, bn) Cundy-Bettoney Co. (score, parts).

————Minuet in G major, arr. by Trinkaus (ob or fl, cl, h, bn) Andraud; Franklin.

————Minuet from Sonata, Op. 49, No. 2 (fl, ob, cl, bn) Andraud; Franklin (arr. by Trinkaus, 2 fl, cl, bn).

————Minuet from Piano Sonata, Op. 22, arr. by Cafarella (fl, ob, cl, bn) Volkwein.

————Quartet, Op. 18, No. 4 (2 cl, alto-cl, bass-cl or 2 Bb cl, Eb cl, bass-cl) MH Boosey-Hawkes (score, parts).

————Rondo from Sonata Pathetique (4 cl; 2 cl, alto-cl or sax, bass-cl or bn; 3 cl, bn or sax, Eb alto-cl) MH Cundy-Bettoney Co. (score, parts); Andraud (arr. for 2 Bb cl, 2 Eb alto-cl or sax).

————Scherzo from Sonata for piano, Op. 26 (4 cl or 2 cl, alto-cl, bass-cl) arr. by Harris. Gornston.

———Three Equales (4 bn) Andraud.

BENNETT, ROBERT RUSSELL, Rondo Capriccioso (4 fl) H New York Flute Club; Andraud; Baxter-Northrup (called Scherzo Capriccioso).

BENTZON, JORGEN, Racconto, Op. 25 (fl, sax, bn, bass) Skandinavisk og Borups; McGinnis & Marx.

BERGER, ARTHUR, Quartet in C Major (fl, ob, cl, bn) VH (rec) Arrow Press.

————Three Poems of Yeats (mezzo-sop, fl, cl, vc) New Music, New York.

BERR, FREDERICH, Six Quartets from Rossini in 2 suites, Andraud.

BLACHER, B., Divertimento (fl, cl, ob, bn) Bote & Bock; Musica Rara, London.

BLUMER, THEODOR, Tanzsuite, Op. 53 (fl, ob, cl, bn) Simrock.

BOCHSA, PERE, Twelve Little Quartets (ob, cl, h, bn) Andraud.

————Little Quartets, Op. 12 (fl or ob, cl, h, bn) First Suite, Andraud.

————Little Quartets, Op. 31 (fl or ob, cl, h, bn) Second Suite, Andraud.

BORODIN, ALEXANDER P., Quartet (fl, ob, va, vc) Leeds.

BRAHMS, JOHANNES, Waltz in Ab (4 cl) Andraud; Fischer (score, parts).

BROD, HENRI, Airs en Quatuor, Book I (ob, cl, h, bn) Pleyel, Paris; Fetis.

CHAMINADE, CECILE, Scarf Dance in Ab, arr. by Louis Pietrini (fl, ob, cl, bn) Ms, copy available from Louis Pietrini, Bassoonist, Met.

CHAVEZ, CARLOS, Soli (ob, cl, bn, tr) Mexico, 1933 Fleisher.

CLEMENTI, MUZIO, Canone Gradus ad Parnassum (2 cl, 2 bn) Andraud.

CORELLI, ARCANGELO, Gigue, arr. by E. Harris (4 Bb cl; 2 Bb cl, 2 Eb alto-cl or sax; 3 Bb cl, bn or Eb alto-cl or sax; fl, ob, Bb cl, bn; 2 Bb cl, Eb alto-cl or sax, bn or

bass-cl) Cundy-Bettoney Co.; Andraud (arr. for 4 cl;
    2 cl, alto-cl, bass-cl; 3 cl, bn; fl, ob, cl, bn).

CORROYEZ, G., See Collections, end of this section.

CUI, CESAR ANTONOVITCH, Orientale, arr. by Harris (fl, ob, cl,
    bn; 4 Bb cl; 3 cl or 2 cl, sax, bn or bass-cl) An-
    draud; Cundy-Bettoney Co.

DAHLHOFF, WALTER, "Sumpf", dramatic dance scene (fl, ob, cl, bn)
    1925, Schmidt, Cefes-Edition; Andraud.

DANZI, FRANZ, Three Quartets, Op. 40 (4 bn) Offenbach; Andre;
    Fetis.

    ---Gypsy Dance, arr. by Quinto E. Maganini (fl, ob, cl, bn)
    Fischer.

DE BUERIS, J., Mozartiana, arr. by De Bueris (4 cl; 3 cl, bass-
    cl; 2 cl, alto-cl, bass-cl) H Belwin.

    ---Gavotte Caprice (3 cl, bass-cl) Fischer.

    ---Six Quartets (4 cl; 2 cl, alto-cl, bass-cl; 3 cl, bn
    or bass-cl) Gavotte Classique, De Bueris; Menuet from
    Fantasia, Op. 78, Schubert; Serenade, Haydn; Canzonetta,
    Mendelssohn; Humoresque, Dvorak; Dance Creole, Chami-
    nade. MH Andraud; Belwin (each published separately).

DEBUSSY, CLAUDE ACHILLE, Nocturne, arr. by Howland (2 cl, alto-
    cl, bass-cl) VH Paul A. Schmitt; Selmer.

    ---Reverie, arr. by Howland (2 cl, alto-cl, bass-cl) VH
    Paul A. Schmitt; Selmer.

DELAMARTER, E., Sketch Book in Eire (fl, ob, cl, bn) ME An-
    draud.

DE LORENZO, LEONARDO, Divertimento Fantastico (fl, ob, cl, bn)
    Ms.

    ---Quartet, Op. 32 (4 fl) Baxter-Northrup; Zimmermann
    (called Capriccio Fantastico, Op. 32); Andraud (called
    I Seguaci di Pan, Op. 32).

DESORMIERE, RODGER, Six Danceries, 16th century (fl, cl, bn,
    eng. h) Baron.

DEVIENNE, FRANCOIS, Deuxieme Symphonie Concertante (fl, ob, h,
    bn) Fetis.

    ---Quartets (4 winds, 4 fl).

DOMANSKY, ALFRED, Divertissement (2 cl, h, bn) 1936, Schmidt,
    Heilbronn, Cefes-Edition; Andraud.

DONEZETTI, GAETANO, Airs from Daughter of the Regiment (fl, cl,
    h, bn) Lemoine, Paris.

DURING, H., Quartet (fl, cl, h, bn) Hedler, Frankfort.

DVORAK, ANTONIN, Humoresque (4 cl; 3 cl, bass-cl; 2 cl, alto-cl,
    bass-cl) ME arr. by De Bueris, Belwin.

    ---Humoreske (fl, ob, cl, bn) in G, arr. by Louis Pietrini.
    Ms, copy available from Louis Pietrini, Bassoonist, Met.

FLEGIER, ANGE, Quartet in G minor (2 ob, 2 bn) MH Enoch; San-
    sone; Andraud.

FOSTER, STEPHEN COLLINS, Quartet "Tioga Waltz" (4 fl) Athens
    Academy.

FRAGALE, FRANK, Quartet "Sprightly Flight" (fl, ob, cl, bn)
    Edition Musicus.

FUCHS, GEORG FRIEDRICH, Trois Quartets, Op. 31 (h, cl, bn, bass)
    Litolff, Paris; Janet & Co.

GALLET, LUCIANO, Suite on Afro-Brazilian Themes (fl, cl, h, bn)
    c/o Mario De Andrade, Rio De Janeiro, Escola Nacional de

Musica.

GOEPFART, KARL, Quartet in D minor, Op. 93 (fl, ob, cl, bn) Andraud; F. Schuberth, Jr. (rec)

HANDEL, GEORGE FREDERICK, Minuet, arr. by del Busto (ob, cl, h, bn) Andraud.

---Rinaldo's Aria, transc. by Georges Grisez (fl, ob, cl, bn) Andraud; Cundy-Bettoney Co.

---Rondo in A (fl, ob, cl, bn) arr. by Louis Pietrini. Ms. copy available from Louis Pietrini, Bassoonist, Met.

---Sarabande from Oboe Concerto in F major (ob, 2 cl, bn) Andraud; Music Publishers Holding Corp. (transc. by Lee M. Lockhart, arr. for 2 ob, 2 bn or ob, 2 cl, bn, score, parts).

---Scherzo in C major (fl, ob, cl, bn) arr. by Louis Pietrini Ms, copy available from Louis Pietrini, Bassoonist, Met.

HARCOURT, MARQUERITE BECLARD D', Peruvian Inca Melodies: Harawi-Baile-Khacampa (mixed cl quartet) Ricordi.

HAYDN, FRANZ JOSEPH, Adagio from Quartet, Op. 64, No. 5, transc. by Marc Tarlow (fl, 2 cl, bn) Andraud (composer listed as Johann Michael Haydn); Music Publishers Holding Corp. (score, parts).

---Adagio No. 300 from a Piano Sonata (fl, ob, cl, bn) Andraud; Cundy-Bettoney Co., (arr. by Harry C. Geiger for 4 Bb cl; 3 Bb cl, bn or Eb alto-cl or sax; fl, ob, cl, bn; 2 Bb cl, Eb alto-cl or sax, bn or bass-cl).

HAYDN, FRANZ JOSEPH, Allegro Con Brio, arr. by L. A. Hahn (fl, ob, cl, bn) Andraud.

---Final Movement from String Quartet in C Major, Op. 33, No. 3 (fl, 2 cl, bn) Masterworks Publications.

---Allegro, Andante and Allegro Molto, from String Quartet, Op. 1, No. 5 (2 ob, 2 h) Haydn Catalogue, Geiringer.

---Divertimento in Bb Major (2 cl, 2h) 1932, Hansen; Kall-meyer (arr. by Hermann Reichenbach; Andraud; AMP.

HAYDN, FRANZ JOSEPH, Menuetto al Rovescio (4 cl) Andraud; Fischer (score, parts).

---Minuet from String Quartet in F, Op. 77, No. 2 (fl, 2 cl, bn) Masterworks Publications.

---Ochsen Menuett (The Ox Minuet) in C (2 ob, 2 bn) (rec) Remick; Gamble-Hinged Music; Music Publishers Holding Corp. (score, parts; transc. by Paul Painter).

---Serenade, arr. by J. De Bueris (4 cl; 3 cl, bass-cl; 2 cl, alto-cl, bass-cl) MH Belwin.

---Theme and Variations from Emperor String Quartet (fl, ob, cl, bn) MH Fillmore Music House.

---Four Trios (fl, ob, vc, bn) Andraud.

HAYDN, JOHANN MICHAEL, Divertimento in D major (fl, ob, h, bn) 1931, Hofmeister (arr. by R. Lauschmann); Andraud; Musica Rara, London; McGinnis & Marx; Eble; New York Public Library (microfilm copies may be obtained by writing Dr. Carleton Sprague Smith).

HERMANN, FRIEDRICH, Three Quartets after Beethoven, Haydn, and Mozart (ob, cl, h, bn) B&H, 1899; Andraud.

HOLBROOKE, JOSEF A., Serenade, Op. 94 in Db major (fl, ob, cl, bn) The Modern Music Library, London; Andraud.

HONEGGER, ARTHUR, Canons (Trois Contrepoints) 1923 (fl, v, eng h, vc or picc or ob) Hansen, Copenhagen; AMP.

---Canon sur Basse Obstinee (picc, v, ob or eng h, vc) AMP; 1926, Hansen (score, parts); Andraud.

HYE-KNUDSEN, JOHAN, Quartet, Op. 3 in A minor (fl, ob or eng h, v, vc) 1926 Hansen (Min score, parts); Andraud; AMP.

IBERT, JACQUES, Quartet, Two Movements (2 fl, cl, bn) VH (fec) 1923 Leduc (score, parts); Baron; Andraud.

KABALEVSKY, DMITRI, Children's Suite, Op. 27, arr. by Seay (fl, ob, cl, bn) Spratt.

KEATS, Rosebuds Dance, Tschaikowsky Dream (4 cl) Andraud.

KNUDAGE-RIISAGER, Sonata (fl, cl, v, vc) Andraud.

KREJEI, ISA, Divertimento (fl, cl, h, bn) H-VH (rec) 1927, Hudebni Matice; Eble; Andraud.

KRUGER, FRITZ, Gay Potpourri (ob, cl, h, bn) 1934, Ehrler; Andraud.

KRUGER, JOHANN PHILIPP, Partie (No. 9) in F major (2 ob, eng h, bn) Kistner & Siegel.

KUHLAU, FRIEDRICH, Quartet, Op. 103 (Grand Quartet) (4 fl) MH-H Andraud; Baron; Richault; Baxter-Northrup (rec)

LA MONACA, JOSEPH, Quartet: Sonata in G Major (4 fl, 2nd and third fl interchanging with piccolos and fl in G, alto-fl)

---Quartet: Scherzo Capriccioso (4 fl; 3 fl and fl in G-alto-fl) Andraud.

LANGE, FRANZ GUSTAVE, Pastorale Quartet (2 ob, eng h or cl, bn) 1880 Erdmann; Andraud.

LAUBER, JOSEPH, Four Intermezzi (fl, eng h, cl, bn) 1922, Henn (min score, parts); Andraud.

MARTINI, GIOVANNI BATTISTA, Les Moutons (The Sheep) Gavotte (2 cl, 2 bn or ob, cl, 2 bn) Andraud.

MASSENET, JULES EMILE FREDERIC, Last Slumber of the Virgin (4 cl; 2 cl, alto-cl, bass-cl; 2 Bb cl, 2 Eb alto-cl or sax; 2 Bb cl, Eb alto-cl or sax, bn or bass-cl) arr. by A. Harris, Cundy-Bettoney Co., Andraud.

MECHIOR, A.J.B., Quartet, Op. 1 (fl, cl, h, bn) Lemoine; Andraud.

---Quartet, No. 6 in G major (fl, cl, h, bn) Costallat.

---Grand Quartet, Op. 8 (fl, cl, h, bn) Lemoine; Andraud.

---Three Little Quartets, Op. 14 (fl, cl, h, bn) Lemoine; Andraud.

---Quartet, Op. 20 in D minor (fl, cl, h, bn) Costallat.

MENDELSSOHN-BARTHOLDY, FELIX, Chorlieder (2 cl, 2 bn) Andraud.

---Lieder and Canon (2 cl, 2 bn) Andraud.

---Three Equales (4 bn) Andraud, arr. by Wittmann.

---Rondo Capriccioso, Op. 14 (2 cl, alto-cl, bass-cl) VH (rec) Paul A. Schmitt (arr. by Howland); Selmer.

---Scherzo (2 cl, alto-cl, bass-cl) H (rec) Paul A Schmitt (arr. by Howland); Selmer.

---Folk Song, arr. by G. Langenus (4 cl) (rec) Fischer.

---Morning Song (4 cl) (rec) Fischer, arr. by G. Langenus.

---Retrospection, arr. by G. Langenus (4 cl) (rec) Fischer.

---Songs Without Words, No. 8 (4 Bb cl) Boosey-Hawkes (score, parts).

MEYERBEER, GIACOMO, Coronation March (4 cl; 2 cl, alto-cl, bass-
          cl or 2 Eb alto-sax; 3 cl, bn or Eb alto-cl or sax; fl,
          ob, cl, bn; 2 Bb cl, Eb alto-cl or sax, bn or bass-cl)
          arr. by A. Harris, Cundy-Bettoney Co. (parts); Andraud.
MIGOT, GEORGES, Quartet (fl, cl, v, harp) Andraud.
MIRANDOLLE, LUDOVICUS, Quartet in D major (4 woodwinds) 1941-2,
          published by author (s'Gravenhage).
MOZART, WOLFGANG AMADEUS, Adagio, transc. by Alexander Richter
          (fl, ob, cl, bn) Music Publishers Holding Corp. (score,
          parts); Remick.
     ---Andante for Mechanical Organ, K616 (fl, ob, va, vc) AMP;
          Schott; Baron.
     ---Cassation or Cassazione (ob, cl, h, bn) H Adagio, Al-
          legro, Minuetto, Adagio, Polacca, Rondo. Baron; Andraud.
     ---Adagio from Clarinet Concerto in A major, Op. 107, K622
          arr. by Laube (2 cl, alto-cl, bass-cl or bn) Cundy-
          Bettoney Co., Inc.
     ---Divertimento No. 11, K 251, arr. by Alexander Richter
          (fl, cl, ob, bn) Kalmus Editions (score, parts).
     ---Minuet from String Quartet in Bb, K458 (fl, 2 cl, bn)
          Masterworks Publications.
     ---Quartet-Minuetto, No. 4 (ob, cl, alto-cl, bn) Andraud.
     ---Final Movement from String Quartet in Bb, K489 (fl,
          2 cl, bn) Masterworks Publications.
     ---Two Quartets (cl, 3 basset-horns) Fetis; Andraud.
     ---Excerpt from Piano Sonata No. 1 (rec) arr. by R. Toll
          (4 cl, 2 Bb cl, 2 Eb cl or sax; 3 Bb cl, bn or Eb alto-
          cl or sax; fl, ob, cl, bn; 2 Bb cl, Eb alto-cl or sax,
          bn or bass-cl) Cundy-Bettoney Co. (score, parts).
     ---Excerpt from Piano Sonata No. 4, arr. by R. Toll (4 cl;
          2 Bb cl, 2 Eb alto-cl or sax; 3 Bb cl, bn or Eb alto-
          cl or sax; 2 Bb cl, Eb alto-cl or sax, bn or bass-cl)
          Cundy-Bettoney Co., (score, parts).
     ---Excerpt from Piano Sonata No. 10, arr. by R. Roll (4
          cl; 2 Bb cl, 2 Eb alto-cl or sax; 3 Bb cl, bn or Eb
          alto-cl or sax; 2 Bb cl, Eb alto-cl or sax, bn or bass-
          cl; fl, ob, cl, bn) Cundy-Bettoney Co. (score, parts)
MOZART, WOLFGANG AMADEUS, Three Excerpts from Piano Sonatas Nos.
          1, 4, and 10 (4 cl; 2 cl, alto-cl, bass-cl; 3 cl, bn)
          (rec) Andraud.
     ---Andante Cantabile in Eb from Second Sonata (2 cl, 2 bn)
          Andraud; Evette & Schaeffer (arr. by G. Wittmann, 2 cl,
          2 bn)
     ---Finale from Fifth Sonata (fl, ob, cl, bn) Andraud; Music
          Publishers Holding Corp. (arr. by A. E. Cafarella, score,
          parts).
     ---Allegro from Eighth Sonata (2 cl, 2 bn) Andraud.
     ---Menuetto from Ninth Sonata (2 cl, 2 bn) Andraud.
     ---Adagio from Eleventh Sonata (2 cl, 2 bn) Andraud.
     ---Theme from Twelfth Sonata (ob, 2 cl, bn) Andraud; Music
          Publishers Holding Corp. (transc. by Lee M. Lockhart, 2
          ob, 2 bn; ob, 2 cl, bn, score, parts).
     ---Adante, Rondo and Allegro from Fifteenth Sonata (2 cl,
          2 bn) Andraud.
     ---Rondo from Seventeenth Sonata (2 cl, 2 bn) Andraud.

---Eight Movements from Sonatas, arr. by del Busto (2 cl, 2
   bn) Andraud.
---Suite in G, arr. by Bellison (2 Bb cl, basset horn inF;
   alternate parts for 3rd Bb cl, Eb alto-cl; Bb bass-cl)
   Ricordi.
---German Dance (ob, cl, h, bn) arr. by del Busto; Andraud.
---Theme and March of the Priests, arr. by G. J. Trinkaus (2
   cl, 2 bn) Franklin; Andraud.
---Rondo, arr. by Maurice Kesnar (fl, ob, cl, bn) Cundy-
   Bettoney Co. (score, parts).
---Minuet from Eb Symphony (fl, ob, cl, bn) Andraud; Cundy-
   Bettoney (4 Bb cl; 2 Bb cl, Eb alto-cl or sax, bn or
   bass-cl).
---Movement from String Quartet, arr. by G. Langenus (fl,
   ob, cl, bn)
MOZART, LEOPOLD, Kleine Suite for Woodwinds, arr. by Karl Marx
OFFENBACH, JACQUES, The Sabre of My Father from "The Grand Du-
   chess", transc. by M.A. Springer (3 Bb cl, bn) Music
   Publishers Holding Corp. (score, parts).
PALESTRINA, GIOVANNI PIERLUIGI DA, Ricercari for Wind Quartet,
   arr. by Fellerer (4 wind instruments) Schott (score,
   parts); Andraud; AMP.
---Alleluia and Choral, arr. by Mendelssohn-Barthody (4
   Bb cl) E Belwin.
PERILHOU, A., Divertissement, Musett. (2 fl, 2 cl; 2 ob, 2
   bn) Heugel; Andraud.
---Divertissement, No. 1 Tale (Conte) (2 fl, 2 cl) Heugel;
   Andraud.
PIERNE, HENRY, March of the Little Tin Soldiers, arr. by G.
   Grisez (fl, ob, cl, bn) ME (rec) Baron; Andraud; EMB;
   Cundy-Bettoney.
PITTALUGA, G., Ricercare (v, cl, bn, tpt) Andraud.
PLEYEL, IGNACE JOSEPH, Symphonie Concertante, No. 5 (fl, ob, h,
   bn) Pleyel; Fetis.
PROKOFIEFF, SERGE, Humoristic Scherzo, Op. 12 (4 bn) Russis-
   cher Musikverlag; Andraud; Baron.
---Fleeting Moments (fl, ob, cl, bn) MH (rec) Cundy-
   Bettoney Co., (score, parts) EMB.
PROKOFIEFF, SERGE, Two Visions Fugitives, Op. 22 (fl, ob, cl, bn)
   Andraud.
PROVINCIALI, EMILIO, Danse Villagoeise in A Major (fl, ob, cl,
   bn) Eschig; Andraud; Baron; AMP.
RAASTED, NILS, Serenade, Op. 40 in F Major (fl, ob, v, vc) An-
   draud; McGinnis & Marx (scored for fl, ob, v, vc); Kist-
   ner & Siegel (min score, parts).
REGER, MAX, Romance (ob, cl, h, bn, fl, and contrabn ad lib) An
   draud.
RIMSKY-KORSAKOFF, NICOLAS ANDRE, Flight of the Bumble Bee, arr.
   by De Bueris (4 Bb cl; 3 Bb cl, bass-cl; 2 Bb cl, Eb
   alto-cl, bass-cl) H Belwin.
ROSSINI, GIOACCHINO ANTONIO, Quartet (fl or ob, cl, h, bn) Andraud; Sansone.
---Six Quartets, Book I and II (fl, ob, cl, bn; fl, cl, h,
   bn) Schott; Baron; Andraud; McGinnis & Marx.
---Stabat Mater (4 fl) Andraud.

---Quartet No. 1, 6 (fl, cl, h, bn) Schott, (arr. by W. Za-
chert); AMP.

---Quartet in F (fl or ob, cl, h, bn) H-VH Ricordi (arr.
by Felice Boghen, min. score, parts); Mercury; Andraud.

RUBINSTEIN, ANTON GREGOROVITCH, The Asra, Op. 32, No. 6, transc.
by M. A. Springer (3 Bb cl, bn) Music Publishers Holding
Corp. (score, parts).

RUDIGER, THEODORE WEIMAR, Intermezzo (fl, ob, cl, bn) Publ. by
composer, 1932, Weimar.

SCARLATTI, DOMENICO, Pastorale, transc. by O. B. Wilson (4 Bb cl;
2 Bb cl, alto-cl, bn) Music Publishers Holding Corp.
(score, parts); Remick.

SCHAFFNER, NICOLAS ALBERT, Three Quartets, Op. 5, in F Major,
D Minor, C Major (fl, ob, cl, bn) B&H; Andraud.

---Three Quartets Concertants, Op. 5, 7, 9 (fl, cl, h, bn)
A.Petite, Paris; Fetis.

SCHMID, HEINRICH KASPAR, Tanze des 16 Jahrhunderts (Seventeenth
Century Dance) (ob, 2 eng h, bn, or various string instruments substituted for the parts) Barenreiter.

SCHUBERT, FRANZ PETER SERAPH, Ave Maria (2 cl, 2 bn) arr. by
Trinkaus. Franklin Co.; Andraud.

---Cantilena and Presto (4 cl, alternate bass-cl) E-ME
Edition Musicus.

---Minuetto from Fantasia, Op. 78, arr. by L.A. Hahn (fl,
ob, cl, bn; 4 cl) Fillmore Music House; Andraud
Belwin (arr. by De Bueris for 4 cl; 3 cl, bass-cl; 2
cl, alto-cl, bass-cl).

---Minuet, arr. by Cafarella (fl, ob, cl, bn) Andraud;
Witmark; Music Publishers Holding Corp. (score, parts).

---Watlz in A Minor, arr. by A. Del Busto (fl, cl, h, bn)
Andraud; Fischer (score, parts).

SCHUMANN, ROBERT ALEXANDER, Choral, Op. 68, No. 4, transc. by
M. A. Springer (2 Bb cl, 2 bn) Music Publishers Holding
Corp. (score, parts).

---Scherzo from Quartet, Op. 41, No. 1 in A Minor (2 cl,
alto-cl, bass-cl) H Schmitt; Selmer (arr. by Howland).

SCHUMANN, ROBERT ALEXANDER, Allegro from Sonata No. 1 (fl, ob,
cl, bn) Andraud.

---Knight Rupert, Op. 68, No. 12 (fl or ob, cl, h or eng h,
bn) arr. by G. J. Trinkaus; Franklin.

---Harvest Song, Canon, Sicilienne (fl, ob, cl, bn) Andraud.

---Fugue (fl, ob, cl, bn) Andraud.

---Allegretto from Sonata No. 1, transc. by Georges Grisez
(fl, ob, cl, bn) Concert Key of F. Cundy-Bettoney Co.
(score, parts). Same piece in Concert Key of Eb (2 Bb
cl, Eb alto-cl or sax, bn or bass-cl) Cundy-Bettoney
Co. (parts only).

SHAW, OLIVER, For the Gentlemen (fl, ob, or cl, cl, bn) ME
(rec) Mercury; EMB.

SPIES, ERNST, A Happy Overture (fl, cl, h, bn) Andraud.

SPOHR, LUDWIG, Concerto No. 1, Op. 26, arr. by J. I. Tallmadge
(2 cl, alto-cl, bass-cl) VH Remick; Gamble Hinged
Music (excerpts); Music Publishers Holding Corp. (score,
parts, arr. for 3 Bb cl, bn).

STAMITZ, JOHANN WENZEL ANTON, Andante, arr. by Mauritz Kesnar
(2 cl, alto-cl, bass-cl; 4 cl; 2 Bb cl, Eb alto-cl or
sax, bn or bass-cl) MH (rec) Cundy-Bettoney Co. (score,
parts).
STAMITZ, KARL, Quartet Op. 8 in Eb Major (ob or cl, corno di caccia, va, bn) (rec) 1914, DTB, Vol. 27, (ed. by Hugo Riemann); 1919, Afas, (ed. by Halmar von Dameck); 1937,
Leuckart (ed. by G. Weigelt, arr. for ob, cl, h, bn);
Andraud (ob, cl, h, bn); B&H; Collegium Musicum, Vol. XV
(ed. by Riemann; Cundy-Bettoney.
STARK, ROBERT, Serenade, Op. 55 in Eb Major (2 cl, bassethorn
or bn, bass-cl or bn; 2 cl, alto-cl, bass-cl; 2 cl, 2
bn) 1922, C. F. Schmidt, Cefes-Edition; Andraud.
STRAVINSKY, IGOR FEDOROVICH, Berceuses du Chat (contralto, 3
cl) Chester; Spratt; Baron, (min. score, parts, pf ad
lib); Concord (arr. by Filippi, for mixed cl quartet);
1925, Wiener Philh. Verlag (called Katzenlieder).
THOMSON, VIRGIL, Five Portraits (4 cl).
TSCHAIKOWSKY, PETER ILITCH, Scherzo from Fourth Symphony (2 cl,
alto-cl, bass-cl) MH H. T. Fitzsimons.
---Chanson Triste, arr. by Hamilton (2 cl, 2 bn) E (rec)
Galaxy.
---Andante Cantabile, arr. by De Bueris (3 Bb cl, bass-cl;
2 Bb cl, alto-cl, bass-cl; 4 cl) MH Belwin.
---Two Little Marches, arr. by R. A. Schumann (4 cl) Andraud;
EMB; Franklin Co. (arr. by Trinkaus).
---The Toy Soldiers' March, Op. 35, No. 5, arr. by G. J.
Trinkaus (4 cl) Franklin Co; Music Publishers Holding
Corp., (transc. by O. B. Wilson).
TUTHILL, BURNET CORWIN, Divertimento in Classical Style, Op. 14,
No. 2 (fl, ob, cl, bn) MH (rec) 1938, Fischer (score,
parts); Andraud.
VERDI, GIUSEPPE, Rigoletto Quartet (4 cl; 2 cl, alto-cl or
sax, bass-cl or bn; 3 cl, bn or sax or Eb alto-cl; 2
Bb cl, 2 Eb cl or sax; fl, ob, cl, bn) Andraud; Cundy-
Bettoney Co., (parts) (arr. by A. Harris, pf acc. ad lib).
VIEIRA BANDAO, JOSE, Choro (fl, eng h, cl, bass-cl) Boletin
Latinoamericano De Musica.
VILLA-LOBOS, HEITOR, Poema da Crianca e sua mama (voice, fl,
cl, vc) Eschig.
---Quartet for Wind Instruments (fl, ob, cl, bn) AMP.
WALCKIERS, EUGENE, Rondo (3 cl, alto or bass-cl) Andraud.
Cundy-Bettoney Co., (arr. by Arthur Brooke, for 3 fl,
alto-cl); Baxter-Northrup.
WASSILENKO, SERGEI NIKIFOROVITCH, Quartet on Turkish Folk
Songs, Op. 65 (fl, ob or eng h, cl, bn, percussion ad
lib) Andraud; Russischer Staatsverlag, Universal Ed-
ition (min. score, parts).
WATERSON, JAMES, Grand Quartet (4 cl) H (rec) Mahillon; An-
draud; Baron.
WETZEL, HERMANN, A Gay Serenade, ed. by Muller (ob, cl, h, bn)
Andraud; Oertel, Hanover (called Humorous Serenade,
arr. for 4 wind instruments.

Collections

Fifth Collection, of 12 Grand Concertant Quartets. Contents:
Concerto in Bb, Handel; Concerto in F, Handel; Concerto in D Minor, Handel; 8 Variations on the Gavotte
from Gluck's Armide, J. N. Hummel; Concertant Quartet,
Fr. Asplmayr (Instrumentation: Part A: fl, ob, cl;
Part B: cl; Part C: cl, fr H in F, Bb ten-sax; Part
D: bn, bar-sax, bass-cl.) Andraud.

CORROYEZ, 19 Celebrated Pieces in Quartet Form, Seventh Collection. Contents: To Elise, Beethoven; Pastorale,
Gretry; Canzonetta, Heller; Gay Spring, Mendelssohn;
Serenade, Andante Espressivo, Schubert; First Sorrow,
Reaper's Song, War Song, Schumann; March Solennelle,
Saint-Saens; Tannhauser, Lohengrin, etc., Wagner.
(Instrumentation: Part A: fl, ob, cl, sop-sax; Part
B: cl, Eb alto-sax; Part C: cl, Bb ten-sax, h, Eb
alto-cl; Part D: bn, bar-sax, bass-cl) Andraud.

TRINKAUS, GEORGE J., G. Schirmer's Select Album for Wind Quartet (2 cl, 2 bn) Contents: Bach, Barnby, Chopin, Dvorak; Gounod, Haydn, Scharwenka, Schumann, Tchaikowsky,
Trinkaus. G. Schirmer.

Piano Quartets

AMBERG, JOHANN, Suite: Seguedille; In Front of the Cathedral; Ronde Villageoise (fl, ob, cl, pf) 1905, Hansen; Andraud.

ANDRAUD, A. J., Four Pieces from Caldara, Rameau, Pergolesi, Vivaldi (fl, cl, bn, harp or pf) Andraud.

AYALA, DANIEL, Vidrios Rotos (Broken Windows) (ob, cl, bn, pf) University of Mexico, Mexico City.

BACH, JOHANN SEBASTIAN, Trio in G Major (2 fl, vc, pf or 2 fl, bn, pf) 1937, Peters; Andraud; 1920, B&H (arr. by Max Seiffert); 1937, in Bach Trio-Sonaten, Vol. I, Peters (arr. by L. Landshoff); Baron (arr. in Bb Major).

   ---Trio Sonata in Bb Major (2 alto reco, pf, vc ad lib) arr, by Woehl, C. F. Peters.

BACH, WILHELM FRIEDEMANN, Three Trios in D Major, D Major and A Minor (2 fl, vc, pf) B&H, ed. by Max Seiffert, 1931.

BEDORD, HERBERT, Night Piece, The Shepherd (voice, fl, ob, pf) 1925, Stainer & Bell.

BELLINI, FERMO, Divertimento on themes of Verdi's Giovanna d'-Arco (eng h, cl, vc, pf) Ricordi, Milan; Fetis.

BONNER, EUGENE, Over the Hills (3 fl, pf) Edition Musicus.

BONONCINI, GIOVANNI BATTISTA, Seven Suites, ed. by F. J. Giesbert (2 fl, vc, pf) 1939, Schott.

BRESGEN, CESAR, Kleine Musik (Folksongs) (2 fl, pf, voice ad lib) 1940, Schott.

BRUNEAU, ERNEST, Quartet (fl, ob, h, pf) 1902, Peregally; Andraud.

CARACCIOLO, PASCAL, Quartet (fl, cl, va, pf) Fetis.

CASTERA, RENE DE, Concerto: Paysage, Interlude, Rondo with variations, in A major (fl, cl, vc, pf) 1924, Rouart; Andraud.

CAVALLINI, ERNESTO, Trio in F Major (fl, ob, cl, pf) 1890, Ricordi; Andraud.

COLBY, CARLETON L., Three Blind Mice, Scherzo in Eb Major (3 cl, or 3 fl, pf ad lib) Remick; Music Publishers Holding Corporation.

CORELLI, ARCANGELO, Trio Sonata, Op. 1, No. 1 (fl, ob, bn, pf) Music Press, Inc.

   ---Trio Sonata, Op. 3, No. 2 (fl, ob, bn, pf) MH-H Music Press, Inc.

   ---Sonatas, Op. 2, Nos. 1, 5, 7 (2 alto reco, pf, vc ad lib) C. F. Peters.

CRAMER, JOHANN BAPTIST, Concertante (woodwind, horns, pf)

DALBERG, JEAN, Quartets (ob, h, bn, pf) Fetis.

DE FESCH, WILLIAM, Three Sonatas (2 fl, pf, vc ad lib) C. F. Peters; McGinnis & Marx.

DOPPLER, FRANZ, Nocturne, Op. 19 (fl, v, h or vc, pf) Andraud.

DOTHEL, NICHOLAS, Six Trios (2 fl, h'chord, vc obbligato) Printed in London; In the British Museum.

EHRHART, J., Valses (Mulhousiennes, Series 1 and 2, Op. 20) MH (fl, ob, cl, pf)

   ---Alsatian Waltzes, Op. 20 (fl, ob, cl, pf) Andraud.

FABRE-D'OLIVET, ANTOINE, Quartets (2 fl, va, pf) Fetis.

FASCH, JOHANN FRIEDRICH, Sonata in B, arr. by Woehl (reco, ob,
v, b.c.) Musica Rara.
---Sonata a 4, in Bb Major (fl or reco, ob, v, pf, vc ad
lib) McGinnis & Marx; Nagel; Barenreiter-Bote (arr.
by Woehl, score, parts).
FOY, JACQUES, Quartet (fl, cl, bn, harp) Fetis.
FRANCAIX, JEAN, Quartet (fl, ob, cl, pf) Andraud.
FRESCOBALDI, GIROLAMO, Five Canzoni for Two Winds, cello, piano
Ed. by H. David (2 fl, vc, pf) Andraud; Schott; AMP;
Baron.
FUCHS, GEORG FRIEDRICH, Trois Quartets, Op. 31 (h, cl, bn, pf)
Litolff, Paris; Janet & Co.
FUX, JOHANN JOSEPH, Nurnberger Partita, 1781 (2 fl or fl, ob,
pf, vc) ed. by Hoffmann, 1939, Kallmeyer.
GABRIELI, GIOVANNI, Sonata (3 fl, pf, vc ad lib) C. F. Peters.
BEGEL, GEORG, Triosonaten in F Major, B Minor (2 fl, vc, pf)
ed. by Max Seiffert, 1926, Kistner & Siegel.
GLUCK, CHRISTOPHE WILLIBALD, Trio Sonata No. 2 in G Minor (fl,
ob, bn, pf) MH Music Press, Inc.
GOEB, ROGER, Concertant I (fl, ob, cl, pf) ACA.
GRAF, FREDERIC HERMANN, Two Quartets (2 fl, va, pf) Fetis.
GREEN, RAY, Holiday for Four (cl, bn, va, pf) American Music
Center, NYC.
GRIMM, C. HUGO, Fantasia in D Minor (2 cl, vc, pf) Andraud.
GROSSMANN, Three Quartets (2 cl, va, pf) Fetis.
GRUNENWALD, J. J., Fantaisie-Arabesque (ob, cl, bn, pf) E. Sala-
bert; Baron.
HAIEFF, ALEXEI, Serenade for Three Woodwinds and Piano (ob, cl,
bn, pf)
HAMM, J. V., Triologue, Introduction and Polonaise (fl, ob, cl,
pf) Andraud; Baxter-Northrup.
HANDEL, GEORGE FREDERICK, Six Trio-Sonatas in Bb Major, D Minor,
Eb Major, F Major, G Major, D Major, ed. by Emil Krause
(2 ob or 2 v, b.c., vc or bn ad lib) Schott; B&H, (ed.
by Max Seiffert for 2 ob or fl, v, pf, vc or bn ad lib).
---Trio No. 1 in Bb Major (2 ob or 2 fl, bn, pf) ed. by Max
Seiffert, 1924, B&H; Andraud (2 ob, bn, pf).
---Trio No. 2 in D Minor, ed. by Max Seiffert (2 ob, or 2
fl, bn or vc, pf) 1919, B&H; Andraud (2 ob, bn, pf).
---Trio No. 3 in Eb Major (ob, v, vc or bn, pf) ed. by Max
Seiffert, 1906, B&H; Music Press, Inc. (fl, ob, bn, pf);
Mercury Music Co. (2 ob, or fl, bn or vc, pf).
---Trio No. 4 in F Major, ed. by Max Seiffert (2 ob or 2 fl,
bn or vc, pf) 1919, B&H; Andraud (2 ob, bn, pf).
---Trio No. 5 in G Major, ed. by Max Seiffert (2 ob or 2 fl,
bn or vc, pf) B&H, 1924; Andraud (2 ob, bn, pf).
---Trio No. 6 in D Major, ed. by Max Seiffert (2 ob or 2 fl,
bn or vc, pf) 1924, B&H; Andraud (2 ob, bn, pf).
---Eight Trio Sonatas, No. 7 in C Minor, No. 9 in F Major,
No. 10 in Bb Major, No. 11 in F Major, No. 12 in G Minor,
No. 13 in G Minor, No. 14 in G Minor, No. 15 in E Major,
ed. by Emil Krause (2 ob or 2 fl or 2 v, vc or bn ad lib,
b.c.) Op. 2, Schott, 1880-1910; B&H (ed. by M. Seiffert).
---Trio No. 7, Op. 2, No. 1 in C Minor (2 ob or 2 vl or 2
v, bn or vc, pf) ed. by Max Seiffert, B&H, 1903; Senart

(ed. by R. Peyrot).

---Trio No. 8, Op. 2, No. 2 in G minor, ed. by Max Seiffert (2 fl or 2 v or 2 ob, vc or bn, pf) B&H; Peters, (ed. by Hans Sitt); International Music Co; Senart (ed. by R. Peyrot); Andraud (2 ob, bn, pf or 2 fl, bn, pf).

---Trio No. 9, Op. 2, No. 3 in F major (2 ob or 2 fl, pb, bn) ed. by Max Seiffert, B&H, 1920.

---Trio No. 10, Op. 2, No. 3 in Bb major (2 v, or fl, ob, vc or bn, pf) ed. by Max Seiffert, B&H, 1920; Andraud (2 ob or 2 fl, bn, pf).

---Trio No. 11, Op. 2, No. 4 in F major, ed. by Max Seiffert (2 fl, vc or bn, pf) B&H; Andraud.
Trio No. 12, Op. 2, No. 5 in G minor (2 v or fl, ob, vc, or bn, pf) ed. by Max Seiffert, B&H, 1919; Andraud (2 ob or 2 fl, bn, pf).

---Trio No. 13, Op. 2, No. 6 in G minor, ed. by Max Seiffert (2 v or fl, ob, vc or bn, pf) B&H, 1920; Andraud (2 ob or fl, bn, pf).

HANDEL, GEORGE FREDERICK, Trio No. 14 in G minor (2 fl, bn, pf or 2 ob, bn, pf) ed. by Max Seiffert, B&H, 1924.

---Trio No. 15 in E major (2 ob or 2 fl, bn, pf) ed. by Max Seiffert, B&H, 1911.

---Seven Trio Sonatas, Op. 5, 1-7, No. 16 in A major, No. 17 in B minor, No. 18 in E minor, No. 19 in G major, No. 20 in G minor, No. 21 in F major, No. 22 in Bb major (2 ob, vc, pf or fl, v, vc, pf, bn ad lib) ed. by Max Seiffert, B&H, 1924.

---Trio No. 16, Op. 5, No. 1 in A major, ed. by Max Seiffert (2 v, vc, pf; 2 vl, vc, pf; 2 ob, vc or bn, pf) B&H 1924; Andraud (2 fl, vc, pf).

---Trio No. 17, Op. 5, No. 2 in B minor, ed. by Max Seiffert (2 ob or 2 fl, bn, pf) B&H, 1924.

---Trio No. 18, Op. 5, No. 3 in E minor (2 v, vc pf or 2 fl, vc, or bn, pf or 2 ob, vc or bn, pf) ed. by Max Seiffert, B&H, 1924; Andraud (2 fl, vc, pf).

---Trio No. 19, Op. 5, No. 4 in G major, ed. by Max Seiffert (2 v or fl, vc or bn, pf; 2 ob, vc or bn, pf) B&H, 1924; Andraud (2 fl, vc, pf); Music Press, Inc. (fl, ob, bn, pf).

---Trio No. 20, Op. 5, No. 5 in G minor (2 v or fl, vc or bn, pf; 2 ob, vc or bn, pf) ed. by Max Seiffert, B&H, 1924; Andraud (2 fl, vc, pf).

---Trio No. 21, Op. 5, No. 6 in F major, ed. by Max Seiffert (2 v or 2 fl, vc or bn, pf; 2 ob, vc or bn, pf) B&H, 1924; Andraud (2 fl, vc, pf).

---Trio No. 22, Op. 5, No. 7 in Bb major (2 v or 2 fl, vc or bn, pf; 2 ob, vc or bn, pf) ed. by Max Seiffert, B&H, 1924; Andraud (2 fl, vc, pf).

---Trio No. 23, in G minor, ed. by Max Seiffert (2 ob or 2 fl or 2 v, bn or vc, pf) B&H, 1934.

---Trio No. 24 in F major, ed. by Max Seiffert (ob, bn, vc, pf) B&H, 1938.

---Trio Sonata, Op. 2, No. 3 in Eb major (2 fl, vc, pf or 2 ob, vc, pf) H ed. by Schikkel, Heugel, 1924.

---Trio Sonata, Op. 1, No. 3 in Eb major (2 ob, bn, pf) Mercury.

HASSE, JOHANN ADOLF PETER, Six Sonatas, Op. 2 (2 fl or 2 v, vc, pf) Fetis.

HERBERT, VICTOR, Three Solitaires (3 cl, pf) Music Publishers Holding Corp.

HONNEGGER, ARTHUR, Rapsodie in C minor (2 fl, cl, pf) Senart, 1923; Sansone; Andraud; Hug.

HUBEAU, JEAN, Quartet, Sonatine Humoresque (fl, cl, h, pf) Baron.

IPPOLITOV-IVANOV, MIKHAIL MIKHAILOVICH, Two Kirghizian Songs (ob, cl, bn, pf) Andraud.

JANITSCH, JOHANN GOTTLIEB, Kammer Sonata, Op. 8 (2 fl, vc, pf or fl, ob, va, pf) B&H, 1937, ed. by Wolff.

KARG-ELERT, SIGFRID, Jugend Musik, Op. 139a in B major (fl, cl, h, pf) 1924, Zimmermann; Andraud; Musica Rara.

KRAFT, WALTER, Hochzeitsmusik (voice, fl, v or 2 fl, and organ, or pf) Barenreiter.

KRAKAMP, EMANUELE, Scherzo, Op. 100 (3 fl, pf) Baxter-Northrup.

KRATZ, ROBERT, Cuckoo, Nightingale, Quail, Joyous Intermezzo (fl, cl, h, pf) Andraud.

KREIN, G., Suite Hebraique (fl, cl, vc, pf) Leeds.

KREISLER, FRITZ, Liebesfreud, Midnight Bells (Heuberger), Schon Rosmarin, arr. by Erik Leidzen (3 cl, pf) EMB; Foley.

LEFEBVRE, CHARLES EDOUARD, Prelude from Second Suite, Op. 122, arr. by Waln (3 cl, pf) Kjos.

LEGRENZI, GIOVANNI, Sonata in D minor (2 fl, pf, vc ad lib) C. F. Peters.

LINIKE, JOHANN GEORG, Suite (2 fl, vc, pf) 1939, Vieweg; Hans Fischer.

LOCATELLI, PIETRO, Quartet, Op. 3, No. 1 in G major (2 fl or 2 v, vc, pf) 1906, B&H, ed. by Hugo Riemann, Collegium Musicum, 21; Andraud; AMP; International Music Co.

LOEILLET, JEAN-BAPTISTE, Three Sonatas (fl, ob, vc, h'chord) London, British Museum Catalogue .

----Sonatas (2 fl, vc, h'chord) London, British Museum Catalogue.

MARECHAL, Quartet (h, cl, harp, pf) Fetis Supplement.

MARIOTTE, A., On the Moutain (fl or ob, cl, eng h or bn, pf) Andraud.

MARTINI, GIOVANNI BATTISTA, Les Moutons, Celebrated Gavotte (ob, 2 bn, pf; ob, vc, bn, pf; cl, 2 bn, pf; cl, vc, bn, pf) Andraud.

MARX, KARL, Botschaft, Cantata with words by Friedrich Georg Junger (sop, 2 fl, pf) Barenreiter.

MAYEUR, L., Trio (fl, ob, cl, pf) Baxter-Northrup.

MIGOT, GEORGES, Quartet, atonal (fl, v, cl, harp) Sansone; Andraud; Sirene Musicale (min score, parts).

MILHAUD, DARIUS, Sonata, polytonal (fl, ob, cl, pf) 1923, Durand; Sansone; Andraud; Elkan-Vogel.

MILLAULT, EDOUARD, Sonata for Four in F major (fl, cl, v, pf) 1880, Lemoine.

MOZART, WOLFGANG AMADEUS, German Dance in A minor (fl, ob, bn, pf) C. F. Peters.

----Quintet for Piano, Oboe, Clarinet, Horn and Bassoon, K 452. Largo-Allegro Moderato, Larghetto, Rondo.

NAUMANN, KARL ERNST, Piano Quartet, Nun lasset uns beginnen (3
fl, pf; 3 ob, pf; 3 cl, pf) 1943, Simrock (score,
parts).
OLENIN, ALEXANDER ALEXEIEVITCH, Preludes Prairiales, Op. 30 (2
ob, v, pf) Andraud; Baxter-Northrup.
PACINI, GIOVANNI, Quartets (wind instruments, pf) Fetis Supplement.
PAGANINI, NICOLO, Perpetual Motion (fl, ob, cl, pf) arr. by
Whitney Tustin, Spratt.
PAISIBLE, JACQUES, Sonatas (2 fl, vc, pf; 2 fl, vc, pf; 2 ob,
vc, pf) No. 1 in D minor, No. 2 in G minor, No. 3 in F
major, No. 4 in C minor, No. 5 in C major. 1931, Moeck
(arr. by W. Friedrich); McGinnis & Marx.
PEPUSCH, JOHANN CHRISTOPHER, Trio Sonata in G minor (reco or fl,
ob or v, pf, vc ad lib) Peters, C. F. (Urtext).
PEZ, JOHANN CHRISTOPHER, Trio-Sonata in C major (2 fl, vc, pf)
arr. by W. Woehl, 1938, Rieter-Biedermann; C. F. Peters
(Urtext, arr. for 2 reco, pf, vc ad lib: Aria, Rondeaux,
Gavotte en Rondeaux, 2 Minuets, Gigue).
PROWO, P., Sonatas No. 5 and 6, in G minor and Bb major (2 fl, vc
pf) ed. by Wilhelm Friedrich, Moeck, 1940.
---Sonata No. 5 in G minor (2 fl or 2 ob, vc, pf) McGinnis &
Marx.
REICHA, ANTON, Grand Quartet, Op. 104 (fl, bn, vc, pf) Andraud;
Boieldieu; Zetter.
REICHERT, MATTHIEU ANDRE, Plaisanterie Musicale on Three German
Airs, Op. 13 (3 fl, pf) Andraud.
RUBENSTEIN, ERNST, Musik, Op. 34 in Eb major (fl, cl, v, pf) An-
draud; 1933, Litolff.
RIEGGER, WALLINGFORD, Three Canons (fl, ob, cl, bn) 1932, New
Music.
RIETI, VITTORIO, Sonata (fl, ob, bn, pf) 1926, Universal Edition;
Andraud.
ROLAND-MANUEL, Suite dans le gout espagnol (ob, bn, tpt, pf) Du-
rand; Elkan-Vogel.
RORICH, KARL, Burleske, Op. 64 in A minor (3 fl, pf) 1922, Zimmer-
mann; Andraud; Baxter-Northrup.
RUDIGER, THEODORE, Sinfonia Intermezzo (fl or ob, cl, bn, pf)
1932, published by author.
SABON, E., Helvetie in Ab (ob, or cl, bn, eng h, pf) Costallat.
SAINT-SAENS, CHARLES CAMILLE, Caprice on Danish and Russian Airs
Op. 79 in Bb major (fl, ob, cl, pf) Andraud; Durand;
Elkan-Vogel.
SALIERI, ANTOINE, Danse from "Tarare" (3 fl, pf or fl, ob, cl, pf)
Edition Musicus.
SAVAGE, H.S., Momento Giojoso (3 cl, pf) Cundy-Bettoney Co., Inc.
SCARLATTI, ALESSANDRO, Quartettino (3 fl, pf; 3 alto reco, pf,
vc ad lib) ed. by W. Woehl, C. F. Peters, (Urtext); 1941,
Rieter-Biedermann (3 fl, pf).
---Sonata (3 fl, pf) Ms, Santini Library, Munster.
SCHADEWITZ, KARL, Liedsinfoni, Op. 20 (sopr, h, fl, pf) 1921,
H. Palz, Wurzburg.
SCHERBER, FERDINAND, Quartet in Bb major (ob, cl, bass-cl, pf)
1914, C. F. Schmidt, Cefes-Edition; Andraud.

SCHICKHARD, JOHANN CHRISTIAN, Twelve Sonatas, Op. 7 (2 ob, bass viol, b.c.) Roger, Amsterdam; Fetis.
---Fourteen Sonatas, Op. 14 (ob, fl, bn, b.c.) Roger, Amsterdam; Fetis.
---Sonatas, Op. 22 (ob, 2 fl, pf) Roger, Amsterdam; Fetis.
SCHMITT, FLORENT, A Tour D'Anches, Op. 97 (ob, cl, bn, pf) MH Eble; Andraud; Durand; Elkan-Vogel.
SCHUBERT, FRANZ PETER SERAPH, Marche Militaire (fl, ob, v, pf) Andraud.
---Rosamunde, Entr'acte (fl, ob, cl, pf or fl, v, va, pf) Andraud; Cundy-Bettoney.
---Impromptu, Op. 142, No. 2 (fl, ob, cl, pf) Andraud; Carl Fischer (score, parts).
SCHUMANN, ROBERT ALEXANDER, Evening Song (fl, ob or cl, bn, pf) Andraud.
SCHUTZ, HEINRICH, Symphoniae Sacrae I (Gerber) No. 6: Jubilate Deo, Omnis Terra (Lob und Ehre gebt dem Herren, alle Volker) (bass, 2 fl or 2 v, b.c.) Barenreiter.
SOLA, CHARLES MICHAEL ALEXIS, Quartet, Op. 19 (fl, cl, vc or bn, pf) Leduc; Fetis.
SOURILAS, TH., Suite in F major (ob, h, vc, harp or pf) Lemoine; Andraud; Sansone; Baxter-Northrup.
STOLZEL, GOTTFRIED HEINRICH, Sonata in C minor, ed. by G. Frotscher (2 ob, bn or vc, pf) 1938, Bisping; Sansone.
---Trio-Sonata in F minor (2 ob, vc, pf) ed. by Helmuth Osthoff, Nagel.
---Trio-Sonata in F minor (2 ob, va, pf) ed. by Helmuth Osthoff, Nagel.
STRUCK, PAUL, Sonate, Op. 17 (cl, 2 h, pf) Leipzig, B&H; Fetis.
---Quartet, Op. 5 (fl, 2 h or 2 va) Mollo, Vienna; Fetis.
TELEMANN, GEORG PHILIPP, Quartet in G major (fl or reco, ob or v, v, pf, vc ad lib) C. F. Peters.
---Tafelmusik II, No. 4 in E minor, ed. by Max Seiffert, Collegium Musicum, No. 55 (fl, ob, vc, pf) 1927, B&H (score, parts); DDT, Vol. I 61/62, 1928; Andraud; AMP; Musica Rara, London.
---Quartet in G major (fl, ob, v, pf) ed. by W. Woehl, 1939, Rieter-Biedermann.
---Trio Sonata in C major (2 fl, vc, ad lib, pf) ed. by Adolph Hoffmann, 1937 B&H.
---Trio-Sonata in C major, ed. by Hugo Riemann, No. 67, Collegium Musicum (2 reco, vc, b.c.) Musica Rara, London; B&H.
---Trio Sonata in F major (2 fl, pf, vc ad lib; fl, ob, pf vc ad lib) McGinnis & Marx; Moeck 1939 (ed. by Rodemann); B&H 1937 (ed. by A. Hoffmann.
---Trio-Sonata in F major, ed. by Hugo Riemann, No. 66, Collegium Musicum (2 reco, vc, b.c.) Musica Rara; B&H.
---Tafelmusik II, No. 2 (D minor quartet) (2 fl, vc, pf) ed. by Max Seiffert, Collegium Musicum, No. 59; B&H, 1931; DDT Bd 61/62; Andraud.
---Trio in C minor (fl, ob, bn, pf) Robert Forberg (ed. by R. Lauschmann; Andraud.
---Quartet in G major (reco or fl, ob, v, pf, vc ad lib) ed.

by W. Woehl, C. F. Peters (Urtext).
---Trio Sonata in C minor (reco or fl, ob or v, pf, vc ad
lib) ed. by W. Woehl, C. F. Peters (Urtext).
---Quartet: Tafelmusik III, No. 2 in E minor (2 fl, vc, pf)
ed. by Max Seiffert, B&H, 1928; AMP.
---Sonata in A major, ed. by H. Schreiter (2 fl, vc, pf)
B&H, 1938.
---Die Kleine Kammermusik, Six Suites (fl, ob, v, pf) 1716;
Fetis.
TSCHAIKOWSKY, PETER ILITCH, Dance des Mirlitons (Dance of the
Reed Flutes, from the Nutcracker Suite, Op. 71) (3 fl,
pf) H Carl Fischer; Baxter-Northrup.
UCCELLINI, DOM MARCO, Die Hochzeit der Henne und des Kuckucks
(The Wedding of the Hen and the Cuckoo) Piano Quartet
(2 ob or cl, ob, or 2 cl, bn or vc, pf) 1930, Vieweg,
ed. by G. Lenzewski; Andraud (v, ob or cl, bn or vc, pf).
VERNIER, JEAN AME, Quartet, Op. 33 (ob, h, harp, pf) Janet;
Fetis.
WEISMANN, WILHELM, Divertimento, Op. 38 (cl, bn, h, pf).
WEISS, FRANZ, Symphonies Concertantes (fl, bn, trom, pf or orch)
Fetis.
WEISS, HANS, Ein Kurioser Kaffee-Klatsch, Op. 32 (fl, cl, v, pf)
Litolff; Andraud.
WEISSMANN, JULIUS, Divertimento, Op. 38 (cl, h, bn, pf)
WITT, CHRISTIAN FRIEDRICH, Suite in F minor (3 fl, pf) Baren-
reiter (score, parts).
WOEHL, WALDEMAR, Frohliche Spielmusik (2 fl or other wind instr,
bn or vc, pf ad lib) Barenreiter.
ZACHOW, FRIEDRICH WILHELM, Trio in F major (fl or ob, bn, pf, vc
ad lib) ed. by Max Seiffert, Kistner, 1929.

Collections

Collegium Musicum, Collection of nearly sixty seventeenth and
eighteenth century chamber music works (2 v, or fl, ob,
pf, vc ad lib) B&H.
Masters of the Baroque, Trio Sonatas by Buxtehude, Reinken,
Foerster, Schop, Becker (2 fl, pf, vc ad lib) C. F.
Peters.

Selective Quintets

ALBISI, Miniature Suite, No. 2 (fl, ob, cl, h, bn) Eble.
AMBROSIUS, HERMANN, Quintet, Op. 57 in B minor (fl, ob, cl, h,
    bn) 1925, Published by author in Leipzig.
ARNOLD, Three Shanties (fl, ob, cl, h, bn) Eble.
BALALEINIKOFF, V., Introduction and Scherzo (fl, ob, cl, h, bn)
    MH Belwin.
BARRAINE, ELSA, Ouvrage de Dame, Theme and Variations (Angelique,
    Berthe, Irene, Barbe--fugato burlesque--Sarah, Isabeau,
    Leocadie) (fl, ob, cl, h, bn) Andraud.
BENNETT, DAVID, Rhapsodette (fl, ob, cl, h, bn) H Fischer.
BENNETT, ROBERT RUSSELL, Dance Scherzo (fl, ob, cl, h, bn) Amer-
    ican Music Center.
BERKOWITZ, SOL, Serenade (fl, ob, cl, h, bn) Ms, Apt. 10F, 190-02
    64th Ave., Flushing, L.I.
BORCH, GASTON, Sunrise on the Mountains, arr. by Riebold (fl, ob,
    cl, h, bn) MH Belwin, Inc.
BOROWSKY, Madrigal to the Moon (fl, ob, cl, h, bn) MH Boosey-
    Hawkes (score, parts).
BOYD, CHARLES N., Suite for Woodwinds (fl, ob, cl, bn, h) trans.
    Corrente, Handel; Adagio, Guilmant; Finale, Haydn; Four
    Minuets in C major, Beethoven. Andraud; Music Publishers
    Holding Corp.
BUCKBOROUGH, JAMES L., Sonatine in Three Movements (fl, ob, cl,
    bn, h) MH Gamble Hinged Music Co.; Music Publishers
    Holding Corp. (score, parts).
BUONONCINI, GIOVANNI BATTISTA, Rondeau (fl, ob, cl, h, bn) An-
    draud.
BYERS, L. J., Suite for Woodwind Quintet, Division V, Op. I, Nos.
    1-7, Sarabande in G minor, Minuet in E major, Trio in E
    minor, Allemande in C major, Gigue in C major, Bourree in
    Ab major, Gavotte in F major (fl, ob, cl, h, bn) Ms. at
    Indiana University School of Music.
CAILLET, LUCIEN, Overture in Bb major (fl, ob, cl, h, bn) Elkan-
    Vogel.
CARTER, ELLIOT COOK, JR., Wind Quintet, 1948 (fl, ob, cl, h, bn)
    ACA.
CAZDEN, NORMAN, Three Constructions for Woodwind Quintet (fl, ob,
    cl, h, bn) Kalmus Editions (score, parts).
CHEMIN-PETIT, Quintet (fl, ob, cl, h, bn) Eble.
CLAPP, PHILIP G., Prelude and Finale (fl, ob, cl, h, bn) VH (rec)
    Boosey-Hawkes (score, parts).
COHEN, SOL B., Woodwind Quintet No. 2 (fl, ob, cl, h, bn) MH
    Belwin; Pro-Art Publications.
COLOMER, B.F., Bourree (fl, ob, cl, h, bn or bass-cl) MH Cundy-
    Bettoney Co.; Andraud.
COPPOLA, CARMINE, Woodwind Quintet (fl, ob, cl, h, bn) Ms. at 217-
    33 77th Ave., Utopia Sta., Flushing, L.I.
DANZI, FRANZ, Three Original Quintets (fl, ob, cl, h, bn) Andraud.
DAVIDOFF, SYDNEY E., Pop Goes the Weasel in A Major (fl, ob, cl,
    h, bn) Ms.
DE BUERIS, J., Petite Pastorale in Eb (fl, ob, 2 cl, bn) Briegel,
    Inc.

DEMUTH, NORMAN, Pastorale and Scherzo (fl, ob, cl, h, bn) Hin-
richsen; McGinnis & Marx.
DESLANDRES, ADOLPHE-EDOUARD-MARIE, Three Pieces (fl, ob, cl, h,
bn) Andante, Scherzo, Allegro. Andraud; Baxter-Northrup.
DITTERSDORF, KARL DITTERS VON, Three Pieces for Winds or Three
Partitas in F (2 ob, 2 h, bn) Collegium Musicum, No. 101;
B&H; McGinnis & Marx (parts).
DOUGLAS, Dance Caricatures: March, Valse, Polka, Country Dance,
Tango, Tarantella (fl, ob, cl, h, bn) C. F. Peters Corp.
(score, parts).
EISLER, HANNS, Op. 5, Palmstrom (voice, fl or picc, cl, v, vc)
1926. Universal Edition.
ELLIOTT, WILLARD, Woodwind Quintet (fl, ob, cl, h, bn) Ms. at
North State Teachers' College, Denton, Texas.
ERLEBACH, PHILIPP HEINRICH, Harmonische Freude Musikalischer
Freunde, Daraus Ausgewahlte Arien u. Duette (1 or 2 voice,
pf, 2 fl, vc or 3 ob, bn) arr. by Max Seiffert, 1929,
Kistner & Siegel.
ESSEX, KENNETH, Wind Quintet (fl, cl, ob, bn, h) Hinrichsen;
C. F. Peters.
FACTOR, DAVID VAN, Gavotte for Five (fl, ob, cl, h, bn)
FINE, IRVING, Partita for Wind Quintet, 1948 (fl, ob, cl, h, bn)
Boosey-Hawkes (rental.
FIORELLO, DANTE, Jigs and Reels (fl, ob, cl, h, bn)
FITELBERG, JERZY, Capriccio Quintet, atonal (fl, cl, bass-cl,
ob, trmb or bar or bn) 1931, Balan (min score, parts);
(fl, ob, cl, bass-cl, trmb) Andraud; Omega; Baron;
Chester; MH
FRANGKISER, CARL, Valse Emilie (fl, ob, cl, h, bn) MH Boosey-
Hawkes-Belwin, Inc.
---Episode from "Dedication" (fl, ob, cl, h, bn) MH Bel-
win, Inc.
FREED, ISADORE, Quintet for Woodwinds (fl, ob, cl, h, bn) Jul-
ius Hart Musical Foundation, Hartford, Conn.
FRICKER, P. RACINE, Woodwind Quintet, Op. 5 (fl, ob, cl, h, bn)
AMP.
FUSSAN, Music for Wind Quintet (fl, ob, cl, h, bn) Eble.
FUSSL, KARL HEINZ, Kleine Kammermusik: Moderately Fast, Song-
like, Fugue, Lively (fl, ob, cl, h, bn) MH 1943, Baren-
reiter (score, parts); Eble.
GERSTER, OTTMAR, Quintet, Jolly Music (fl, ob, cl, h, bn) 1938
Schott (score, parts); Andraud.
GIANNINI, VITTORIA, Quintet (fl, ob, cl, h, bn) 1903.
GRIMM, CARL HUGO, Quintet for Winds (fl, ob, cl, h, bn)
GUENTHER, R., Rondo (fl, ob, cl, h, bn) MH Cundy-Bettoney Co.
GUENTZEL, "Bas-Bleu", Air de Ballet (fl, ob, cl, h, bn) MH
C. L. Barnhouse.
GUILMANT, ALEXANDER, Canzonetta, arr. by Lawrence Taylor (fl,
ob, cl, h, bn) ME Gamble Hinged Music Co.; Music Pub-
lishers Holding Corp. (score, parts); Remick.
GUION, D. W., The Harmonica-Player (fl, ob, cl, h, bn)
HAAS, PAUL, Quintet, Op. 10 (fl, ob, cl, h, bn) 1935, Sadlo.
HALL, PAULINE, Suite for Woodwind Quintet in C. Major (fl, ob,
cl, h, bn) MS., Photostats from scores from Norwegian
Composers Society.

HAMERIK, EBBE, Woodwind Quintet (fl, ob, cl, h, bn) McGinnis & Marx (score, parts).

HARTLEY, GERALD, Divertissement (fl, ob, cl, h, bn) AMP.

HILLMANN, KARL, Capriccio, Op. 57 (fl, ob, cl, h, bn) VH Andraud; Belwin, Inc; Andre (min score, parts).

HIRSCHBACH, HERMANN, Quintet, Op. 40 in Bb major (v, va, vc, cl, h) Fetis; Kistner & Siegel.

 ---Quintet, Op. 41 in Bb major (v, va, vc, cl, h) Fetis; Kistner & Siegel.

 ---Quintet, Op. 48 in Eb major (v, va, vc, cl, h) Fetis; Kistner & Siegel.

HUFFNAGLE, Candlelight and Crystal (fl, ob, cl, h, bn) MH D. Gornston.

HUGHES, HERBERT, Three Satirical Songs (voice, fl, v, c., bn) Enoch.

HUGUENIN, CHARLES, Two Pieces in G major (fl, ob, cl, h, bn) Huguenin, Paris.

JOHN, FRITZ, Six Transcribed Quintets from the Masters: Menuett, Haydn; Dittersdorf, Deutscher Tanz; Kuhlau, Rondo Burlesco; Mozart, Menuett; Gossec, Gavotte; Mozart, Deutscher Tanz (fl, ob, cl, h, bn) Andraud.

KEITH, GEORGE D., Woodwind Quintet (fl, ob, cl, h, bn) MH Boosey-Hawkes.

KENNEN, KENT, Woodwind Quintet (fl, ob, cl, h, bn) Ms., University of Texas.

KOTSCHAU, JOHANN, Quintet, Op. 14 (fl, ob, cl, h, bn) Andraud; Zimmermann.

KROL, Eight Pieces for Woodwinds (fl, ob, cl, h, bn) Eble.

KUHNEL, EMIL, A Little Suite, Op. 29 (fl, ob, cl, h, bn) Grosch; Deutsche Ostseebilder.

LABATE, BRUNO, Intermezzo, Scherzino (fl, ob, 2 cl, bn) Spratt.

LABEY, MARCEL, Quintet for Wind Instruments (fl, ob, cl, h, bn) 1923, Eschig; 1923, Rouart.

LAURISCHKUS, MAX, Quintet, Op. 23, Lithanian Suite (fl, ob, cl, h, bn) H (rec) 1914, Simrock (score, parts); Andraud; Hug.

LECLAIR, JEAN MARIE, Three Petite Pieces de Concert (fl, ob, cl, h, bn) 1. Pfeiffer Pastoral; 2. Menuet; 3. Hunting Scene. H Andraud.

LEFEBVRE, CHARLES EDOUARD, Allegretto Scherzando, Suite, Op. 57 (fl, ob, cl, h, bn) MH 1910, Hamelle (score, parts); Pro-Art Publications; Sansone; Cundy-Bettoney.

LEFEBVRE, CHARLES EDOUARD, Canon from Suite, Op. 57 (fl, ob, cl, h, bn) MH Pro-Art Publications; Sansone; Hamell, (score, parts); Cundy-Bettoney.

 ---Finale, Allegro Leggiero, from Suite Op. 57 (fl, ob, cl, h, bn) MH Pro-Art Publications; Sansone; Hamelle, (score, parts); Cundy-Bettoney.

 ---Prelude from Second Suite for Woodwinds, Op. 122, arr. by W. Waln (fl, ob, cl, h, bn) ME-MH Neil A. Kjos.

LEMARE, E. H., Andantino (fl, ob, cl, h, bn) Arr. by G. J. Trinkhaus, Andraud; Franklin.

LIST, KURT, Quintet (fl, ob, cl, h, bn)

LONGAZO, GEORGE, Woodwind Quintet: Allegro, Moderato, Rondo (fl, ob, cl, h, bn) Indiana University School of Music.

LOURIE, ARTHUR, Pastoral de la Volga (ob, bn, 2 va, vc) Eschig;
        Baron; Andraud; AMP.
LUIGINI, A.C.L.J., Ballet Egyptian, March Miniature, Woodwind
        Quintet, No. 1, arr. by G. E. Holmes (fl, ob, cl, h, bn)
        ME C. L. Barnhouse, Inc.
MAGANINI, QUINTO E., FoxTrot Burlesque on "Simple Aveu" (fl, ob,
        cl, h, bn) Andraud; Carl Fischer (score, parts).
MAHMOUD, PARVIZ, Woodwind Quintet, based on a Persian Folk Song
        (fl, ob, cl, h, bn) Indiana University School of Music;
        19 W. 85 St., NYC.
MARECHAL, HENRI, Air du Guet in C Major (fl, ob, cl, h, bn) Mer-
        cury; Heugel, Paris.
MARTIN, FRANK, Prestissimo (fl, ob, cl, h, bn) MH Boosey-Hawkes
        (score, parts).
MCBRIDE, ROBERT, Cuatro Milpas Por Un Quinteto (fl, ob, cl, bn,
        contra-bn) ACA
MCKAY, GEORGE FREDERICK, Woodwind Quintet, 1932 (fl, ob, cl, h,
        bn)
MILLER, RALPH DALE, Three American Dances (fl, ob, cl, h, bn) C.
        Fischer.
NECKE, Mills of Sans-Souci (fl, ob, cl, h, bn) E Mills Music,
        Inc.
NIELSEN, CARL AUGUST, Serenata-Invato (cl, bn, h, vc, contra-bn)
        MH Eble; Skandinavisk Musikforlag; McGinnis & Marx.
        (score, parts); Musica Rara (called Serenata-Invana).
OUBRADOUS, FERNAND, Fantaisie Dialogue in D Major (fl, ob, cl,
        h, bn) L'Oiseau Lyre.
PALMER, ROBERT, Concerto (fl, v, cl, eng h, vc) in blueprint.
PERISSAS, MADELEINE, A Scotch Suite: Pibroch, Reel, Hornpipe,
        Stathspey, Coronach, Jig (fl, ob, cl, h, bn) Andraud.
PIERNE, PAUL, Suite Pittoresque (fl, ob, cl, h, bn) 1936,
        Buffet, Crampon.
PLEYEL, IGNACE JOSEPH, Rondo. (fl, ob, cl, h, bn) arr. by Harry
        C. Geiger, Remick; Music Publishers Holding Corp; An-
        draud.
POLDOWSKI, LADY DEAN PAUL, Suite Miniature, arr. by G. Barrere
        (fl, ob, cl, h, bn) ME-H (rec) Andraud; Galaxy Music
        Corp.
PRAGER, HEINRICH ALOYS, Quintet, Op. 12 in Bb major (fl, 2 cl,
        va, bn) B&H.
REICHEL, A., Two Quintets (fl, ob, cl, h, bn) Andraud.
RUBBRA, EDMUND, The Buddha, Op. 64 (fl, ob, v, va, vc) Mills;
        Lengnick.
RUBENSTEIN, ANTON GREGOROVITCH, Quintet, Op. 5 (h, bn, ob, cl,
        fl) Sansone.
SCHAEFER, T., Quintet (fl, ob, cl, h, bn) 1940, Pazdirek.
SEKLES, BERNHARD, Fifteen Little Chamber Pieces (fl, cl, va, vc,
        percussion)
SEMMLER, ALEX, Quintet for Winds (fl, ob, cl, h, bn)
SHARMAN, GRANT, Woodwind Quintet (fl, ob, cl, h, bn) Publ. in
        facsimile Ms. New Music, 2305 Red River, Austin, Texas.
SHULMAN, ALAN, Folk Songs (fl, ob, cl, h, bn)
SIEGMEISTER, ELIE, Wind Quintet, 1932 (fl, ob, cl, h, bn)
SIMON, JOSEPH, Quintett (fl, ob, cl, h, bn)
SKILTON, CHARLES SANFORD, Sarabande for Winds (fl, ob, cl, h, bn)

SOBECK, JOHANN, Quintet, Op. 11 (fl, ob, cl, h, bn) H Belwin
    (each movement published separately).
  ---Quintet, Op. 14 (fl, ob, cl, h, bn) H Belwin (each move-
    ment published separately).
  ---Andante Sostenuto, Op. 11, 1st mvt in Eb major (fl, ob,
    cl, h, bn) H Bosworth; Belwin, Inc.
  ---Larghetto Finale, Op. 11 in Eb major (fl, ob, cl, h, bn)
    H Bosworth; Belwin, Inc.
  ---Allegretto Giojoso, Op. 11, 3rd mvt in Eb major (fl, ob,
    cl, h, bn) Bosworth; Belwin, Inc.
  ---Allegro Mosso, Op. 14 in G minor, 1st mvt (fl, ob, cl, h,
    bn) H Bosworth; Belwin, Inc.
  ---Tarantelle Finale, Op. 14 in G minor (fl, ob, cl, h, bn)
    H Bosworth; Belwin, Inc.
SPENCER, O.W., Playtime in Bb (fl, ob, cl, h, bn) Briegel.
STARER, ROBERT, Serenade for Wind Quintet (fl, ob, cl, h, bn)
STEIN, LEON, Quintet for Winds (fl, ob, cl, h, bn) ACA; De Paul
    University, 64 E. Lake St., Chicago, Ill.
STICH, JOHANN WENZEL, Quintet (h, fl, strings)
STRINGFIELD, LAMAR, A Moonshiner Laughs (fl, ob, cl, h, bn) An-
    draud.
TARP, SVEND ERIK, Serenade (fl, cl, v, va, vc) 1934, Edition
    Dania (min score, parts); Kistner & Siegel; Andraud;
    McGinnis & Marx (score, parts).
TARTINI, GIUSEPPE, Largo, Quintet from violin sonata in G minor
    arr. by G. J. Trinkaus (fl, ob, cl, h, bn) Andraud; Mu-
    sic Publishers Holding Corp.(score, parts).
TAYLOR, LAWRENCE, Suite Miniature in F Major (fl, ob, cl, h, bn)
    E Gamble Hinged Music Co; Music Publishers Holding
    Corp. (score, parts).
TOCCHI, GIANLUCCA, Arlecchino (fl, cl, v, va, vc) Carisch 1938.
TREMBLAY, GEORGE, Wind Quintet (fl, ob, cl, h, bn)
TURNER, GODFREY, Suite for Wind Quintet (fl, ob, cl, h, bn)
TUTHILL, BURNET CORWIN, Quintet, Op. 9, Variations on "When Johnny
    Comes Marching Home" (fl, ob, cl, h, bn) Sansone.
WASSILENKO, SERGIE NIKIFOROVITCH, On Turkish Folk Songs, Op. 65
    (fl, ob, cl, bn, percussion) 1932, Universal Editions;
    Peters.
VON WEBER, CARL MARIA, Rondo (fl, ob, cl, h, bn) H Gamble Hinged
    Music Co; Remick; Music Publishers Holding Corp. (score,
    parts, transc. by Maruits Kesnar).
WEBER, JOSEPH MIROSLAV, Quintet, 1900 (fl, cl, ob, h, bn)
WEBER, LUDWIG, Quintet (fl, cl, ob, h, bn)
WEBERN, ANTON VON, Six Songs, Op. 14 (cl, bass-cl, v, vc, voice)
WEIGEL, EUGENE, Short, Slow and Fast for Woodwind Quintet (fl,
    ob, cl, h, bn) University of Illinois, Urbana; ACA.
WEINGARTNER, FELIX VON, Quintet, Op. 40 in C Major (2 v, 2 ob,
    vc) B&H.
WELLONES, PIERRE, Le Cantique des Cantiques, Adaptation Poetique
    de Jean Labor (3 voices, fl, bn) 1926, Senart.
WHARTON, JOHN, Woodwind Quintet (fl, ob, cl, h, bn) H. Carbon-
    dale, Illinois.
WHITE, FELIX HAROLD, Four Proverbs, 1925 (fl, ob, v, va, vc)
    Stainer & Bell.
WHITNEY, Adagio and Fugue (fl, cl, v, va, vc) Composers Press.

WOOLETT, HENRY, Quintette in E Major (fl, ob, cl, h, bn) Ms.
  at Eastman.
ZILCHER, HERMANN, Quintet, Op. 91 (fl, ob, cl, h, bn) W. Muller.

Cumulative Quintets

BADINGS, HENK, Quintet No. 1, 1929 (fl, ob, cl, bn, h) Stich-
  ting Donemus.
  ---Quintet No. 2, 1948 (fl, ob, cl, bn, h) Stichting Done-
  mus.
BARROWS, JOHN R., JR., Woodwind Quintet (fl, ob, cl, h, bn) 117
  MacDougal St., NYC.
BEACH, MRS. H.H.A., Pastorale (fl, ob, cl, h, bn) MH The Com-
  posers Press, Inc.
BEEKHUIS, HANNA, Elegie en Humoreske, 1939 (fl, ob, cl, h, bn)
  Stichting Donemus.
BEETHOVEN, LUDWIG VAN, Allegro from Symphony No. 5 (fl, ob, cl,
  h, bn) MH C. L. Barnhouse, Inc.
  ---Adagio and Minuetto from Sonata Op. 2, No. 1 (fl, ob, cl,
  h, bn) MH Witmark; Music Publishers Holding Corp.
  (arr. by G. J. Trinkaus, score, parts).
BESOZZI, CARLO, 24 Sonatas for Quintet (2 ob, 2 h, bn)
BEYER, J.M., Quintet for Winds (fl, ob, cl, h, bn)
  ---A Movement for Wind Quintet (fl, ob, cl, h, bn)
BIZET, GEORGES, Minuetto from Second L'Arlesienne (fl, ob, cl,
  h, bn) H C. L. Barnhouse, Inc; Andraud; Fischer; EMB,
  (arr. by G. E. Holmes).
BLANC, ADOLPHE, Quintet (fl, cl, h, ob, bn) Fetis.
BOOCHERINI, LUIGI, Menuet (fl, ob, cl, h, bn) Andraud.
BRANDL, JEAN, Quintettes Pour le Basson et Pour la Flute, Fetis.
BRESCIA, DOMENICO, Dithyrambic Suite (fl, ob, h, cl, bn)
BRUNMAYER, ANDRE, Six Quintets (5 wind instruments) Fetis.
BUTTING, MAX, Quintet, Op. 22 (ob, cl, v, va, vc) 1926, Tis-
  cher & Jagenberg.
CHANDLER, Valse Emilie in C major (fl, ob, cl, h, bn) Boosey
  & Hawkes (score, parts).
COHEN, SOL B., Minuet-Fantasy (fl, ob, cl, h, bn) MH (rec)
  C. Fischer; Eble.
  ---March-Miniature (fl, ob, cl, h, bn) ME Carl Fischer.
COLACO OSORIO, Suite Voor Blazers, 1948 (Reine Swaab) (fl, ob,
  cl, h, bn) Stichting Donemus).
CORBETT, WILLIAM, Six Sonatas (2 ob or tpt, 2 v, bass)
CROUSE, E., A Grecian Ballet in C Major (fl, ob, cl, bn, h) Ms.
DANZI, FRANZ, Gypsy Dance, from Quintet, Op. 56, No. 2 in G Mi-
  nor (fl, ob, cl, h, bn) MH (rec) Fischer, (arr. by Mag-
  anini, score, parts); Andraud.
DAQUIN, LOUIS CLAUDE, The Cuckoo, Quintet in E Minor (fl, ob, 2
  cl, bn) Andraud; Music Publishers Holding Corp. (arr.
  by Phillip Gordon, score, parts).
DAVISE, HUGO, Danse Suite (fl, ob, cl, h, bn)
DENARDIS, CAMILLO, Allegro Giocoso in Eb Major (Thematic Bass)
  (fl, ob, cl, h, bn) Ms., copy available from composer
  who is a bassoonist at Met.

DORNAUS, LUCAS, Six Petites Pieces, Op. 2 (bn, 2 h, 2 cl) Fetis; Offenbach.
DRAESEKE, FELIX, Quintet, Op. 48 (fl, v, va, vc, h) Andraud.
DUBOIS, CLEMENT FRANCOIS THEODORE, Premiere Suite (fl, ob, cl, h, bn) Mercury.
---Deuxieme Suite (fl, ob, cl, h, bn) Leduc (score, parts).
EGGE, KLAUS, Quintettes, 13 (fl, ob, cl, h, bn) Ms., Photostats available from scores with Norwegian Composers Society.
EMBORG, J. L., Quintet, Op. 47 (fl, ob, cl, h, bn) Edition Dania.
ERDLEN, HERMANN, Quintet, Op. 27, No. 1, Little Variations on A Spring Song (fl, ob, cl, h, bn) 1932, Zimmermann, (min score, parts); Andraud.
FARLEY, R., The Night Wind (fl, ob, cl, h, bn).
FELTRE, ALPHONSE CLARKE, Quintets (wind instruments) Fetis.
FIORILLO, FREDERIC, Quintet (h, fl, ob, or cl, v, va, bass) Sieber; Fetis.
FLOTHIUS, MARIUS, Quintet, Op. 13, (fl, ob, cl, bn, bass-cl) Stichting Donemus.
FRID, GEZA, Serenade, Op. 4, 1928 (fl, 2 cl, bn, h) Stichting Donemus.
GABRIEL-MARIE, Berceuse (fl, ob, cl, h, bn) Andraud.
GEBAUER, FRANCOIS RENE, Wind Quintets (wind instruments) Fetis.
---Six Works (wind instruments) Hentz-Jouve; Sieber; Fetis.
GODARD, BENJAMIN LOUIS PAUL, Gigue (fl, ob, cl, h, bn) arr. by George J. Trinkaus; Andraud; Franklin.
GOEPFERT, CHARLES ANDRE, Twelve Pieces of Harmony, Op. 26, Books I and II (2 cl, 2 h, bn) Offenbach; Andre; Fetis.
GRIMM, CARL HUGO, A Little Serenade, Op. 36 in D Major (Intrada, h; Alla Sarabanda, cl, bn; Scherzino, fl, ob; Finale, fl, cl, ob, h, bn) Andraud.
GUENTZEL, Scherzo, Op. 17 (fl, ob, cl, h, bn) H C. L. Barnhouse, Inc.
---Tarantella (fl, ob, cl, h, bn) H C. L. Barnhouse, Inc.
GYROWETZ, ADALBERT, Serenade, Op. 3 (2 cl, 2 h, bn) Fetis.
---Serenade, Op. 32 (2 cl, 2 h, bn) Offenbach; Andre; Fetis.
HAMM, JOHANN V., Abenstaendchen Lied in F Major (4 h, cl) C. F. Schmidt.
HAYDN, FRANZ JOSEPH, Presto in C Major (fl, ob, cl, h, bn) Andraud.
---Minuet from Symphony No. 11 (fl, ob, cl, h, bn) MH Andraud; C. L. Barnhouse, Inc.
---Allegretto from Symphony No. 11 (fl, ob, cl, h, bn) ME C. L. Barnhouse, Inc.
HENKEMANS, HANS, Kwintet, 1934 (fl, ob, cl, bn, h) Stichting Donemus.
HERMANN, FRIEDRICH, Zur Ubung im Zu in D Major (fl, ob, cl, h, bn) B&H.
HOSMER, JAMES B., Fugue in C Major (fl, ob, cl, h, bn) H Music Publishers Holding Corp. (score, parts); Gamble Hinged Music Co.; Music Publishers Holding Corp., (score, parts).
HUFFER, FRED K., Sailor's Hornpipe, Concert Paraphrase (fl, ob, cl, h, bn) Andraud; Music Publishers Holding Corp., (score, parts).

JACOBSON, MAURICE, Four Pieces (fl, ob, v, va, vc) Curwen.
KANKAROWITSCH, Aquarelles (fl, ob, cl, h, bn) 1942, Andraud.
KERN, FRIDA, Woodwind Quintet (fl, ob, cl, h, bn) Grosch.
KING, HAROLD C., Kwintet, 1940 (fl, ob, cl, bn, h) Stichting
  Donemus.
KLUGHARDT, AUGUST FRIEDRICH, Quintet in C major (fl, ob, cl, h,
  bn) H (rec) Zimmermann, 1901; Andraud.
  ---Finale from Quintet in C major (fl, ob, cl, h, bn) H
   Rubank.
KOLB, JEAN BAPTISTE, Quintets and Trios (ob, cl, bn) Fetis.
LACHNER, FRANZ, Two Quintets for Wind Instruments, Fetis.
LANDRE, GUILLAUME, Quintetto (fl, ob, cl, bn, h) 1930, Stich-
  ting Donemus.
LANGE, HANS, Quintet, Op. 40 in Ab major (Bohmische Musikanten)
  (fl, ob, cl, h, bn) 1937, Published by author, Berlin.
  ---Quintet, Op. 14 in D major (fl, ob, cl, h, bn) 1937,
   Published by author, Berlin.
LEWIN, G., Quintet (fl, ob, cl, h, bn) Andraud.
LICKL, JOHANN GEORG, Quintet (fl, ob, cl, h, bn) Haslinger;
  Fetis.
LILGE, HERMANN, Variations and Fugue, Op. 67 (fl, ob, cl, h, bn)
  1937, Kistner and Siegel (min score, parts); Andraud.
LINDNER, FRIEDRICH, Quintet for Wind Instruments, Op. 1 in Bb
  major (fl, ob, cl, h, bn) Fetis; Hofmeister.
LINDPAINTNER, PETER JOSEF, Symphonie Concertante, Op. 36 (fl,
  ob, cl, h, bn) Schott; Fetis.
  ---Symphonie Concertante, Op. 4 (fl, ob, cl, h, bn) Schott;
   Fetis.
LISZT, FRANZ, Pastorale from "Les Preludes" (fl, ob, cl, h, bn)
  H Galaxy Music Corporation (arr. by Hamilton); Andraud.
MAGANINI, QUINTO E., Reverie, arr. by Harris (fl, ob, cl, h, bn)
  Andraud.
MALZAT, JOHANN MICHAEL, Four Quintets (fl, ob) Fetis.
MANDIC, JOSEPH, Woodwind Quintet (fl, ob, or eng h, cl, h, bn)
  1933, Universal Edition.
MANGOLD, WILHELM, Quintet for Wind Instruments, Schott; Fetis.
MARIE, GABRIEL, Berceuse in Bb, arr. by Harris (fl, ob, cl, h,
  bn) Cundy-Bettoney.
MASSON, FERNAND, Quintet (ob, bn, v, va, vc) 1917, Selva.
MATTIE-KLICKMAN, Victoria Gavotte in Ab major (fl, ob, cl, h,
  bn) Standard.
MCCOLLIN, FRANCES, Diversion for Five Winds (fl, ob, cl, h, bn)
MCKINLEY, CARL, Suite for Five (fl, ob, cl, h, bn)
MEDERACKE, JURT, Bohmische Suite, Op..43, Praludium, Scherzo,
  Adagio, Polka, Finale (fl, ob, cl, h, bn) MH Eble; Hof-
  meister.
MEEK, CHARLES, Slumber Suite: Relaxation, Day Dream, Awakening
  (fl, ob, cl, h, bn).
MENEAU, LEON, Quintettes (strings and winds) Fetis Supplement.
MENGAL, MARTIN JOSEPH, Three Quintets (fl, ob, cl, h, bn) Ple-
  yel; Fetis.
MILLS, CHARLES, Chamber Concertante for Wind Quintet (fl, ob,
  cl, h, bn).
MORITZ, KURT, Quintet, Op. 12, Heitere Suite (fl, ob, 2 cl, bn)
  1938, Ries & Erler; Eble; Andraud.

MORTENSEN, OTTO, Quintette in C major (fl, ob, cl, h, bn) Hansen.
MORTENSEN, Quintet, (fl, ob, cl, h, bn) McGinnis & Marx.
MOYZES, ALEXANDER, Woodwind Quintet, Op. 17 in Bb major (fl, ob, cl, h, bn) 1943, Simrock.
MUFFAT, GEORG, Suiten aus dem Blumenbuschlein (5 winds) ed. by W. Woehl, Barenreiter, 1938.
MULLER-RUDOLSTADT, WILLY, Quintet (fl, ob, cl, h, bn) 1933, Grosch.
NERO, Monsoon in Bb (fl, ob, cl, h, bn) Fischer.
NEVIN, ETHELBERT W., Gondolieri, arr. by Phillip Gordon (fl, ob, cl, h, bn) Presser.
NOHR, CHRISTIAN FRIEDRICH, Pot-pourri, Op. 3 (fl, ob, cl, h, bn) Fetis; Leipzig, B&H.
NORMAND, A., Quintet, Op. 45 in E major (fl, ob, cl, h, bn) Andraud; Baxter-Northrup; 1890, Vernede, Versailles (score parts).
NYMAN, UNO, Arctic Suite (fl, ob, cl, h, bn).
PESSARD, EMILE LOUIS FORTUNE, Prelude and Minuet from "Captain Fracasse" (fl, ob, cl, h, bn) Baron; Andraud.
---Aubade, Op. 6 in D major (fl, ob, cl, h, bn) MH 1880, Leduc; Cundy-Bettoney Co; Sansone; Baron; Andraud.
PFEIFFER-LECLAIR, JEAN MARIE, Three Petite Pieces de Concert (fl, ob, cl, h, bn) H Andraud.
PIERCE, EDWIN H., Quintet in Bb major: German Dance, Dittersdorf; Rondeau, Steibelt; Gavotte, Wesley (fl, ob, cl, h, bn) H Gamble Hinged Music Co; Music Publishers Holding Corp., (score, parts).
---Allegro Piacevole and Scherzo (fl, ob, cl, h, bn) MH Gamble Hinged Music Co; Remick; Music Publishers Holding Corp. (score, parts).
PIERNE, GABRIEL, Pastorale, Op. 14, No. 1 (fl, ob, cl, h, bn) MH Cundy-Bettoney Co; Sansone; Baron; Andraud.
---March of the Little Tin Soldiers (fl, ob, cl, h, bn) ME Andraud; Cundy-Bettoney (fl, ob, cl, bn or 4 Bb cl, with pf acc, trans. by Georges Grisez.)
PIJPER, WILLEM, Quintet, 1929 (fl, ob, cl, bn, h) Stichting Donemus.
PINSUTI, CIRO, Scherzino, transc. by M. A. Springer (2 fl or fl and ob, 2 Bb cl, bn) Music Publishers Holding Corp., (score, parts).
PITICCHIO, PETER PAUL, Fifteen Quintets (2 ob, 2 h, bn) Fetis.
POLDOWSKI, LADY DEAN PAUL, Miniature Suite in Five Parts, arr. by Georges Barrere (fl, ob, cl, h, bn) MH Galaxy Music Corp.
PONSE, LUCTOR, Deux Pieces Pour Quintette a Vent, 1943 (fl, ob, cl, h, bn) Stichting Donemus.
PORSCH, GILBERT, Suite Modique for Quintet: Prelude, Valse Caprice, Scherzo Legere (fl, ob, cl, h, bn) H Remick; Gamble Hinged Music Co; Music Publishers Holding Corp., (score, parts).
PRAAG, HENRI C. VAN, Kwintet, 1938 (fl, ob, cl, h, bn) Stichting Donemus.
---Kwintet, 1948 (fl, ob, cl, h, bn) Stichting Donemus.

PRAEGER, HENRI ALOYS, Quintet, Op. 12 (va, 2 cl, fl, bn) Fetis.
PYLE, FRANCIS, Pastorale and Allegro for Woodwind Quintet (fl,
        ob, cl, h, bn) Ms, Dr. Paul Oberg, Univ. of Minnesota.
RANDERSON, HORACE EDWARD, Quintet for Wind Instruments (fl, ob,
        cl, h, bn).
RAPAPORT, EDA, Indian Legend (fl, ob, cl, h, bn) AMP; Baron.
RUMLER, JOHANN, Quintet, Op. 6 (2 cl, 2 h, bn) Gombart; Fetis.
RUMMEL, CHRISTIAN, Quintuor, Op. 41 in Bb major (ob, cl, h, bn,
        basset-h) Schott; Fetis.
    ---Quintet, Op. 42 (basset-h, eng h, cl, fl, bn) Fetis;
        Schott.
SANTO, SAMUEL BENJAMIN, Twenty-Four Pieces for Four and Five
        Wind Instruments. Fetis.
SCHMITT, NICOLAS, Three Quintets of Concert Airs, arr. (cl, bn,
        2 va, vc) Pleyel; Fetis.
    ---Three Quintets (fl, ob, cl, h, bn) Pleyel; Fetis.
SCHMUTZ, ALBERT D., Scherzo Poetique (fl, ob, cl, h, bn) MH
        Cundy-Bettoney Co.
SCHWARZ, LEONID, Oriental Suite (fl, ob, cl, h, bn) 1932, Rus-
        sicher Musikverlag; Universal Edition (score, parts);
        Andraud (fl, ob, cl, bn, drums or perc.).
SHEPERD, ARTHUR, Divertissement for Winds (fl, ob, cl, h, bn).
SIERING, MORITZ, Serenade, Op. 15 in G major (v, va, vc, fl, ob
        or cl) 1860, Hoffarth.
SMETACEK, VACLAV, Suite, Aus dem Leben der Insekten (fl, ob, cl,
        h, bn) 1939, Editions Continental, Prague (score, parts).
SOATTA, G., Quintet (fl, 2 va, bn, vc) Ricordi.
SOBECK, JOHANN, "Lucia di Lammermoor" Quintet (solo-cl, fl, ob,
        bn, h) Andraud.
SODERO, CESARE, Valse Scherzo (fl, ob, cl, h, bn) MH Baron;
        Andraud; AMP.
    ---Morning Prayer (fl, ob, cl, h, bn) MH Andraud; AMP.
STRAESSER, EWALD, Quintet (fl, ob, cl, h, bn) Ms, Berlin Ton-
        kunstlerverein prize.
THEUSS, KARL THEODORE, Serenade, Op. 21 (fl, cl, 2 h, bn) Fe-
        tis; Gombart.
TURECHEK, EDWARD, Introduction and Scherzo (fl, ob, cl, h, bn)
        H Witmark; Andraud; Music Publishers Holding Corp.
        (score, parts).
VALEN, FARTEIN OLAV, Serenade, Op. 42, atonal (fl, ob, cl, h,
        bn) Ms., Photostats available from scores, Norwegian
        Composers Society.
VALLENTIN, ARTHUR, Quintet, Op. 30 in G major (ob, cl, 2 h, bn)
        1941, published by author.
WEIS, FLEMING, Serenade, Uden Reele Hensigter (fl, ob, cl, h,
        bn) 1941, Hansen (min score, parts).
WIJDEVELD, WOLFGANG, Kwintet, 1934 (fl, ob, cl, h, bn) Stich-
        ting Donemus.
WILDSCHUT, CLARA, Kleine Serenade, 1946 (fl, ob, cl, h, bn)
        Stichting Donemus.
WOLF, FRANZ XAVIER, Two Quintets (2 cl, 2 h, bn) Hulaeufer;
        Fetis.
WOOD, THOMAS, Scherzo, The Brewhouse at Bures (fl, ob, cl, h,
        bn) 1929, Stainer and Bell (score, parts).
WUILLEUMIER, Quintet in D minor (fl, ob, cl, h, bn) Andraud.

ZAGWIJN, HENRI, Quintetto, 1948 (fl, ob, cl, h, bn) Stichting
        Donemus.
ZOLLER, CARL, Quintet, Op. 132 in F major (fl, ob, cl, h, bn)
        1883, Cubitt, London.

Collections

Collection of Four Quintets: 1. Jongen, Op. 98, Preambule and
        Dances; 2. Grimm, C. H., Op. 36, A Little Serenade: In-
        trado for Horn alone, Alla Sarabanda (cl, bn), Scherzino
        (fl, ob), Finale (fl, ob, cl, h, bn); 3. Leclair, Min-
        uet and Hunting Scene; 4. Liszt, Pastoral, Longing for
        Home, Eclog (fl, ob, cl, h, bn) Andraud.

Training Quintets

BACH, JOHANN SEBASTIAN, Saraband, arr. by Henschel (fl, ob, cl, h, bn) Eble.
   ---Sarabande in D minor from 1st French Suite (fl, ob, cl, h, bn) ME Boosey-Hawkes (score, parts); arr. by T.M. Finney.
BARGIEL, WOLDEMAR, Meditation, arr. by Harris (fl, ob, cl, h, bn) E Cundy-Bettoney Co; Andraud.
BARNBY, JOSEPH, Now the Day is Over, transc. by O. B. Wilson (fl, 3 Bb cl, bn) Music Publishers Holding Corp. (score, parts).
BARRERE, GEORGES, Twelve Transcriptions, Books I and II, arr. (fl, ob, cl, h, bn) ME-MH (rec) Schirmer; Andraud; Juilliard Series of Music for Wind Ensemble. Book I: Bach, Davis, Delibes, Loomis, Rameau, Schubert. Book II: Beethoven, Farley, Grieg, Guion, Mozart, Stravinsky.
BEETHOVEN, LUDWIG VAN, Country Dance (fl, ob, cl, h, bn) ME Carl Fischer; Andraud.
   ---Gavotte in F major (fl, ob, cl, h, bn) ME Fischer; Andraud.
BUECHE, Woodwind Holiday (fl, ob, cl, h, bn) ME Bourne, Inc.
CARABELLA, EZIO, Woodwind Suite (fl, ob, cl, h, bn) H-VH 1933, Ricordi (score, parts); Andraud.
CHAILLEY, JACQUES, Barcarolle (fl, ob, cl, h, bn) ME Eble; Alphonse Leduc.
COHEN, SOL B., Forest Lullaby, Part I (fl, ob, cl, h, bn) E Fischer.
   ---Suite in Three Parts, Parts I and III (published separately) ME-E (fl, ob, cl, h, bn) Fischer.
COLOMER, B. F., Menuet (fl, ob, cl, h, bn or bass-cl) ME Andraud; Cundy-Bettoney Co.
CORELLI, ARCANGELO, Sarabande and Courante, arr. by G. J. Trinkaus (fl, ob, cl, h, bn) ME Kay & Kay Music Publishing Co; Franklin; Andraud.
DURAND, MARIE AUGUSTE, Rococo Menuet (fl, ob, cl, h, bn or bass-cl) Arthur P. Schmidt Co.
GAYFER, Suite (fl, cl, ob, h, bn) Boosey & Hawkes.
GROFE, FERDE, Huckleberry Finn, from Mississippi Suite, arr. by G. E. Waln (fl, ob, cl, h, bn).
GUENTZEL, In the Meadow, Pastorale (fl, ob, cl, h, bn) ME C. L. Barnhouse.
   ---Intermezzo, Op. 68 (fl, ob, cl, h, bn) ME Pro-Art Publications.
HIRSH, HARRY S., The Turtle Dove, English Folk Song (fl, ob, cl, h, bn) E Andraud; Leeds; Sprague-Coleman, Inc.
   ---Nocturne in Bb major (fl, ob, cl, h, bn) Briegel.
JESU, JAMES DE, Clarinet Choir, arr. (3 Bb cl, 1 alto-cl, bass-cl) White & Smith.
JOHNSON, ELEANOR, A Legend of Erin (fl, ob, cl, h, bn) ME Belwin, Inc; arr. by Riebold.
JOHNSON, Quintet in C major (fl, ob, cl, h, bn) ME Fischer.
KIRBY, SUZANNE THUOT, Elfin Dance (fl, ob, cl, h, bn) AMP.
LAMAR, A Moonshiner Laugh (fl, ob, cl, h, bn) Andraud.

LEFEBVRE, Prelude, arr. by Waln (fl, ob, cl, h, bn) Eble.
LEVY, Lovelette, arr. by Riebold (fl, ob, cl, h, bn) ME Bel-
       win, Inc.
MACDOWELL, EDWARD, To a Wild Rose (fl, ob, cl, h, bn or bass-
       cl) Arthur P. Schmidt Co.
MCKAY, FRANCIS, Bainbridge Island Sketches (fl, ob, cl, h, bn)
       ME (rec) C. L. Barnhouse.
MCKAY, GEORGE FREDERICK, Joyful Dance (fl, ob, cl, h, bn) ME
       Mercury Music Corp.
NOCKE, The Mill of Sans-Souci, arr. by Lawrence Taylor (fl, ob,
       cl, h, bn) Mills Music.
PIERCE, EDWIN H., Romance (fl, ob, cl, h, bn) MH Pro Art.
   ---In Merry Mood (fl, ob, cl, h, bn) ME Gamble Hinged
       Music Co; Music Publishers Holding Corp. (score, parts).
RATHAUS, K., Gallant Serenade (fl, ob, cl, h, bn) ME-MH Boo-
       sey & Hawkes (score, parts).
SCARMOLIN, LOUIS, By the Sleepy Nile (fl, ob, cl, h, bn) ME
       Gamble Hinges Music Co; Music Publishers Holding Corp.
       (score, parts).
   ---Scherzino All'Antica (fl, ob, cl, h, bn) ME Pro-Art
       Publications.
SCHUBERT, FRANZ, Allegretto, arr. by G. E. Holmes (fl, ob, cl, h,
       bn) ME C. L. Barnhouse, Inc.
SENAILLE, JEAN BAPTISTE, Rondo Serioso, arr. by Lawrence Taylor
       (fl, ob, cl, h, bn) ME Mills Music, Inc; Eble.
SOMIS, GIOVANNI BATTISTA, Adagio and Allegro, arr. by Robert
       Hernried (fl, ob, cl, h, bn) ME Fischer.
STRINGFIELD, LAMAR, An Old Bridge (fl, ob, cl, h, bn) Leeds.
TARTINI, GIUSEPPE, Arioso in E minor, arr. by George J. Trink-
       aus (fl, ob, cl, h, bn) ME Kay & Kay; Franklin; An-
       draud.
   ---Evening Song, arr. by G. J. Trinkaus (fl, ob, cl, h, bn)
       ME Kay & Kay; Franklin; Andraud.
TAYLOR, LAWRENCE, Petite Suite from the Eighteenth Century, af-
       ter Corelli, arr. (fl, ob, cl, h, bn) E-ME Mills Music.
TORJUSSEN, TRYGVE, Norwegian Wedding Dance (fl, ob, cl, h, bn
       or bass-cl) Arthur P. Schmidt Co.
ULRICH, HUGO, Masterworks for Woodwinds, album, arr. (fl, ob, cl,
       h, bn) VE Boston Music Co; EMB.
VINTER, Two Miniatures (fl, ob, cl, h, bn) Eble.
WALTERS, H., Waggery for Woodwinds (fl, ob, cl, h, bn).
WARD, ROBERT, Little Dance Suite (fl, ob, cl, h, bn) E-ME
       Mills Music, Inc.
WEIS, FLEMMING, Serenade for Quintet (fl, ob, cl, h, bn) Mc-
       Ginnis & Marx.
ZAMECNIK, Allegro Giubiloso (fl, ob, cl, h, bn) ME Sam Fox
       Publishing Co.

Collections

MASTER WOODWIND ENSEMBLE SERIES, Irving Cheyette and Charles J.
  Roberts (fl, ob, 2 Bb cl, bn, parts for Eb cl, Eb alto-cl
  or alto sax, h in F, Bb tenor sax or bass-cl, Eb bar-sax)
  Contents: I. Scherzo, Op. 166, Schubert; Rondeau, G. B.
  Buononcini. II. Humoresque, Op. 101, No. 7, Dvorak;
  Two Dances, J. A. Hasse. III. Finale from Symphony "La
  Reine", Haydn; Menuet, J. S. Bach. IV. Tambourine, F.
  J. Gossec; Knight Rupert, R. Schumann; V. Minuetto,
  from L'Arlesienne Suite No. 1, Bizet; VI. Larghetto
  from Second Symphony, Beethoven; Londonderry Air, Irish
  Folk Song; VII. Air Louis XIII, H. Ghys; New Year's
  Song, R. Schumann. ME (rec) Carl Fischer.
FOX Chamber Music Folio of Wood-Wind Ensembles, Arr. by J. S. Za-
  mecnik (Instrumentation: fl, cl, ob, h, bn or bass-cl,
  pf ad lib) Contents: Knight Errant, Zamecnik; Madri-
  gal, Zamecnik; Roundelay, F. Van Norman; Menuet Melodi-
  que, Zamecnik; Twilight, Reverie, J. Reynard; Allegro
  Giubiloso, Zamecnik; Dance Sylvan, G. Wellesley; Ga-
  votte Naive, R. L. Creighton; Idylle, G. Wellesley; La
  Gondoliera, Serenade, Zamecnik; Etude, F. Van Norman;
  Ballet Pirouette, J. Reynard. MD Sam Fox Publishing Co.

Classic Quintets

BACH, JOHANN SEBASTIAN, Adagio, arr. by H. Sarlit (fl, ob, cl,
  h, bn) Baron.
 ---Badinerie, arr. by Presser (fl, ob, cl, h, bn) Presser.
 ---Bouree from Overture No. 3 in D major, arr. in F major by
  Orem (fl, ob, cl, h, bn) Presser, 1940.
 ---Menuet (fl, ob, cl, h, bn) Andraud.
 ---Prelude and Fugue in E minor, arr. by Moehlmann (fl, ob,
  cl, h, bn).
 ---Prelude No. 22, Vol. I, Well-Tempered Clavichord (fl, ob,
  cl, h, bn) arr. by C. S. Kessler MH Rubank.
 ---Quintette Fugue, No. 22, Vol. I, Well-Tempered Clavichord
  arr. by C. S. Kessler (ob, eng h, bar, 2 bn) Rubank.
 ---Sonata (fl, ob, cl, h, bn) arr. by H. Sarlit; Baron.
 ---Sarabande, arr. by H. Sarlit (fl, ob, cl, h, bn) Baron.
 ---Unschuld, Kleinod Reiner Seelen, Aria (sop, fl, ob, v,
  va) McGinnis & Marx; Hortus Musicus, Musica Rara.
BACH, JOHANN CHRISTOPH FRIEDRICH, Allegro Brillante, origin-
  ally for fl, ob, cl, h, bn, trans. by Quinto Maganini (fl,
  ob, cl, h, bn) Fischer.
BACH, JOHANN CHRISTIAN, Allegretto Piacevole, originally for
  fl, cl, bn, trans. by Quinto Maganini (fl, ob, cl, h, bn)
  Fischer.
BALAY, GUILLAUME, Quintet (fl, ob, cl, h, bn) Buffet-Crampon.
 ---Dawn in the Forest (L'Aurore sur la Foret) (solo h, fl,
  cl, ob, bn) Andraud.
 ---Petite Suite Miniature: Minuet, Gavotte, Saraband,
  Petit Rondeau (fl, ob, cl, h, bn) MH (rec) Leduc; An-
  draud; Kjos.

---The Peaceful Valley, Reverie (La Vallee Silencieuse)
(solo fl, ob, cl, h, bn) Andraud.
BALAY, GUILLAUME, Menuet and Rondo from Petite Suite Miniature
arr. by Waln (fl, ob, cl, h, bn) MH (rec) Neil A. Kjos;
Eble.
BARROWS, JOHN R., JR., March for Woodwind Quintet (fl, ob, cl,
h, bn) G. Schirmer.
BARTHE, A., Passacaille and Aubade (fl, ob, cl, h, bn) MH
Leduc; Andraud; Baron; Sansone.
---Passacaille (fl, ob, cl, h, bn) MH (rec) Ruband.
---Aubade (fl, ob, cl, h, bn) Pinatel; Andraud.
BARTOK, BELA, Geyermekeknek, Suite based on Hungarian Folksongs
(I Look for the Needle; Czardas; My Daughter Lidi;
Above the Tree; My Little Rosebud; They Killed the Lad
for Gold; Mockery; Drinking Song) transc. by Ross Taylor
(fl, ob, cl, h, bn).
BARTOS, FRANTISEK, Le Bourgeois Gentilhomme (Mestak Slechticem)
Intrada, Carillon, Bourree, Menuet, Gigue, Marcia Alla
Turca (fl, ob, cl, h, bn) MH Hudebni Matice; Eble.
BECK, FREDERICK W., Two Movements of Woodwind Quintet (fl, ob,
cl, h, bn) Introduction and Dance; Song.
BEETHOVEN, LUDWIG VAN, Allegro from Sixth Symphony in Eb, arr.
by G. E. Holmes (fl, ob, cl, h, bn) Barnhouse.
---Cavatina from String Quartet, Op. 130, transc. (ob, 2 cl,
h, bn) Andraud.
---Gavotte in F, Country Dances (fl, ob, cl, h, bn) Andraud;
Carl Fischer (score, parts). Published Separately.
---Larghetto from Second Symphony and Londonderry Air (fl,
ob, cl, h, bn) Andraud.
---Minuet, Andante and Variations, Op. 25 (fl, ob, cl, h,
bn) Andraud.
---Divertimento, Op. 12, arr. by George J. Trinkaus (fl, ob,
cl, h, bn) Andraud; Music Publishers Holding Corp.,
(score, parts).
---Quintet, Op. 29 (fl, ob, cl, h, bn) Andraud.
---Sextet, Op. 71, transc. by R. Stark for Quintet. Adagio-
Allegro, Adagio, Menuetto: Quasi Allegretto, Rondo: Alle-
gro (fl, ob, cl, h, bn) MH-H (rec) Sikorski; Sansone;
Andraud; A. E. Fischer; Benjamin; Andraud; B&H, Crit-
ical Edition, 1862-5, Supplementary Vol., 1904.
---String Quartet, Op. 59, No. 1, arr. by Jerome Roth (fl,
ob, cl, h, bn).
---String Quartet, Op. 18, No. 5, variations arr. (fl, ob,
cl, h, bn) Andraud.
---Variations on a Theme from Mozart's Don Juan, arr. by
Bellison (fl, ob, cl, h, bn) Ricordi.
BENNETT, ROBERT RUSSELL, Toy Symphony for Five (fl, ob, cl, h,
bn) 530 Park Ave., NYC.
BENTZON, JORGEN, Racconto No. 5, Op. 46 (fl, ob, cl, h, bn)
Skandinavisk Musikforlag; McGinnis & Marx.
---Variazioni Interrotti, Op. 12 (cl, bn, v, va, vc) Han-
sen (score, parts); Andraud; AMP.
BEREZOWSKY, NICOLAI T., Suite No. 1, Op. 11 (fl, ob, cl, h, bn)
Boosey-Hawkes; Russicher Musikverlag. (rec)
---Wind Quintet No. 2, Op. 22 (fl, ob, cl, h, bn) VH (rec)

Mills Music, Inc; Eble; Andraud; Mills Music, Inc.

BEVERSDORF, THOMAS, Prelude and Fugue (fl, ob, cl, h, bn) H
939 Woodland Ave., Houston, Texas.

BEYTHIEN, KURT, Quintet, Op. 7 in F major (fl, ob, cl, h, bn)
Published by author, Dresden (score, parts).

BLISS, ARTHUR, Conversations (fl or bass-fl, ob or eng h, v, va,
vc) Curwen (score, parts); Universal Edition; Andraud.

BLUMER, THEODOR, Quintet in F major, Op. 34, Woodwind Suite:
Serenade and Theme with Variations (fl, ob, cl, h, bn)
MH-H (rec) Simrock (score, parts); Sansone; Andraud;
AMP.

---Quintet in Bb major, Op. 52 (fl, ob, cl, h, bn) H-VH
(rec) Zimmermann, (min score, parts); Sansone; Andraud.

---Dance Suite, Op. 53 Rigaudon, Sarabanda, Menuet, Hungarian Dance, Valse Boston, Onestep, in D major (fl, ob,
cl, h, bn) Simrock (min score, parts); AMP; Andraud.

BOELIMANN, LEON, Gothic Minuet (ob, eng h, cl, h, bn) Sansone;
Andraud; Durand; Elkan-Vogel.

BORKOVEC, PAUL, Quintet Suite (fl, ob, cl, h, bn) Hudebni Matice; Andraud.

BORODIN, ALEXANDRE, Chorus of Villagers, in Bb major, arr. by
H. S. Hirsch (fl, ob, cl, h, bn) Presser.

BOZZA, EUGENE, Scherzo, Op. 48 (fl, ob, cl, h, bn) Baron; Andraud; Leduc.

---Andante, Op. 48 (fl, ob, cl, h, bn) Baron; Andraud;
Leduc.

---Variations Sur Un Theme Libre, Op. 42 (fl, ob, cl, h,
bn) H-VH (rec) Eble; Baron; Leduc.

BRICCIALDI, GIULIO, Quintet, Op. 124 in D major (fl, ob, cl, h,
bn) Schott.

BROD, HENRI, Quintetti, Nos. 1 and 2 (fl, ob, cl, h, bn) Lemoine; Andraud.

---Trois Quintetti (fl, ob, cl, h, bn) Pacini, Paris; Fetis.

CASELLA, ALFREDO, Serenata in C major (cl, bn, tpt, v, vc) Andraud; Universal Edition.

CHAMINADE, CECILE, Scarf Dance, arr. by A. Hicks (fl, ob, cl, h,
bn).

CRETIEN, HEDWIGE (Madame) Quintet for Woodwinds in Bb major
(fl, ob, cl, h, bn) Andraud; Baxter-Northrup.

---Arabesque (fl, ob, cl, h, bn) Andraud.

CHRIST, WILLIAM, Quintet (fl, ob, cl, h, bn) H Indiana University School of Music.

COLOMER, Bourree and Menuet (fl, ob, cl, h, bn) Andraud.

COWELL, HENRY, Suite for Woodwind Quintet (fl, ob, cl, h, bn)
VH Mercury Music Corporation; McGinnis & Marx (score,
parts).

CUI, CESAR ANTONOVITCH, Orientale, arr. by A. Del Busto (fl, ob,
cl, h, bn) Andraud; Fischer (score, parts).

DAHL, INGOLF, Allegro and Arioso (fl, ob, cl, h, bn).

DAHLHOFF, WALTER, Waldegeheimnisse (Secrets of the Wood)(fl, ob,
2 cl, bn) Schmidt, Cefes-Edition; Andraud.

---Der Choral von Leuthen (fl, ob, cl, h, bn) Schmidt, Cefes-
Edition; Andraud.

DANZI, FRANZ, Quintets (fl, ob, cl, h, bn) Offenbach Press.

---Quintet, Op. 56, No. 2 in G minor (fl, ob, cl, h, bn) MH
(rec) DTB, Bd. 27 (arr. by Riemann); Leuckart (arr. by
Weigelt, parts); Andraud; B&H, 1914; XV Jahrgang Mann-
heimer Kammermusik des 18 Jahrhunderts 1. Tiel, transc. by
Weigelt; Schlesinger; Fetis; Blue print available from
Roy Houser, Indiana University.

---Gypsy Dance from Quintet, Op. 56, No. 2 in G minor (fl,
ob, cl, h, bn) MH Fischer.

DANZI, FRANZ, Quintet, Op. 56, No. 1 (fl, ob, or cl in C, cl in
Bb, h, bn) XVI, Jahrgang Mannheimer Kammermusik des 18
Jahrhunderts II Tiel, Trios und Duos; Schlesinger; Fetis.

---Quintet, Op. 56, No. 3 (fl, ob, or cl in C, cl in Bb, h,
bn) XVI, Jahrgang Mannheimer Kammermusik des 18 Jahrhunderts II Tiel, Trios und Duos; Schlesinger; Fetis.

---Quintet, Op. 67, No. 2 in E minor (fl, ob, cl, h, bn) No.
9 in Das Erbe dt. Musik, Vol. 14; Nagel (arr. by Helmut
Schultz).

---Trois Quintetti, Op. 67, G major, E minor and Eb major
(fl, ob, cl, h, bn) Offenbach; Andre.

---Triois Quintetti, Op. 68, A major, F major, D minor (fl,
ob, cl, h, bn) Offenbach; Andre.

DEBUSSY, CLAUDE ACHILLE, Children's Corner Suite (fl, ob, cl, h,
bn) New Art Wind Quintet, arr.

---Le Petite Suite (fl, ob, cl, h, bn) New Art Wind Quintet,
arr.

---Le Pas Sur La Neige (fl, ob, cl, h, bn) New Art Wind
Quintet, arr.

---Romance (fl, ob, cl, h, bn) New Art Wind Quintet, arr.

---Le Petit Negre, arr. by Eugene Bozza (fl, ob, cl, h, bn)
Baron.

---Suite for Winds, arr. by John McGrosso: Prelude, Menuet,
Claire de Lune (fl, ob, cl, h, bn) Department of Music,
University of Texas, Austin.

DELIBES, LEO, Petite Marche, arr. by G. Barrere, (fl, ob, cl, h,
bn) Juilliard Edition; G. Schirmer.

DE LORENZO, LEONARDO, Divertimento Flautistico (5 fl; 3 picc, 2
fl in G) Ms.

DESORMIERES, ROGER, Six Danceries from the Sixteenth Century (fl,
eng h, cl, h, bn) Baron.

DESPORTES, YVONNE, Prelude, Variations and Finale on a Gregorian
Chant (fl, ob, cl, h, bn) VH Baron; Andraud.

DILLON, ROBERT M., Nocturne and Dance (fl, ob, cl, h, bn) Director of Music at Bethany, Oklahoma Public Schools.

D'INDY, PAUL VINCENT, Quintet, Op. 24, Suite in D major (2 fl,
tpt and string quartet).

DOMANSKY, ALFRED, Quintets, 1. Vorspiel, 2. Scherzo, 3. Schluss-
satz (fl, ob, cl, h, bn) Schmidt, Cefes-Edition; Eble;
Andraud (parts).

---Quintet No. 2 (fl, 2 cl, h, bn) Schmidt, Cefes-Edition;
Eble; Andraud.

DVORAK, ANTONIN, Humoreske, Quintet, Op. 101, No. 7, arr. by G. J.
Trinkaus (fl, ob, cl, h, bn) Andraud; Franklin.

EGIDI, ARTHUR, Quintet, Op. 18 in Bb major (fl, ob, cl, h, bn)
Verlag fur Musikalische Kultur.

EISLER, HANS, Quintet, Op. 4 (fl, ob, cl, h, bn) Andraud.

ELGAR, EDWARD, Salut d'Amour, Quintet, Op. 12, arr. by G. J.
    Trinkhaus (fl, ob, cl, h, bn) Andraud; Franklin.
EPPERT, CARL, A Little Symphony, Quintet, Op. 52 (fl, ob, cl, bn,
    alto-cl) Andraud; Music Publishers Holding Corp. (score,
    parts).
ERLEBACH, RUPERT O., Rhapsody, Op. 17 (fl, ob, or eng h, v, va,
    vc) 1927, Stainer & Bell (score, parts); Andraud.
ESHPAY, A., Quintet, Marische Melody (fl, ob, cl, bn, eng h) An-
    draud.
FAURE, GABRIEL URBAIN, Barcarolle (fl, ob, cl, h, bn) New Art
    Wind Quintet, arr.
FAURE, GABRIEL URBAIN, Les Presents (fl, ob, cl, h, bn) New
    Art Wind Quintet, arr.
FERNANDEZ, OSCAR, Suite in F major, Op. 37 (fl, ob, cl, h, bn)
    VH Baron; AMP.
FOERSTER, JOSEF BOHUSLAV, Quintet in D major, Op. 95 (fl, ob,
    cl, h, bn, pf ad lib) H Hudebni Matice (score, parts);
    Eble; Andraud.
FRAGALE, FRANK, Woodwind Quintet (fl, ob, cl, h, bn) H Baron;
    AMP.
FRANCAIX, JEAN, Quintet (fl, vn, va, vc, harp) Eble; Schott.
GERSHWIN, GEORGE, Summertime (fl, ob, cl, h, bn) New Art Wind
    Quintet, arr.
CHEDINI, F., Quintet, Concerto for Five (fl, ob, cl, h, bn)
    Ricordi; Eble.
GIFFELS, ANN, Quintet (fl, ob, cl, h, bn) MH Indiana Univer-
    sity School of Music.
GILLIS, DON, Three Quintets (fl, ob, cl, h, bn).
GLUCK, CHRISTOPH W. VON, Gavotte from Paris and Helena in C ma-
    jor (fl, ob, cl, h, bn) Andraud; Fischer (score, parts).
GOEB, ROGER, Prairie Songs (fl, ob, cl, h, bn).
    ---Quintet No. 1 (fl, ob, cl, h, bn) ACA.
GOULD, MORTON, Pavane from American Symphonette, No. 2 (fl, ob,
    cl, h, bn) ME (rec) arr. by L. Taylor. Mills Music,
    Inc.; New Art Wind Quintet, arr.
GOUNOD, CHARLES FRANCOIS, Funeral March of a Marionette, arr. by
    Teague (fl, ob, cl, h, bn) ME Baron; AMP; EMB; Broad-
    cast Music, Inc.
GRAINGER, PERCY A., Walking Tune (Wanderlied) ME-MH (fl, ob, cl,
    h, bn) Schott; Andraud.
GRANT, PARKS, Soliloquy and Jubilation, Op. 40 (fl, ob, cl, h,
    bn) ACA.
GRIEG, EDWARD H., Sailors' Song (fl, ob, cl, h, bn) New Art
    Wind Quintet, arr.
    ---Norwegian Dance, Op. 47, No. 28 (fl, ob, cl, h, bn) arr.
    by A. E. Cafarella, Volkwein.
    ---Dance of the Elves, Op. 12, No. 4 (fl, ob, cl, h, bn) arr.
    by G. J. Trinkaus, Franklin; Andraud.
    ---Birdling, Op. 43, No. 4 in G major (fl, ob, cl, h, bn)
    Ditson.
    ---Erotikon, No. 5, Op. 43 (The Muse of Erotic) arr. by G.
    J. Trinkaus (fl, ob, cl, h, bn) Franklin; Andraud.
    ---Morning Mood, from Peer Gynt Suite, Op. 46, No. 1, arr.
    by Trinkaus (fl, ob, cl, h, bn) Franklin; Music Pub-
    lishers Holding Corp. (score, parts).

     ---Rigaudon, Op. 40 from Holberg Suite (fl, ob, cl, h, bn)
        Andraud; Franklin.
HANDEL, GEORGE FREDERICK, Two Marches (2 tpt or v, 2 ob or cl,
        bn or vc) Baron; Mercury Music Corp. (arr. by Sidney
        Beck).
     ---Suite for Woodwinds in C major (fl, ob, cl, h, bn) Arr.
        by C. J. Boyd, Witmark.
     ---Marches (2 tpt, 2 v, or cl, ob, vc or any bass instru-
        ment) Mercury.
     ---Six Little Fugues, arr. by Bauer, Vol. I and II (fl, ob,
        cl, h, bn) MH Baron; AMP; Broadcast Music, Inc.
HAUBIEL, CHARLES, Five Pieces: Flowingly; In 5/8; Canon; In
        7/8: With Animation (fl, ob, cl, h, bn) Composers
        Press; M&H Publications.
HAUFRECHT, HERBERT, Woodland Rondo (fl, ob, cl, h, bn).
HAYDN, FRANZ JOSEPH, Divertimento in Bb major (fl, ob, cl, h, bn)
        Allegro con spirito, Andante, "Chorale St. Antoni", Minu-
        etto: Trio, Rondo ME (rec) Boosey-Hawkes (parts), arr.
        by E. Perry.
     ---Symphony No. 11,. second movement (fl, ob, cl, h, bn) EMB.
     ---Finale, La Reine Symphony (fl, ob, cl, h, bn) Andraud.
     ---Violin Concerto, No. 1 in C major (fl, ob, cl, h, bn) New
        Art Wind Quintet, arr.
     ---Largo from String Quartet, Op. 76, No. 5 (fl, ob, cl, h,
        bn) Ditson.
     ---Nach Einem Klavier-Trio, arr. by Muth, in C major (fl, ob,
        cl, h, bn) MH-H (rec) Zimmermann; Andraud (collection).
HAYDN, JOHANN MICHAEL, Divertimento in G major (fl, h, v, va, bn)
        DTO, 14, Jg. 2., (arr. by L. H. Perger); B&H.
     ---Quintet (2 cl, 2 h, bn) Fetis.
HEIDEN, BERNHARD, Sinfonia for Quintet (fl, ob, cl, h, bn) H
        Very Slow; Lively - Indiana University School of Music.
HEIM, MAX, Quintet in Eb major (fl, ob, cl, h, bn) Allegro Vi-
        vace, Andante, Rondo Presto. C. F. Schmidt, Cefes-Edi-
        tion; Eble; Andraud; Sansone.
HERMANN, FRIEDRICH, Three Quintets after Beethoven, Haydn, Mo-
        zart, Book II: Beethoven, Theme with Variations from
        String Quartet, Op. 18, No. 5; Mozart, Minuet from String
        Quartet in D minor, K421; Haydn, Presto from String Quar-
        tet in C major (fl, ob, cl, h, bn) ME-H (rec) Andraud;
        B&H.
HINDEMITH, PAUL, Quintet, Op. 24, No. 2, Kleine Kammermusik:
        Playful, Waltz, Placid, Rapid, Lively (fl, ob, cl, h, bn)
        VH (rec) Schott; Baron; AMP; Andraud.
     ---Tafelmusik (fl, tpt or cl, 2 v, vc) Schott (score, parts)
        AMP.
HOFFDING, FINN, Quintet, Op. 35 (fl, ob, cl, h, bn) H Eble;
        Carl Fischer; Skandinavisk Musikforlag; McGinnis &
        Marx (score, parts).
HOFFER, Blaser Quintet (fl, ob, cl, h, bn) Eble.
HOLBROOKE, JOSEPH, Quintet, Op. 33b, Characteristic Miniature
        Suite (fl, ob, cl, h, bn) Andraud; Sansone; Rudall,
        Carte & Co.
HOWDEN, BRUCE, Three for Five (fl, cl, ob, h, bn).
HOYER, KARL, Serenade, Op. 29 in F major (fl, ob, cl, h, bn)

MH-H (rec) Simrock (min. score, parts); Andraud; AMP; Sansone.

HUGHES, LOUIS, Intermezzo, Op. 92 (2 fl, ob, cl, bn) Andraud.

HUGHES, LOUIS, Allegro Scherzoso, Op. 92 in D major (2 fl, ob, cl, bn) Ricordi.

HUGENIN, CHARLES, Gavotte and Musette, Op. 21 (fl, ob, cl, h, bn) Andraud.

---Souvenir d'Auvergne, Op. 69 (fl, ob, cl, h, bn) Andraud.

HUNTER, EUGENE, Danse Humoresque, Op. 1, No. 3 (fl, ob, cl, h, bn) Fischer (score, parts); Andraud;

IBERT, JACQUES, Trois Pieces Breves: Allegro, Andante, Assez Lent: Scherzando (fl, ob, cl, h, bn) VH (rec) Leduc (min score, parts); Baron; Eble; Sansone; Andraud.

---The Gardener of Samos (fl, cl, tpt, v, vc, drum) Andraud.

INGENHOVEN, JAN, Quintet in C major (fl, ob, cl, h, bn) H Wunderhorn-Verlag (score, parts); Andraud; Fischer & Jagenburg.

JACOBI, FREDERICK, Scherzo (fl, ob, cl, h, bn) VH Fischer; Andraud.

JAMES, PHILLIP, Quintet, Suite in Four Movements: Praeludium, Gavet, Introspection, Variations and Fugue (fl, ob, cl, h, bn) VH (rec) Carl Fischer (score, parts); Andraud.

JIRAK, KAREL B., Quintet, Op. 32 (fl, ob, cl, h, bn) Andraud.

JONGEN, JOSEPH, Concerto for Woodwinds, Op. 124 (fl, ob, cl, h, bn) VH (rec) Andraud; Baron.

---Preamble and Dances, Op. 98 (fl, ob, cl, h, bn) VH Andraud.

JUON, PARUL, Quintet, Op. 84 in Bb major (fl, ob, cl, h, bn) H-VH (rec) Birnbach (min score, parts); Andraud.

---Divertimento, Op. 41 (fl, ob, cl, h, bn) Eble; Schlesinger.

KAMINSKI, HEINRICH, Quintet in F# minor (v, va, cl, h, vc) Andraud; Universal Edition (score, parts).

KARG-ELERT, SIEGFRIED, Quintet Op. 30 in Eb major (ob, 2 cl, h, bn) Kahnt (score, parts); Andraud.

---Quintet No. 1 (fl, ob, cl, h, bn) Eble.

KARREN, L., A Little Tale from Brittany (fl, ob, cl, h, bn) Andraud.

KAUFFMANN, FRITZ, Quintet Op. 40 in Eb major (fl, ob, cl, h, bn) MH-H Heinrichshofen (score, parts); Andraud.

KLEINSINGER, GEORGE, Frenchy, The French Horn (fl, ob, cl, h, bn) New Art Wind Quintet, arr.

KLUGHARDT, AUGUST, Quintet, Op. 79 in C major (fl, ob, cl, h, bn) MH-H (rec) Zimmermann; Andraud; Andraud Collection; Sansone; Giessel (score, parts).

---Finale from Quintet, Op. 79 in C major (fl, ob, cl, h, bn) MH-H (rec) Rubank.

KNUDAGE-RIISAGER, Quintet (fl, ob, cl, h, bn) Andraud.

KRAFT, WALTER, Concertante Musik (2 fl, ob or eng h, v, vc) Barenreiter.

KREUTZER, KONRADIN, Quartet in Eb major, First Movement (fl, ob, cl, bn, bass-cl ad lib) arr. Alfred.

KUBIK, GAIL T., Woodwind Quintet (fl, ob, cl, h, bn) Alumni Office, Eastman School of Music.

LABATE, BRUNO, Quintet (fl, ob, 2 cl, bn) Andraud.

LEFEBVRE, CHARLES EDOUARD, Suite, Op. 57: Canon, Allegro, Fi-
nale (fl, ob, cl, h, bn) MH Hamelle (score, parts);
Eble; Andraud.
LENDVAI, ERWIN, Quintet, Op. 23 in Ab major (fl, ob, cl, h, bn)
Theme with Variations, Intermezzo, Finale H-VH (rec)
Simrock (min score, parts); Andraud; Sansone; AMP.
LISZT, FRANZ, Trois Morceaux in Eb major, arr. by E. Lassen (fl,
ob, cl, h, bn) Schott.
---Pastoral, Nostalgia, Eglog (fl, ob, cl, h, bn) Andraud.
arr. from "Annees" for pf.
LUENING, OTTO, Fuguing Tune for Winds (fl, ob, cl, h, bn) VH
Baron; AMP.
MACDOWELL, EDWARD, Idyl, Op. 28, No. 2 (fl, ob, cl, h, bn) Mu-
sic Publishers Holding Corp. (arr. by G. J. Trinkaus,
score, parts); Andraud.
MARECHAL, Night Watch Tune of King Rene (fl, ob, cl, h, bn) An-
draud.
MARX, KARL, Achtzehn Variationen, Op. 30, on an Old English Folk-
song (2 fl, ob, v, vc) Barenreiter.
MASON, DANIEL G., Divertimento: March and Fugue (fl, ob, cl, h,
bn) H Witmark; Andraud; Music Publishers Holding Corp.
(score, parts: March in D minor, Op. 26a, Fugue, Op. 26b).
---Fugue, Op. 26b (fl, ob, cl, h, bn) Witmark; Andraud;
Music Publishers Holding Corp; Fischer.
MCBRIDE, ROBERT GUYN, Jam Session (fl, ob, cl, h, bn) VH Com-
posers Press; Lyon & Healy.
MCCALL, H. E., Two Tunes from Mother Goose; Three Blind Mice Go
Modern, Rock-a-Bye, Swing-a-Bye, Baby (fl, ob, cl, h,
bn) VH Andraud.
MELLIN, G., Menuet Badin (fl, ob, cl, h, bn) Andraud.
MENDELSSOHN-BARTHOLDY, FELIX, Figurate Humn in Bb major (fl, ob,
cl, h, bn) Fischer.
---Song Without Words, Op. 62, No. 4, arr. by A. E. Cafarella,
(fl, ob, cl, h, bn) Volkwein.
---Krakowiak in C major (fl, ob, cl, h, bn) arr. by Jospe,
Briegel.
---Menuet, arr. by H. Sarlit (fl, ob, cl, h, bn) Baron.
MILHAUD, DARIUS, La Cheminee of King Rene, Modern Suite in 7
Short Movements: Cortege, Aubade, Jugglers, La Maousin-
glade, Jousts on the River, Hunting at Valabre, Madrigal-
Nocturne (fl, ob, cl, h, bn) H-VH (rec) Baron; Andraud.
---Two Sketches: Madrigal and Pastorale (fl, ob, cl, h, bn)
MH-H Mercury.
MONTEUX, PIERRE, Arrieta and March (fl, ob, cl, bn, tpt, per-
cussion) Andraud.
MOORE, DOUGLAS, Quintet for Winds (fl, ob, cl, h, bn) H (rec)
Schirmer; Society for Publication of American Music.
MORITZ, EDWARD, Quintet, Op. 41 (fl, ob, cl, h, bn) H (rec)
Zimmermann (min score, parts); Andraud; Sansone.
MOUSSORGSKY, MODEST, Selections from Pictures at an Exhibition
(fl, ob, cl, h, bn) New Art Wind Quintet, arr.
---Ballet of the Chickens in Their Shells, F major (fl, ob,
cl, h, bn) Rubank.
MOZART, WOLFGANG AMADEUS, Adagio in Bb major, K411, transc. by
Weigelt (fl, ob, cl, h, bn) MH (Leuckart; Marks (score,

parts); Musica Rara; McGinnis & Marx (arr. by Goldman); Andraud (arr. for 2 cl, 3 alto-cl); B&H (arr. for 2 cl, 3 bassethorns); Mercury (arr. for 3 cl, alto-cl, bass-cl); Offenbach (arr. for 2 cl, 3 bassethorn); Sansone (5 cl).

---Adagio and Rondo, K 617 (fl, ob, va, vc, pf or celeste) Baron; Andraud.

---Adagio in F major, arr. by J. Sobeck (fl, ob, cl, h, bn) Lehne & Komp.

---Allegro Concertante, from Sonata in D minor for violin and piano (fl, ob, cl, h, bn) MH Witmark; Andraud. Music Publishers Holding Corp., (transc. by Campbell-Watson, score, parts).

---Divertimento, No. 8, K213, transc. by G. Weigelt, in F major (fl, ob, cl, h, bn) MH Leuckart; Andraud.

---Divertimento, No. 9, K240, transc. by G. Weigelt in Bb major (fl, ob, cl, h, bn) Andraud; Leuckart.

---Divertimento, No. 13, K253, transc. by G. Weigelt in F Major (fl, ob, cl, h, bn) MH Leuckart; Andraud.

---Divertimento, No. 14, K270, transc. by G. Weigelt in Bb major (fl, ob, cl, h, bn) MH Leuckart; Andraud.

MOZART, WOLFGANG AMADEUS, German Dance in D major (fl, ob, cl, h, bn) Andraud.

---March of the Priests (fl, ob, cl,h, bn) New Art Wind Quintet, arr.

---Minuet from Divertimento, No. 17 in C major, arr. by Lee M. Lockhart (fl, ob, cl, h, bn) Music Publishers Holding Corp. (score, parts).

---Minuet from Symphony in G minor (fl, ob, cl, h, bn) arr. by F. H. Klickmann, Standard.

---Menuet, K. 421, in F major (fl, ob, cl, h, bn) Andraud.

---Menuet from Quintet in D minor, arr. by W. A. Waln (fl, ob, cl, h, bn) ME Kjos Music Co.

---Rondo from Serenade No. 11, K375 in Eb major (fl, ob, cl, h, bn) Ditson.

---Serenade, Op. 27 (2 cl, 2 h, bn) Offenbach; Andre; Fetis.

---Quintet in F major, trans. from String Trio by Lucien Cailliet (fl, ob, cl, h, bn) MH-H Elkan-Vogel.

MULLER, PETER, Three Quintets, Eb major, C minor, A major (fl, ob, cl, h, bn) Ruhle; Andraud; Praeger & Meier.

MUTH, FRITZ, Quintet after a Haydn Trio (fl, ob, cl, h, bn) Eble; Andraud.

NIELSEN, CARL A., Quintet, Op. 43 in A major (fl, ob, cl, h, bn) Hansen (min score, parts); Eble; Andraud; McGinnis & Marx (score, parts).

NORTH, ALEX, Woodwind Quintet (fl, ob, cl, h, bn).

ONSLOW, GEORGES, Quintet, Op. 81 in F major: Allegro non Troppo, Scherzo, Andante, Allegro Spiritoso (fl, ob, cl, h, bn) MH-H Kistner & Siegel; Andraud.

PERSICHETTI, VINCENT, Pastorals for Wind Quintet, Op. 21 (fl, ob, cl, h, bn) G. Schirmer.

PFEIFFER, GIOVANNI, Pastorale, Op. 71 (fl, ob, cl, h, bn) Andraud.

PFEIFFER-LECLAIR, Three Short Concert Pieces: Pastoral, Pfeiffer, Minuet and Hunting Scene, Leclair (fl, ob, cl, h, bn).

PIETSCH, EDNA FRIDA, Suite for Wind Quintet (fl, ob, cl, h, bn)
PLEYEL, IGNACE JOSEPH, Quintet, Op. 48, arr. by Harris (fl, ob,
     cl, h, bn) Cundy-Bettoney.
     ---Three Quintets, Op. 10 (fl, v, ob, va, bn) Haviesen.
PORTER, COLE, Can't Help Loving That Man (fl, ob, cl, h, bn)
     New Art Wind Quintet, arr.
PRESSER, WILLIAM, Passacaglia (cl, h, v, va, vc) Composers
     Press, Inc.
PROKOFIEFF, SERGE, Quintet, Op. 39 in G minor (ob, cl, v, va, bn)
     Gutheil; Marks; Russicher Musikverlag; Baron; B&H;
     Andraud.
PURCELL, HENRY, Trumpet Voluntary (fl, ob, cl, h, bn) New Art
     Wind Quintet, arr.
RAMEAU, JEAN PHILLIPE, Tambourin (fl, ob, cl, h, bn) arr. by Lee
     M. Lockhart, Music Publishers Holding Corp. (score,
     parts); Andraud.
     ---Acante et Cephise, Airs de Ballet, arr. by Roger Desor-
     miere (fl, ob, cl, h, bn) Baron.
     ---La Poule, arr. by H. Sarlit (fl, ob, cl, h, bn) Baron.
RAVEL, MAURICE JOSEPH, Mother Goose Suite (fl, ob, cl, h, bn)
     New Art Wind Quintet, arr.
     ---Piece en forme de Habanera, arr. by C. S. Kessler
     (fl, ob, cl, h, bn) VH Leduc (score); Baron; Andraud.
     ---Pavanne Pour Une Infante Defunte, arr. by Intravaia (fl,
     ob, cl, h, bn) H Elkan-Vogel.
READ, GARDNER, Quintet, (fl, ob, cl, h, bn) Ms, Boston Univer-
     sity, School of Music.
REICHA, ANTON, Six Quintets, Op. 100, No. 19 in F major, No. 20
     in D minor, No. 21 in Eb major, No. 22 in E minor, No. 23
     in A minor, No. 24 in Eb major, No. 6 in Bb major (fl,
     ob, cl, h, bn) Costallat; Andraud; Boieldieu; Schott;
     Zetter.
     ---Introduction and Allegro from Quintet, Op. 88 (fl, ob,
     cl, h, bn) ME-H Mercury Music Corp; Boieldieu; Janet.
     ---Six Quintets, Op. 88, No. 1 in E minor, No. 2 in Eb ma-
     jor, No. 3 in G major, No. 4 in D minor, No. 5 in Bb ma-
     jor, No. 6 in F major (fl, ob, cl, h, bn) MH Leuckart
     (arr. by G. Weigelt); Andraud; Boieldieu; Simrock;
     Schott; Janet.
     ---Quintet, No. 1, Op. 88 in E minor (fl, cl, ob, h, bn)
     Andraud.
     ---Quintet No. 2, Op. 88 in Eb major (fl, ob, cl, h, bn)
     ed. by G. Weigelt, Leuckart.
     ---Six Quintets, Op. 91, No. 7 in C major, No. 8 in A mi-
     nor, No. 9 in D major, No. 10 in G minor, No. 11 in A
     major, No. 12 in C minor (fl, ob, cl, h, bn) MH An-
     draud; Simrock; Boieldieu; Janet.
     ---Quintet No. 13, Op. 99 in C major (fl, ob, cl, h, bn)
     AMP.
     ---Six Quintets, Op. 99, No. 13 in C major, No. 14 in F mi-
     nor, No. 15 in F major, No. 16 in D major, No. 17 in B
     minor, No. 17 in G major (fl, ob, cl, h, bn) Janet; An-
     draud; Simrock; Boieldieu.
REIZENSTEIN, FRANZ, Quintet (fl, ob, cl, h, bn) Boosey-Hawkes-
     Belwin, Inc; B&H Andraud.
RIEGGER, WALLINGFORD, Woodwind Quintet (fl, ob, cl, h, bn)

Blueprint, 506 W. 113th St., NYC.

---Three Canons for Woodwinds (fl, ob, cl, h, bn) Durand.

RIMSKY-KORSAKOFF, NICOLAS ANDRE, Flight of the Bumble-Bee, arr.
    by Trinkaus (fl, ob, cl, h, bn) Franklin; Andraud.

ROPARTZ, J. GUY, Deux Pieces (fl, ob, cl, h, bn) H-VH (rec)
    Durand (score, parts); Eble; Andraud; Elkan-Vogel.

RORICH, KARL, Quintet, Op. 58 in E minor (fl, ob, cl, h, bn)
    Zimmermann (score, parts); Andraud; Sansone.

ROUSSEL, ALBERT, Divertissement (fl, ob, cl, h, bn) H Eble.

SACHSSE, HANS, Suite, Op. 32 in C major (fl, ob, cl, h, bn)
    Bohm & Son (min score, parts); Andraud (score, parts).

SAUER, E., Music-Box (picc. fl, ob, 2 cl) Andraud.

SCARLATTI, DOMENICO, Sonata in D major (ob, cl, bn, v, vc)
    Baxter-Northrup.

SCARMOLIN, A. LOUIS, Badinage (fl, ob, cl, h, bn) ME Lyon &
    Healy; Boosey-Hawkes.

SCHICKHARDT, JOHANN CHRISTIAN, Konzerte (4 fl, pf) Barenreiter.

SCHMID, HEINRICH KASPAR. Quintet, Op. 28 in Bb major (fl, ob, cl,
    h, bn) MH-H Schott (min score, parts); Andraud; AMP.

SCHONBERG, ARNOLD, 6 Lieder, Op. 14 (voice, cl, bass-cl, v, vc)
    Universal Edition.

---Quintet, Op. 26 (fl, ob, cl, h, bn) VH Universal Edi-
    tion (min score, parts); Andraud; AMP.

SCHUBERT, FRANZ, Ballet Music from Rosamunde (fl, ob, cl, h, bn)
    Andraud; EMB.

---Hark! Hark! The Lark, transc. by M. A. Springer (fl, 3 Bb
    cl, bn) Music Publishers Holding Corp. (score, parts).

---March Hongroise, arr. by L. Taylor (fl, ob, cl, h, bn) E
    Mills Music, Inc.

---Minuet (fl, ob, cl, h, bn) Andraud.

---Scherzo, Op. 166 (fl, ob, cl, h, bn) Andraud.

SCHUMANN, ROBERT A., New Year's Song, Air Louis XIII (fl, ob, cl,
    h, bn) Andraud.

---Knight Rupert (fl, ob, cl, h, bn) Andraud.

---Fughette and Gigue, arr. by H. Sarlit (fl, ob, cl, h, bn)
    Baron.

SEHLBACH, Kortum-Serenade (fl, ob, cl, h, bn) Eble.

SHOSTAKOVICH, DMITRI, Polka (fl, ob, cl, h, bn) New Art Wind
    Quintet, arr.

SIBELIUS, JAN, Pastorale from Pelleas and Melisande, Op. 46 (fl,
    ob, cl, h, bn) ME-MH Fischer (arr. by G. Langenus); An-
    draud.

SLAVENSKI, JOSPI S., Suite, Op. 6, From the Village (fl, cl, v,
    va, bass) Schott; AMP; Andraud.

SOBECK, JOHANN, Quintet, Op. 9 in F major (fl, ob, cl, h, bn) H
    (rec) Bote & Bock; Sansone; Andraud; Boosey-Hawkes.

---Quintet, Op. 11 in Eb major (fl, ob, cl, h, bn) H Bos-
    worth; Sansone; Andraud; Belwin.

---Quintet, Op. 14 in G minor (fl, ob, cl, h, bn) H Bos-
    worth; Sansone; Belwin; (first and fourth movements);
    Andraud.

---Quintet, Op. 23 in Bb major (fl, ob, cl, h, bn) H Ehr-
    ler (score, parts); Andraud (score, parts, arr. by Lehne);
    Leduc (arr. by Cobbett).

SOWERBY, LEO, Quintet (fl, ob, cl, h, bn) Schirmer (score, parts);
     Society for the Publication of American Music.
    ---Quintet: Jauntily, Elegiac Mood, A Steady Trot (fl, ob,
     cl, h, bn) Andraud.
    ---Pop Goes the Weasel (fl, ob, cl, h, bn) VH Fitzsimons
     (score, parts); Andraud; Schirmer.
STAINER, CHARLES, Scherzo, Op. 27 (fl, ob, cl, h, bn) H-VH
     (rec) Rudall, Carte & Co; Eble; Andraud.
STARK, ROBERT, Quintet Concertant, Op. 44 (fl, ob, cl, h, bn)
     Andraud.
STRAVINSKY, IGOR FEDOROVICH, Pastorale, Chanson sans paroles
     (v, ob, eng h, cl, bn) Schott (score, parts, arr. for
     voice, ob, eng h, cl, bn as well as above); Baron; An-
     draud; AMP.
STRUBE, GUSTAVE, Quintet (fl, ob, cl, h, bn).
SULLIVAN, ARTHUR S., Quintett Madrigal, (Yeoman of the Guard) in
     G major (fl, ob, cl, h, bn) Ms.
    ---Quintett Madrigal from the Mikado in F major (fl, ob, cl,
     h, bn) Ms.
SWANSON, HOWARD, Night Music for Woodwinds.
TAFFANEL, CLAUDE PAUL, Quintette in G minor (fl, ob, cl, h, bn)
     MH-H (rec) Leduc; Baron; Andraud; Sansone.
TELEMANN, GEORG PHILIPP, Ouverture-Suite in D major (2 ob, 2 h,
     bn) Leuckart; Andraud (fl, ob, cl, h, bn).
THOMAS, CHARLES, Gavotte from Mignon, arr. by G. J. Trinkaus (fl,
     ob, cl, h, bn) Franklin; Andraud.
THOMSON, VIRGIL, Sonata da Chiesa (Eb cl, tpt, va, h, tromb)
     New Music Editions, XVIII, No. 1, 1944.
TOLDI, JULIUS, Little Suite for Woodwinds and Horn (fl, ob, cl,
     h, bn) Ms.
TOMASI, Quintet (fl, cl, h, ob, bn) Eble.
TOMASI, HENRI, Variations on a Corsican Theme (fl, ob, cl, h, bn)
     VH (rec) Leduc (min score, parts); Baron; Eble; An-
     draud.
TSCHAIKOVSKY, PETER ILITCH, Nutcracker Suite (fl, ob, cl, h, bn)
     New Art Wind Quintet, arr.
    ---April, Op. 37, No. 4 (fl, ob, cl, h, bn) transc. by G. J.
     Trinkaus, Franklin; Andraud.
    ---June, Op. 37, No. 5 (fl, ob, cl, h, bn) transc. by G. J.
     Trinkaus, Franklin; Andraud.
    ---Melodie, Op. 42, No. 3 in Eb major (fl, ob, cl, h, bn)
     Carl Fischer.
    ---Andante Cantabile from String Quartet, Op. 11 in C major
     (fl, ob, cl, h, bn) Fischer (score, parts), arr. by L.
     Pietrini.
TURECHEK, EDWARD, Quintet (fl, ob, cl, h, bn) Music Publishers
     Holding Corp.
TUTHILL, BURNET CORWIN, Sailors' Hornpipe, Op. 14, No. 1 (fl,
     ob, cl, h, bn or fl, 2 Bb cl, h, bn) Fischer (score,
     parts); Andraud.
VERNEUIL, RAOUL DE, Quintet for Wind Instruments, Lima, Peru.
VERRALL, JOHN, Serenade for Five Instruments (fl, ob, cl, h, bn)
     MH-H Music Press, Inc; Mercury.
VIDAL. P., Christmas Prelude (fl, ob, vc, v, va) Andraud.
VILLA-LOBOS, HEITOR, Quintet (fl, ob, eng h, cl, bn).

WAGNER, WILHELM RICHARD, March from Tannhauser (fl, ob, cl, h, bn) New Art Wind Quintet, arr.

WATERSON, JAMES, Quintet in F major (fl, ob, cl, h, bn) MH-H Lafleur; Andraud; Sansone; Boosey-Hawkes.

WEBER, CARL MARIA VON, Minuet from Clarinet Quintet, Op. 34 in Bb major (3 cl, alto-cl or sax, bass-cl or bn) Cundy-Bettoney.

WEISS, ADOLPH, Quintet (fl, ob, cl, h, bn) VH ACA; 3267 Blair Rd., Hollywood, California.

WESTON, P., Arbeau Suite (fl, ob, cl, h, bn) MH Concord Music Publishing Co., Inc.

WOOD, CHARLES, Quintet in F major (fl, ob, cl, h, bn) Boosey-Hawkes-Belwin, Inc. (score, parts); Sonsone; Andraud.

Collections

ANDRAUD, Twenty-One Quintets, arr. by Andraud (fl, ob, cl, h, bn) ME-VH (rec) Andraud; Baron. Contents: Beethoven, Op. 71, Quintet; Beethoven, Minuet, Andante, Variations: Beethoven, Op. 18, No. 5, Variations; Barraine, Ouvrage de Dame; Barthe, Passacaille; Colomer, Minuet; Colomer, Bourree; Chretien, Quintet; Deslandres, Quintet; Goepfart, Quartet (fl, ob, cl, bn) Haydn-Muth, Quintet; Haydn, Menuet; Haydn, Presto; Lefebvre, Op. 57, Suite; Moritz, Quintet, Op. 41; Mozart, Minuet; Mozart, German Dance; Normand, Quintet in E major; Pfeiffer, Musette, Trio; Pierne, Pastorale; Taffanel, Quintet.

ANDRAUD, Sixth Collection, 12 Concert Pieces in Quintet Form, Contents: Haydn, Andante from Surprise Symphony; Beethoven, Scherzo from Seventh Symphony; Chopin, Nocturne, Op. 15, No. 3; Chopin, Mazurka, Op. 7; Intermezzo, Op. 13, Mendelssohn; Mendelssohn, Canzonetta, Op. 12; Beethoven, Andante Cantabile, with variations, Op. 18, No. 5; Beethoven, Symphonie Pastorale (Reunion Joyeuse de Villageois; Corroyez, Faunes et Nymphes (Divertissement et Danse); Bizet, Intermezzo from Carmen; Weber, Invitation to the Waltz, Op. 65; Corroyez, Marche de M. le Marechat de Saxe (18th Century Reconstituee et Harmonisee) (Instrumentation: Part A: fl or v; Part B: ob, v or cl; Part C: cl, or v; Part D: cl, v, or h in F; Part E: bn, vc or bass-cl) Andraud.

FOUR QUINTETS: Jongen, Preambule and Dances, Op. 98; C. H. Grimm, A Little Serenade, Op. 36: Intrade for Horn Alone, Alla Sarabanda, duo for cl and bn, Scherzino, duo for fl and ob, Finale for entire ensemble; Leclair, Minuet and Hunting Scene; Liszt, Pastoral, Longing for Home, Eclog. (fl, ob, cl, h, bn) H-VH Andraud; Baron.

Piano Quintets

ABRAMSKY, ALEXANDER, Concertino (fl, cl, h, bn, pf) Russicher
       Staats Verlag; Universal Edition; Andraud.
ALBINONI, TOMMASO, Douze Concerts a Deux Hautbois, alto violon-
       celle et orgue, Op. 9 (2 ob, va, vc, organ) Fetis.
BACH, JOHANN CHRISTIAN,Quintett in D major (fl, ob, v, vc,
       harpsichord) arr. by Ermeler, Musica Rara; McGinnis &
       Marx; Barenreiter-Bote.
    ---Quintets, Op. 11 in Eb major, No. 4, and D major, No. 6
       (fl, ob, v, va, pf) ed. by R. Steglich, Nagel, (score,
       parts).
    ---Deux Quintetti (fl, ob, va, vc, pf) Fetis.
BAUSSNERN, WALDEMAR VON, Quintet in F major (v, cl, h, vc, pf)
       Simrock; Andraud; AMP.
BEDFORD, HERBERT, Lyric Interlude, Pathways of the Moon, Op.
       50 (fl, ob, v, va, pf) Goodwin & Tabb.
BEETHOVEN, LUDWIG VAN, Menuet from the Septet, Op. 20 (fl, ob,
       cl, bn, pf) Fischer, (score, parts).
    ---Quintet, Op. 16 in Eb major (ob, cl, h, bn, pf) VH
       Costallat; Sansone; B&H, Critical Edition; Litolff;
       Schott; Andraud; E. B. Marks; International Music Co;
       AMP; Andre; Simrock; Cranz (ed. by L. Lee and Louis
       Winkler); Sander (min score, Eulenburg).
BLANC, ADOLPHE, Quintet, Op. 37 (fl, cl, h, bn, pf) Costallat;
       Richault.
BONNER, EUGENE, Flutes, Op. 10 (voice, fl, cl, bn, harp or pf)
       La Chanson du Porcepic, La Complainte de Monsieur Benoit,
       Chameaux, Paysage de Neige. Chester.
CAPLET, ANDRE, Quintet, 1898 (fl, ob, cl, bn, harp or pf).
CETTIER, PIERRE, Quintet in G major (fl, ob, cl, bn, pf) 1927,
       Senart.
CORBETT, WILLIAM, Six Sonatas (2 ob or tromb, 2 v, b.c.) Roger;
       Fetis.
COUPERIN, FRANCOIS, 6 Concerts Royeaux (ob, v, bn, vc, h'chord)
       L'Oiseau Lyre (in score form only in a complete edition
       of Couperin's works).
COUPERIN, FRANCOIS, Adolescentulus sum, Motet (sop. 2 fl, v, or-
       gan (L'Oiseau Lyre; Musica Rara.
DANZI, FRANZ, Quintetto, Op. 53, 54 (fl, ob, h, bn, pf) Andre;
       Fetis; Offenbach.
    ---Premier Quintet in F major, Op. 53 (fl, ob, cl, bn, pf)
       Offenbach; Andre; Dresden, Konig Bibliothek.
    ---Deuxieme Quintet in D major, Op. 53 (fl, ob, cl, bn, pf)
       Offenbach; Andre; Dresden, Konig Bibliothek.
    ---Quintet, Op. 41 (ob, cl, h, bn, pf) Andraud; B&H;
DE BUERIS, J., Basson Fantasie in F (4 bn, pf) Boosey & Hawkes.
DENZA, L., Funiculi-Funicula, arr. by A. Harris (4 Bb cl; 2 Bb
       cl, 2 Eb alto-cl or sax; 3 Bb cl, bn or Eb alto-cl or
       sax; fl, ob, Bb cl, bn; 2 Bb cl, Eb alto-cl or sax, bn
       or bass-cl; all with pf accompaniment) Cundy-Bettoney
       Co., Inc. (parts).
DONATO, VINCENZO DI, Pastorale (ob, cl, eng h, sax, pf) Edi-
       zioni De Santis, Rome.

DUKELSKY, VLADIMIR, Three Pieces in C: Humn, Waltz, Paso Doble
    (fl, ob, cl, bn, pf) Fischer.
DUNCAN, WILLIAM E.,Quintet, Op. 38 (fl, cl, h, bn, pf) Andraud;
    Rudall & Carte; Boosey & Hawkes.
DUNHILL, THOMAS FREDERICK, Quintet, Op. 3 in Eb major (v, vc, cl,
    h, pf) Rudall, Carte & Co; Boosey & Hawkes.
EHRENBERG, Choeur with 2 cl, 2 h, h'chord, Fetis.
FASCH, JOHANN FRIEDRICH, Sonata a 4 in Bb major (fl, ob, v, vc,
    pf, vc ad lib) Nagel; McGinnis & Marx.
FIBICH, ZDENKO, Quintet, Op. 42 in D major (v, cl, h, vc, pf)
    A. Urbanek; Andraud.
FINGER, GODEFROID, A Set of Sonatas in Five Parts for Flutes and
    Oboes (2 fl, 2 ob, pf) Roger; Fetis.
GABRIELI, GIOVANNI, Sonata (3 fl, vc ad lib, pf) C. F. Peters.
GHEDINI, GIORGIO F., Concerto for Five (fl, ob, cl, bn, pf) An-
    draud; Ricordi.
GIESEKING, WALTER, Quintet in Bb major (ob, cl, h, bn, pf) Oer-
    tel; Sansone; Andraud; Furstner.
GRUND, WILHELM FRIEDRICH, Quintet, Op. 8 (ob, cl, h, bn, pf) An-
    draud; Peters; Fetis.
HAMM, JOHANN VALENTINE, Dialogue (fl, ob, cl, h, pf) Andraud.
HARRIS, A., A Kerry Tune, Farewell to Cucullain (4 Bb cl; 2 Bb
    cl, 2 Eb alto-cl or sax; or 3 Bb cl, bn or Eb alto-cl or
    sax; fl, ob, Bb cl, bn; 3 fl, alto-fl or Bb cl; 2 Bb
    cl, Eb alto-cl or sax, bn or bass-cl, all with pf acc't)
    Cundy-Bettoney Co., Inc. (score, parts).
HARRIS, ROY, Quintet, 1932 (fl, ob, h, bn, pf).
HAYDN, FRANZ JOSEPH, Symphony Concertante, Op. 84 (ob, bn, v,
    vc, pf) ed. by Hans Sitt, Andraud; International Mu-
    sic Co.; Baron; B&H; AMP.
   ---Divertimenti (v, 2 h, bn, pf or other combinations)
    Geiringer.
HERZOGENBERG, HEINRICH VON, Quintet, Op. 43 in Eb major (ob, cl,
    h, bn, pf) Peters; Andraud.
HOLBROOKE, JOSEF A., Quintet, No. 2 (4 winds, pf) Andraud;
    Modern Music Library.
HUBER, HANS, Quintet, Op. 136 (fl, cl, h, bn, pf) Hug; Andraud.
HUMMEL, JOHANN NEPOMUK, Serenade, Op. 63, No. 1 (pf, v, guitar,
    cl, bn) Fetis; Artaria; Richault.
   ---Serenade, Op. 66, No. 2 (pf, v, guitar, cl, bn) Fetis;
    Artaria; Richault.
HUTTEL, JOSEF, Divertissement Grotesque (ob, cl, bn, h, pf) 1929,
    Library of Congress, Washington.
IPPOLITOV-IVANOV, MIKHAIL, Quintet, Op. 71, Evening in Georgia
    (fl, ob, cl, bn, pf or harp) Russicher Staats-Verlag;
    Universal Edition; Andraud; Peters.
JADIN, LOUIS EMMANUEL, Three Quintets Concertant (fl, ob, h, bn,
    pf) Janet; Fetis.
JANITSCH, JOHANN GOTTLIEB, Kammersonate, Op. 8 (fl, ob or 2 fl,
    va, vc, pf) B&H, ed. by C. Wolff.
KAHN, ROBERT, Quintet, Op. 54 in C minor (cl, v, h, vc, pf) Bote
    & Bock; Andraud.
KALKBRENNER, FRIEDRICH, Quintet, Op. 81 in A minor (cl, h, vc,
    bn, pf) B&H; Fetis.
KALMAN, EMMERICH, Un Coin Sous Les Toits, Tango (4 cl, pf) AMP;
    Eschig; Baron.

KANITZ, ERNEST, Quintettino, 1944 (ob, cl, h, bn, pf) Ms, University of Southern California.
   ---Sonate de Danse, Quintet (fl, cl, bn, tpt, pf) Andraud; University of Southern California.
KARG-ELERT, SIEGFRIED, Jugond in Bb (fl, cl, bn, h, pf) Zimmerman.
KETELBY, A. W., Quintet (fl, cl, h, bn, pf).
KOSPOTH, ORHON, C. E., Baron De, Serenade, Op. 19 (ob, 2 basset-h, bn, pf) Fetis; Andre; Offenbach.
KREUTZER, KONRADIN, Divertissement, Op. 37 (fl, h, bn, bass, pf) Gombart; Fetis.
KRIEGER, JOHANN PHILIPP VON, Partie Feldmusik, III (ob, 2 eng h bn, pf).
   ---Suite, Old Style, Partie Aus Feldmusik, No. 9 in F major (2 ob, eng h, bn, pf) Kistner & Siegel (ed. by Max Seiffert); Andraud.
LACOMBE, LOUIS B., Quintet, Op. 26 in F# minor (v, ob, vc, bn, pf) Costallat.
LANNOY, EDOUARD, Baron De, Quintet, Op. 2 (ob, cl, h, bn, pf) Fetis; Andre; Offenbach.
LAUBE, P. X., Alsatian Dance, arr. by A. Harris (4 cl; fl, ob, cl, bn; 2 Bb cl, 2 Eb alto-cl or sax; 2 Bb cl, Eb alto-cl or sax, bn or bass-cl; all with pf acc't) Cundy-Bettoney Co. (parts, score).
LAUBER, JOSEPH, Quintet (fl, cl, eng h, bn, pf) Andraud.
LEIDESDORF, MAX, Quintet, Op. 66 in Eb major (v, cl, vc, bn, pf).
   ---Rondo Brilliant, Op. 128 (fl, cl, va, vc, pf) Artaria; Fetis.
LESLIE, HENRY, Quintet in G minor (ob, cl, h, bn, pf) Fetis.
LIEBERSON, GODDARD, Quintet (va, vc, ob, bn, pf or harp).
LOEFFLER, CHARLES, Ballade Carnevalesque (fl, ob, sax, bn, pf).
LONGO, ACHILLE, Scenetta Pastorale (fl, ob, cl, bn, pf) Curci; Andraud.
LUTZ, HENRY, Fantaisie Japon (2 fl, v, vc, harp) Paxton.
MACBETH, A., Intermezzo, Forget-Me-Not, arr. by A. Harris (4 Bb cl; 2 Bb cl, 2 Eb alto-cl or sax; 3 Bb cl, bn or Eb alto-cl or sax; fl, ob, Bb cl, bn; 2 Bb cl, Eb alto-cl or sax, bn or bass-cl; all with pf acc't) Cundy-Bettoney Co., Inc.
MAGNARD, ALBERT, Quintet, Op. 8 in D minor (fl, ob, cl, bn, pf) Rouart; Andraud.
MANUEL, Suite for Piano Quintet (fl, ob, cl, bn, pf) McGinnis & Marx.
MARTINI, GIOVANNI BATTISTA, Les Moutons, Celebrated Gavotte (ob, cl or 2 cl, 2 bn, pf) Andraud.
MEYER, KARL HEINRICH, Fantasy Concertant, Op. 20 (fl, cl, h, bn and orchestra) Hofmeister; Fetis.
MOLLOY, J., Kerry Dance, arr. by A. Harris (4 Bb cl; 2 Bb cl 2 Eb alto-cl or sax; 3 Bb cl, bn or Eb alto-cl or sax; fl, ob, Bb cl, bn; 2 Bb cl, Eb alto-cl or sax, bn or bass-cl; all with pf acc't) Cundy-Bettoney Co. (parts).
MORILLO, ROBERTO GARCIA, Goya Suite, Las Pinturas Negras de Goya (pf, vc, fl, cl, bn) Performed at University of Montevideo, Uruguay, Mary 27, 1940.
MORINI, FERDINAND, Quintet, Op. 16 (wind instruments, pf) Fetis.

MORTARI, VIRGILIO, Concertino (v, cl, tpt, bn, pf).
MOZART, WOLFGANG AMADEUS, Second Quintet, Op. 20 (fl, ob, va, vc, pf) Andraud.
---Symphony Concertante (ob, cl, h, bn, pf), in Eb major, K 297b Sansone; Andraud; B&H; Cundy-Bettoney Co., Inc.; Musica Rara.
---Quintet in Eb major, K 452, Largo-Allegro Moderato, Larghetto, Rondo (ob, cl, h, bn, pf) Andre; Schott; Litolff; B&H, Critical Edition; Sander (min score, Eulenburg; Marks; International Music Co; Andraud; Baron; AMP.
---K 616 (fl, ob, va, vc, pf).
---Adagio and Rondo in C, K 617 (fl, ob, va, vc, pf or celeste) B&H; Andraud; Schweers & Haake (ed. by Czerny); Baron; AMP.
MUFFAT, GEORG, Die Suiten aus dem Blumenbuschlein, ed. by Woehl (4 or 5 wind instruments, pf) Barenreiter.
OLDBERG, ARNE, Woodwind Piano Quintet (fl, ob, cl, bn, pf), Op. 18, Northwestern University.
ONSLOW, GEORGE, Quintet, Op. 30 in Eb major (fl, cl, h, bn, pf)
PAUER, ERNST, Quintet, Op. 44 in F major (ob, cl, h, bn, pf) Andraud; Schott.
PIERNE, HENRY, March of the Little Tin Soldiers (fl, ob, cl, bn; 4 Bb cl, with pf acc't) transc. by G. Grisez, Cundy-Bettoney Co., (parts).
PFEIFFER, GIOVANNI, Sonata in G major (fl, ob, h, bn, pf) Hofmeister (ed. by R. Lauschmann); Eble; Andraud; Hug, (ed. by R. Lauschmann).
PONCHIELLI, AMILCARE, Quartetto (fl, ob, Eb cl, cl, pf) Andraud; Ricrodi.
PORTA, BERNARDO, Quintets, Books I, II, III, Iv (2 fl, v, va, pf) Naderman; Fetis.
PROKOFIEFF, SERGE, Quintet, Op. 39 in G minor (ob, cl, v, va, pf) Gutheil; Russicher Musikverlag (score, parts); International Music Co; E. B. Marks; Baron; Andraud; B&H.
PURCELL, HENRY, Music for Midsummer Night's Dream and from the Fairy Queen (4 wind instruments, pf) Hockner, Musica Rara.
---Music for Midsummer Night's Dream II (continuation of Book I, 4 wind instruments, pf) Musica Rara; Barenreiter.
REICHARDT, JOHANN FRIEDRICH, Quintet (2 fl, 2 h, pf) Fetis.
REICHEL, A., Quintet (ob, cl, h, bn, pf) Andraud.
RICCIO, GIOVANNI BATTISTA, Jubilent Omnes (voice, fl, v, bn, pf) Text, Latin and German, ed. by Dr. Adam Adrio, Nagel.
RICE, H. H., Quintet, Op. 2 in Bb major (ob, cl, h, bn, pf) Andraud; Simrock.
RIMSKY-KORSAKOFF, NICOLAS ANDRE, Quintet in B major (h, bn, cl, fl, pf) Sansone; Belaiev; Andraud; Musica Rara; Russicher Verlag; McGinnis & Marx.
ROGOSKI, GUSTAVE, Quintet (4 wind instruments, pf) Fetis Supplement.
RON, MARTIN VON, Quintet, Op. 1 (fl, cl, h, bn, pf) B&H; Fetis.
RORICH, CARL, Quintet, Op. 58 (4 wind instruments, pf) Zimmerman.

ROTA, NINO, Quintetto (fl, ob, va, vc, harp) Ricordi.
ROUSSEAU, SAMUEL ALEXANDER, Bergers et Mages, Bb major (ob, v,
    bn, harp and organ, arr. for ob, bn, v, vc, pf) Mercury.
RUBINSTEIN, ANTON GREGOROVITCH, Quintet, Op. 55 in F major (fl,
    cl, h, bn, pf) Schuberth & Co; Hamelle; Andraud.
RUYNEMAN, DANIEL, Divertimento (fl, cl, va, h, pf) Andraud;
    Chester.
SATTER, GUSTAV, Quintet, Op. 6 in Eb major (2 fl, alto-h, bn,
    pf, or 2 cl, alto-h, bn, pf) Hoffarth.
SAUGUET, HENRI, Pres du Bal, Divertissement (fl, cl, bn, v, pf)
    Rouart.
    ---Divertissement de chambre (fl, cl, bn, va, pf) Andraud;
    Eschig.
SCARLATTI, ALESSANDRO, Quartetino (3 alto reco or 3 fl, pf, vc
    ad lib, ed. by Woehl, C. F. Peters (Urtext); Baron.
    ---Sonata (2 fl, 2 v, pf) Santini Library, Ms.
SCHEIDT, SAMUEL, Suite (4 wind instruments, pf) Nagel.
SCHICKHARDT, JOHANN CHRISTIAN, Konzerte (4 fl, pf) Barenreiter,
    (score, parts).
    ---3 Concerti (4 alto reco, pf) McGinnis & Marx (score).
    ---Sonata, Op. 5 (fl, 2 ob, bass viol, b.c.) Roger; Fetis.
SCHMIKERER, J. A., Suite in Two Parts, F major and D minor (4
    wind instruments, pf) ed. by W. Woehl, Barenreiter.
SCHOECK, OTHMAR, Wanderspruche, Liederfolge nach Eichendorff,
    Op. 42 (ten or sop, cl, h, pf, perc.) B&H; Universal
    Edition.
SCHULZE, JOHANN CHRISTOPHER, Suite in D minor (2 fl, vc, pf,
    gambe), ed. by W. Friedrich, Schott.
SCHUTZ, HEINRICH, Symphoniae Sacrae, No. 7, Anima Mea; No. 8,
    Adjuro Vos (2 ten, 2 eng h, pf) Barenreiter.
    ---Deutsches Konzert, Der Herr Ist Mein Licht (ten, bar,
    2 wind instruments, pf or organ) ed. by H. Hofmann,
    Nagel.
SLAVENSKI, JOSIP S., Suite, Op. 6, From the Village (fl, cl, v,
    va, pf) Schott (score, parts); AMP; Andraud.
SPINDLER, FRITZ, Quintet, Op. 360 in F major (ob, cl, h, bn, pf)
    Leuckart; Andraud.
    ---Quintet, Op. 2 (ob, cl, bn, h, pf) Andraud.
SPOHR, LOUIS, Grand Quintet, Op. 52 in C minor (fl, cl, h, bn,
    pf) Andraud; Barenreiter; Musica Rara; McGinnis &
    Marx (score, parts); Peters.
STEPHEN, DAVID, Quintet, Op. 3 in D minor (ob, cl, bn, h, pf)B&H.
TANSMAN, ALEXANDRE, Divertimento (ob, cl, tpt, vc, pf) AMP.
TAUBERT, ERNST EDUARD, Quintet, Op. 48 in Bb major (fl, cl, h,
    bn, pf) Bote & Bock; Andraud.
TEIL, ZWEITER, 9 Weitere Stucke (4 wind instruments, pf) Baren-
    reiter (score, parts).
TELEMANN, Georg Philipp, Chambersonata "Echo" (fl, ob, va, vc,
    b.c.) Musica Rara, London; Collegium Musicum, No. 68,
    B&H (ed. by Hugo Riemann).
    ---Quartet in D minor (reco, 2 fl, vc, b.c.) Musica Rara;
    Collegium Musicum, No. 59, B&H (ed. by Hugo Riemann).
    ---Quartet in G major (reco or fl, ob, or v, v, pf, vc ad
    lib) C. F. Peters (Urtext, ed. by Woehl) Rieter-
    Biedermann.

---Kanarienvogel-Kantate, Tragikomische Kantate (voice, 2 fl,
    2 strings, b.c.) Barenreiter.

---Tafelmusik II, No. 2 in D minor (3 fl, bn, pf) ed. by
    Max Seiffert, B&H; D.D.T. (arr. for 3 fl, vc, pf).

THIERIOT, FERNINAND, Quintet, Op. 80 in A minor (ob, cl, h, bn,
    pf) Simrock; Andraud.

TRIEBENSEE, JOSEPH, Grand Quintet (cl, eng h, basset-h, bn, pf)
    Haslinger; Fetis.

TURECHEK, EDWARD, Flute Quintet in D minor (4 fl, pf) VH An-
    draud; Witmark; Music Publishers Holding Corp., (score,
    parts).

VERDI, GIUSEPPE, Rigoletto Quartet (4 cl; 2 cl, alto-cl or sax,
    bass-cl or bn; 3 cl, bn or sax or Eb alto-cl; 2 Bb cl,
    2 Eb cl or sax; fl, ob, cl, bn; all with pf acc't).
    arr. by A. Harris, Cundy-Bettoney Co., Inc. (parts); An-
    draud.

VERHEY, THEODOR, Quintet, Op. 20 in Eb major (ob, cl, h, bn, pf)
    B&H; Andraud.

VILLERS, BARON DE, Quintet (harp, ob, h, bn, pf) Chatot.

VIVALDI, A., Concerto in D major "Del Gardellino," F. XII, No.
    9, ed. by Malipiero (fl, ob, v, bn, pf) Hug.

---Concerto in G major, F XII, No. 13, ed. by Malipiero
    (fl, ob, v, bn, b.c.) Hug.

---Concerto in G minor, F XII, No. 6, ed. by Malipiero (fl,
    ob, v, bn, pf) Hug.

VOLBACH, FRITZ, Quintet, Op. 24 in Eb major (ob, cl, h, bn, pf)
    B&H; Sansone; Andraud; Musica Rara; AMP.

WIDERKEHR, JACQUES CHRETIEN MICHEL, Six Quintets (fl, cl, h, bn,
    pf) Janet; Fetis.

WITT, L. FRIEDRICH, Grand Quintet, Op. 6 (ob, cl, h, bn, pf)
    B&H; Fetis.

WOLF, ERNST WILHELM, Two Quintets (fl, v, va, bn, pf) Fetis.

WOOLETT, HENRY, Five Pieces (2 fl, cl, h, pf).

Sextets

ABEL, CLAMER-HEINRICH, Concerto in Eb (2 v, va, 2 fl, pf) C.F.
    Peters (Urtext).

ACHRON, JOSEPH, Sextet, Op. 73 (fl, ob, cl, h, bn, tpt) New
    Music, XV, No. 4, 1942.

ARTSIBOUSHEV, NICOLAI V., Mazurka in F major (fl, ob, 2 cl, h,
    bn) arr. by H. Klickmann, Standard.

AURIC, GEORGES, Five Bagatelles on Marlborough (fl, bn, tpt, v,
    vc, pf) Andraud.

---Incidental music to Marcel Achard's play "Malbrouck s'en
    va-t-en guerre" (cl, bn, tpt, v, vc, pf).

BACH, JOAHNN CHRISTIAN, Sextet, Op. 11, No. 1-6, C major, G ma-
    jor, F major, Eb major, A major, D major (fl, ob or v, v,
    va, vc, pf) ed. by R. Steglich, 1936, Nagel.

BACH, JOHANN GEORG, Sextuor, Op. 3 (ob, v, vc, 2 h, pf) Fetis;
    Offenbach; Andre.

BACH, JOHANN SEBASTIAN, Musical Offering XIII, Ricercar a 6 (6-
    part fugue) (3 reeds, 3 strings) G. Schirmer.

BACH, WILHELM FRIEDEMANN, Sinfonia in D major (2 fl, 2 v, va,
    pf) Fetis.
BAUER, MARION, Concertino, Op. 32b (ob, cl, 2 v, va, vc, pf ad
    lib) Arrow.
BEETHOVEN, LUDWIG VAN, Sextet. Scherzo, Op. 2, No. 2 from the
    pf sonata, arr. by A. E. Cafarella (fl, ob, cl, 2 h, bn)
    Andraud; Music Publishers Holding Corp. (score, parts).
  ---Scherzo, Op. 2, No. 3, from the pf sonata, arr. by Wm. C.
    Schoenfeld (fl, ob, 2 cl, h, bn) Andraud; Music Pub-
    lishers Holding Corp. (score, parts).
  ---Scherzo, Op. 10, No. 2, from the pf sonata in F minor,
    arr. by Wm. C. Schoenfeld (fl, ob, 2 cl, h, bn) Andraud;
    Music Publishers Holding Corp. (score, parts).
  ---Finale, Op. 10, No. 2, from the pf sonata in F minor,
    arr. by Wm. C. Schoenfeld (fl, ob, 2 cl, 2 bn) Music Pub-
    lishers Holding Corp. (score, parts); Andraud (fl, ob,
    2 cl, h, bn).
  ---Scherzo from Grand Sonata, Op. 26 (2 cl, 2 alto-cl, 2
    bass-cl) E David Gornston.
  ---Scherzo from pf sonata, Op. 27, No. 2, arr. by Wm. C.
    Schoenfeld (fl, ob, 2 cl, h, bn) Music Publishers Hold-
    ing Corp. (score, parts); Andraud.
  ---Sextet for wind instruments, Op. 70, in Eb major (6
    wind instruments) International Music Corp.; Musica
    Rara.
  ---Sextet, Op. 71 in Eb major (2 cl, 2 h, 2 bn) MH-H (rec)
    B&H (score); Sander (min score); Andraud; Sansone;
    Costallat (parts); Eulenburg; AMP; International Mu-
    sic Co; B&H Critical Edition, Supplementary Volume;
    Educational Music Service, Inc.
  ---Sextet, Op. 81b in Eb major (2 v, va, vc, 2 h) Litolff;
    Louis Oertel; Sander (min score); Sansone (2 h, 2 vc,
    2 v); Andraud (2 h, 2 vc, 2 v); Costallat (parts);
    B&H (score, parts).
  ---March in B major (2 cl, 2 h, 2 bn) arr. by Emil Kahn
    MH-H (rec) E. B. Marks; Andraud.
  ---March in Bb major, B&H.
  ---Minuet (2 cl, 2 h, 2 bn) arr. by Emil Kahn MH-H (rec)
    E. B. Marks; Andraud.
BENJAMIN, ARTHUR L., Jamaican Rumba (fl, ob, cl, bn, h, pf) H
    Boosey-Hawkes (score, parts).
BILLINGS, B., Chester (fl, ob, 2 Bb cl, h in F, bn, pf ad lib)
    Carl Fischer (score, parts).
BIZET, GEORGES, Quintet from Carmen, arr. by Wilson (fl, ob, cl,
    h, bn, pf) H-VH Carl Fischer.
BLUMER, THEODORE, Sextet, Op. 45, Original Theme and Variations
    in F major (fl, ob, cl, h, bn, pf) Simrock; Andraud; AMP.
  ---Sextett, Op. 92 (fl, ob, cl, h, bn, pf) Wilke.
BOCCHERINI, LUIGI, Six Sinfonie, Op. 22 (2 v, va, ob or fl, h,
    pf) Fetis; Sieber.
  ---Sextet, Op. 42, No. 2 (v, va, bn, ob or fl, h, pf) Fe-
    tis; Pleyel.
BOISDEFFRE, RENE DE, Scherzo, Op. 49, arr. by Altmann (fl, ob,
    cl, h, bn, pf) MH J. Hamelle; Fischer; Andraud.

BOSSI, RENZO, Sextet, Op. 10a, Theme and Variations (fl, ob, cl, bn, h, tpt) Bohm (score, parts).

BRANDL, JEAN, Sextuors (6 bn or 6 fl) Fetis.
---Sextuor in C major, Op. 16 (v, bn, h, 2 va, vc) Fetis; Offenbach.

BRAUER, MAX, Sextet in G minor (fl, ob, cl, h, bn, pf) B&H; Sansone; Andraud; AMP.

BRETON, TOMAS, Sextet (fl, ob, cl, h, bn, pf) Union Music, Espanola.

BRUNEAU, ERNEST, Sextet in C major (fl, ob, cl, h, bn, pf) Andraud; Schneider.

BULLERIAN, HANS, Sextet in Gb major, Op. 38 (fl, ob, cl, h, bn, pf) Andraud; Simrock; AMP.

BUMCKE, GUSTAV, Sextet, Op. 19 in Ab major (cl, eng h, sax, h, bass-cl, bn) Diem (score, parts); Andraud; Eisoldt & Rohkramer; Saturn-Verlag.

CARMICHAEL, HOAGI, Stardust, arr. by F. H. Klickmann (fl, ob, 2 cl, h, bn) Mills Music.

CASTILLO, RICARDO, The Fairy of the Blue Mountain (2 fl, ob, cl, bn, pf) Fleisher.

CHOULET, CHARLES, Sextet, Op. 18 (fl, ob, h, v, vc, pf) Costallat.

CORDS, GUSTAV, Sextet (fl, ob, cl, h, bn, pf) Andraud.

CROES, HENRI-JACQUES DE, Symphonies d'eglise, Sonatas 2-13 (2 v, va, vc, 2 ob) Fetis Supplement.

DALLAPICCOLA, LUIGI, Divertimento in 4 Exercizi (voice, 5 winds) Carisch.

D'ANDRIEU, JEAN FRANCOIS, Musette in G major (fl, ob, eng h, cl, 2 bn) Andraud; Ricordi.

DANZI, FRANZ, Sextet, Op. 10 (ob, 2 va, 2 h, vc, pf) Schott; Fetis.

DAVID, JOHANN NEPOMUK, Divertimento on Old Folksongs, Op. 24 (fl, ob, cl, h, bn, pf) ed. by W. Bohle, B&H.

DEFESCH, WILLIAM, Deux Concerts (2 ob, 2 v, bass viol, pf) Roger; Fetis.

DELLA JOIO, NORMAN, Sextet (3 rec or 3 winds, 3 strings) Hargail.

DESPORTES, YVONNE, Prelude and Pastorale (fl, ob, cl, h, bn, pf) Andraud.

DEVASINI, G., Sextet (fl, ob, 2 cl, h, bn) Ricordi; Fetis.

DIETHE, Romance (2 ob, cl, 2 bn, h, bass-cl) Andraud.

D'INDY, PAUL VINCENT, Sarabande in D major, Menuet in D minor, Op. 72, arr. from suite for pf, Op. 24 (fl, ob, cl, h, bn, pf) H Andraud; Hamelle; Sansone.

DOHNANYI, ERNST VON, Sextet, Op. 37 (v, va, vc, cl, h, pv) Universal Music Co.
---Sextet, Op. 57 in C major (cl, h, v, va, vc, pf) Lengnick; Mills Music.

DONOVAN, RICHARD FRANK, Sextet (5 winds, pf).

DRESDEN, SEM, Suite Naar Rameau, 1916 (fl, ob, cl, bn, h, pf) Stichting Donemus.
---Kleine Suite in C major, No. 2 (fl, ob, cl, bn, h, pf) Stichting Donemus.
---Derde Suite, 1920 (fl, ob, cl, h, bn, pf) Stichting Donemus.

DUKELSKY, VLADIMIR (Vernon Duke) Nocturne (fl, ob, cl, h, bn, pf) VH Carl Fischer.

---Three Pieces (6 woodwinds, no horn) H-VH Carl Fischer.

EBERS, CHARLES FREDERIC, Twelve Little Pieces (2 basset-h, 2 h, 2 bn) Hummel; Fetis.

EICHNER, ERNST, Sextetto in A major, Op. 12 (fl, ob, v, va, bn, pf).

EISLER, HANS, Palmstrom, Op. 5 (voice, fl, cl, v, va, vc) Universal Edition.

EMMANUEL, MAURICE, Trois Airs Rhythmes (2 fl, eng h, vc, 2 harps) Hayet.

EMMERT, ADAM JOSEPH, Harmonie, Premiere Recueil (2 cl, 2 h, 2 bn) Fetis.

ERLANGER, GUSTAV, Sextet, Op. 41 in Eb major (cl, h, bn, v, va, vc) Kistner & Siegel (score, parts); Andraud.

ERNST, Collection of Works, some by Ernst, some arr. from various operas and symphonies (2 cl, 2 h, 2 bn) Fetis.

FALLA, MANUEL DE, Concerto for Harpsichord or Piano (fl, ob, cl v, vc, pf or h'chord) Eschig (min score, parts).

FARRENC, MME. JEANNE LOUISE, Sextet, Op. 40 in C minor (fl, ob, cl, h, bn, pf) Fetis.

FIBICH, ZDENEK, Poeme, ed. by Trinkaus (2 cl, 2 h, bn, tuba; 2 cl, h, 2 bn, tuba; 3 cl, h, bn, tuba; 3 cl, 2 bn, tuba) Franklin Co.

FICHER, JACOBO, Suite en Estilo Antiquo (6 winds).

FISCHER, JOHANN, Suite, No. 3 in Bb major, No. 4 in D minor, No. 5 in G major, No. 6 in F major, ed. by Wohl (5 winds, pf) Barenreiter.

FOERSTER, EMMANUEL A., Sextet, Op. 9 (v, va, vc, fl, bn, pf) Fetis; Offenbach.

FRANCK, CESAR AUGUSTE, Panis Angelicus, from Messe Solennelle, arr. by G. J. Trinkaus (2 cl, 2 h, bn, tuba; 2 cl, h, 2 bn, tuba; 3 cl, h, bn, tuba; 3 cl, 2 bn, tuba) Franklin Co.

FRENSEL WEGENER, Emmy, Sextet, 1928 (fl, ob, cl, h, bn, pf) Stichting Donemus.

FUCHS, GEORG FRIEDRICH, Sextet, Op. 34 (cl, h, bn, v, va, pf) Imbault; Fetis.

FUHRMEISTER, FRITZ, Gavotte and Tarentelle, Op. 6 (fl, ob, cl, h, bn, pf) Sansone; Andraud.

GALINDO, BLAS, Sextet (fl, cl, bn, h, tpt, tromb) c/o Carlos Chaves, Orquesta Sinfonica de Mexico, Mexico City.

GARNEFELT, Berceuse, arr. by Theodore Rosch (fl, 2 cl, alto-cl, 2 bass-cl) T. Rosch, Band Director, State Normal Teacher's College, Ypsilanti, Michigan.

---Praeludium, arr. by Theodore Rosch (fl, 2 cl, alto-cl, 2 bass-cl) Ypsilanti, Michigan.

---White Peacock, arr. by Theodore Rosch (fl, 2 cl, alto-cl, 2 bass-cl) Ypsilanti, Michigan.

---The Ancient, arr. by T. Rosch (fl, 2 cl, alto-cl, 2 bass-cl) Ypsilanti, Michigan.

GASTINEL, LEON GUSTAVE CYPRIEN, Sextet (wind instruments, pf) Fetis Supplement.

GENIN, T., Sextuor in Eb major (fl, ob, cl, h, bn, pf) Andraud; 1906, Eschig (arr. by Demets, parts).

GERSTBERGER, KARL, Kammer-Kantate on "Gesang von der Lowengrube,"
    Goethe, Op. 24 (voices: sop, alto, bass, 3 ob) Barenreiter.
GOSSEC, FRANCOIS JOSEPH, Six Serenades (v, fl, h, bn, va, pf) Fet-
    is; Sieber; Vernier; Bailleux; La Chevardiere.
GRABNER, HERMANN, Sextet, Op. 33 (fl, ob, cl, alto-sax, h, bn)
    1932, Kistner & Siegel (score, parts).
GRAGNINI, FILIPPO, Sextet, Op. 9 (fl, cl, v, 2 guit, vc) Fetis;
    Carli; Richault.
GRIEG, EDVARD, Anitra's Dance, Sextet in A minor, arr. by W. C.
    Schoenfeld from Peer Gynt Suite (fl, ob, 2 cl, h, bn) An-
    draud; Music Publishers Holding Corp. (score, parts).
HANDEL, GEORGE FREDERICK. Concerto Grosso in C major (2 ob, 2 v, 2
    va, b.c. or 2 ob, 2 v, va, vc b.c.) B&H, XXI, 1858.
    ---Allegro from Fifth Concerto (4 strings, 2 ob) Andraud.
    ---Andante, Minuet, from Fourth Concerto (4 strings, ob, bn)
    Andraud.
HANKE, CHARLES, Sextets and Serenades (various combinations) Fetis.
HARRIS, ROY, Sextet, 1932 (fl, ob, cl, h, bn, pf).
HASSLER, HANS LEO, Intraden, from Lustgarten (6 woodwinds) arr. by
    Hockner, Barenreiter; Musica Rara, London.
HAUER, JOSEPH MATTHIAS, Seven Variations, Op. 35 (fl, cl, v, va,
    vc, b.c.).
HAYDN, FRANZ JOSEPH, Cassazione, No. 1 (fl, ob, 2 v, vc, pf)
    Haydn Catalogue, Geiringer.
    ---Cassazione, No. 5 in G major (2 v, fl, ob, vc, pf) Fetis.
    ---Cassazione, No. 11 (fl, ob, 2 v, vc, pf) Haydn Catalogue,
    Geiringer.
    ---Capriccio (fl, c., v, va, vc, harp) arr. by G. Tocchi, De
    Santis.
    ---Divertimento in C major, arr. by A. Sandberger, Jr. (2 ob,
    2 h, 2 bn) Munich.
    ---Divertissement (v, va, fl, 2 h, pf) Fetis; Sieber; Janet;
    Porro; Offenbach; Andre.
    ---Divertissement, No. 5 in C major (2 v, fl, ob, vc, pf)
    Fetis; Breitkopf.
    ---Sextet in E minor (v, ob, h, bn, va, pf) Fetis; Sieber;
    Janet; Porro; Offenbach; Andre.
HAYDN, GIUSEPPE, Divertimento No. XV in F major (2 ob, 2 h, 2 bn)
    Ms., Friends of Music Library, Vienna.
HERRMANN, EDUARD, Sextet, Op. 33 in G minor (ob, cl, 2 v, va, vc)
    Andraud; Raabe & Plothow; Afas-Verlag Hans Dunnebeil.
HILL, EDWARD B., Sextet, Op. 39 in Bb major (fl, ob, cl, h, bn,
    pf) Schirmer; Society for the Publication of American Music.
HOFFMEISTER, FRANZ ANTON, Variations (2 cl, 2 h, 2 bn) Leipzig;
    Fetis.
    ---Two Suites in harmonies of six and eight parts: Suite I
    (six instruments, including winds) Fetis.
HOLBROOKE, JOSEPH A., Sextet, Op. 33a in F minor (fl, ob, cl, h,
    bn, pf) Chester; Andraud; Modern Music Library; Hug.
HOLZBAUER, IGNAZ JAKOB, Sextuor, Op. 5 (fl, ob, v, va, bn, pf)
    Sieber, arr. by Meysey.
HONEGGER, ARTHUR, Concerto da Camera (fl, eng h, strings) Mc-
    Ginnis & Marx (score).
HUBER, HANS, Sextet in Bb major (fl, ob, cl, bn, h, pf) Andraud;
    Hug.

HUFFER, FRED K., Sailor's Horn Pipe in C major (fl, ob, cl, h, bn, pf) Witmark.

IBERT, JACQUES, The Gardener of Samos, Suite (fl, cl, tpt, v, vc, drums) Andraud; Heugel.

IMBRIE, ANDREW, Divertimento (fl, bn, tpt, v, vc, pf) UCLA, Berkeley.

INDY, VINCENT D'., Sarabande et Menuet, Op. 72 (from Op. 24) (fl, ob, cl, h, bn, pf) Hamelle.

IRELAND, JOHN, Sextet (cl, h, 2 v, va, vc).

JADIN, LOUIS EMMANUEL, Harmonie (2 cl, 2 h, 2 bn) LeDuc; Fetis.
---Three Sextets Concertant (2 cl, 2 h, 2 bn) Dufaut & Dubois; Fetis.

JANACEK, LEOS, Miade Jugend Suite (Youth Suite) (fl, ob, cl, h, bn, bass-cl) VH (rec) Hudebni Matice (min score, parts); B&H; Eble; Sansone; Andraud; Chester.

JAUNEZ, A., Sextet, Op. 4 in A major (2 h, 2 va, 2 vc) Costallat.
---Sextet, Op. 5 in F major (fl, v, 2 vc, 2 h) Costallat.

JAVAULT, LOUIS, Sextets, Nos. 1-6 (cl, fl, ob, h, 2 bn) Fetis; G. Gaveaux.

JENSEN, NIELS PETER, Bridal Song in D major, arr. by F. H. Klickmann (fl, ob, 2 cl, h, bn) Standard.

JENTSCH, WALTER, Kleine Kammermusik, Op. 5 (fl, ob, cl, h, bn, pf) Ries & Erler.

JONGEN, JOSEPH, Rhapsody, Op. 70 (fl, ob, cl, h, bn, pf) VH Andraud; Dogilbert.

JUON, PAUL, Divertimento in F major, Op. 51 (fl, ob, cl, h, bn, pf) Lienau; Andraud; Schlesinger; E. C. Schirmer.

KANITZ, ERNEST, Sextet, 1932 (fl, ob, cl, h, bn, v) University of Southern California, School of Music, Ms.

KARREN, L., Humoristic Scenes: Untimely Awakening, Painful Pavane, Weeping Menuet (fl, ob, cl, h, bass-cl, bn or pf) Andraud.

KEITH, GEORGE D., Journey of the Swagmen in C major (fl, ob, cl, h, bn, pf) Remick Music Corp; Gamble Hinged Music; Music Publishers Holding Corp. (score, parts).

KLEINSINGER, GEORGE, Design for Woodwinds (fl, ob, 2 cl, h, bn) MH (rec) Broadcast Music, Inc; Baron; AMP.

KLENGEL, AUGUSTE ALEXANDRE, Polonaise Concertante, Op. 35 (fl, cl, va, vc, bn, pf) Fetis.

KOEHLER, BENJAMIN FRIEDRICH, Jeu de dez D'ecossaises (2 cl, 2 h, tpt, bn) Breslau, Leuckart; Fetis.

KOPPEL, HERMAN D., Sextet, Op. 36 in C major (fl, ob, cl, h, bn, pf) Eble; Skandinavisk Musikforlag; McGinnis & Marx (score, parts).

KRAFT, WALTER, Die Beste Zeit im Jahr ist Mein, Cantata (sop, 4 winds, pf or organ) Barenreiter.

KUBIK, GAIL T., Trivialities, Op. 5, 1934 (fl, h, 2 v, va, vc)

KURPINSKI, CHARLES, Paysage Musical, Pot-Pourri, Op. 18 (h, bn, string quartet) Brzczina, Varsovie; Fetis.

LABATE, BRUNO, Intermezzo and Scherzino in A major (fl, ob, 2 cl h, bn) Labate, N.Y.

LACROIX, Sextet (fl, ob, cl, h, bn, pf) Ms., at Curtis Institute of Music, Philadelphia, Pa.

LAKE, MAYHEW L., Ludwig Miniature Ensembles, arr. by Lake: Cleveland, March; Madeline, Waltz; Long, Long Ago, Reverie;

Louisiana, Fox Trot; Andantino; Iron Mountain, March.
(Woodwind Ensemble: cl, bn, contra-bn) Ludwig Music Pub-
lishing Co.
LEFEBVRE, CHARLES EDWARD, Second Suite, Op. 122 (fl, ob, 2 cl, h,
bn) MH (rec) Léduc; Andraud.
LEYE, L., Sextet, Op. 3 (2 h, fl, basset h or cl, bn, pf) Sinner,
Coburg, 1844.
LORENZINI, RAIMOND, Six Nocturnes (2 cl, 2 h, bn, serpent) Fetis.
LUENING, OTTO, Sextet, Op. 2 (fl, cl, h, v, va, vc).
LULLY, JEAN BAPTISTE DE, Menuet from Le Bourgeois Gentilhomme
(4 cl, 2 bn, with contra-bn ad lib) Andraud.
MALHERBE, EDMOND, Sextet (fl, ob, cl, h, bn, eng h) H Ms. at
Curtis Institute of Music, Philadelphia, Pa.
MALZAT, JOHANN MICHAEL, Three Sextets for Oboe, Fetis.
MAPES; GORDON, Passacaglia (fl, ob, cl, h, bn, eng h) Ms. at
Curtis Institute of Music, Philadelphia, Pa.
MARTINU, BOHUSLAV, Cuisine Parade: Prologue, Tango, Charleston
and Finale (cl, bn, tpt, v, vc, pf) Leduc; Andraud;
Spratt; Baron (min score, parts).
---Serenada I, in A minor (cl, h, 3 v, va) Allegro Moder-
ato, Larghetto, Allegro; Melantrich.
MARX, KARL, Sextet, Op. 30, 18 Variations on an Old English Folk-
song (2 fl, ob or v, v, va, vc) Barenreiter (score, parts).
MEDER, JEAN GABRIEL, Six Marches (2 cl, 2 h, 2 bn) Hummel; Fe-
tis.
MEL-BONIS, Mme. Albert Domange, Sextet for Winds, Ms.
MELNIK, Clarinet Holiday (6 cl) EMB.
MENDELSSOHN-BARTHOLDY, FELIX, Intermezzo from Midsummer Night's
Dream, transc. (fl, ob, cl, h, bn, pf or fl, 2 Bb cl, h,
bn, pf) E Carl Fischer (score, parts).
---Scherzo, Op. 118 (fl, ob, cl, h, bn, pf) Andraud.
---Scherzo, Op. 110, transc. by Jospe (fl, ob, cl, h, bn, pf)
E Carl Fischer (score, parts).
MENTER, Serenade (fl, ob, 2 cl, h, bn) Andraud.
MIGNONE, FRANCISCO, Urutau; O Passaro Fantastico (picc, fl, cl,
bn, 2 pf) Boletin Latinoamericano de Musica, VI.
---Sextet (fl, ob, cl, bn, h, pf) University of Rio de Jan-
eiro.
MILLER, RALPH DALE, Three American Dances, Op. 25 (fl, ob, cl,
h, bn, pf) VH Carl Fischer.
MOHR, ADOLPHE, Die Dormusikanten, Humoresque (2 picc, cl, bn,
tromb, va) Andraud.
MONTEUX, PIERRE, Sextet (fl, ob, cl, bn, tromb, pf) Mathot.
MORAWETZ, JOHANN, Sextet (2 v, ob, fl, va, vc) Fetis.
MOSCHELES, IGNAZ, Grand Sextet, Op. 35 in Eb major (v, fl, 2 h,
vc, pf) Fetis; Schlesinger.
MOUQUET, JULES, Suite (fl, ob, 2 cl, h, bn) Lemoine.
MOZART, WOLFGANG AMADEUS, Five Divertissements, Op. 91 (2 ob, 2
h, 2 bn) Offenbach; Andre; Fetis.
---Divertimento No. 6 in C major, K 188
1880, B&H (score).
---Divertimento No. 7, K 205 in D major (v, va, bn, 2 h pf)
Andraud; B&H (score, parts); Sander (min score); Eulen-
burg (min score); AMP (2 h, string quintet--see Septets).

MOZART, WOLFGANG AMADEUS, Divertimento No. 8 in F major, K 213
(2 ob, 2 h, 2 bn) MH (rec) B&H (parts); Andraud; B&H
(score); AMP.
---Divertimento No. 9 in Bb major, K 240 (2 ob, 2 h, 2 bn) MH
(rec) B&H (parts); Andraud.
---Divertimento No. 10 in F major, K 247 (2 v, va, 2 h, pf)
B&H (score) Sander (min score, parts); Andraud; Heckel
(min score); Simrock, (arr. by F. David, parts); Senff,
(arr. by F. David, parts); Eulenburg (min score).
---Divertimento No. 12, in Eb major, K 252 (2 ob, 2 h, 2 bn)
MH (rec) B&H (parts, score); Andraud.
---Divertimento No. 13 in F major, K 253 (2 ob, 2 h, 2 bn) MH
(rec) B&H (parts, score); Sander (min score); Andraud.
---Divertimento No. 14 in Bb major, K 270 (2 ob, 2 h, 2 bn)
MH (rec) B&H (score, parts); Sander (min score); An-
draud; Masterworks Publications (parts); Marks; Musica
Rara.
---Divertimento No. 15 in Eb major, K 287 (2 v, va, 2 h, pf)
B&H (score, parts); Sander (min score); Andraud; Heckel
(min score); Simrock (arr. by F. David, parts); Senff,
(arr. by F. David, parts); Eulenburg (min score).
---Divertimento No. 16 in Eb major, K 289 (2 ob, 2 h, 2 bn)
MH (rec) B&H (parts, score); Andraud.
---Divertimento No. 17, K 334 in D major (2 v, va, 2 h, pf)
B&H (score, parts); Sander (min score); Eulenburg; An-
draud; Heckel (min score); Simrock (arr. by F. David,
parts); Senff (arr. by F. David, parts).
---Serenade No. 11 in Eb major, K 375 (2 cl, 2 h, 2 bn) B&H
(score).
---March, K 445 in F major (2 v, 2 va, vc, 2 h) B&H.
---Die Dorfmusikanten, K 522 in F major (2 v, va, 2 h, pf)
Schlesinger (score, parts); Andre (parts); B&H (score,
parts); Erdmann (parts); Heckel (min score); Sander,
(min score); Seeling; Eulenburg (min score).
---Three Pieces for Wind (2 cl, 2 bn, 2 h) B&H.
---Contradance in Rondo Form (2 ob, 2 h, 2 bn) arr. by Emil
Kahn; MH E. B. Marks.
MUFFET, GEORG, Die Suiten aus dem Blumenbuschlein (5 winds, pf)
arr. by W. Woehl, 1938, Barenreiter.
MULDER, ERNEST W., Sextett, 1946 (fl, ob, or eng h, cl, bn, h,
pf) Stichting Donemus.
MULLER, JOHANN MICHAEL, Twelve Sonatas, Op. 1 (concert ob, 2 ob,
or v, tenor ob, bn, pf) Fetis.
OLIVER, J. A., 40 Divertimenti (2 cl, 2 h, 2 bn) Fetis.
ONSLOW, GEORGE, Sextet in Eb major, Op. 30 (fl, cl, h, bn, bass,
pf) Andraud; B&H; AMP.
---Sextet in A minor, Op. 77 (fl, cl, h, bn, bass, pf) Kist-
ner & Siegel.
OSBORNE, GEORGE ALEXANDER, Sextet in E major, Op. 63 (fl, ob, h,
vc, bn, pf) Lemoine.
PAER, FERDINAND, La Douce Victoire, Fantasy (2 fl, 2 h, bn, pf)
Schoenenberger; Fetis.
PANIZZA, GIACCOMO, Sextet (fl, 2 cl, 2 h, bn) Artaria; Fetis.
PAZ, JAUN CARLOS, Second Concerto (ob, tpt, 2 h, bn, pf) Andraud.

PECHACZEC, FRANZ, Twelve Pieces, Laendler (2 cl, 2 h, 2 bn) Has-
 linger; Fetis.
PEMBAUR, K., Mountain Pictures (fl, ob, cl, h, bn, pf) Andraud.
PEPUSCH, JOHANN CHRISTOPHER, Six Concertos (2 fl a bec, 2 fl tra-
 versieres, ob, b.c.) Fetis.
PESSARD, EMILE LOUIS FORTUNE, Sextet (6 wind instruments) Fetis
 Supplement.
PHILIDOR, ANNE, Premier Livre de Pieces (fl traversiere, flute a
 bec, violins, oboe, b.c.) Fetis Supplement.
PHILIDOR, FRANCOIS-ANDRE, Ariettes Periodiques (voice, v, va, ob,
 h, pf) Fetis Supplement.
PIERE, HENRY GABRIEL, Giration, Divertissement Choregraphique
 for strings (fl, cl, bn, tpt, tromb, pf) Andraud.
 ---The March of the Little Lead Soldiers, transc. (fl, ob, cl,
 h, bn, pf) ME Andraud.
PIJPER, WILLEM, Sextet, 1923 (fl, ob, cl, bn, h, pf) Stichting
 Donemus; McGinnis & Marx.
PINSUITI, CIRO, Scherzino in G major, arr. by M..A. Springer (fl,
 ob, 2 cl, tpt, bn) Gamble Hinged Music Co.
PORSCH, GILBERT, Americana, Potpourri of War Medlodies (fl, ob,
 2 cl, h, bn)
POULENC, FRANCIS, Sextet (fl, ob, cl, bn, h, pf) H Andraud;
 Eble; McGinnis & Marx; Chester; Hug.
PRAAG, HENRI, C. VAN, Divertimento, 1938 (v, fl, ob, cl, bn, h)
 Stichting Donemus.
PROWO, P., Sextet, Concerto in C major (2 bass strings, 2 ob, 2
 bn) Nagel (score).
PUSCHMANN, JOSEPH, Three Pieces in Harmony (2 cl, 2 h, 2 bn)
 Fetis.
QUEF, CHARLES, Sextet, Op. 4, Suite (fl, ob, cl, h, bn, pf) An-
 draud; Noel.
RAFF, JOSEPH JOACHIM, Sextet (5 instruments, pf) Fetis Supple-
 ment.
READ, GARDNER, Two Songs for Voice and Woodwind Quintet, Boston
 University School of Music.
REBNER, EDWARD W., Sextet for Woodwinds, A. F. of M., Los Angeles,
 California.
 ---Sextet for Woodwinds and Piano, Los Angeles Conservatory
 of Music.
REDLICH, HANS F., Opus 10, Slovakische Lieder (voice, 5 instru-
 ments) 1932, Bote & Bock.
REICHA, ANTON, Sextet (2 cl, string quartet).
REINECKE, CARL, Sextet in Bb major, Op.271 (fl, ob, cl, bn, 2 h)
 H Zimmermann (score, parts); Sansone; Andraud.
REUCHSEL, AMEDEE, Sextet in G major (fl, ob, cl, h, bn, pf) An-
 draud; Lemoine.
RHEINBERGER, JOSEF GABRIEL, Sextet in F major, Op. 191b (fl, ob,
 cl, h, bn, pf) Leuckart; Andraud.
RICCI-SIGNORINI, ANTONIO, Fantasia Burlesca in C major (fl, ob,
 cl, h, bn, pf) Carisch.
RIES, FERDINAND, Sextett in G minor, Op. 142 (cl, h, bn, bass, pf,
 harp) Schott; Fetis.
RIETZ, JULIUS, Concertstuck, Op. 41 (fl, ob, cl, h, bn, pf) An-
 draud.
RIGHINI, VINCENT, Serenade (2 cl, 2 h, 2 bn) Gombart; Fetis.

ROLDAN, AMADEO, Ritmicas, First Four (fl, ob, cl, bn, h, pf)
    Grupo de Musical Renovacion.
ROOS, ROBERT DE, Sextuor, 1935 (fl, ob, cl, bn, h, pf) Stich-
    ting Donemus.
ROSETTI, FRANZ ANTON, Sextet, Parthia in Bb major (ob, 2 cl, 2
    h, bn) DTB, Vol. 33 (arr. by O, Kaul, score); B&H.
ROUSSEL, ALBERT CHARLES PAUL, Divertissement in G major, Op. 6
    (fl, ob, cl, h, bn, pf) H Rousart; Baron; Andraud.
ROUSSELOT, SCIPION, Sextet (ob, cl, h, bn, vc, pf) Catelin;
    Fetis Supplement.
RULOFFS, BARTHOLOME, Pieces of Harmony (2 cl, 2 h, 2 bn) Hum-
    mel; Fetis.
SAUER, E., Sextet (2 fl, ob, 2 cl, harp or picc, fl, ob, 2 cl,
    harp) Schott.
SCARLATTI, ALESSANDRO, Sonata (2 fl, 2 v, pf, vc or 2 fl, 2 v,
    pf) Ms., Santini Library, Munster.
   ---Sinfonia No. 4 in E minor (reco or fl, ob, strings) Mc-
    Ginnis & Marx (score, parts).
SCHEIDT, SAMUEL, Suite (2 v, 3 fl, va) Nagel. (5 winds, pf).
SCHERRER, HEINRICH, Old French Dance Suite, Op. 11 (fl, ob, 2
    cl, h, bn) Bouree, I, II, Sarabande, Menuett, Gavotte,
    Musette MH-H Sansone; Eble; Andraud; Schmidt,
    (score, parts).
SCHICKHARD, JOHANN CHRISTIAN, Concerts, Op. 13 (2 ob, 2 v, bn,
    b.c.) Roger; Fetis.
SCHOENBERG, ARNOLD, Pierrot Lunaire (21 tiny poems) (reciting
    voice, fl, cl, v, vc, pf) Op. 21 Universal Edition.
   ---5 Geistliche Lider, Op. 15 (voice, fl, cl or bass-cl,
    tpt, harp, v, or va) Universal Edition.
SCHUMANN, ROBERT ALEXANDER, Romance from Childhood Scenes, arr.
    by G. J. Trinkaus (2 cl, 2 h, bn, tuba; 2 cl, h, 2 bn,
    tuba; 3 cl, h, bn, tuba;) Franklin Company.
   ---Little Hunting Song, Op. 68, No. 7 in F major (fl, ob,
    cl, h, bn, tpt) Andraud; Music Publishers Holding Corp.
    (arr. by A. E. Cafarella, score, parts).
   ---Romanza in Bb major, arr. by Briegel (fl, 2 cl, 2 h, bn)
    Briegel.
SEITZ, ALBERT, Two Sextets, Op. 22 (fl, ob, cl, h, bn, pf) An-
    draud; Carl Geist.
SHANKS, ELLSWORTH, Sextet, Night Music for Six (fl, ob, cl, h,
    bn, pf) VH Gamble Hinged Music Co.; Music Publishers
    Holding Corp. (score, parts).
SMIT, LEO, Sextuor, 1933 (fl, ob, cl, bn, h, pf) Stichting Don-
    emus.
SOWERBY, LEO, Pop Goes the Weasel (fl, ob, cl, h, bn, pf) Fitz-
    simons.
STABINGER, MATTHIAS, Sextets Concertants, Op. 5 (fl, 2 v, 2 h,
    pf) Fetis.
STEVENSON, Phantom Visions, arr. by Reibold (fl, ob, 2 cl, alto-
    cl, bn) E Belwin.
STICH, JOHANN WENZEL, Sextet, Op. 34 (cl, bn, h, v, va, pf) Le-
    duc; Fetis.
STOHR, RICHARD, Sextet in E major, Op. 2 (cl, 2 h, v, va, vc)
    Eulenburg.
STRANG, GERALD, Cello Concerto (fl, ob, cl, bn, pf).

STUMPF, JOHANN CHRISTIAN, Pieces of Harmony, Books I, II, III,
If (2 cl, 2 h, 2 bn) Offenbach; Andre; Fetis.
TANSMAN, ALEXANDRE, The Witch's Dance, from the Ballet Le Jar-
din de Paradis (fl, ob, cl, h, bn, pf) VH Eschig; AMP;
Baron; Andraud; Schott (called Hexantanz).
TARTINI, GIUSEPPE, Largo from Sonata in G minor (fl, ob, 2 cl,
h, pf) Witmark.
TAUSCH, FRANZ, Six Quartets, Op. 5 (2 basset-horns, 2 bn, 2 h
ad lib) Fetis; Dunker.
THOMSON, VIRGIL, Barcarolle (fl, ob, eng h, bn, cl, bass-cl)
Mercury.
THUILLE, LUDWIG, Sextet in Bb major, Op. 6 (fl, ob, cl, h, bn,
pf) VH B&H; Sansone; Andraud; Musica Rara; AMP.
---Gavotte from Sextet in Bb major, Op. 6 (fl, ob, cl, h,
bn, pf) Carl Fischer.
TOCH, ERNST, Dance Suite, Op. 30 (fl, cl, v, va, perc., pf)
Schott (score, parts).
TOESCHI, CARLO GIUSEPPE, Trois Sextuors (fl, ob, v, va, bn, pf)
Hugard.
TOESCHI, JOHANN BAPTISTE, Six Symphonies, Op. 12 (2 ob, 2 h, 2
bn) Fetis; Bailleux.
TOURNEMIRE, CHARLES, Sextet, Op. 40 For an Epigram of Theocritus
(3 fl, 2 cl, harp) Andraud; Les Editions Musicales,
(score, parts).
TUTHILL, BURNET CORWIN, Variations on When Johnny Comes Marching
Home, Op. 9 (fl, ob, cl, h, bn, pf) Galaxy Music Corp.
Andraud.
UBER, CHRISTIAN BENJAMIN, Eleven Concertinos (fl, va, 2 h, bn,
pf) Fetis.
VAN BUSKIRK, CARL, Esoteric Suite (fl, ob, cl, h, bn, harp) 1950,
Indiana University School of Music.
VANDER HAGEN, ARMAND, Duos for 6 Flutes, in album of airs from
comic operas, by Folie, Mehul, Picaros, Diego, and Dalay-
rac (6 fl) Fetis Supplement; Janet.
---Three Suites of Italian Operatic Airs (2 cl, 2 h, 2 bn)
Fetis; Janet.
VELLONES, PIERRE, Sextet, A Versailles (fl, ob, cl, h, bn, pf)
Baron.
VINEE, ANSELME, Sextet (5 winds, pf).
WAGNER, WILHELM RICHARD, An Album Leaf, transc. by Boyd (fl, ob,
cl, h, bn, pf) ME (fl, 2 Bb cl, h in F, bn, pf) Carl
Fischer (score, parts).
WAGNER-REGENY, RUDOLF, Kleine Gemeinschaftsmusik in C major (v,
va, vc, ob, cl, bn) Universal Edition (score, parts).
WALTON, WILLIAM TURNER, Facade, Recitation (fl, cl, sax, tpt,
vc, perc) Oxford University Press.
WEBERN, ANTON VON, 5 Geistliche Lieder (voice, fl, cl, tpt, v,
harp) Op. 15, Five Sacred Songs.
WEILL, KURT, Op. 10, Frauentanz (sop, fl, va, cl, h, bn) Uni-
versal Edition
WEISS, ADOLPH, Sextette for Winds and Piano (fl, ob, cl, bn,
contra-bn, pf) ACA.
WILLNER, ARTHUR, Sextet (fl, ob, cl, h, bn, pf) Andraud.
WILSON, MORTIMER, Pipes and Reeds (2 fl, 2 cl, ob, bn) Andraud.
WINTER, PETER VON, Sextet, Op. 10 (2 v, 2 h, cl, va, pf) B&H; Fetis.

WINTER, PETER VON, Sextet (2 v, va, bn, ob, 2 h) Fetis; Naderman.
WOLF, FRANZ XAVIER, Two Serenades, Op. 1 (2 cl, 2 h, 2 bn) Fe-
    tis; Offenbach.
ZAGWIGN, HENRI, Suite, 1912 (fl, ob, cl, bn, h, pf) Stichting
    Donemus.
    ---Scherzo, 1946 (fl, ob, cl, bn, h, pf) Stichting Donemus.

Septets

AUBERY DU BOULLEY, PRUDENT LOUIS, Septuor, Op. 69 (v, va, fl, h,
    c., guit, pf) Richault; Fetis.
BACH, CHRISTOPH, FRIEDRICH, Septet, Op. 3 in C minor (2 h, ob,
    v, va, vc, pf) Kistner & Siegel (ed. by G. Schunemann);
    Andraud.
BACH, JOHANN SEBASTIAN, Overture in D major (2 v, va, 2 ob, tpt,
    pf) Fetis.
BACH, JOHANN SEBASTIAN, Overture in C major (2 v, va, 2 ob, bn,
    pf) Fetis.
    ---Sonate, arr. by Johann Lorenz (2 fl, 2 cl, 2 h, bn).
    ---Three Little Sonatas, ed. by C. A. V. Oberdorffer (2 fl, 2
    cl, bn, 2 h).
BACH, KARL PHILIPP EMANUEL, Sonatine in C major (2 fl, 2 v, va,
    vc, pf) Afas-Verlag Hans Dunnebeil; Andraud; Raabe &
    Plothow.
    ---Six Sonatas, No. 1 in G major, No. 2 in F major, No. 3 in
    A major, No. 4 in D major, No. 5 in Eb major, No. 6 in C
    major (2 fl, 2 cl, bn, 2 h) MH-VH (rec) Ricordi (ed. by
    Johann Lorenz); E. B. Marks; Litolff (arr. by U. Leupold
    for 2 fl, pf, string quartet, score, parts).
    ---Six Marches (2 ob, 2 cl, 2 h, perc ad lib) ME-MH An-
    draud, Mills Music.
BAUSSNERN, WALDEMAR VON, 8 Kammergesange, German, French, and
    Italian (voice, fl, cl, string quartet) Schott.
BAX, ARNOLD E., Concerto (fl, ob, harp, string quartet).
BEETHOVEN, LUDWIG VAN, Scherzo from Sonata in F minor, Op. 10,
    No. 2 (fl, ob, bn, 2 cl, h, pf) H-VH Witmark.
    ---Septet, Op. 20 in Eb major (v, va, h, cl, bn, vc, pf) VH
    Millereau; Universal Edition (parts); E. B. Marks; An-
    draud; Baron (parts); International Music Company; San-
    sone; B&H (parts, score); Ricordi (min score); Costal-
    lat (parts, score); Schott (score); Litolff (parts,
    score); Peters (parts, score); Sander (min score); Eul-
    enberg (min score); Hoffmeister; B&H Critical Edition,
    Supplementary Volume; Universal Music Company; Wiener
    Philharmonischer Verlag.
    ---II Viennese Dances (2 fl, or cl, 2 h, 2 v, pf, with bn
    in one movement) B&H, 1907.
BERWALD, FRANZ ADOLF, Septet in Bb major (v, va, cl, h, bn, vc,
    pf) Musikaliske Konstforeningen, Stockholm.
BILLINGS, B., Chester, (fl, ob, 2 Bb cl, h in F, bn, pf acc't.
    ad lib) Carl Fischer (score, parts).
BLANC, ADOLPHE, Septet, Op. 40 in E major (v, va, cl, h, bn,
    vc, pf) Costallat; Richault.

BLANC, ADOLPHE, Septet, Op. 54 in E major (fl, ob, cl, h, vc, bn,
pf) Costallat; Richault.
BLISS, ARTHUR, Septet (fl, ob, 2 v, va, vc, pf or bn) Andraud.
---Madame Noy (sop, fl, cl, bn, harp, va, pf) Chester.
BOCCHERINI, LUIGI, Serenade (2 v, 2 ob, 2 h, pf) Fetis.
BOISDEFFRE, CHARLES HENRI, Sepuor, Op. 49 in Eb major (fl, ob,
cl, h, bn, contra-b, pf) Hamelle, Paris; Andraud.
BOLZONI, GIOVANNI, Minuetto, arr. by Conn (fl, ob, bn, 2 cl, alto-
cl, bass-cl) MH Carl Fischer.
BOUFIL, JACQUES-JULES, Ouverture, 6 Airs Varies, and Potpourri of
National Airs, Book I and II (fl, 2 cl, 2 h, 2 bn) Fetis;
Gambaro.
BRAND, MAX GOTTLIEB, 5 Ballades, Op. 10 (fl, ob, cl, h, v, vc,
voice) Universal Edition.
BUMCKE, GUSTAV, Love and Sorrow, Op. 24, Tone Poem in G major (fl,
ob, cl, 2 h, bn, harp) Andraud; Diem (score, parts);
Saturn-Verlag.
BUSCH, C., An Ozark Reverie (fl, ob, bn, 2 cl, 2 h) ME Andraud;
Fitzsimons Co.
CAMBINI, JEAN JOSEPH, Several Patriotic Ayres (voice, 2 cl, 2 h,
2 bn) Fetis.
CATURLA, ALEJANDRO GARCIA, Primera Suite Cubana (6 wind instru-
ments, pf) Grupo de Musical Renovacion.
COPPOLA, PIERO, Five Poems (fl, cl, tr, string quartet) Durand
(parts, score).
DALLEY, ORIEN E., Serenade (2 fl, ob, 2 cl, 2 bn) ME Witmark;
Music Publishers Holding Corp. (score, parts).
D'ANDRIEU, JEAN FRANCOIS, Musetta, arr. by Vinardi (fl, ob, eng h,
cl, 2 bn).
DOST, RUDOLF, Septet, Op. 55 in G major (fl, ob, cl, h, bn, tymp,
pf, also triangle and tamborine) Zimmermann; Andraud;
Sandone.
---Septet, Op. 56 (fl, ob, cl, bn, h, tymp, pf) MH Baxter-
Northrup.
DUBOIS, CLEMENT FRANCOIS THEODORE, In the Garden, Suite: Birds,
Playing House, Drops of Rain (2 fl, ob, 2 cl, h, bn) An-
draud.
EBERS, CHARLES FREDERIC, Nine Variations (2 cl, 2 h, 2 bn, pf)
Fetis; Andre; Offenbach.
EISLER, HANNS, Palmstrom (Morgenstern), Op. 5 (voice, fl, picc,
cl, v, va, vc).
FASANOTTI, FILIPPO, Settimino in Eb major (ob, cl, h, 2 bn, vc,
pf) Ricordi.
FESCA, ALEXANDER ERNST, First Septet, Op. 26 in C minor (v, ob,
va, h, vc, bn, pf) Litolff; Costallat; Andraud.
---Second Septet, Op. 28 in D minor (v, ob, va, vc, h, bn,
pf) Costallat; Andraud; Litolff.
FIEDLER, C. H., March (2 cl, 2 h, tpt, 2 bn) Boehme; Fetis.
FLAMENT, EDWARD, Fantasia Con Fugua, Op. 28 (fl, ob, eng h, cl,
h, 2 bn) Andraud.
FLEISCHER, HANS, Concerto, Op. 35 in F# major (2 v, va, vc,
fl, cl, pf) Schultheiss (score, parts).
FRANZ, ETIENNE, Septet (v, ob, fl, h, etc...source does not in-
dicate full instrumentation) Fetis.

FREUNDTHALER, CAJETAN, Regina Coeli (bass voice, 2 vl, fl, 2 h,
    organ) Traeg, Vienna; Fetis.
FUX, JOHANN JOSEPH, Six Overtures in F major (2 v, va, 2 ob, bn,
    pf) Fetis.
GENZMER, HARALD, Septet (fl, cl, h, v, va, vc, harp) Schott;
    Barom; AMP; Hug.
GHEDINI, GIORGIO FEDERICO, Adagio e Allegro di Concerto (fl, cl,
    h, v, va, vc, harp) Ricordi.
GLEISSNER, FRANCOIS, Six Pieces (fl, 3 cl, 2 h, bn) Offenbach;
    Andre; Fetis.
GLINKA, MICHAEL IVANOVITCH, A Serenade, on the themes of "Anna
    Bolena" (harp, h, bn, va, vc, bn, pf) Fetis.
GLUCK, ARMIDE, Gavote No. 4 in F major (2 bn, 2 v, va, vc, pf)
    Durand.
HABA, KAREL, Septet, Op. 16 (va, v, vc, cl, h, bn, pf) Andraud.
HABERT, JOHANNES EVANGELISTA, Scherzo, Op. 107a (fl, ob, cl, 2 bn,
    2 h) Andraud; B&H; AMP.
HANDEL, GEORGE FREDERICK, Concerto No. 4, Op. 3 in F major (2 v,
    2 ob, va, bn, b.c.) B&H.
   ---Concerto Grosso in C major (2 ob, 2 v, va, vc, b.c., also
    scored for sextet) B&H, Werke XXI.
   ---Zwolf Marsche, ed. by Rudolf Steglich (2 ob, va, bn, tromb,
    h, tpt) Nagel.
HAYDN, FRANZ JOSEPH, Divertissement No. 4 in D major (2 v, 2 fl,
    2 h, pf) Fetis.
   ---Divertissement No. 3 in C major (2 v, va, fl, 2 h, pf)
    Fetis.
HEINZ, AUGUSTE HIMBERT, Six Variations (cl, fl, 2 v, 2 h, pf) Fe-
    tis.
HINDEMITH, PAUL, Septet (fl, ob, cl, bass-cl, bn, h, tpt) H
    Schott & Co; AMP.
   ---Die Junge Magd, Six Poems, Op. 23, No. 2 (contralto voice,
    fl, cl, string quartet) Schott.
HIRSCHBACH, HERMANN, Septet, Op. 5 (v, va, vc, cl, h, bn, pf)
    Fetis.
HOLLAND, JEAN-DAVID, Air, in the manner of a Polonaise (2 v, cl,
    2 h, va, vc) Fetis Supplement.
   ---Deux Airs (v, 2 cl, 2 h, bn, vc) Fetis Supplement.
   ---Divertimento, in the manner of a waltz (2 v, 2 cl, 2 h,
    vc) Fetis Supplement.
HUMMEL, JOHANN NEPOMUK, Grand Military Septet, Op.114 in C major
    (fl, v, cl, tpt, vc, bn, pf) Haslinger; Andraud; Fetis.
   ---Grand Septet, Op. 74 in D minor (fl, ob, h, va, vc, bn,
    pf; also fl, ob, h, bn, vc, bass, pf) Andre; Andraud;
    Ricordi (min score); J. Schuberth (ed. by F. Liszt, score,
    parts); Joubert; Peters; Schott; Fetis.
IBERT, JACQUES, Le Jardinier de Samos, suite (fl, cl, tpt, v, vc,
    tambourin, tamb, milit) Heugel (score, parts).
INDY, VINCENT D', Suite in Old Style, Op. 24 in D major (2 fl, tpt,
    string quartet) Hamelle (score, parts); Andraud; Univer-
    sal Music Company; International Music Co.
   ---Chanson et Danses, Op. 50 in Bb major (fl, ob, 2 cl, h, 2
    bn) MH Durand (score, parts); Andraud; Sansone; Elkan-
    Vogel.

JANACEK, LEOS, Concertino (2 v, va, cl, h, bn, pf) Hudebni Matice; B&H; Andraud; Sansone.

KALKBRENNER, FRIEDRICH WILHELM MICHAEL, Septet, Op. 132 in A major (ob, cl, h, bn, vc, bass, pf) B&H.

KAREL, HABA, Septet, Op. 16 (va, v, vc, cl, h, bn, pf) Andraud.

KITTL, JOHANN FRIEDRICH, Septet, Op. 25 in Eb major (fl, ob, cl,
h, bn, bass, pf) Kistner & Siegel.

KOECHLIN, CHARLES, Septet (fl, ob, cl, bn, h, sax, eng h) ME
Eble.
---Septuor d'instrument a vent (7 winds) C major. L'Oiseau
Lyre.

KOESSLER, HANS, Chamber Songs (voice, ob, h, string quartet)
Simrock.

KOMMA, KARL MICHAEL, Music for Seven Instruments, 1940, Ullmann.

KRENEK, ERNST, Two Movements, Op. 11 (cl, bn, pf, string quartet)
Ms.

KREUTZER, KONRADIN, Septet, Op. 62 in Eb major (v, va, cl, h, bn,
vc, pf).

KRUMPHOLTZ, JOHANN BAPTIST, Two Symphonies for Harp (harp, fl, 2
h, 2 v, vc).

LACOMBE, Serenade, Op. 47 in G major (fl, ob, h, 2 v, va, vc) Hamelle.

LECHANTRE, Mlle., Two Concerti, Op. 1 (2 v, 2 ob, va, bn, pf)
Fetis Supplement.

LEGRAND, WILHELM, Six Pieces of Harmony, Book I, taken from the
operas of Meyerbeer and Nicolini (fl, 2 cl, 2 h, 2 bn)
B&H; Fetis.
---Six Pieces of Harmony, Book II, taken from the operas of
Rossini, Nicolini and Pacini (fl, 2 cl, 2 h, 2 bn) B&H;
Fetis.

LIEBAU, FRIEDRICH WILHELM, Quintet (2 fl, 2 v, vc, ad lib, pf)
Fetis.

MALZAT, JOHANN MICHAEL, Septet (various winds) Fetis.

MARCELLI, NINO, Music Box Minuet (picc, 2 fl, ob or fl, 2 cl,
bells) MH Mills Music, Inc.

MATTHEWS, THOMAS, Music for Seven Woodwinds, Oklahoma University,
Oklahoma City, Oklahoma.

MAYR, S., In the Morning, Idyl (tpt or h, fl, ob, 2 cl, 2 bn)
Andraud.

MEL-BONIS, MME. ALBERT DOMANGE, Septet (2 fl, pf, string quartet)
Ms.

MENDELSSOHN-BARTHOLDY, FELIX, Andante, Op. 7, arr. by Fitzgerald
(fl, ob, 3 cl, bass-cl, bass or bn) University of Texas.

MENEAU, LEON, Septets (7 woodwinds).

MILHAUD, DARIUS, Symphonie No. 2, Pastorale (v, va, vc, bass, fl,
eng h, bn) Andraud; Mercury; Universal Edition (score,
parts).
---Symphonie No. 3, Serenade (v, va, vc, bass, fl, cl, bn)
Universal Edition (score, parts); Andraud.

MIROUZE, MARCEL, Piano and Winds in A major (fl, ob, cl, bn, h,
tpt, pf) Leduc (parts); Andraud.

MONTEUX, PIERRE, Arietta and March (fl, ob, cl, bn, tpt, bass,
perc) Mathot; Andraud.

MONTEVERDI, CLAUDIO, Scherzi Musicali, ed. by H. Trede (3 voices,
3 winds, pf) Barenreiter.

MORAWETZ, JOHANN, Eight Nocturnes (fl, d'amounr, fl traversiere, 2 v, 2 h, pf) Fetis.
MOSCHELES, IGNAZ, Septet, Op. 88 in D major (v, va, cl, h, vc, vc, pf) Fetis; Kistner & Siegel; Schlesinger.
MOUQUET, JULES, Adagio, Aubade and Scherzo, Suite (fl, ob, 2 cl, 2 bn, h) Lemoine (min score, parts); Andraud.
MOUSSORGSKY, MODEST, Ballet of the Chickens in Their Shells, arr. by Quinto E. Maganini (fl, ob, 2 cl, 2 tpt, bn) Musicus, NYC.
MOZART, WOLFGANG AMADEUS, Cassazione, K99 (2 v, or 2 va, bass, 2 ob, 2 h) B&H; Andraud.
---Serenade No. 2, Contradanse, K101 (2 v, 2 ob, 2 h, fl or bn) Andraud.
---Cassazione in G major, K163 (2 v, or 2 va, bass, 2 ob, 2 h) B&H; Andraud.
---Divertimento No. 5, K187 in C major, arr. by Emil Kahn (2 cl, 2 tpt, tromb, tymp) MH E. B. Marks.
---Divertimento, No. 6 in C major, K188, arr. by Emil Kahn (2 cl, 2 tpt, tromb, tymp) MH E. B. Marks.
---Divertimento in D major, No. 7, K205 (v, 2 va, bn, bass, 2 H) Sander (min score); B&H (parts); AMP.
---Divertimento in F major, No. 10, K247 (2 v, va, vc, bass, 2 H) B&H.
---Divertimento in D major, No. 11, K251 (ob, 2 h, 2 v, va, bass) Sander (ed. by R. Gerber, min score); Andraud; B&H (score, parts).
---Divertimento in Bb major, No. 15, K287 (2 v, va, vc, 2 h, bass) B&H.
---Divertimento in D major, No. 17, K334 (2 v, va, vc, 2 h, bass) B&H.
---Serenade-Minuetto, K361 (ob, 2 cl, 2 alto-cl, bn, bass) Andraud;
NEUBAUER, JOHANN, Two Nocturnes (2 h, 2 va, 2 fl, vc) Fetis.
ONSLOW, GEORG, Septuor, Op. 79 in Bb major (fl, ob, cl, h, bn, cfgt, pf), Kistner & Siegel.
PHILIPP, FRANZ, Four Lenaulieder, Op. 1 (alto, cl, bn, string quartet) Bohm (score).
PIERNE, HENRI CONSTANT GABRIEL, March of the Little Tin Soldiers (fl, ob, bn, cl, h, pf, tambur ad lib) Leduc; Andraud.
---Pastorale Variee, Op. 30 in Bb major (fl, ob, cl, 2 bn, tpt, h) Andraud; Durand; Sansone; Elkan-Vogel.
---Preludio and Fughetta, Op. 40, No. 1 in C minor (2 fl, ob, cl, h, 2 bn) VH Andraud; Hamelle (score, parts).
PIJPER, WILLEM, Septet, 1920 (fl, or picc, ob or eng h, cl, bn, h, bass, pf) Stichting Donemus.
PLEYEL, IGNACE JOSEPH, Symphonie Concertante, No. 4 (2 v, va, vc, fl, ob, bn) Pleyel; Fetis; Sieber.
POPOW, GABRIEL, Septet, Op. 22 (fl or picc, cl, bn, tpt, v, vc, bass) Russicher Staats-Verlag; Universal Edition; Andraud.
POULENC, FRANCIS, Rapsodie Negre (2 v, va, vc, fl, cl, voice) Spratt; Baron (score, parts); Chester (scored for pf, fl, cl, 2 v, va, vc, voice ad lib).
RAMEAU, JEAN PHILIPPE, Tambourin (3 cl, 2 h, 2 bn) Andraud.
---Musette en Rondeau (3 cl, 2 h, 2 bn) Andraud.

131

RAVEL, MAURICE JOSEPH, Introduction and Allegro in Gb major
        (fl, cl, harp, 2 v, va, vc) Sansone; Durand.
REBNER, EDWARD W., Septet for Pf and winds, Los Angeles Conser-
        vatory of Music.
REMBT, JOHANN ERNST, Choral Varie (organ, 2 cl, 2 h, 2 bn) Fe-
        tis.
RHENE-BATON, Aubade, Op. 53 in G major (fl, ob, 2 cl, h, 2 bn)
        Andraud; Durand; Elkan-Vogel.
RIES, FERDINAND, Septet, Op. 25 in Eb major (cl, 2 h, v, vc,
        bass, pf) Andraud; Simrock.
RONTGEN, JULIUS, Serenade, Op. 14 in A major (fl, ob, cl, 2 h, 2
        bn) B&H (score, parts); Andraud.
ROOTHAM, CYRIL B., Septet (va, fl, ob, cl, bn, h, harp) Andraud.
ROSETTI, FRANZ ANTON, Parthia in D major (2 ob, 2 cl, 2 h, bn)
        DTB, Vol. 33, ed. by O. Kaul.
SAINT-SAENS, CHARLES CAMILLE, Septuor, Op. 65 (tpt, 2 v, va, vc,
        bass, pf) Andraud.
SANTORO, CLAUDIO, Musica de Camara, 1944 (fl, picc, cl, bass-cl,
        pf, v, vc) Boletin Latinoamericano de musica, VI.
SCHOECK, OTHMAR, Ten Songs, based on poems by Gottfried Keller
        (bar, fl, ob, bass-cl, tpt, perc, pf) B&H, Cobbett.
SCHONBERG, ARNOLD, Suite, Op. 29 (2 cl, bass-cl, v, va, vc, pf)
        Cobbett; Universal Edition.
SCHUMANN, ROBERT ALEXANDER, Knight Rupert, from Album for Young
        for pf, Op. 68, No. 12, arr. by Irving Cheyett and Charles
        J. Roberts (fl, ob, cl, bn, cl, alto-cl, bass-cl) Carl
        Fischer.
SIBELIUS, JEAN, Suite Mignonne, Op. 98a in G minor (2 fl, 2 v, va,
        vc, bass), arr. by Johann Oertel, Chapell. (parts, and also
        arr. for pf, 2 hands).
SPOHR, LOUIS, Septet, Op. 147 in A major (v, vc, fl, cl, h, bn,
        pf) Peters (score, parts); Andraud; Costallat.
STEINBACH, FRITZ, Septet, Op. 7 in A major (ob, cl, h, v, va, vc,
        pf) Schott.
STRAVINSKY, IGOR FEDOROVICH, The Soldier's Tale (v, cl, tpt, bn,
        tromb, bass, perc) Andraud; Philharmonia; AMP.
TAG, CHRISTIAN GOTTHILF, Four Preludes de Chorals (2 cl, 2 h, 2
        bn, organ) Fetis.
TAK, P. C., Duo (fl, cl, string quintet) Stichting Donemus.
TARAS, BULBA, Concertino (pf, 2 v, va, cl, h, bn) Hudebni Matice.
TELEMANN, GEORG PHILIPP, Matthias Weckmann: Gegrusset Seist Du,
        Holdselige (sop, ten, 2 reeds, 2 fl, b.c.) Barenreiter.
TIESSEN, HEINZ, Septet, Op. 20 (2 v, va, vc, fl, cl, h).
TOJA, G., Serenata (fl, ob, 2 cl, 2 h, bn) Ricordi.
TRICON, JULES, Suite, Song d'une nuit d'ete (sextet, pf) Senart.
UBER, ALEXANDER, Septet, Op. 17 (cl, h, v, 2 va, 2 vc) Andre;
        Fetis; Offenbach.
UBER, CHRISTIAN BENJAMIN, Nine Divertissements (pf, fl, v, 2 h,
        va, bass) Wienbrack; Fetis.
VERETTI, ANTONIO, Divertimeno (6 instruments, pf) Ricordi(score,
        parts, min. score).
VILLA-LOBOS, HEITOR, Choros, No. 7 (fl, ob, cl, sax, bn, v, vc,
        large tam-tam) Eschig; Schott; Andraud; Fleisher.
WARLOCK, PETER, The Curlew, Song Cycle (tenor, fl, eng h, string
        quartet) Stainer & Bell.

WATSON, W.C., Divertimento (fl, ob, 2 cl, 2 h, bn) MH Witmark.
WEBER, JOSEPH MIROSLAV, Aus Meinem Leben, in E major (v, va, vc,
  cl, bn, 2 h) Andraud; Universal Edition (score, parts).
WECKMANN, MATTHIAS, Gegrusset Seist Du, Holdeselige (sop, ten,
  2 v, 2 reco or fl, pf) McGinnis & Marx; Barenreiter;
  Musica Rara, London.
WELLESZ, EGON, Dance Suite (solo v, va, vc, fl, cl, eng h, bn)
WEILL, KURT, Frauentanz, Op. 10 (sop, fl, va, cl, h, bn) Uni-
  versal Edition.
WIDERKEHR, JACQUES CHRETIEN MICHEL, Symphony Concertante, No. 4
  (fl, ob, cl, h, 2 bn, vc) Janet; Cotelle; Fetis.
WIND, BLASIUS, Serenade Amusante, Op. 1339 (fl, ob, 2 cl, bn, 2
  h) Andraud.
WINTER, PETER VON, Septet Concertante, Op. 20 (v, va, ob, cl,
  bn, vc, pf or orch) B&H; Fetis.
 ---Septet (v, va, vc, cl, bn, 2 h) Fetis; B&H.
WITT, L. FRIEDRICH, Septet (2 v, va, bass, cl, h, bn) Fetis;
  Schott.
WOOD, CHARLES, Septet (winds and strings).
ZAGWIJN, HENRI, Nocturne, 1918 (fl, eng h, cl, bn, h, harp, ce-
  lesta) Stichting Donemus.

Octets

ABEL, CLAMER-HEINRICH, Concerto in Eb major (pf, 2 v, va, vc or
  bass, 2 fl, C.F. Peters (Urtext).
ABRAHAM, Pieces (2 v, 2 fl, 2 c, 2 bn) Fetis.
ALLEN, P. H., The Muses (fl, ob, 2 cl, bn, h, tpt, tromb) Whitney
  Blake.
ANDRIESSEN, JURRIAAN, Octuor, Divertissement (fl, 2 ob, 2 cl, 2
  bn, bass-cl) Stichting Donemus.
ASIOLI, BONIFACE, Serenade (2 v, 2 va, 2 fl, bn, bass) Fetis.
BACH, JOHANN SEBASTIAN, Brandenburg Concerto No. 2 in F major
  (solo tpt, fl, ob, v, string quartet; also fl, ob, tpt,
  string quartet, pf) Andraud.
 ---Brandenburg Concerto No. 4 in G major (solo v, 2 fl, 2
  v, va, vc, pf or bass) Andraud; Peters; Fetis.
 ---Concerto in F major (2 fl, pf, string quintet) Andraud.
 ---Cantate Comique, No. 1 (sop, bass, 2 v, va, fl, h, pf)
  Klemm; Fetis (ed. by S. W. Dehn).
 ---Cantate Comique, No. 2 (sop, ten bass, 2 v, va, fl, pf)
  "Schlendrian et sa Fille la Petite Lisette" Berlin, Cranz;
  Fetis (ed. by S. W. Dehn).
 ---Musical Offering, ed. by Hans T. David (fl, ob, eng h, bn,
  2 v, va, vc) G. Schirmer.
BACH, KARL PHILIPP EMANUEL, Six Marches (2 ob, 2 cl, bn, 2 h,
  perc) E. B. Marks.
BARBER, SAMUEL, Capricorn Concerto in C major (fl, ob, tpt, 2
  v, va, vc, bass) Schirmer.
BAZELAIRE, PAUL, Greek Suite (2 fl, ob, v, va, 2 vc, harp or pf)
  Andraud; P. Schneider.
BEETHOVEN, LUDWIG VAN, Octet, Op. 103 in Eb major, arr. by Beet-
  hoven after the Quintet (2 ob, 2 cl, 2 bn, 2 h) H (rec)
  B&H (score, parts); Sander (ed. by W. Altmann); Broude

Bros; Sansone; Andraud; Eulenburg (min score); B&H
Critical Edition, Supplementary Volume; International
Music Co; AMP; International Music Corp; Musica Rara.
---Rondino, Op. 146 in Eb major (2 h, 2 ob, 2 cl, 2 bn) H
(rec) B&H (score, parts); Sander (min score); Mercury
Music Corp; Sansone; Andraud; Eulenburg (min score);
AMP; Diabelli; B&H Critical Edition, Supplementary Vol-
ume; International Music Corp; Music Rara; Mercury
(2 ob, or fl, ob, 2 cl, 2 h, 2 bn or bn, bass-cl).
---Klavierkonzert in D major (3 v, vc, fl, harmonium, bass,
pf) Vieweg (min score, parts).
---Serenade in Eb major (2 ob, 2 cl, 2 bn, 2 h) Broude
Bros.
BESSEL, A.M.S.E.DE, Menuets and Trios (2 v, 2 fl, 2 h, bass, pf)
Fetis.
BLISS, ARTHUR, Madame Noy (fl, cl, h, bn, va, bass, harp, voice)
Baron.
BOCCHERINI, LUIGI, Op. 41, Symphonie Concertante (2 v, 2 vc,
fl, or ob, h, bn, alto) Fetis.
BRANDL, JEAN, Serenade, Op. 4 (v, 2 fl, 2 va, 2 h, bn) Fetis;
Heilbronn.
CAMPBELL-WATSON, FRANK, Divertimento for Eight Wind Instruments
(fl, ob, 2 cl, bass-cl, 2 h, bn) MH-H Witmark; Music
Publishers Holding Corp. (score, parts).
CODIVILLA, F., Ottetto in Eb major (fl, ob, bn, cl, 2 h, cornet
or tpt, tromb) Pizzi; Andraud.
CONTRERAS, SALVADOR, Suite (chamber orchestra: cl, bn, tpt, pf,
strings) Fleisher.
CROES, HENRI-JACQUES DE, Sonata II (2 v, va, vc, 2 ob, 2 h)
Fetis Supplement.
---Sonata III (2 v, va, vc, 2 ob, 2 h) Fetis Supplement.
---Sonatas IX-XVI (2 v, va, vc, 2 ob, 2 h) Fetis Supplement.
DALLEY, ORIEN E., Reverie, Serenade (2 fl, ob, 2 cl, h, 2 bn) MH
Andraud; Witmark; Music Publishers Holding Corp. (score,
parts).
DOLMETSCH, FRIEDRICH, Octet in F minor, Op. 27 (pf, v, ob, or
fl, va, cl, h, vc, bass) Costallat.
DUBOIS, CLEMENT FRANCOIS, First Suite: Petite Mazurka, Canzon-
etta, Chaconne (2 fl, ob, 2 cl, 2 bn, h) Heugel (score,
parts); Andraud; Leduc.
---Second Suite: Archers Patrol, Lesbien Song, Little Waltz,
Stella Matuttina, Minuet (2 fl, ob, 2 cl, 2 bn, h) MH
Leduc (score, parts); Baron; Andraud.
DUPONT, JACQUES, Octet, Op. 4 (bn, cl, h, string quaret, pf)
Hamelle; Andraud.
DEPUY, L., Une Soiree d'ete, Elegie (fl, ob, bn, 2 v, va, vc,
bass) Self published by author in Paris.
---Serenata (fl, ob, bn, 2 v, va, vc, bass) Self published
by author in Paris.
DUREY, LOUIS EDMOND, Images a Crusoe, Op. 11 (Seven Songs)
(voice, string quartet, fl, cl, celesta or harp) Chester.
EBERS, CHARLES FREDERIC, Six Marches, Op. 18 (2 cl, 2 ob, 2 h, 2
bn) Fetis.
ELIAS, ALFONSO DE, Suite (chamber orchestra: cl, bn, tpt, pf
strings) 1. Preludio, 2. Clare de Luna en Tlalmanalco,
3. Allegretto Vivace. Fleisher.

ENSLIN, PHILIPPE, Andante with Variations (2 v, 2 fl, 2 h, bass,
    pf) Offenbach; Fetis.
FERGUSON, HOWARD, Octet (cl, bn, h, 2 v, va, vc, bass) VH An-
    draud; Boosey-Hawkes (min score, parts).
FISCHER, VOLBERT, Six Symphoneis (2 v, va, bass, 2 ob, 2 h) Fe-
    tis; M. J. Traeg.
FREDERICK THE GREAT, Overture, Allegro, Andante, Finale (1st mvt:
    string quartet, 2 ob, 2 h; 2nd mvt: 2 fl 2 v; 3rd mvt:
    string quartet, 2 ob, 2 h).
FROMMEL, GERHARD, Blaser Suite, Op. 18 in C major (fl, ob, 2 cl,
    2 h, bn, dfgt) Mueller.
GABRIELI, GIOVANNI, Kanzone and Sonatas (8 wind Instruments)
    Barenreiter.
GAL, HANS, Divertimento, Op. 22 (fl, ob, 2 cl, tpt, 2 h, bn) An-
    draud; Leuckart (score, parts).
GLEISSNER, FRANCOIS, Symphonies Faciles, Op. 15 (2 v, va, bass,
    2 ob, 2 h) Nos. 1, 2, 5. Fetis.
GODECHARLE, EUGENE CHARLES JEAN, Symphonie Nocturne (2 v, 2 ob,
    2 h, picc, tambourine) Ceulemans; Fetis.
---Six Symphoneis (2 v, va, 2 ob, 2 h, bass) Huet; Fetis.
GOEPFERT, CHARLES ANDRE, Eighteen Pieces of Harmony (2 cl, 2 h,
    ob or fl, tpt, bn, serpent) Offenbach; Andre; Fetis.
GOOSSENS, EUGENE, Octet, Op. 3 (fl, cl, h, harp, string quartet)
    Andraud.
GOUVY, LOUIS THEODORE, Octet, Op. 71, in Eb major (fl, ob, 2 cl,
    2 h, 2 bn) Kistner & Siegel (score, parts); Andraud.
GRAINGER, PERCY ALDRIDGE, My Robin is to the Greenwood Gone (fl,
    eng h, six strings) Schott, London.
GREEN, RAY, Three Pieces for a Concert (fl, 2 cl, 2 tpt, tromb,
    pf, perc) MH E. B. Marks.
HANDEL, GEORGE FREDERICK, Concerti No. 5 and 6 from Six Concerti
    Op. 3, in D minor and D major (2 ob, 2 v, va, vc, vc, b.c.)
    B&H, Werke XXI.
---Concerto Grosso in Bb major, ed. by G. Dasch (2 ob, pf,
    strings) Barenreiter-Bote (parts, score).
---Italienische Kantaten: Em die Flamme (Tra le Fiamme)
    (sop, solo v, fl, ob, h, 2 v, pf) Barenreiter.
HARTMANN, E. Serenade, Op. 43 (fl, ob, 2 cl, 2 bn, 2 h) Ries
    & Erler.
HASSLER, HANS LEO, Two Canzonas (8 woodwinds) Barenreiter;
    Musica Rara.
HAYDN, FRANZ JOSEPH, Six Divertissements, Op. 31 (fl, 2 h,
    string quartet, bass) Artaria, 1781; Haydn Catalogue,
    Geiringer.
---Divertisssement for winds in B minor (2 ob, 2 h, 3 bn,
    serpent) Fetis; Sieber; Janet; Porro; Offenbach;
    Andre.
---Divertissement for winds, No. 2 in B minor (2 ob, 2 cl,
    2 h, 2 bn) Fetis; Sieber; Janet; Porro; Offenbach;
    Andre.
---Divertissement for winds, No. 3 in E minor (2 ob, 2 cl, 2
    tpt, 2 bn) Fetis; Sieber; Janet; Porro; Offenbach;
    Andre.
---Divertissement for winds, No. 4 in F major (2 ob, 2 h, 3
    bn, serpent) Fetis; Sieber; Janet; Porro; Offenbach.
    Andre.

---Divertissement for winds, No. 5 in B minor (2 ob, 2 cl, 2 tpt, 2 bn) Fetis; Sieber; Janet; Porro; Offenbach; Andre.

---Divertissement for winds, No. 6 in F major (2 ob, 2 h, 3 bn, serpent) Fetis; Sieber; Janet; Porro; Offenbach; Andre.

---Divertissement No. 2 in G major (2 v, 2 va, bass, fl, 2 h) Fetis.

---Six Scherzandi: Allegro, Minuet, Andante or Adagio, Presto (fl, 2 ob, 2 h, 2 v, bass) Haydn Catalogue, Geiringer.

---Six Feldpartitas (2 ob, 2 cl, 2 h, 2 bn; also 2 ob, 2 h, 3 bn, serpent) Haydn Catalogue, Geiringer.

---Octet, No. 16 (2 v, 2 eng h, 2 bn, 2 h) Haydn Catalogue, Geiringer.

---Octet, Divertimento in Bb major (2 ob, 2 cl, 2 h, bn, contra bn) arr. by Emil Kahn MH E. B. Marks; Andraud; Universal; F. Schuberth, Jr. (Geiringer, score, parts).

---Octet for Woodwinds (2 ob, 2 cl, 2 h, 2 bn) Masterworks Publications.

---Octet in F Major, arr. by F. Grutzmacher (2 ob, 2 cl, 2 h, 2 bn) MH (rec) Kahnt (score, parts); Andraud; E. B. Marks; Musica Rara; International Music Co.

---Allegro from Octet in F Major (2 ob, 2 cl, 2 h, 2 bn) MH Mills Music Co; E. B. Marks.

HAYDN, GIUSEPPE, Divertimento VI, Vol. I, Arr. by R. Phillip (2 ob, 2 cl, 2 h, 2 bn).

---Divertimento VI, Vol. 2 (2 ob, 2 h, 3 bn, cfgt).

HERSCHEL, FREDERIC GUILLAUME, Two Concertos Militaires in B minor (2 ob, 2 h, 2 tpt, 2 bn) Fetis; Royal Astronomical Society Library.

HILIMANN, CARL, Impromptu, Op. 54 (2 v, vc, bass, fl, cl, tpt, pf) C. F. Schmidt, Cefes-Edition.

HINDEMITH, PAUL, Die Junge Magd (voice, fl, cl, harp, string quartet).

HIRSCHBACH, HERMANN, Octet, Op. 26 (v, va, vc, bass, fl, cl, bn, h) Fetis.

HOFFMEISTER, FRANCOIS ANTOINE, Two Suites, Suite II (8 winds) Fetis.

HOFMANN, HEINRICH KARL JOHANN, Octet, Op. 80 in F major (2 v, va, vc, fl, cl, h, bn) B&H; Andraud; AMP; Sansone (arr. for 2 v, 2 vc, fl, cl, h, bn).

HONEGGER, ARTHUR, Pastorale d'ete, 1920 (fl, ob, cl, h, string quartet); Senart; Universal Editions.

INGALLS, ALBERT M., Woodwind Octet, Largo Movement (fl, ob, bn, 2 cl, bass-cl, 2 h) Albert M. Ingalls, 6551 24 Ave., NE Seattle 5, Washington.

JUON, PAUL, Octet, Op. 27a in Bb major (v, va, vc, ob, cl, h, bn, pf) Lienau; Andraud; Schlesinger; E. C. Schirmer.

KALLENBERG, SIEGRIED GARIBALDI, Vom Himmel hoch ihr Engel Kommt (string quartet, fl, bn, h, voice) Bohm & Sohn.

KAUN, HUGO, Octet, Op. 34 in F major (cl, h, bn, 2 v, va, vc, bass) Ruhle (score, parts); Kaun.

KLING, HENRI, Spring Poetry, Idyl (h, fl, 2 ob, 2 cl, 2 bn) Andraud.

KNUDAGE-RIISAGER, Sinfonietta (fl, cl, 2 bn, 2 tpt, 2 tromb) An-
draud.
KORNAUTH, EGON, Octet, Op. 31 (fl, ob, cl, h, string quintet)
Andraud.
KRAUS, JOSEPH MARTIN, Andante (2 v, 2 fl, 2 h, va, vc) Fetis.
KRENEK, ERNST, Octet, Op. 11 (winds and strings) Universal Edi-
tion.
KRIEGER, ADAM, Gay Fieldmusic (5 ob, eng h, 2 bn) Municipal
Library of Hamburg.
KROMMER, FRANZ, Concertino, Op. 18 (fl, ob, 2 va, 2 h, vc, bass)
Offenbach; Andre; Fetis.
LACHMANN, ROBERT, Hungarian Minuet (2 v, va, vc, bass, fl, cl,
bn) Andraud.
LACHNER, FRANZ, Octet, Op. 156 in Bb major (fl, ob, 2 cl, 2 h,
2 bn) Kistner (score, parts); Andraud.
LAUBER, JOSEPH, Octette in Bb major (2 fl, ob, 2 cl, 2 bn, cfgt)
Ms., Luetzinger Bassoonist Zurich, Switzerland.
LAZZARI, SYLVIO, Octet, Op. 20 in F major (fl, ob, eng h, cl, 2
h, 2 bn) Buffet-Crampon; Andraud; Evette & Schaeffer.
LIADOV, ANATOL CONSTANTINOVITCH, Octet, Op. 32, A Musical Snuff-
box (picc, 2 fl, 3 cl, harp, campanelli) Belaieff; An-
draud; Baron; AMP.
LOEFFLER, CHARLES MARTIN TORNOV, Octet (2 cl, harp, string quin-
tet; 2 v, va, vc, bass).
LOUCHER, RAYMOND, Wind Octet (cl-Eb, 2 cl-Bb, cl-A, bass-cl-B,
contra bass-cl-E, bn, contra bn).
LOUIS, FERDINAND, Prince of Prussia, Octet in F minor, Op. 12
(pf, cl, 2 h, 2 v, 2 vc) B&H; Fetis.
LULLY, JEAN BAPTISTE DE, Menuet du Bourgeois Gentilhomme (Eb
cl, 4 cl, 2 bn, cfgt) Andraud.
MAIER, L., Six Symphonies (2 v, va, bass, 2 ob, 2 h,) Fetis.
MARX, KARL, Kantate, Op. 41a (sop, 2 fl, string quintet) Baren-
reiter.
MASCHEK, VINCENT, Six Pieces (8 wind instruments) Fetis.
MILHAUD, DARIUS, Machines Agricoles, Six Pastorales (voice, 7
instruments) Universal Edition.
MIRANDOLLE, LUDOVICUS, Octet in D major (2 v, va, vc, bass, cl,
h, bn) Self published, 1944.
MITSCHA, FRANCOIS ADAM DE, Pieces in Harmony (2 ob, 2 cl, 2 h,
2 bn) Fetis.
MOLBE, HEINRICH FREIHERR VON BACH, Octet, Op. 20 in F major (cl,
bn, h, 2 v, va, vc, bass) Hofmeister (score, parts).
---Octet, Op. 45 in D minor (ob, h, basset h, 2 v, va, vc,
bass) Hofmeister (score, parts).
---Octet, Op. 46 in Bb major, Serenata (2 v, va, vc, bass, ob,
h, basset h) Hofmeister (score, parts).
---Octet, Op. 47 in G major (cl, eng h, bn, 2 v, va, vc,
bass) Hofmeister (score, parts).
MOZART, WOLFGANG AMADEUS, Symphony Concertant in E minor (v, ob,
cl, h, bn, vc, va, bass) Gombart; Fetis.
---Cassazione in G major, K63 (2 v, va, bass, 2 ob or 2 fl,
2 h) B&H; Andraud.
---Cassazione in Bb major, K99 (2 v, va, bass, 2 ob, 2 h)
B&H (score, parts); Andraud.
---Symphonie in D major, K133, ed. by Fendler (ob, h, tpt,
string quintet) Barenreiter-Bote (score, parts).

---Serenade No. 2 in F major, K101 (2 ob, 2 h, 2 v, vc, bass) B&H; AMP.

---Serenade No. 11, K375 in Eb major (2 ob, 2 cl, 2 h, 2 bn) (rec) Peters; Broude; Offenbach; Andre; B&H.

---Serenade No. 12, K388 in C minor (2 ob, 2 cl, 2 h, 2 bn) Peters; Broude; Offenbach; Andre; B&H; Musica Rara (score, parts).

---Serenade No. 11 in Eb major, K375 (2 ob, 2 cl, 2 h, 2 bn) VH Adagio, Menuetto, Allegro. Andre (parts); B&H, (score, parts); Sander (min score); Broude Bros; Andraud; Offenbach.

---Serenade No. 12 in C minor, K388 (2 ob, 2 cl, 2 h, 2 bn) Sander (min score); Broude Bros; Andraud; Andre (parts); B&H (score); Offenbach.

---Five Pieces for Winds (2 cl, 2 ob, 2 h, 2 bn) B&H.

---Divertimento in Eb major, K113, No. 1 (2 v, va, bass, 2 cl, 2 h) B&Y (score).

---Divertimento No. 4 (2 ob, 2 cl, 2 eng h, 2 bn) MH Baxter Northrup Co.

---Divertimento No. 5 in C major, K187 (2 fl, 5 tpt, tymp) Andraud; White & Smith; E. H. Morris & Co.

---Divertimento in Eb major, K 196 E (Anh 226) (2 ob, 2 cl, 2 h, 2 bn) Ms., Christlieb, c/o Woodwind Magazine, Ozalid parts).

---Divertimento in Bb major, K 196 F (Anh 227) (2 ob, 2 cl, 2 h, 2 bn) Ms., Christlieb, c/o Woodwind Magazine, Ozalid parts).

---Anh, 228, interesting but not authentic, in Bb major (2 ob, 2 cl, 2 h, 2 bn) Ms., Christlieb, c/o Woodwind Magazine, Ozalid parts.

---Divertimento No. 11 in D major K251 (ob, 2 v, va, vc, 2 h, bass) B&H; AMP.

---Organ Sonatas, No. 12 in G major, K274, No. 14 in C major K336 (2 ob, 2 tpt, 2 v, vc, tymp) Mercury.

NEUHAUSER, LEOPOLD, Four Nocturnes, No. 3 (2 v, 2 ob, 2 h, va, bass) Fetis.

NIELSEN, LUDOLF, Bagpipe, Op. 30 (2 fl, 2 ob, 2 cl, 2 bn, perc) H Andraud.

NOVACEK, RUDOLF, Sinfonietta, Op. 48 in D minor (fl, ob, 2 cl, 2 bn, 2 h) B&H (score, parts); Andraud; Sansone.

PACINI, GIOVANNI, Octet (3 v, ob, bn, h, vc, bass) Fetis Supplement.

PASCAL, CLAUDE, Octet: Ouverture, Scherzo, Andante, Mouvement Perpetuel (2 fl, ob, cl, 2 bn, h in F, tpt in C) Elkan-Vogel; Eble; Durand & Cie.

PAZ, JAUN CARLOS, Octet, 1930 (8 winds).

PETERS, GUIDO, Nocturne, in F major (2 v, va, vc, ob, cl, bn, h) Universal Edition (min score, parts); Andraud; Peters.

PETYREK, FELIX, Divertimento in Bb major (2 fl or 2 picc, ob, cl, 2 bn, 2 h) Andraud; Universal Edition.

PIERLOT, DENIS, Three Symphonies, Op. 1 (2 v, va, bass, 2 ob, 2 h) Imbault; Fetis.

PIERNE, HENRI CONSTANT GABRIEL, Pastorale Variee in Bb major (2 fl, ob, cl, 2 bn, tpt, h) Durand; Andraud.

---Petite Gavotte (fl, ob, cl, h, string quartet) Spratt; Baron.

PITICCHIO, PETER PAUL, Six Pieces in Harmony (4 ob, 2 h, 2 bn)
Fetis.

POLDOWSKI, LADY DEAN PAUL, Octet, (2 fl, ob, oboe d'amore, eng h,
cl, basset-h, bass-cl) Ms.

PONIRIDY, G., 2 Poemes Dans le Style Populaire Grec: 1. Le
chant de l'exile, 2. Le chant du metier (fl, cl, string
quartet, pf, voice) Senart.

POULENC, FRANCIS, Le Bestiaire ou le cortege d'Orphee, Six Poemes (mezzo sop, fl, cl, bn, string quartet) La Sirene
Musicale.

----Rapsodie Negre (voice, pf, 2 v, va, vc, fl, cl) Chester.

PURCELL, HENRY, Lament from Dido and Aeneas, arr. by Theodore M.
Finney (fl, ob, cl, bn, string quartet) Music Publishers Holding Corp; Witmark.

RAFF, JOSEPH JOACHIM, Octet (7 instruments, pf) Fetis Supplement.

RAYMOND, EDWARD, Nocturne (v, va, vc, bass, fl, cl, bn, h)
Fetis.

REBNER, EDWARD W., Suite (ob, eng h, bn, cfgt, h, 2 tpt, perc)
Fine Arts Foundation of Glendale, California.

REICHA, ANTON, Octet, Op. 96 in Eb major (2 v, va, vc, ob, cl,
h, bn) Janet.

REICHEL, FREDERIC, Octets (8 winds) Fetis Supplement.

REINECKE, KARL, Octet in Bb major, Op. 216 (fl, ob, 2 cl, 2 h,
2 bn) Kistner & Siegel (score, parts); Andraud.

REUSS, AUGUST, Octet, Op. 37 in B major (2 ob, 2 cl, 2 h, 2 bn)
Zimmermann (min score, parts); Andraud; Halbreiter.

REVUELTAS, SILVESTRE, Ocho por Radio (8 Musicians over the Air)
(cl, bn, tpt, perc, strings) Fleisher.

REYMANN, F. G., Three Serenades for Eight Instruments, Fetis.

RIES, FERDINAND, Octet, Op. 128 in Ab major (pf, v, va, cl, h,
bn, vc, bass) Andraud; Kistner & Siegel.

RIISAGER, KNUDAGE, Sinfonietta (fl, cl, 2 bn, 2 tpt, 2 tromb)
Andraud.

RUBENSTEIN, ANTON GREGOROVITCH, Octet, Op. 9 in D major (pf, v,
va, vc, bass, fl, cl, h) Hamelle; Andraud; Peters.

RUDOLF, JOHANN ANTON, Theme with Six Variations (solo v, 2 v,
fl, ob, 2 h, bass) Fetis.

SAINT-LUBIN, LEON DE, Octet, Op. 33 in E minor (pf, fl, cl, bn,
v, va, vc, bass).

SAINT-SAENS, CHARLES CAMILLE, Album Leaves, Op. 81, arr. by C. P.
Taffanel (fl, ob, 2 cl, 2 h, 2 bn) Durand; Andraud;
Elkan-Vogel.

SCARLATTI, ALESSANDRO, Allegro from Eighth Suite in Bb major (fl,
2 ob, 2 cl, 2 bn, h) Ricordi; Andraud.

SCHERER, HEINRICH, Old French Dance, Op. 2 (fl, ob, 2 cl, 2 bn,
2 h) MH Baxter-Northrup Co.

SCHMITT, NICOLAS, Airs Italiens in eight parts, Books I. and II.
(8 winds) Pleyel; Fetis.

SCHOLL, CHARLES, Introduction and Variations Brilliant (solo fl,
2 v, va, bass, horns, ob) Op. 19, 20, 26, 28 Fetis;
Diabelli; Haslinger.

SCHOLZ, ROBERT, Landliche Weisen in A major (2 ob, 2 cl, 2 h, 2
bn) Ms., Robert Scholz, 55 W. 55th Street, NYC.

SCHONBERG, ARNOLD, Serenade, Op. 24 (voice, cl, bass-cl, mandolin,
guitar, v, va, vc) Hansen; Universal Edition.

SCHUBERT, FRANZ, Octet, Op. 166 in F major (cl, h, bn, string
  quartet, bass) H Wiener Philharmonischer Verlag; AMP;
  Baron; Andraud; International Music Co; B&H (score, parts)
  Costallat; Cranz; Peters; Sander (min score); Eulenburg.
---Minuett and Finale in F major, Series 3, No. 2 (2 ob, 2 cl,
  2 h, 2 bn) B&H (score, parts); AMP.
---Minuet in F major, Series 3, No. 2 (2 ob, 2 cl, 2 h, 2 bn)
  Marks; Musica Rara.
SIEVERS, JOHANN FRIEDRICH LUDWIG, Symphonie for Piano (pf, 2 v,
  2 fl, 2 h, bass) Fetis.
SIMONET, FRANCOIS, Suite de Morceaux du "Jockey" (2 fl, 2 cl, 2
  h, 2 bn) Fetis.
SPOHR, LOUIS, Octet, Op. 32 in E major (v, 2 va, vc, bass, cl,
  2 h) Costallat; Sander (min score); Eulenburg; An-
  draud; Peters.
STRAVINSKY, IGOR FEDOROVICH, Octet for Winds (fl, cl, 2 bn, 2
  tpt, 2 tromb) Boosey Hawkes; Edition Russe de Musique
  (min score, parts); Andraud; Keynote Music Service. VH
---Parthia in F major (2 ob, 2 cl, 2 h, 2 bn) Nagel.
---Trois Poesies de la Lyrique Japonaise (voice, pf, fl, cl,
  string quartet) Russicher Musikverlag.
STURMER, BRUNO, Suite, Op. 9 in G minor (fl,ob, cl, bn, string
  quartet) Andraud.
TAILLEFERRE, GERMAINE, Image, Prelude (fl, cl, ob, celeste, string
  quartet) Andraud; Chester (scored for pf, fl, cl, string
  quartet, celesta).
TANSMAN, ALEXANDER, Four Impressions for Octet (2 fl, 2 ob, 2 bn,
  2 cl) MH Leeds Music Corp.
THIERIOT, FERDINAND, Octet, Op. 62 in Bb major (2 v, va, vc, bass,
  cl, h, bn) Rieter-Biedermann; Peters.
TOESCHI, JOHANN BAPTISTE, Three Symphonies, Op. 6 (2 v, 2 ob, 2 h,
  va, bass) Fetis; Huberti.
UMSTADT, JOSEF, Symphonies (2 v, va, bass, 2 ob, 2 h) Fetis.
VANDER HAGEN, ARMAND, Pot-pourri (8 instruments) Janet; Fetis.
VAN MALDERE, PIERRE, Six Symphonies (2 v, va, bass, 2 ob, 2 h)
  Fetis.
VARESE, EDGAR, Octet (fl, cl, ob, bn, h, tpt, tromb, string bass)
  Curwen & Sons (score).
WAGENAAR, BERNARD, Concertino for Eight Instruments (fl, ob, cl,
  bn, h, v, va, vc) Fischer.
WAILLY, PAUL DE, Octet (fl, ob, 2 cl, 2 bn, h, tpt) Ro art.
---Second Movement from Octet (fl, ob, 2 cl, 2 bn, h, tpt)
  Rouart; Salabert.
WALTER, AUGEST, Octet, Op. 7 in Bb major (v, va, vc, ob, cl, h,
  bn, bass) Kistner & Siegel; Cobbett.
WANHAL, JOHANN BAPTISTE, Six Symphones, Op. 4 (2 v, va, bass, 2
  of, 2 h) Leduc; Fetis.
---Three Symphonies, Op. 10 (2 v, va, bass, 2 ob, 2 h) Fetis;
  Sieber.
---Three Symphonies, Op. 16 (2 v, va, bass, 2 ob, 2 h) Fetis;
  Sieber.
WEBBE, SAMUEL, Divertissements Militaires (2 cl, 2 h, 2 bn, picc,
  tpt, bugle, serpent) Fetis.
WEINGARTNER, FELIX VON, Octet, Op. 73 in G major (2 fl, ob, cl,
  2 bn, 2 h) Andraud; Chester; Birnbach (scored for cl,
  h, bn, 2 v, va, vc, pf).

WEISSE, HANS, Octet, 1929 (strings and winds).
WELLESZ, EGON, Octet (3 winds, 5 strings).
WESTMEYER, GUILLAUME, Octet (8 winds) Fetis Supplement.
WHITE, PAUL, Fantastic Dance in C major (2 fl, 2 cl, ob, 2 bn,
        castanets) Ms.
WILDER, ALEC, Mixed Wind Octets: Walking Home in Spring; Such
        a Tender Night; She'll be Seven in May; Seldom the Sun;
        Neurotic Goldfish; A Debutante's Diary (8 winds) Andraud.
WINTER, PETER VON, Partita (2 ob, 2 cl, 2 h, 2 bn) Bureau D'Art
        et D'Industrie, Wien.
WOLF-FERRARI, ERMANNO, Suite-Concertino, Op. 16 in F major (bn,
        2 h, 2 v, va, vc, bass) G. Ricordi & Co.
ZICH, OTOKAR, Octet (2 v, va, vc, bass, cl, h, bn) or (h, bn, pf,
        string quintet) Hudebni Matice.
ZOPF, Serenade, Op. 35, No. 2 in C major (2 fl, ob, 2 cl, 2 h,
        bn) Ms.

Nonets

ASIOLI, BONIFACE, Serenade (2 v, fl, 2 h, va, bn, bass, pf)
        Fetis.
BACH, JOHANN SEBASTIAN, Prelude from English Suite, No. 5
        (fl, ob, cl, bn, tpt, v, va, vc, bass) Andraud.
    ---Second Brandenburg Concerto (fl, ob, tpt, v, 2 v, va, vc, pf)
        Fetis.
    ---Chorale Preludes, arr. by R. Landes (fl, 2 ob, 2 bn, 2 cl,
        bass-cl, contra-bass-cl, ad lib) Richard Landes, Music
        Department, Buena Vista College, Storm Lake, Iowa.
BAX, ARNOLD E., Nonett (2 v, va, vc, bass, fl, cl, ob, harp)
        Murdoch (score, parts).
BECK, CHRETIEN-FREDERIC, Concerto (pf, 2 v, va, bass, 2 fl, 2 h)
        Schott; Fetis.
BEETHOVEN, LUDWIG VAN, Rondino in Eb (2 ob, 2 cl, 2 h, 2 bn,
        bass-cl) MH-H Mercury.
BERNARD, EMILE, Divertissement (2 h, bn, 2 cl, 2 ob, 2 fl) San-
        sone).
BERTINI, HENRI JEROME, Nonett, Op. 107 in D major (pf, fl, ob,
        va, vc, h, bn, tpt, bass) Lemoine.
    ---Three Nonets (pf, 8 winds) Fetis Supplement.
BIRD, WILLIAM, Pavane (2 fl, 2 ob, 2 cl, 2 bn, h) ME (rec)
        Ricordi; Andraud.
BIZET, GEORGES, Minuet from "L'Arlesienne Suite" arr. by Cheyette
        and Roberts (fl, ob, Eb cl, 2 cl, alto-cl, bass-cl, bar-
        sax, h) Carl Fischer.
BLISS, ARTHUR, Rhapsody (fl, eng h, string quartet, bass, sop,
        ten) Stainer & Bell.
BOEHNER, JEAN-LOUIS, Serenade (2 v, viola, fl obbligato, 2 h,
        bn, vc, contra bass) B&H; Fetis.
BONVIN, LUDWIG, Romance, Op. 19a for Winds (fl, 2 ob, 2 cl, 2
        h, 2 bn) B&H; Andraud.
    ---Melodie, Op. 56b (fl, 2 ob, 2 cl, 2 bn, 2 h) B&H; Andraud.
BRANDL, JEAN, Grande Serenade, Op. 7 (v, ob, vc, bn, 2 v, 2 h,
        bass accompaniment) Heilbronn; Fetis.
BRAUTGAM, HELMUT, Nonet, Op. 11, Kleine Jagdmusik (fl, 2 ob, 2
        cl, 2 h, 2 bn) B&H (score, parts).

BRUN, Passacaille, Op. 25 (2 fl, ob, 2 cl, bn, 2 h, string bass
    or contra-bn) Lemoine; Andraud.
BUMCKE, GUSTAV, Promenades, Op. 22, Tone Poem in F major (fl, ob,
    eng h, cl, alto-cl, h, bar sax, bn, harp) Andraud; Ries
    & Erler (score, parts).
BURGMEIN-MUGNONE, Noel! Noel! Pastorale (picc, fl, 2 ob, eng h,
    2 cl, 2 bn) B&H.
    ---O Mamma Cara (Holy Virgin) and Preghiera (Prayer) (2 fl,
    2 cl, 2 ob, bn, h, harp) B&H.
CARDON, LOUIS, Deux Concertos, Op. 10 (harp, 2 v, 2 ob, 2 h, va,
    bass) Fetis.
CATURLA, ALEJANDRO GARCIA, Nonet, No. 10 New Music Orchestra
    Series; Andraud.
    ---Primera Suite Cubana (8 winds, pf) New Music Orchestra
    Series; Fleisher.
    ---Bembe, Tres danzas cubanas (wind instruments, perc, pf)
    1. Danza del tambor, 2. Motivos de danzas, 3. Danza Lu-
    cumi. Elkan-Vogel; Fleisher.
CHAVEZ, CARLOS, Energia (6 winds, va, vc, contra-bass) Fleisher.
CHEMIN-PETIT, HANS, Kleine Suite (ob, cl, bn, drums, 2 v, va, vc,
    bass) Lienau (parts, score).
CIANCHI, EMILIO, Nonetto (2 ob, 2 bn, 2 cl, 2 h, cfgt) Paoletti.
COGAN, PHILIPPE, Concerto Favori Pour le Piano (pf, 2 v, alto,
    bass, 2 fl, 2 h) Op. 6 Fetis.
COLERIDGE-TAYLOR, SAMUEL, Nonet, Op. 2 in F minor (winds, strings,
    pf).
COSSART, L. A., Suite, Op. 19 (harp, 2 fl, 2 ob, 2 h, 2 fag) Hein-
    richshofen.
COUPERIN, FRANCOIS, Louis XIV Suite Premier des "Concerts Royeaux"
    (fl, ob, bn, h'chord or pf, string quintet) Music Publish-
    ers Holding Corp.
CROES, HENRI-JACQUES DE, Sonata No. 1 (2 v, va, vc, 2 ob, 2 tpt,
    tymp) Fetis Supplement.
    ---Sonata No. V (2 v, va, vc, 2 ob, 2 tpt, tymp) Fetis Sup-
    plement.
CUPIS, JEAN BAPTISTE, Air de l'Aveugle de Palmyre et Menuet de
    Fischer, variations for violoncello (vc, 2 va, 2 v, bass,
    2 ob, 2 h) Fetis.
DRUZECHY, GEORGES, Pieces (2 cl, 2 ob, 2 h, 2 bn, tpt) Fetis.
DUBOIS, CLEMENT FRANCOIS THEODORE, Nonetto (fl, ob, cl, bn,
    string quintet) Heugel (min score, parts); Andraud.
DVORAK, ANTONIN, March from Serenade, Op. 44 (2 ob, 2 cl, 2 bn,
    3 h, cfgt, v c, bass ad lib) E. B. Marks.
FARRENC, MME. JEANNE LOUISE, Nonetto, Op. 38 (v, va, vc, bass,
    fl, ob, cl, h, bn) Fetis.
FAURE, GABRIEL URBAIN, Nocturne Nonet, Op. 33, No. 1 (fl, 2 ob,
    2 cl, 2 h, 2 bn) Andraud, arr. by G. Grovlez.
FICHER, JACOBO, The Guests Ballet, Op. 26 (fl, cl, alto-sax, ten
    sax, 2 tpt, perc, pf) Fleisher Collection (unpublished).
FINZI, GERALD, Nonet, A Severn Rhapsody (fl, ob, 2 cl, h, strings)
    Stainer & Bell (score, parts); Andraud.
FOERSTER, JOSEF BOHUSLAV, Nonet, (fl, ob, cl, h, bn, v, va, vc,
    bass) Hudebni Matice.
GILCHRIST, WILLIAM WALLACE, Nonet (fl, cl, h, pf, string quintet)
GILSE, JAN VAN, Nonet, 1916 (ob, cl, bn, h, 2 v, va, vc, bass)
    Stichting Donemus.

GIVOTOFF, A., Framments Nonetto, Op. 2 (fl, cl, bn, tpt, 2 v, va, vc, pf) Russicher Staats-Verlag (score, parts); Andraud; Universal Edition.

GOOSSENS, EUGENE, Petite Symphonie (fl, 2 ob, 2 cl, 2 bn, 2 h) Costallat.

---Fantasy for Nine Wind Instruments, Op. 40 (fl, ob, 2 cl, 2 bn, 2 h, tpt) VH Curwen (score, parts); Andraud.

GOSSEC, FRANCOIS JOSEPH, Tambourine, arr. by Cheyette and Roberts (fl, ob, bn, 2 cl, alto-cl, bass-cl, bar sax, Eb cl) MH Carl Fischer.

GOUNOD, CHARLES FRANCOIS, Petite Symphonie in Bb major (fl, 2 ob, 2 cl, 2 h, 2 bn) MH (rec) Costallat (score, parts); Andraud; Sansone; Baron.

GOUVY, LOUIS THEODORE, Petite Suite Gauloise, Op. 90 (fl, 2 ob, 2 cl, 2 bn, 2 h) VH Universal Edition (score, parts); Andraud; Peters.

GROVLEZ, GABRIEL, Nocturne (2 h, 2 bn, fl, 2 ob, 2 cl) Sansone.

GRUENBERG, LOUIS T., The Creation, Op. 23 (voice, fl, cl, bn, h, kettledrums, perc, va, pf) Universal Edition.

---The Daniel Jazz, Op. 21 (voice, 8 instruments).

GYROWETZ, ADALBERT, Serenade, Op. 7 in nine parts (9 instruments) Andre:; Offenbach; Fetis.

HARSANYI, TIBOR, Nonett (fl, ob, cl, bn, h, string quartet) La Sirene Musicale; Andraud; Lemoine (min score, parts).

HARTMANN, EMIL, Serenade, Op. 43 in Bb major (fl, ob, 2 cl, 2 h, 2 bn, vc, or bass) Ries & Erler.

HAUER, JOSEPH MATTHIAS, Tanzsuite, Op.70 (fl, ob, cl, bn, 2 v, va, vc, pf) Universal Edition.

HAYDN, FRANZ JOSEPH, Nonet, No. 20 (2 ob, 2 h, 2 v, va, vc, bass) Haydn Catalogue, Geiringer.

---Two Marches (2 cl, 2 bn, serpent, 2 h, 2 tpt) Fleisher Collection (unpublished).

---Symphonie in Bb major, ed. by Alfred Einstein (fl, ob, bn, h, string quintet) Barenreiter-Bote (score, parts).

---Konzert in G major for Cembalo or Piano solo (pf, 2 v, va, vc, 2 ob, 2 h) Ed. by K. Schubert, Nagel.

---Divertissement No. 1 in F major (2 v, 2 va, bass, 2 h, 2 ob) Fetis; Breitkopf.

---Divertissement No. 2 in F major (2 v, 2 fl, 2 h, 2 bn, bass) Fetis; Breitkopf.

---Divertissement in D major (2 v, 2 va, bass, 2 fl, 2 h) Fetis.

---Cassazione, No. 2 in G major (2 v, 2 va, bass, 2 h, 2 ob) Fetis.

---Cassazione, No. 3 in G major (2 v, 2 va, bass, 2 h, 2 ob) Fetis.

---Eight Nocturnes (2 h, 2 lire organizzate, 2 cl, 2 va, bass) seven listed by Pohl, an eighth in C major, Ms. owned by W. W. Manning of London.

---Nocturne, No. 7 in C major, ed. by Ernst Fritz Schmid (fl, ob, 2 v, 2 h, 2 va, bass) Schmid.

---Nocturne, No. 5 in C major, ed. by Geiringer (fl, ob, 2 v, 2 h, 2 va, bass) Pohl.

---Nocturne, No. 6 in G major, ed. by Edward Fendler (fl, ob, 2 v, 2 h, 2 va, bass) Pohl; Barenreiter-Bote (score,parts).

HEINZ, AUGUSTE HIMBERT, Variations (cl, 2 v, 2 fl, 2 h, va, bass)
    Fetis; J. P. Spehr.
HESELTINE, PHILIP, An Old Song, ed. by P. Warlock (fl, ob, cl, h,
    String quintet).
HOFFMEISTER, FRANCOIS ANTOINE, Serenade (2 ob, 2 cl, 2 h, 2 bn,
    bass) Simrock; Fetis.
HOLBROOKE, JOSEF A., Nocturne (2 fl, 2 ob, eng h, 2 cl, 2 bn) An-
    draud; Modern Music Library.
HUE, GEORGES ADOLPHE, Serenade (solo fl, ob, cl, bn, string
    quintet) Andraud.
JUON, PAUL, Kammersinfonie, Op. 27 (ob, cl, h, bn, v, va, vc,
    bass, pf).
KIRNBERGER, JOHANN PHILIPP, Twelve Minuets (2 v, 2 ob, 2 fl, 2
    h, basso continuo) Fetis.
KITTL, JOHANN FRIEDRICH, Nonet (pf, fl, ob, cl, 2 h, va, vc,
    bass) Fetis; Kistner & Siegel.
KLEBANOV, D., Ukrainian Concertino (ob, cl, bn, h, pf strings)
    Leeds.
KLEINSINGER, GEORGE, Design for Woodwinds (2 fl, 2 ob, 2 bn, 2
    cl, h) MH Boston Music Co.
KLUGHARDT, AUGUSTE FRIEDRICH MARTIN, Nonetto (2 v, va, vc, fl,
    ob, cl, bn, bass) Fetis Supplement.
KORNAUTH, EGON, Nonet, Op. 31 in F minor, Kammermusik (fl, ob,
    cl, h, string quintet) Doblinger (score, parts); An-
    draud; Universal Editions.
KOZELUH, LEOPOLD ANTON, Two Suites for Wind Nonet (2 ob, 2 cl,
    2 h, 2 bn, bass) Simrock; Fetis.
KRAFFT, ANTOINE, Nocturne (2 vc, 2 v, 2 fl, 2 h, bass) Fetis.
KRENEK, ERNST, Symphony Music in Two Movements, Op. 11 (fl, ob,
    cl, bn, 2 v, va, vc, bass) Universal Edition (score);
    Andraud.
   ----Symphony Music Divertimento, Op. 23 (fl, cl, bn, h, 2 v,
    va, vc, bass) Andraud.
KROMMER, FRANZ, Armonia in F major (2 ob, 2 cl, 2 h, 2 bn, cfgt)
    Lorenzi.
   ---Concertante, Op. 38 and 39 (fl, ob, v, 2 va, 2 h, vc,
    bass) Offenbach; Andre; Fetis.
LACHNER, FRANZ, Nonet (winds and strings) Fetis.
LANGE, GUSTAVE FRIEDRICH, Nonet in F major (2 ob, fl, 2 cl, 2 h,
    2 bn) Erdmann (score, parts); Andraud; Seeling.
LEEMANS, Aria: Le Songe (harp, 2 v, 2 bn, 2 h, bass) Fetis
    Supplement.
LIBER, ANTON JOSEPH, Divertimento in Bb major (2 cl, 2 h, 2 bn,
    2 va, bass) Ms.
LOESENER, J.G., Variations for the basset-horn, Op. 3 (basset h,
    2 v, va, bass, 2 fl, 2 h) B&H; Fetis.
LUIGINI, A.C.L.J., Andante Cantabile, Op. 41 in C major (3 fl,
    ob, 2 cl, h, bn, harp) Grus.
   ---Aubade, Op. 13 (3 fl, ob, 2 cl, h, bn, harp or pf) An-
    draud.
MARTEAU, HENRI, Serenade, Op. 20 in D major (2 fl, 2 ob, 2 cl,
    bass-cl, 2 bn) Steingraber-Verlag (min score, parts);
    Andraud.
MARTINI, JEAN PAUL EGIDE, Ancient pieces composed for the French
    Regiment (9 winds) Naderman; Fetis.

MASSENET, JULES, EMILE FREDERIC, Introduction and Variations (fl, ob, cl, h, bn, string quartet) Heugel.

MC PHEE, COLIN, Concerto (pf, wind octet) New Music Edition, IV, No. 2, 1930.

MERIKANTO, AARRE, Concerto (v, cl, h, strhg sextet) Schott, (min score); Andraud; AMP.

MILHAUD, DARIUS, First Symphony, The Spring (picc, fl, ob, cl, 2 v, va, vc, harp) Andraud; Mercury; Universal Edition (score, parts).

MOLBE, HEINRICH FREIHERR VON BACH, Nonet, Op. 26 Tanzweisen (ob, cl, h, bn, string quintet) 1896 Hofmeister (score, parts).
---Nonett, Op. 61 in Eb major (cl, eng h, h, bn, 2 v, va, vc, bass) Hofmeister (score, parts).
---Intermezzo, Op. 81 in G minor (ob, cl, h, bn, 2 v, va, vc bass) Hofmeister (score, parts).
---Nonet, Op. 83 in F major, Scherzo (ob, cl, h, bn, 2 v, va, vc, bass) 1900, Hofmeister (score, parts).
---Nonet, Op. 84 in G major, Andante Pensieroso (ob, cl, h, bn, 2 v, va, vc, bass) 1900, Hofmeister (score, parts).
---Nonet, Op. 89 in Eb major, Tanzweisen (ob, cl, h, bn, 2 v, va, vc, bass) 1900 Hofmeister (score, parts).

MOZER, FRANZ JOSEF, Sinfonie, Op. 40 in F major (fl, ob, cl, bn, h, v, va, vc, bass) 1924, Doblinger (socre, parts); Andraud.

MOZART, JOHANN CHRYSOSTOMUS WOLFGANG GOTTLIEB, Zwei Zwischenakts-musiken zu Konig Thamos (ob, bn, h, kettledrums, string quintet) ed. by Alfred Einstein, Barenreiter-Bote, (score, parts).
---Grand Serenade (9 winds) Simrock; Fetis.
---Cassazione, No. 1 in G major, K63 (2 ob, 2 h, string quintet) B&H, 1880; AMP
---Cassazione No. 2 in Bb major, K99 (2 ob, 2 h, string quintet) B&H, 1830; AMP.
---Divertimento, No. 1 in Eb major, K113 (2 cl, 2 h, string Quintet) B&H, 1878; AMP.

NAUMANN, ERNSTGUIDO, Serenade, Op. 10 in A major (fl, ob, bn, h, 2 v, va, vc, pf or bass) Simrock (score, parts); Andraud; AMP.

NEUMANN, H., Premiere Harmonie, Op. 30 (2 cl, 2 ob, 2 h, 2 bn, cfgt).

NIELSEN, Bagpipe, Op. 30, No. 3 in Bb major (2 fl, 2 ob, 2 cl, 2 bn, perc; Also picc, fl, 2 ob, 2 cl, 2 bn, triangles, pietti) Andraud.

ONSLOW, GEORGE, Nonett, Op. 77 in A minor (fl, ob, cl, h, bn, 2 v, va, vc, bass ad lib) Joubert; Kistner & Siegel; Andraud.

PARRY, SIR CHARLES HUBERT HASTINGS, Nonet for Wind Instruments, Op. 70 in Bb major (fl, ob, eng h, 2 cl, 2 bn, 2 h).

PEZEL, JOHANN, Bicinia Variorum (v, h, fl, cl, bn, with 2 Bombardinis Vulgo Chalumean, cl, bn) Fetis.

PIERNE, HENRI CONSTANT GABRIEL, March of the Little Lead Soldiers (fl, cl, tpt, drum, harp, strings) Andraud.

PISTON, WALTER, Divertimento for Nine Instruments (fl, ob, cl, bn, string quintet) VH Broadcast Music, Inc; AMP; Baron.

PLAYEL, IGNACE JOSEPH, Serenade (3 winds, bass, strings) Rudall & Carte.

REVUELTAS, SILVESTRE, Planos, A Geometric Dance (cl, bass-cl, bn, tpt, pf, strings without va) Fleisher.

RHEINBERGER, JOSEF GABRIEL, Nonett, Op. 139 in Eb major (fl, ob, cl, h, bn, v, va, vc, bass) Kistner & Siegel (score, parts) Andraud.

RICCI-SIGNORINI, ANTONIO, Fantasia Burlesca in C major (fl, ob, h, bn, xylophone, triangle, pf--4 hands) Carisch, 1925.

RIDKY, JAROSLAV, Nonett, Op. 32 (v, va, vc, bass, fl, ob, cl, bn h) Sadlo, 1941.

RIES, FERDINAND, Nonet (cl, bn, h, v, va, vc, pf, harp or 2 pf) Andraud.

ROSETTI, FRANZ ANTON, Six Symphonies (2 v, va, bass, fl, 2 ob, 2 H) Sieber; Fetis.
  ---Three Symphonies, Op. 5 (2 v, va, bass, fl, 2 ob, 2 h) Artaria; Fetis.
  ---Two Symphonies, Op. 13 (2 v, va, bass, fl, 2 ob, 2 h) Andre; Offenbach; Fetis.

RUDOLF, JOHANN ANTON, Theme with 12 Variations (solo v, 2 v, 2 h, 2 cl, va, bass) Fetis.

RUYNEMAN, DANIEL, Hieroglyphics (2 fl, 2 mandolins, guitar, pf, harp, celesta, cup-bells).

SIANT-SAENS, CHARLES CAMILLE, Deuxieme Suite (2 fl, ob, 2 cl, 2 bn, 2 h) H Baxter-Northrup.

SALVIUCCI, GIOVANNI, Serenata (string quartet, fl, ob, cl, bn, tpt) Ricordi (min score, parts).

SAMAZEUILH, GUSTAVE, Divertissement and Musette in G minor (fl, ob, cl, h, bn, 2 v, va, vc) Durand (score, parts); Andraud.

SCHEIN, JOAHNN HERMANN, Dances from Banquetto Musicale (9 winds) McGinnis & Marx.

SCHOECK, OTHMAR, Serenade, Op. 1 (fl, ob, cl, bn, h, string quartet) Hug, 1907.

SCHOLZ, ROBERT, Second Divertimento for Nine Wind Instruments (fl, 2 ob, 2 cl, 2 h, 2 bn) Ms., Robert Scholz, 55 West 55th St., NYC.

SCHONBERG, ARNOLD, Pierrot Lunaire (voice, pf, fl, picc, cl, bass-cl, v, va, vc).

SCHRECK, GUSTAVE, Divertimento, Op. 40 in E minor (2 fl, with picc, ob, 2 cl, 2 h, 2 bn) B&H (score, parts); Andraud; AMP; Sansone.

SCHUBERT, FRANZ, A Short Funeral Piece (Eine Kleine Trauermusik) in Eb major (2 cl, 2 bn, cfgt, 2 h, 2 tromb) B&H (score, parts); Andraud; AMP; Sansone, (scored for 2 cl, 2 bn, cfgt, 2 h, 2 tpt).

SETACCIOLI, GIACOMO, Nonet (9 winds).

SHEHERBACKER, Nonet, Op. 10 (winds, strings, pf) Universal Edition.

SILAS, EDOUARD, Nonet (strings, winds).

SPAETH, ANDREW, Nonetto (string and wind instruments) Fetis.

SPOHR, LOUIS, Nonett, Op. 31 in F major (v, va, vc, bass, fl, ob, cl, h, bn) Costallat; Haslinger; Litolff; Sander, (min score); Andraud (scored for v, va, vc, fl, ob, cl, h, bn, pf); Sansone; Eulenburg.

STANFORD, SIR CHARLES V., Serenade for Strings and Winds, Op. 95 in F major (fl, cl, 2 bn, horn, strings) Andraud.

STOHR, RICHARD, Kammersymphonie, Op. 32 in F major (string quar-
      tet, ob, cl, h, bn, harp) Kahnt (score, parts).
STRANG, DR. GERALD, Concerto Grosso (fl, cl, bn, h, v, va, vc,
      pf).
STRAVINSKY, IGOR FEDOROVICH, Priaboutki, Chansons Plaisantes (med
      voice, fl, ob, cl, bn, string quartet); Spratt; Baron,
      (score, parts); Chester (scored for voice, fl, ob, or eng
      h, cl, bn, v, va, vc, bass).
STRIEGLER, KURT, Nonet, Op. 14 in E minor, Kammer Sinfonie (fl,
      ob, cl, bn, h, string quartet) Junne (score, parts).
STURMER, BRUNO, Suite in G minor, Op. 9 (fl, ob, cl, bn, string
      quintet) Schott (score, parts); Andraud; AMP.
VILLA-LOBOS, HEITOR, Nonet (fl, ob, cl, sax, bn, harp, celesta,
      perc, mixed choir) Max Eschig, Paris.
WEBERN, ANTON VON, Sinfonie, Op. 21 (cl, bass-co, 2 h, harp, 2
      v, va, vc) 1929, Universal Edition (score, parts).
---Two Songs: Du, der ich's nicht sage, and Du machst mich
      allein, Op. 8, words by R. M. Rilke (voice, cl or bass-cl,
      h, tpt, celesta, harp, v, va, vc) Universal Edition.
WELLER, AUGUSTE HEinrich, Concerto (pf, 2 v, va, bass, 2 ob, 2 h)
      Fetis; German Edition.

Dixtuors

AUBERY DU BOULLEY, PRUDENT LOUIS, Grand Serenade, Op. 48 (2 v,
      va, bass, fl, 2 cl, 2 h, bn) Richault; Fetis.
BACH, JOHANN SEBASTIAN, Symphony in D major (2 v, va, 2 ob, bn,
      3 tpt, bass) Catalogue of C.P.E. Bach; Fetis.
BEETHOVEN, LUDWIG VAN, Overture to Coriolanus (2-3 v, pf, har-
      monium, va, vc, bass, fl, kettledrums) Vieweg (min
      score, parts).
BERNARD, EMILE, Divertissement, Op. 36 in F major (2 fl, 2 ob, 2 cl,
      2 h, 2 bn) Durand (score, parts); Andraud; Sansone;
      Elkan-Vogel.
BYRD, WILLIAM, Pavane (2 fl, 2 ob, 2 cl, 2 h, 2 bn) Andraud.
---Suite in D major (2 fl, 2 ob, 2 cl, 2 h, 2 bn) Ms., Libra-
      ry of Congress, Washington, D.C.
BLATTNER, ORRIN, Two American Sketches. 1. Rural, 2. Urban (2 fl,
      2 ob, 2 cl, 2 h, 2 bn) MH Witmark; Music Publishers
      Holding Corp. (score, parts).
BOCCHERINI, LUIGI, Concerto, Op. 8, 1769 (2 v, ob, vc, alto and
      bass obligati, 2 v, h, tpt for ripieno) Fetis.
BRAUER, MAX, Suite (10 woodwinds, with bass) B&H (parts, score).
BRESGEN, CESAR, Woodwind Music, Op. 17 (10 winds) Vieweg (score),
      parts).
BRITTEN, BENJAMIN, Sinfonietta, Op. 1 in F major (fl, ob, cl, bn,
      h, 2 v, va, vc, bass) Boosey & Hawkes.
BRUNMAYER, ANDRE, Petite Cantate (4 voices, 2 cl, 2 h, 2 bn)
      Fetis.
CAPLET, ANDRE, Suite Persane (2 fl, 2 ob, 2 bn, 2 cl, 2 h) Ms. at
      Curtis Institute of Music, Philadelphia, Pa.
CASADESUS, FRANCIS LOUIS, London Sketches, Humorous Suite. 1.
      The Policeman in the Zoo, 2. Trafalgar Square Idyl, 3.
      Children at Play (2 fl or 2 picc, 2 ob, 2 bn, 2 cl, 2 h)
      H (rec) Diess & Co., (score, parts); Andraud; Baron.

CASTILLON DE SAINT-VICTOR, Allegretto (2 v, va, vc, bass, fl, ob,
cl, h, bn) Ms., Fetis Supplement.
COSME, LUIZ, Bombo, Canto Onomatopeyico-mimico (fl, 2 cl, bn,
tromb, bass drum, small tambourine, 2 tambourines, bar)
Boletin Latinamericano de Musica VI.
DESTENAY, E., Op. 12 in Eb major (wind quintet, string quartet,
harp) 1906, Hamelle.
DITTERS VON DITTERSDORF, KARL, Concertino (2 ob, bn, 2 h, 2 v, 2
va, bass) Ms. at Traeg, Vienna; Fetis.
DOLEZALER, JEAN EMMANUEL, Twelve Ecossaises (2 v, 2 cl, 2 h, fl,
2 bn, bass) Artaria; Fetis.
DUBOIS, CLEMENT FRANCOIS THEODORE, Dixtuor in D minor (fl, ob,
cl, h, bn, string quintet) Leduc; Heugel (min score,
parts); Andraud.
---Suite No. 2 (10 instruments) Heugel; Andraud.
DVORAK, ANTONIN, March Serenade, Op. 44 (2 ob, 2 cl, 2 bn, 3 h,
cfgt) H Mills Music, Inc.
ENESCO, GEORGES, Dixtuor, Op. 14 in D major (2 fl, ob, eng h, 2
cl, 2 h, 2 bn) Ms., copy at Curtis Institute of Music
Philadelphia, Pa.
---Intermezzo for Ten Wind Instruments, Op. 12.
FICHER, JACOBO, Dos Poemas, No. 16 and 42, from "The Gardener" of
Rabindranath Tagore, Op. 10 (fl, ob, cl, h, bn, 2 v, va,
vc, bass) Fleisher.
FLEGIER, ANGE, Dixtuor in F minor (fl, ob, cl, h, bn, string
quintet) Lemoine (score, parts); Andraud; Grus.
GASTINEL, LEON GUSTAVE CYPRIEN, Adagio and Allegretto in the manner
of saltarello (10 wind instruments) Fetis Supplement.
GYROWETZ, ADALBERT, Serenade (10 instruments) Offenbach; Andre;
Fetis.
HANDEL, GEORGE FREDERICK, Concerto No. 2 in Bb major, Op. 3 (2
first v, 2 second v, 2 ob, va, 2 vc, continuo) B&H.
---Concerto Grosso, No. 1 in Bb major (2 ob, 2 v, va, 2 vc,
b.c.) B&H.
---Firework Music, Part II (2 ob, bn, 3 tpt, 3 h, timp) E.
B. Marks.
HARTMANN, EMIL, Serenade, Op. 43 in Bb major (fl, ob, 2 cl, 2 h,
2 bn, vc, bass) Ries & Erler (score, parts); Andraud.
HAYDN, FRANZ JOSEPH, Feldpartituer, Chorale St. Antoine (2 ob, 2
cl, 2 h, 3 bn, cfgt.) Ms., Friends of Music Library, Vienna.
---Notturno I in C major (fl, ob, 2 h, 2 v, 2 va, vc, bass)
E. F. Schmid (score, parts).
---Notturno II in C major (2 fl, 2 h, 2 v, 2 va, vc, bass)
E. F. Schmid (score, parts).
---Notturno II in F major (fl, ob, 2 h, 2 v, 2 va, vc, bass)
E. F. Schmid (score, parts); Hohler & Schafler.
---Notturno V in C major (fl, ob, 2 h, 2 v, 2 va, vc, bass)
Universal Edition (ed. by Geiringer, score, parts).
---Partita in F major (fl, ob, 2 h, 2 v, 2 va, vc, bass) Uni-
versal Edition (ed. by Geiringer, score, parts).
---Divertissement, No. 1 (fl, ob, bn, 2 v, va, bass, ob, 2 h)
Ms. held by Fetis.
HONNEGGER, ARTHUR, Pastorale d'Ete (fl, ob, cl, h, bn, string quin-
tet) Andraud.

IBERT, JACQUES, Capriccio (fl, ob, cl, bn, tpt, harp, string quintet) Andraud; Leduc (score, parts); Baron (min. score,
   parts).
IPPOLITOV, IVANOV, MIKHAIL M., Dans la Mosquee, in D major (2 fl,
   ob, cl, 2 bn, 3 h, tymp) Ms.
ITIBERE, BRASILIO, Contemplacao (fl, ob, cl, 2 h, strings and wo-
   men's chorus) Boletin de Latinoamericano Musica.
JADASSOHN, SALOMON, Serenade, Op. 104c (2 fl, 2 ob, 2 cl, 2 h, 2
   bn) Andraud.
KLINGLER, KARL, Variations in A major (fl, ob, cl, bn, h, 2 v, va,
   vc, bass) 1938, self published by author in Berlin, score,
   parts.
KUNSTMANN, JOHANN GOTTFRIED, Six Quadrilles (2 v, fl, picc, cl, 2
   h, bn, tromb, bass) B&H; Fetis.
LALO, EDWARD VICTOR ANTON, Two Aubades (fl, ob, cl, h, bn, strings)
   Andraud.
   ---Aubade, Morning Serenade (fl, ob, cl, h, bn, string quin-
   tet) Heugel.
LILIEN, IGNACE, Apollinisch Sonatine, in C major (2 fl, 2 ob, 2
   cl, 2 bn, 2 h) Stichting Donemus.
LOUIS, FERDINAND, Prince of Prussia, Rondo, Op. 9 in Bb major (2
   v, va, vc, bass, fl, cl, 2 h, pf) B&H.
MASCHEK, VINCENT, Concertino (2 fl, 2 cl, 2 h, 2 bn, pf, 4 hands)
   B&H; Fetis.
MASSENET, JULES EMILE FREDERIC, Introduction and Variations, Op.
   19, (2 v, va, vc, bass, fl, ob, cl, bn) Fetis Supplement.
MELIN, Menuet Badin (2 fl, 2 ob, 2 cl, 2 bn, 2 h) Evette; An-
   draud.
MIGNONE, FRANCISCO, Ao Anoitecer, Lullaby (2 fl, 2 ob, harp, ce-
   lesta, strings) Fleisher.
MILHAUD, DARIUS, Symphonie No. 5 (picc, fl, ob, eng h, cl, bass-
   cl, 2 bn, 2 h) VH 1922, Universal Edition (score, parts);
   Andraud.
MOLBE, HEINRICH FREIHERR VON BACH, Dezett, Op. 21 in C minor (3
   v, va, vc, bass, cl, eng h, h, bn) Hofmeister (score,
   parts).
   ---Hymm de Printemps, Op. 31 (cl, eng h, h, bn, harp, 2 v,
   va, vc, bass) Hofmeister, 1902.
   ---Dezett, Op. 91 in Eb major (cl, eng h, h, bn, harp, 2 v,
   va, vc, bass) Hofmeister (score, parts).
   ---Dezett, Op. 104 in F major (cl, eng h, h, bn, harp, 2 v,
   va, vc, bass) Hofmeister (score, parts).
   ---Dezett, Op. 109 in Eb major (cl, eng h, h, bn, harp, 2 v,
   va, vc, bass) Hofmeister (score, parts).
   ---Intermezzo, Op. 110 in Bb major (cl, eng h, h, bn, harp,
   2 v, va, vc, bass) Hofmeister (score, parts).
   ---Intermezzo, Op. 111 in F major (cl, eng h, h, bn, harp, 2
   v, va, vc, bass) Hofmeister (score, parts).
   ---Dezett, Op. 113 in Ab major (cl, eng h, h, bn, harp, 2 v,
   va, vc, bass) Hofmeister (score, parts).
   ---Dezett, Op. 118 in C major (cl, eng h, h, bn, harp, 2 v,
   va, vc, bass) Hofmeister (score, parts).
   ---Dezett, Op. 124 in Bb major (cl, eng h, h, bn, harp, 2 v,
   va, vc, bass) Hofmeister (score, parts).

---Dezett, Op. 129 in C major (cl, eng h, h, bn, harp, 2 v, va, vc, bass) Hofmeister (score, parts).

---Grune Klange, Op. 141 (cl, eng h, h, bn, harp, string quintet) Hofmeister (score, parts).

MOOR, EMANUEL, Dixtuor, Op. 103 in A major, Suite for Double Quintette (fl, ob, cl, h, bn, string quintet) Salabert (score, parts); Andraud; Sansone.

MOZART, WOLFGANG AMADEUS, Divertimento No. 3 in Bb major, K166 (2 ob, 2 cl, 2 eng h, 2 h, 2 bn) (rec) B&H (score, parts); Andraud; AMP.

---Decett, Divertimento No. 3 in Bb major, KV 166 (2 eng h, 2 ob, 2 cl, 2 h, 2 bn) B&H.

---Divertimento No. 4 in Bb major, K186 (2 ob, 2 cl, 2 eng h, 2 h, 2 bn) (rec) B&H (score); Andraud; AMP.

---Divertimento No. 5 in C major (2 fl, 5 tpt, 4 kettledrums) B&H (score, parts), K187.

---Serenade, K100 (2 v, va, bass, 2 ob or 2 fl, 2 h, 2 tpt) Andraud.

---Serenade, K185 (2 v, va, bass, 2 ob, or 2 fl, 2 h, 2 tpt) Andraud.

---Serenade, K204 (2 v, va, bass, 2 ob or 2 fl, 2 h, 2 tpt) Andraud.

PIERNE, HENRY CONSTANT GABRIEL, March of the Little Lead Sol- diers (fl, tpt, cl, drum, pf, strings) Andraud.

---March of the Little Fawns (wind quintet, string quintet) Andraud.

---Farandolle (fl, ob, cl, bn, h, tpt, tambourine, strings) Baron (score, parts, pf-conductor).

---Petite Gavotte (fl, ob, cl, h, strings) Baron (score, parts, pf-conductor).

PITTALUGA, GUSTAVO, Petite Suite (fl, cl, bn, tpt, tromb, harp, string quartet) Spratt; Baron (min score, parts).

PRATELLA, FRANCESCO BALILLA, Per un Dramma Orientale, Op. 40, (woodwind quintet, string quartet, pf) Ricordi (score, parts, min score).

PROKOFIEFF, SERGE, Suite from Music for Children, Op. 65, arr. by Wilson (fl, ob, eng h, 3 cl, alto-cl, bass-cl, alto-sax, bass or bn) University of Texas.

RAFF, JOSEPH JOACHIM, Sinfonietta, Op. 188 in F major (2 fl, 2 ob, 2 cl, 2 h, 2 bn) Kistner & Siegel; Andraud; Rudall, Carte & Co.

RAVEL, MAURICE JOSEPH, Three Poems of Mallarme (female voice, pf, string quartet, 2 fl or picc, 2 cl, or bass-cl) Durand.

REICHA, ANTON, Dixtuor (5 winds, 5 strings).

RIETI, VITTORIO, Madrigal in Four Movements (fl, ob, cl, bn, h, tpt, string quartet) Andraud.

SAINT-SAENS, CHARLES CAMILLE, Bacchanale from Samson & Delilah (2 fl, ob, eng h, 2 cl, 2 h, 2 bn) Andraud.

SCARLATTI, DOMENICO, Pastorale from Clavicembal Sonata, arr. by J. Hasselmans (2 fl, 2 ob, eng h, 2 cl, 2 bn, h) Schott; Andraud; Ricordi.

SCHMITT, FLORENT, Lied and Scherzo, Op. 54 (2 fl, ob, eng h, 2 cl, h, 2 bn, or fl, picc) VH (rec) Andraud; Duradn (scored for double wind quintet); Elkan-Vogel.

SCHUMAN, ROBERT ALEXANDER, Dixtour (2 ob, eng h, 2 bn, 2 cl, 2 h, bass-cl).

SPORCK, GEORGES, Landscapes of Normandy (2 fl, 2 ob, 2 cl, 2 h, 2 bn) Andraud.

STRAUSS, RICHARD, Serenade for Woodwinds (2 fl, 2 bn, 2 cl, 4 h) International Music Co.

STRAVINSKY, IGOR FEDOROVICH, 3 Poesies de la Lyrique Japonaise (sop, 2 fl, 2 cl, pf, 2 v, va, vc) Russsicher Music-Verlag; Edition Russe de la Musique.

STRIEGLER, KURT, Kammer-Sinfonie, Op. 14 in E minor (fl, ob, cl, bn, h, string quintet) Junne (score, parts).

STURMER, BRUNO, Suite: Ouverture, Intermezzo, Passacaglia, Rondo (3 v, vc, bass, fl, cl, pf, 4 hands, harmonium) Vieweg, (score, parts, min score).

TANEIEV, SERGIUS, Andante (2 fl, 2 ob, 2 cl, 2 h, 2 bn) arr. by Lamm, Leeds.

TOESCHI, JOHANN BAPTISTE, Three Symphonies, Op. 7 (2 v, 2 ob, 2 h, va, bass, 2 bn) Fetis; Huberti.

VANDER HAGEN, ARMAND, Suites of Military Harmony (Deux Suites de pas Redoubles), Op. 14, 17, 20, 21 (10 instruments) Fetis; Frere, Paris; Leduc.

WELLESZ, EGON, Aurora (coloratura, string quartet, fl, cl, bn, h, harp) Curwen, 1926.

WOLF-FERRARI, ERMANNO, Kammersymphonie, Op. 8 in Bb major (fl, ob, cl, bn, h, string quartet, pf) Andraud; Rahter.

More Than Ten Instruments

AIBLINGER, JOSEPH GASPARD, Six Messes Solennelles ou Breves (4 voices, organ, wind and stringed instruments ad lib) Fetis.

ASSMAYER, IGNACE, Messe Solennelle in C major (4 voices, violins, va, vc, bass, 2 ob, 2 bn, 2 h, 2 tpt, timbales, organ) Mechetti; Fetis.

BACH, JOAHNN SEBASTIAN, Brandenburg Concerto, No. 1 (v, 3 ob, 2 h, 2 v, va, vc, bass, pf) Peters; Fetis.
---Ach Bleib, arr. by Don Christlieb (fl, picc, 2 ob or ob d'amour, eng h, bar oboe, 2 cl, bass-cl, 3 bn, cfgt).

BACH, JOHANN SEBASTIAN, Jesu, Joy of Man's Desiring, arr. by Fitzgerald (ob solo, 2 cl, 2 alto-sax, 2 alto-cl, bass-cl, bass, 2 tpt, 2 tromb, men's chorus) University of Texas.
---Suite in C minor (2 fl, 2 ob, 3 cl, alto-cl, bass-cl, bn, bass) University of Texas.
---Ein Feste Burg, arr. by L. Mortan (2 fl, picc, 2 ob, eng h, bar oboe, 2 cl, bass-cl, 3 bn, cfgt).

BEETHOVEN, LUDWIG VAN, Allegretto from Sonata, Op. 27, No. 2, arr. by Robert Russell Bennett (2 fl, 2 ob, 2 bn, 3 cl, alto-cl, bass-cl, 2 alto-sax, ten sax, bar sax, bass) University of Texas.
---Sonata, Op. 10, No. 2, arr. for Reed Band (16 reeds) MH Gamble Hinged Music; Music Publishers Holding Corp., (transc. by G. Strickling, scored for fl, ob, bn, 3 1st cl, 2 2nd cl, 2 3rd cl, alto-cl, bass-cl, alto-sax, ten sax; bar sax and bass sax ad lib., Score, parts).

    ---Sonata, Op. 10, No. 2, Allegretto, arr. by Fitzgerald (2 fl, 2 ob, 3 cl, 2 bn, alto-cl, bass-cl, 2 alto-sax, ten sax, bar sax, bass) University of Texas.

    ---Bundeslied, Op. 122, words by Goethe (2 solo voices, chori, 2 cl, 2 h, 2 bn) Fetis.

BERG, ALBAN, Chamber Concerto (13 winds, pf, v).

BYRD, WILLIAM, Serenade for Woodwind Instruments in Eb major (2 fl, 2 ob, eng h, 2 cl, 2 h, 2 bn) Ms., Library of Congress, Washington, D.C.

BLISS, ARTHUR, Rout (sop, fl, cl, harp, string quartet, bass, side drum, glockenspiel) Goodwin & Tabb.

    ---The Women of Yueh, Five Songs (fl, ob, cl, bn, string quartet, bass, glockenspiel, triangle, side drums) Chester.

BLOCH, ERNEST, Four Episodes (fl, ob, cl, h, bn, 2 v, va, vc, bass, pf or harp) Birchard.

BOCCHERINI, LUIGI, Ouverture a Grand Orchestre, Op. 43 (2 v, 2 altos, vc, contra bn, 2 ob, 2 h, bn) Pleyel; Fetis.

BOLZONI, GIOVANNI, Menuet for Woodwind Band, arr. by Righter, State University of Iowa.

BRAHMS, JOHANNES, Fugetta Super: Dies Sind Die Heil'gen Zehn Gebot (fl, picc, fl, 2 ob, eng h, bar, ob, 2 cl, bass-cl, 3 bn, contrabn) arr. by L. Mortan.

    ---Serenade, Op. 16 (2 fl, 2 ob, 2 cl, 2 bn, 2 h, va, vc, bass) Andraud.

    ---Herlich tut Mich Verlangen (fl, alto-fl, ob, eng h, bar ob, 2 cl, bass-cl, 2 bn, contra bn) arr. by L. Mortan.

BRAUER, MAX, Pan, Suite in Bb major (2 fl, 2 ob, 2 cl, 2 h, 2 bn, bass) B&H.

BROER, ERNEST, Vepres, Op. 3 (4 voices, 2 v, va, organ, 2 ob, 2 h) Grosser; Fetis.

BUSCH, ADOLF GEORG W., Divertimento (fl, ob, cl, bn, 2 h, tpt, tymp, string quintet) Andraud.

CARTELLIERI, CASIMIR-ANTOINE, Nocturne (2 v, va, bass, fl, ob, cl, bn, 2 h, 2 tromb, timbales) Ms. at Traeg, Vienna; Fetis.

CASELLA, ALFREDO, Introduzione, Corale, Marcia (3 fl, 3 ob, 3 cl, 3 bn, 4 h, 3 tpt, 3 tromb, tuba, perc, pf, 4 bass) Universal Edition.

CATURLA, ALEJANDRO GARCIA, Bembe, Three Cuban Dances (fl or alto picc, ob or alto eng h, cl, bass-cl, bn, 2 h, tpt, ten tromb, tuba, perc, pf) Elkan-Vogel; Senart (scored for fl, ob, eng h, 2 cl, bn, tpt, 2 h, tromb, perc, pf; also fl, ob, eng h, 2 cl, bn, string quartet, perc, pf).

CAZDEN, NORMAN, On the Death of a Spanish Child, Op. 20 (3 fl, 2 ob, 5 cl, 3 bn, 2 alto-sax, ten sax, 4 h, 3 tpt, 3 tromb, 2 tubas, bar, tymp, bass drum, cy) Fleisher Collection, Unpublished.

COSSART, LELAND A., Two Suites, Op. 19 in F major (2 fl, 2 ob, 2 cl, 2 h, 2 bn, harp) Andraud; Heinrichshofen (score, parts).

DEVIENNE, FRANCOIS, Overtures Pour Instruments a Vent a l'usage des Fetes Nationales, No. 1-7, Ozy, Paris; Fetis.

DIEREN, BERNARD VAN, Sonnet VII, Demund Spenser, "Amoretti" (string quartet, c'bass, fl, cl, corno di bassetto, bn, h, voice).

DOST, RUDOLF, Le Bal de Beatrice D'Este (2 fl, 2 cl, ob, 2 bn, 2 h, tpt, 2 harp) Baxter-Northrup.

DEPUY, L., Une Soiree D'Ete.

DVORAK, ANTONIN, March, Op. 44 (2 ob, 2 cl, 2 bn, cfgt ad lib, 3
    h, vc, double-bass) MH E. B. Marks.
  ---Serenade, Op. 44 in D minor (2 ob, 2 cl, 2 bn, cfgt ad
    lib, 3 h, vc, double-bass) MH Simrock; Andraud.

EICHHEIM, HENRY, Oriental Impressions (pf, harp, violins, fl,ob,
    eng h, bells, perc) G. Schirmer.

FICHER, JACOBO, Sinfonia de Camara, Op. 20, Symphony No. 1 (wind
    instruments, tympany, strings) Fleisher.

FINZI, GERALD, A Severn Rhapsody (fl,ob, 2 cl, 2, strings) (fl,
    ob, eng h, cl, bass-cl, h, 2 v, va, vc, bass) Andraud.

FRIED, OSKAR, Adagio and Scherzo, Op. 2 (3 fl or 3 picc, 3 ob, 3
    cl, 3 bn, 3 h, 2 harps, tymp) B&H; Andraud.

GALLIARD, Sonata for Chamber Orchestra, arr. by F. Sevitsky (fl,
    ob, cl, bn, horns, strings, timpany) Ricordi (score,
    parts).

GANZ, R., Woody Scherzo for Thirteen Instruments, Op. 33 No. 3
    (picc, 2 fl, 2 ob, eng h, 2 bn, cfgt, 3 cl, bass-cl) MH
    Mills Music Co.

GIANNETTI, RAFFAELE, Stabat Mater (4 voices, fl, 2 cl, strings)
    Fetis Supplement.

GILSON, PAUL, Norwegian Melody--Humoresques (woodwinds, horns)

GOSSEC, FRANCOIS JOSEPH, A Symphonie Concertante (11 instruments)
    Venier; Bailleux; La Chevardiere; Sieber; Fetis.
  ---Three Symphonies for Wind Instruments, Venier; Bailleux;
    La Chevardiere; Sieber; Fetis.

GRABNER, HERMANN, Perkeo Suite for Wind Orchestra, Op. 15 (2 fl,
    or alt picc, 2 ob, 2 cl, 3 bn, 4 h, small drum) Kahnt.

GRAINGER, PERCY ALDRIDGE, Ye Banks and Braie O' Bonnie Doon
    (picc, fl, ob, eng h, bn, cl, alto-cl, bass-cl, alto-sax,
    ten-sax, bass-sax, h, bar-sax) E. G. Schirmer.

GRAVINA, GILBERTO, Preludio e Fuga in C major (12 fl).

GRIEG, EDVARD, Heart Wounds, arr. by Holvik (2 fl, 2 ob, eng h,
    2 bn, 3 cl, 4 h, alto-sax, alto-cl, ten-sax, bass-cl,
    bar sax) Music Dept., Iowa State Teachers College.
  ---The Last Spring, arr. by Holvik (2 fl, 2 ob, eng h, 3 cl,
    alto-sax, ten sax, bar sax, bass-cl, 2 bn, cfgt) Music
    Dept., Iowa State Teachers College.

GRIMM, KARL HUGO, Byzantine Suite (fl, ob, cl, h, bn, tpt, string
    quintet) Andraud.

GROSSE, FRIEDRICH DER, Sinfonie in D major (2 fl, 2 ob, 2 h,
    strings, pf) ed. by Dr. Helmuth Osthoff, Nagel.

GUARNIERI, CAMARGO, Tostao de Chuva, Lundu (fl, eng h, cl, bn, 2
    h, harp, strings, voice) Boletin Latinoamericano de Mu-
    sica, VI.

HABERT, JOHANNES EVANGELISTA, Four Funeral Marches (2 cl, 10
    brass) Andraud.

HAHN, REYNALDO, La Bal de Beatrice D'Este (2 fl, 2 cl, ob, 2 bn,
    2 h, tpt, perc, 2 harps, perc--tympani, cymbals, triangle)
    Heugel; Fleisher; Baron (with string quartet, score,
    parts).

HANDEL, GEORGE FREDERICK, Firework Music, Part I (3 ob, 2 bn, 3
    tpt, 3 h, tymp) Part II (see Dixtours) E. B. Marks.
  ---Concerto No. 1 in Bb major, Op. 3 (2 v, 2 ob, 2 fl, 2 va,
    2 bn, b.c.) B&H, 1858.

HANDEL, GEORGE FREDERICK, Concerto Grosso, No. 2 in G minor (ob,
 2 fl, 2 v, 2 va, 2 bn, vc, b.c.) B&H.
----Notturno V in C major, Universal Edition.
----Partita in F major, Universal Edition.
----Divertissement, Concertante (v, vc, bass, fl, bn, 2 v, va,
 bass, 2 ob, 2 h) Fetis; Sieber; Janet; Porro; Andre;
 Offenbach.
----Symphonie Concertante, Concertino (4 v, va, vc, bass, 2
 ob, fl, bn) Boyer; Offenbach (entitled Serenade); Fetis.
----Cassazione, No. 1 in C major (2 v, bass, 2 fl, 2 ob, 2 h,
 2 bn) Fetis.
HEATH, JOHN RIPPINER, The Lamp, a chamber music drama (3 solo
 voices, chorus, string quartet, fl, cl, bn, h).
HENNIG, JEAN CHRETIEN, Six Pieces (5 cl, fl, 2 h, 2 tpt, 2 bn,
 tromb, serpent) Haecker; Fetis.
HERBERIGS, ROBERT, Concert Champetre (winds).
HINDEMITH, PAUL, Spielmusik, Op. 43, No. 1 (2 fl, 2 ob, string
 orchestra; also fl, ob, cl, bass-cl, bn, tpt, h, tromb,
 v, va, vc, bass, pf) Andraud.
----Concert Music for Wind Orchestra, Op. 41 (fl, ob, 4 cl, 6
 h, baritone, 3 tpt, 3 tromb, 2 tubas, perc) Andraud.
----Concert Music, Op. 36, No. 1 (fl, ob, cl, bass-cl, bn, h,
 tpt, tromb, v, va, vc, bass, pf) Andraud.
HOFER, FRANZ, Sinfonietta No. 1 in C major, Op. 63 (2 v, va, vc,
 bass, pf, harmonium, 2 fl, cl, tpt, h, kettledrums) Vieweg (score, parts, min score).
HOLBROOKE, JOSEF A., Serenade, Op. 61b (5 alto sax, ob, cl, eng
 h, va, cornet, bar or 2 saxhorns, harp) Andraud; Modern
 Music Library.
HOLLAND, JEAN-DAVID, Deux Serenades (2 v, 2 va, clarinets, 2 h,
 bassoons, violincelli) Fetis Supplement.
HOLST, GUSTAV THEODORE, Savitri, chamber opera (double string
 quartet, c'bass, 2 fl, eng h, chorus).
HORN, JEAN GASPARD, Musicalische Tugend und Jugend-Gedichte,
 musical poems (1, 2, 3, 4, and 5 voices, 5 v or fl, b.c.)
 Fetis.
IVES, CHARLES EDWARD, The Unanswered Question (4 fl, chamber-
 orch).
----Central Park in the Dark (4 fl, chamber orch).
KANIITZ, ERNEST, Concerto Grosso (fl, ob, sop, sax, cl, bn, 2
 h, tpt, pf, perc., strings) University of Southern Cal.
----Serenade (2 fl, ob, 2 cl, alto-sax, 2 bn, h, 2 tpt, pf,
 perc) University of Southern California, ms.
KALLENBERG, WILHELM, Six Chants (sop, cont, ten, bass, with fl,
 2 cl, 2 h, 2 tpt, tromb, organ) Hoffmann; Fetis.
KNIPPER, LEV K., Little Concerto (3 ob, 3 tpt, 4 tymp, 3 harps,
 strings) Leeds.
KRENEK, ERNST, Kleine Blasmusik, Op. 70a (2 fl, 2 ob, 3 cl, 3 bn,
 2 h, 2 tpt, 2 tromb, tuba, perc) Universal Edition.
----Drei Lustige Marsche, Op. 44 (fl, ob, 4 cl, 2 h, 2 tpt,
 tromb, tuba, perc) Universal Edition.
KRENN, FRANCOIS, O Deus Ego Amare, offertory, Op. 23 (sop or ten,
 bass, with 2 v, va, bass, organ, 2 cl, 2 h) Haslinger;
 Fetis.
LALANDE, MICHEL RICHARD DE, Sinfonies, The Suppers of the King
 (2 fl, or 2 picc, 2 ob, 2 bn, 3 tpt, 3 tromb, cym, strings)

LAMPE, WALTHER, Serenade, Op. 7 for Fifteen Instruments (2 fl, 2
  ob, eng h, 2 cl, bass-cl, 4 h, cfgt, 2 bn) Simrock; Andraud; Broude Bros., (score, parts).
LAUBER, JOSEPH, Serenade for Fourteen Wind Instruments (fl, picc,
  ob, eng h, 2 cl, 2 h, 2 bn, 2 tpt, 2 tromb) Ms., Luetzinger, Bassoonist, Zurich, Switzerland.
LELEU, JEANNE, Suite Symphonique (2 fl, ob, eng h, cl, bn, h, 2
  tpt, tromb, perc, pf) Baron; Leduc; Andraud.
LENDVAI, ERWIN, Kammersuite, Op. 32 in F# minor, ed. by Schluss
  (fl, ob, cl, bn, h, harp, string quintet) Rahter (score,
  parts).
MALIPIERO, G. FRANCESCO, Ricercari for Eleven Instruments (fl,
  ob, cl, bn, h, 4 va, vc, bass, picc) Universal Edition,
  (score, parts); Andraud; Peters.
  ---Ritrovari for Eleven Instruments (fl, picc, ob, cl, bn,
  h, 4 va, vc, bass) Andraud; Universal Edition; Peters.
MAZZINGHI, JOSEPH, Some Pieces in Harmony, Op. 33 (4 cl, 2 picc,
  2 bn, 2 h, tpt, serpent, tromb) Fetis.
MEDERITSCH, JOHANN, Choeur de Chaveliers du Temple (4 voices, 2
  fl, 2 cl, 2 bn, 2 tromb, organ) Fetis; Ms.
MENDELSSOHN, ARNOLD LUDWIG, Suite, Op. 62 (2 fl or alto picc, 2
  ob, 2 cl, 2 bn, 2 h, 2 tpt, 3 tromb, tymp, triangle, tam-
  bourine) Leuckart.
MENDOZA, VICENTE T., Jalisco, Part 1 (8 wind and percussion in-
  struments, pf, strings) Fleisher.
MEYERBEER, GIACOMO, Entri'acte in D major (2 v, va, flutes, oboe,
  clarients, bassoons, horns, basses) Fetis Supplement.
MILAHUD, DARIUS, Serenade (2 v, va, vc, bass, 2 fl, 2 ob, 2 cl,
  2 bn, 2 h, 2 tpt, tymp) Andraud.
MOLBE, HEINRICH FREIHERR VON BACH, Scherzo, Op. 83 in F major
  ---Andante Pensieroso, Op. 84 in G major.
  ---Tanzweisen, Op. 89 in Eb major.
MOSER, F., Serenade, Op. 35 for Fifteen Instruments (2 fl, 3 ob, 3
  cl, 3 bn, 4 h) Universal Edition; Andraud.
MOZART, WOLFGANG AMADEUS, Divertimento K113 (2 v, va, bass, 2
  cl, 2 h, 2 ob, 2 eng h, 2 bn) Andraud.
  ---Divertimento, No. 35 (2 fl, 5 cl, 5 tpt, 4 tymp) MH
  Baxter Northrup Co.
  ---Haffner Serenade, K250, in D major (2 v, va, vc, bass, 2
  ob or 2 fl, 2 bn, 2 h, 2 tpt) Andraud.
  ---Serenade in D major, K320 (2 v, va, bass, 2 fl, 2 ob, 2
  bn, 2 h, 2 tpt, tymp) Andraud.
  ---Serenade No. 5 in D major, K 204 (2 v, va, bass, 2 ob or 2
  fl, 2 h, 2 tpt) Andraud; (2 ob, 2 h, 2 tpt, string quintet) B&H; AMP.
  ---Serenade No. 4 in D major, K 203 (2 v, va, bass, 2 ob or
  2 fl, 2 h, 2 tpt, bn) Andraud; (2 ob, bn, 2 h, 2 tpt,
  string quintet) B&H; AMP.
  ---Serenade in D major, No. 3, K 185 (2 v, va, bass, 2 ob,
  or 2 fl, 2 h, 2 tpt) Andraud; (2 ob, 2 h, 2 tpt, string
  quintet) B&H; AMP.
  ---Serenade No. 1 in D major, K 100 (2 v, va, bass, 2 ob, or
  2 fl, 2 h, 2 tpt) Andraud; (2 ob, 2 h, 2 tpt, string quintet) B&H; AMP.

MOZART, WOLFGANG AMADEUS, Divertimento No. 2 in D major, K 131 (2 v, 2 va, vc, bass, fl, ob, bn, 4 h) B&H (parts, score); Andraud; AMP.
---Divertimento No. 5 in C major, K 187 (2 fl, 2 tpt, 4 tymp) (rec) B&H; AMP.
---Divertimento No. 6 in C major, K 188 (2 fl, 5 tpt, 4 tymp) (rec) B&H; AMP.
---Serenade in Bb major, No. 10, K 361 (2 ob, 2 cl, 2 alto-cl, 4 h, 2 bn, cfgt or bass) VH (rec) Sander (ed. by R. Gerber, min score); Andraud; Broude Bros; B&H (score, parts); Eulenburg (min score); AMP.
ORDONEZ, CARLOS, Five Chamber Symphonies (string quartet, 2 ob, 2 h, 2 tpt, drums) Ms., Brussels Conservatoire.
PAZ, JAUN CARLOS, Overture for 12 Solo Instruments (winds and strings) Fleisher.
---Variations for 11 Wind Instruments, Fleisher.
PEREIRA, ARTHUR, Poemas Da Negra, No. 1 (2 fl, 2 ob, 2 cl, 2 bn, 4 h, 2 tpt, harp, voice, strings) Boletin Latinoamericano De Musica, VI.
PERILHOU, ARMAND, Divertissement, Tale, Musette, Hunting and Bourree (2 fl, 2 ob, 2 cl, 2 bn, 4 h) Heugel; Andraud.
PETYREK, FELIX, Arabian Suite (2 fl or alto picc, ob, 2 cl, 2 bn, 2 h, tromb, tymp, perc, harp, pf) Universal Edition.
PIERENE, HENRY CONSTANT GABRIEL, Frandolle (fl, ob, cl, bn, h, tpt, tambourine, strings,) Baron.
REBNER, EDWARD W., Suite 1492 (tpts, woodwinds, percussion) Los Angeles, California, A.F. of M.
REVUELTAS, SILVESTRE, Homenaje a Federico Garcia Lorca (7 winds, percussion, pf, strings) Fleisher.
REZNICEK, EMIL N. VON, Traumspiel (fl, picc, ob, eng h, cl, bass-cl, bn, h, tpt, va, v, vc, perc, harp, celeste or pf) Simrock.
RIETI, VITTORIO, Madrigal in Four Parts (fl, ob, cl, bn, h, tpt, string quintet, pf) Andraud.
ROSETTI, FRANZ ANTON, La Chasse, Symphonie (2 v, va, bass, fl, 2 ob, 2 h, 2 tpt, bn) Sieber; Fetis.
ROSSI, LAURO, Piece (20 wind instruments) Fetis Supplement.
RUYNEMAN, DANIEL, Hieroglyphs, (3 fl, cel, tpt, cup-bells, pf, 2 mandolins, 2 guitars) Chester.
SALMHOFER, FRANZ, Kammersuite, Op. 19 (fl, picc, 2 ob, cl, cl and bass-cl, 2 bn, 2 h, harp, string quintet) Universal Edition.
SANJUAN, PEDRO, Sones de Castilla: Crepusculo en la Meseta, Baile de Pandero, Paramera, Ronda (5 winds, tpt, perc, pf, strings) AMP; Fleisher.
SCARLATTI, DOMENICO, Pastorale and Capriccio, arr. by Hasselmans (2 fl, 2 ob, 2 cl, 2 h, 2 bn, tpt, bass) Andraud.
SCHONBERG, ARNOLD, Chamber Symphony, in E major, Op. 9 (fl, ob, eng h, cl in D, cl in A, bass-cl, bn, cfgt, 2 h, string quartet) ed and simplified by Anton von Webern, Universal Edition.
SEKLES, BERNHARD, Serenade Op. 14 in Eb major (fl, cl, ob, bn, h, 2 v, va, vc, bass, harp) Rahter (score, parts).
SIQUEIRA, JOSE, Pregao for 11 Instruments (fl, ob, cl, bn, h, pf, string quintet) Boletin Latinoamericano de Musica, VI.

SPISAK, MICHEL, Concerto for Bassoon (bn, fl, ob, cl, h, tpt, tromb, tuba, string quintet) Baron.

SPITZMULLER-HARMERSBACH, ALEXANDER, Marschmusik, Op. 13 (2 fl, 2 ob, 2 cl, 2 bn, 3 h, 2 tpt, tuba, 2 tromb, perc, pf) Universal Edition.

STAMITZ, KARL, La Chasse, Symphonie (2 v, va, bass, fl, 2 ob, 2 bn, 2 h, 2 tpt) Sieber; Fetis.

STOHR, RICHARD, Kammersymphonie, Op. 32.

STRAUSS, RICHARD, Serenade in Eb major, Op. 7 for Thirteen Instruments (2 fl, 2 ob, 2 cl, 2 bn, cfgt or doublebass, tuba, 4 h) Universal Edition (score, parts); Andraud; International Music Co.

---Serenade for Wind Instruments (2 fl, ob, 2 cl, 4 h, 2 bn, cfgt or tuba) VH International.

---Orchesterstudien for Wind Instruments (3 cl, ob, 2 eng h, h, bass tuba, tpt, bass tpt, bn, contra bn) Peters.

---Suite for Thirteen Instruments, Op. 4 in Bb major (2 fl, 2 ob, 2 cl, 3 bn, 4 h, 2 bn, cfgt) Leuckart (score, parts).

STRAVINSKY, IGOR FEDOROVICH, Song of the Hauleurs on the Volga (picc. fl, ob, cl, bn, 2 h, 3 tpt, 3 tromb, tuba, perc) Andraud; Chester.

---Ragtime for Eleven Instruments (fl, cl, h, cornet, tromb, 2 v, va, bass, cymb, perc) Andraud; Chester.

STRINGHAM, E. J., Nocturne (2 fl, 2 ob, 2 cl, 2 h, harp, alto-cl, 2 bn) Fleisher Collection (unpublished).

TOMASI, HENRI, Jeux de Geishas, Petite Suite Japonaise (woodwind quintet, percussion, harp or pf, string quartet) Durand (score, min score, parts).

TSCHAIKOWSKY, PETER ILICH, Canzonetta, Andante from Violin Concerto (2 fl, 2 ob, 4 cl, alto-cl, bass-cl, bass) University of Texas.

VARESE, EDGAR, Intergrales for Small Orchestra and Percussion (2 fl, ob, cl, Eb cl, h, tpt in C, tpt in D, tenor tromb, bass tromb, contra bass tromb, perc--4 players) Curwen & Sons.

WOLF-FERRARI, ERMANNO, Kammersymphonie, Op. 8 in Bb major (fl, ob, cl, bn, h, string quintet, pf) Rahter; Andraud.

ZOLL, PAUL, Hessische Spielmusic (fl, cl, tpt, string orchestra) Barenreiter.

BIBLIOGRAPHY

GENERAL REFERENCE BOOKS

1. Agricola M. Musica Instrumentalis Deudsch. (Wittemberg: 1528 und 1545), Leipsic: Breitkopf, 1896.

2. Apel, W. Harvard Dictionary of Music. Cambridge, Mass. Harvard University Press, 1944.

3. Baker Biographical Dictionary of Musiciana. New York: G. Schirmer, Inc., 1940

4. Bekker, P. The Story of the Orchestra. New York: W. W. Norton & Co., 1936.

5. Bessaraboff, N. Ancient European Musical Instruments. Cambridge, Mass. Harvard University Press, 1941.

6. Brancour, R. Histoire des Instruments de Musique. Paris: Laurens, 1921. Page 117.

7. Bukofzer, M. Music in the Baroque Era. New York: W. W. Norton & Co., 1947.

8. Carse, A. Horniman Museum. London. London: London City Council, 1947.

9. Carse, A. The Orchestra from Beethoven to Berlioz. New York: Broude Bros., 1949.

10. Carse, A. The Orchestra in the XVIII Century. Cambridge, England: W. Heffer & Sons, 1940.

11. Carse, A. Musical Wind Instruments. London, Macmillan & Co., 1939.

12. Cobbett, W. W. Cyclopedic Survey of Chamber Music. London: Oxford University Press, 1929.

13. Dannreuther, E. Musical Ornamentation. London: Novello & Co., 1891.

14. Davison, A. T. and Apel, W. Historical Anthology of Music. Cambridge, Mass. Harvard University Press, 1946.

15. Dolmetsch, A. The Interpretation of Music of the Seventeenth and Eighteenth Centuries. London: Novello & Co., 1915.

16. Dunhill, T. F. Chamber Music. London: Macmillan & Co., 1913.

17. The Edwin A. Fleisher Music Collection. Philadelphia: Innes and Sons, 1945.

Bibliography, Continued.

18. Einstein, A. Music in the Romantic Era. New York: W. W.
        Norton & Co., 1947.

19. Galpin, F. W. Old English Instruments of Music. Chicago:
        A. C. McClurg and Co., 1911.

20. Gleason, H. Examples of Music Before 1400. Rochester: The
        Eastman School of Music of the University of
        Rochester, 1942.

21. Goldman, Richard The Band's Music. New York: Pitman
        Publishing Co., 1938. Pgs. 19-63.

22. Grove Dictionary of Music and Musicians. New York:
        Macmillan, 1944.

23. Helm, S. Catalogue of Chamber Music for Wind Instruments.
        Ann Arbor, Michigan: 1952.

24. Houser, R. Catalogue of Chamber Music for Woodwind Instru-
        ments. Indiana University School of Music.

25. Kinsky, G. A History of Music in Pictures. London & Toronto:
        J. A. Dent & Sons, Ltd., 1930.

26. Koechel, L. R. Mozart-Verzeichnis. Ann Arbor: J. W.
        Edwards, 1947.

27. Laing, M. The Woodwind Quintets of Anton Reicha. Ph. D.
        Dissertation, University of Michigan, 1952.

28. Mersemann, Hans Die Kammermusic. Leipsic: Breitkopf, 1933.
        Band I, II, III, IV.

29.   Musical Instruments in the South Kensington Museum.
        (essay on the History of Musical Instruments by
        Carl Engel) Eyre & Spottiswoode, London: 1874.

30. Mazzeo, Rosario A Brief Survey of Chamber Music. Cundy-
        Bettoney, 1938.

31.   Musical Materials for Small Instrumental Ensembles.
        Music Supervisors National Conference, Chicago:
        1934.

32. Morlind, T. Musikinstrumentens Historia. Stockholm: Nordisk,
        1941.

33.   Oxford History of Music and Musicians. London:
        Oxford University Press, 1929.

                Introduction, Pgs, 85-116- 216-218.
                Vlm. III, Chapter 8, Pgs. 308-375.
                Vol. IV, Pgs. 166-189; 342-343.
                Vol. V, Chapter 2, Pgs, 19-56.

Bibliography, Continued

Vol. VI, Chapters 6, Pg. 80
7, Pg. 111
10, Pg. 225.
Vol. VII, Chapter 5, Pgs. 134-164.
Chapters 3 and 4 optional.

34. Pierre, C. Les Facteurs d'Instruments de Musique. Sagot:
Paris, 1893.

35. Praetorius, M. De Organographia. (Vol. 2 of Syntagma Musicum
Wolf. 1619) English Translation by H. Blumenfeld,
Chinese Printing Office: Yale University.

36. Praetorius, M. De Organographia. (Vol. 2 of Syntagma Musicum
Wolf. 1619) Kassel: Barenreiter, 1929.

37. Profeta, R. Storia e Letteratura degli Strumenti Musicali.
Marzocco: Firenze, 1942.

38. Reese, G. Music in the Middle Ages. New York: W. W.
Norton & Co., 1940.

39. Rowen, R. Early Chamber Music. New York: Columbia
University Press, 1949.

40. Ruth-Sommer, H. Alte Musikinstrumente. Berlin: Carl
Schmidt & Co., 1920.

41. Sachs, C. The Rise of Music in the Ancient World.
New York: W. W. Norton & Co., 1943.

42. Sachs, C. The History of Musical Instruments. New York:
W. W. Norton & Co., 1940.

43. Schlesinger, K. The Greek Aulos. London: Methuen & Co.,
1939.

44. Solo Literature for the Wind Instruments.
Bulletin of NASM: 1951.

45. Terry. C. S. Bach's Orchestra. London: Oxford University
Press, 1948.

46. Ulrich, H. Chamber Music. New York: Columbia University
Press, 1948.

47. Van Slyke, J. The Development and Use of Woodwind Instruments
in Chamber Music. University of Illinois Thesis,
1946.

48. The Woodwind Anthology. New York: Woodwind
Magazine, 1952.